PREFACE.

*Alius alio plura invenire potest,
nemo omnia.*

AUSONIUS.

The history of the mercenary companies in Italy no longer remains to be told; it having been published in 1844 by Ercole Ricotti; however, several successive monographs on the same subject have produced such a wealth of information from new sources that Ricotti's work, estimable as it is, almost requires to be rewritten. The *Archivio Storico Italiano* has already recognised this by dedicating an entire volume to *Documents for the history of Italian warfare from the 13th to the 16th centuries* collected by Giuseppe Canestrini.

These are of great importance; but even taking into account all we owe to them, and to all that later historical researches have brought to light, the theme is not yet exhausted: truth is like happiness, and though as we approach we see it shining more intensely, and becoming clearer in outline, yet we can never feel, that we have obtained full possession of it.

One of the most celebrated condottieri was the Englishman John Hawkwood, or as contemporary Italian chroniclists put it "Giovanni Acuto;" whom Filippo Villani proclaims as "grand master of war." Giovio with elegant laconism defines him *acerrimus bellator et cunctator egregius,* while Muratori recognises him as a "brave and wary captain," qualifying his praise however by adding "a brigand of the first rank;" and Ammirato says "by many proofs he showed himself valiant and courageous in his own person, astute in reaping advantages, and a man who could wait the results of action without hurrying to obtain fame."

As for popular tradition, we have the testimony of Franco Sacchetti, who (in his 181st Novella) tells the story of certain monks

1

who gave Hawkwood the greeting of " Peace " on which he replied :
" May the Lord take away your alms." The alarmed monks excused
themselves, by saying they " meant only to be kind," and he explained: " Do you not know that I live by war, and that peace would
be my undoing ? " and the story-teller adds : " It certainly is true that
Hawkwood fought in Italy longer than any other man ever fought,
and nearly every part of it became tributary to him : so well did he
manage his affairs that there was little peace in Italy in his days."
Warrior by trade, in peace his occupation was gone. This truly characteristic story was paraphrased in Latin : *De co qui pacis nomine ro-*
ganti pauperi nihil dare voluit. (*Faccezie* di Filitimo Ermotimo, 1560).

It was said that if he had wished, he might easily have cut a
principality out of Tuscany for himself, or perhaps have become Lord
of the whole province, — a new Castruccio or Uguccione della Fag-
giuola ; — but either he lacked the ambition, or else he knew the place
and the times well enough to realise how impossible it would have
been to found a lasting dynasty.

In any way he was for more than thirty years one of the most
effective dominators of Italian affairs, and in her history, — military,
political, and social, — he figures as a personage whose character and
actions have an importance more than sufficient to justify the simple
curiosity of biographical erudition.

It is now evident that there is more than a little to add and to
rectify in his history; and — taking into account several inedited documents corroborating that which has, it is true, been already nar-
rated, though neither clearly nor precisely — it would seem that a new
monograph of John Hawkwood may well be attempted.

Paolo Giovio gave a place to the English Condottiere in the *Elo-*
gia virorum bellica virtute illustrium; but it is a short record with
more rhetoric than biography in it, — more romance than history; it
is a sketch in fine Latin prose with an ugly woodcut, and two unhappy verses by Giulio Feroldo ; and as to truth, the famous bishop
of Como always had (since Benedetto Varchi shewed up Paolo Giovio's
errors in history) the most justifiable reputation of giving it quite a
secondary importance.

Domenico Maria Manni collected many valuable facts edited and
inedited, and formed a praiseworthy biography (published in 1760,
in Vol. II of the appendix to *Rerum Italicarum Scriptores*), but it was
incomplete and not always exact.

From the literary correspondence in 1640-1641 between Sir William
Boswell English ambassador to the Hague, and J. de Laet of Leiden
(British Museum, *additional MSS.* 6395) it results that Mr. John

SIR
JOHN HAWKWOOD

(L'ACUTO).

STORY OF A CONDOTTIERE

TRANSLATED FROM THE ITALIAN

OF

JOHN TEMPLE-LEADER, Esq. & Sig. GIUSEPPE MARCOTTI

BY

LEADER SCOTT.

London,

T. FISHER UNWIN

26, PATERNOSTER SQUARE.

1889.

Publishing Statement:

This important reprint was made from an old and scarce book.

Therefore, it may have defects such as missing pages, erroneous pagination, blurred pages, missing text, poor pictures, markings, marginalia and other issues beyond our control.

Because this is such an important and rare work, we believe it is best to reproduce this book regardless of its original condition.

Thank you for your understanding and enjoy this unique book!

Maurice had compiled, and written in English, a life of Sir John Hawkwood, profiting by the Italian authors existing in the ambassador's library, and by Sir William Boswell's own observations. It is possible that this is the MS. biography of Hawkwood, which is preserved in the *Ashmolean Collection* of Oxford (N° 749). It consists of 100 pages folio, and diverges from the subject in long digressions on general contemporary history, complacently quoting Tacitus and other Latin writers. The author thus metaphorically announces his subject on page 21: "I nowe applie my selfe to my intended theme, the life of the valiant and fam'd Sir John Hawkwood, or rather some few discourses, considerations, and observations on several passages of his life, and acts, for these we have growing at our own home, and th' other must chiefly be imported from forraine parts where they grow too thinne." In any case the book would only have a very limited biographical value were it not for the documents which were furnished by the Italian archives.

Thus if our subject is not without precedent, neither is it yet exhausted.

For the rest, in narrating and documenting the life of this soldier of fortune, it is enough merely to indicate, and not reproduce entire, those general facts of the time which are well known, or easily found in accredited histories. Our labours refer to the career of the classical Condottiere in the midst of his soldiers, and to his relations with the princes and republics to whom he sold his sword; and it will suffice for this, if we throw some of the modern lights on the social and military conditions of Italy, during the second half of the 14th century.

To simplify chronology we have indicated the dates by marginal numbers. Dates of the old Florentine and Pisan styles have been reduced to modern style.

I.

THE HAWKWOOD FAMILY. — FIRST ENGAGEMENTS IN FRANCE.

[MORANT, *Hist. of Essex* [1768] which cites the feudal registers of the Earls of Oxford — CAMDEN's *Britannia* — FULLER, *Worthies of England* [1663] — STOWE, *Annals* — Will of Gilbert Hawkwood existing in the *Harleyan Charters* 51, D. 6, pub. in *Gentleman's Magazine*, Vol 58, p. 1061 — FILIPPO VILLANI, *Cronica* — AMMIRATO, *Istorie Fiorentine* — SAMUEL SMILES, *Life and Labour* — MATTEO VILLANI, *Cronica* — BECKER, *Adventurous Lives* — LAROUSSE, *Dictionnaire universel du XIX siècle* — FROISSART, *Chroniques* — GUILELMUS DE NANGIS, *Chronica* — PERRENS, *Histoire de Florence.*]

On the left bank of the little river Colne in Essex, in the parish of Sible Hedingham not far from the ancient city of Colchester, there still exists an old house and estate named Hawkwood Manor, — once a feudal dependance on the Castle of Hedingham belonging to the Earls of Oxford, and which was in the possession of the Hawkwoods as far back as the reigns of John Lack-Land and Edward III.

Tradition says that our John Hawkwood was born here, and we have no reason to doubt it.

The epoch of his birth is not proved: we only know that he died very old in 1394, and that in 1360 he was already a captain of assured reputation; we may therefore conclude that he came into the world in the beginning of Edward the Third's reign, about the year 1320.

John's father was named Gilbert and he was by trade a tanner; a fact perfectly compatible with his well-to-do condition as a landowner.

There are not wanting fabricators of marvellous genealogies, which make Hawkwood's ancestry originate with

Memprecius King of the Frisians. On the other hand Filippo Villani and Ammirato believe Hawkwood to be a personal cognomen, rather than a family surname, recounting that " the mother being about to give birth to a child, had herself carried into a forest, and here the boy was born," — hence the name *hawk* and *wood*.

The Florentine historians were better informed in saying that his parents " were well born although not of grand lineage (gentil' huomini mercatanti e antichi borghesi)." The fact that they used the aristocratic particle " de," and that they possessed lands, goods, and money, is proved by some English documents, among which is the Will of Gilbert de Hawkwood himself.*

1340.   In this his last testament Gilbert de Hawkwood declares his wish to be buried in the church of Sible Hedingham ; then in the first place he leaves 2 *solidi* to the building fund of St. Paul's in London ; then 17 *marks* 10 *solidi* for his obsequies on the day of the funeral, and on the seventh and thirtieth days after it.

He had three sons : John the elder, John the younger, and Nicholas. The elder no doubt inherited, by right of seniority, the Manor of Hedingham Sible, of which the Will makes no mention, it being only a series of legacies in money, goods or furniture :

to John senior 10 pounds, the cart and six horses, two oxen, 10 quarters of wheat and 10 of oats ;

to John junior 20 pounds and 100 *solidi ;*

to Nicholas 10 marks ;

to each 5 quarters of wheat, 5 of oats, with bed and maintenance for a year.

There were besides four daughters : Agnes and Jane, married ; Alice and Margaret still spinsters, to each of

---

* Tommaseo, in his Comments on the Letters of St. Catherine of Siena, has romanced too much in attributing to " Acuto " the title of Count.

them Gilbert left 100 *solidi* and to the two spinsters 10 pounds besides, with bed and maintenance for a year.

Then follows a long list of petty legacies to priests, menservants, and maidservants, abbesses, and nuns; with a general legacy of " all the remainder " to his executors to be employed in charity and prayers for his soul.

The executors were his sons, the two Johns, and the Vicar of Gosfield: this indicates that those two sons were both at home in 1340; in fact they obtained, after Gilbert's death in that same year, the official documents giving them legal possession and power of administration of the property mentioned in the Will.

Of the three sons, the least favored, Nicholas, embraced the ecclesiastical career, with such success that in 1363 we find him in holy orders, and holding a territorial benefice of such value that it placed him on an equal rank with John senior, who as head of the family was Squire of Sible Hedingham.

The other cadet John junior, being provided with his 20 pounds and 100 *solidi* (in those times a considerable sum), lived for a year at his brother's expense, as legally enjoined, — he might even have prolonged the visit in fraternal fashion, — but after that he began to think, as cadets must do, of making a career for himself.

Now at that time there was war in France, and thither went many Englishmen to seek their fortunes, and gain money, lands, and titles, while King Edward III on his part appropriated whole provinces, — and these temptations induced our hero to become a soldier.

This seems the most probable version of his story; nevertheless the tradition was generally accepted in England that John's first weapons were needle and scissors, and that they were wielded during an apprenticeship to a London tailor. Fuller gives this as a fact adding: " Now that mean men bred in manual and mechanick trades, may arrive at great skill in martiall performances, that Hawkwood, though an eminent, is not the only instance of our English nation."

On this account a popular modern writer, Smiles, registered Hawkwood among the illustrious men of the working classes in his *Life and Labour.*

It is also noteworthy that some French authors give John Hawkwood the cognomen of Jean de L'Aiguille. But all this is not at all authentic, and accords ill with the condition of the family de Hawkwood. As to the real Jean de L'Aiguille, Matteo Villani is our best informant; he says that "after having shewn himself a brave man of great spirit in feats of arms, Gianni della Guglia, English tailor, in the summer of 1359, got together a company of English plunderers and swordsmen; and either pillaging open lands or protecting them for money, he made a great fortune in a few months, and returning to his allegiance to the King of England placed a great part of the wealth he had accumulated at his sovereign's disposal."

When in later times Hawkwood appeared as hero of the Tuscan wars, Filippo Villani, who continued Matteo's history, while trying to throw light on the origin of the Condottiere, does not even dream of identifying Giovanni Acuto with Gianni della Guglia: and Froissart, on his side, assures us that in 1360, Giovanni Haconde was still "a poor knight, having gained nothing but his spurs."

Skippon, an English writer, on reading in Florence the name of Johannes Acutus,* translated it literally into

---

* The numberless variations in the spelling of this name in ancient documents, contemporaneous chronicles, and later historians is incredible. Every possible combination of the letters which do or do not compose it, as long as they approximated to the sound of *Hacoud,* were experimented upon by secretaries, and authors, learned or popular. Even his own amanuensis signing for him (as we see in several letters in the Archives of Mantua) indulged in the most fantastic aberrations of orthography. It would be useless to give a long list, suffice it to state that we can ring all the changes between *Aguto* and *Kauchcole* and that S. Antonino constantly calls him *Agostino.*

English as " John Sharp," without even suspecting that
it referred to Hawkwood. Some mistake of this sort may
have given rise to the metamorphose of " Acuto " into
Giovanni dell'Ago, and thence to the legend of his exploits
in a tailor's shop.

It has been frequently asserted that Hawkwood was
enrolled by a press-gang, but it has also been said that he
made his own choice of the career of arms, and that he was
educated for it by his uncle who was an expert warrior.

Some declare that his first campaign in France in 1343
was made as a vassal of John de Vere, 7th earl of Oxford;
and it is probable that he fought in the famous battles 1346, 1356.
of Cressy and Poitiers, for it is an accepted tradition, that
he so distinguished himself in those actions, as to win the
favour of the Black Prince, and receive from the King
the honor of knighthood.

All considered however, there is much less documentary
proof for the story of his early career than even that of
his origin; while the history of his vocation as Captain
of Mercenaries is on the contrary sufficiently recounted
by the French chronicles.

During the war, many companies of mercenary adventurers had multiplied on the disputed soil of France, some
fighting on their own account, others for belligerent potentates.

The peace of Bretigny being concluded, a great number 1360.
of the troops were dismissed and returned to their homes
across the sea. Many of the Englishmen however were
too much accustomed to the excitement of fighting and
setting ransoms in an enemy's country, to willingly return
to peaceful occupations in their own; they preferred following up the career, and finding numerous adherents, —
Germans, men of Brabant, Flemings, Gascons, and French,
they formed into companies both great and small, known

by the common name of *Tards-venus,* to distinguish them
from other troops which had preceded them, or to express
that they gleaned the little that was left in France, which
had already been devastated by so many years of war.*

English captains of the higher rank being laden with
spoil and full of honors, after victorious campaigns fought
for the right; obeyed the proclamation of peace, and
declined to mix themselves up with the *Tards-venus,* who
therefore elected new leaders, " choosing," says· Froissart,
" the worst among them." **

John Hawkwood may have been " a poor knight," but
he must have won reputation as a man of war, because
one of these companies placed him at their head.

II.

THE ENGLISH IN PIEDMONT. — THE ' CONTE VERDE.'
THE DEATH OF COUNT LANDO.

[FROISSART, *Chroniques* — MATTEO VILLANI, *Cronica* — BALUZIO, *History of the Popes at
Avignon* — MARTENE, *Thesaurus Anecdotorum, II* — *Chronique de Saroie* — AZARIO,
Cronaca — The slaughter of Savigliano in the *Archivio Storico Italiano,* 1st series.
v. 13 — GUICHENON, *Histoire généalogique de la maison de Savoie.*]

The *Tards-venus* under Bernardo de la Sale, after having
desolated Champagne and Burgundy, and made a rendez-

---

* The ingenuous latin of the chronicler Guilelmus de Nangis is worthy
of quotation. Peace proclaimed, he writes, *gaudebant quasi omnes et merito
exceptis forsitan illis qui in tempore guerrarum et in factis earum, aliis per-
dentibus, reperiunt magna lucra, sicut sunt armifactores, et aliqui alii qui ra-
pinas illicitas et opera nefaria in tali tempore, Dei timore postposito, cupiunt
exercere, et de rebus non suis sua replere marsupia minus juste; de quibus in
die judicii districtam eis oportebit reddere rationem....*

*Item insurrexerunt filii Belial et viri iniqui, videlicet multi guerratores de
diversis nationibus, non habentes titulum aliquem neque causam aliquos invadendi,
nisi proprio motu sive nequitia affectata sub spe depredandi.*

** Perrens would give us to understand that the nucleus of these companies was composed of Gascons and Normans, who had served England
and hence the name of English. But from their own documents in Italy we
find that the element of real English blood existed, especially in the knights
and constables.

vous at Lyons, descend the Rhone by long nocturnal mar- ches, surprise the bridge and fort of Saint Esprit, and take it by assault, thereby gaining both women and spoil; establishing themselves there they command the whole river, and menace Avignon itself; John Hawkwood gives great assistance in this enterprise.

Pope Innocent VI to defend himself has recourse to arms temporal, spiritual and moral: he fortifies Avignon, proclaims a crusade with liberal indulgences, writes to Conte Verde *atleta e difensore della Chiesa,* and other tran- salpine princes, that they may oppose the companies, and prevent their passage; for already a troop got toge- ther by the Countess of Harcourt to avenge the murder of her husband by the King of France, and another large company of Englishmen are hastening to new prey in Provence.

The Cardinal of Ostia succeeds in collecting a few men; but they do not remain staunch, on the contrary several go over to the enemy.

Not being able to brave the storm, the Pope carefully takes the opportunity of turning it aside, by putting his hand in his purse. He comes to an understanding with the Marquis of Montferrat who requires soldiers to fight against the Visconti: so counselled by Conte Verde,* and backed up by the money of the Church, the Marquis takes into his pay the larger part of the great company of *Tards- venus* as well as the brigand-paladins of the Countess, — in all 6000 horse.

How much did this financial operation cost the Pope, besides the plenary indulgence?

Froissart says that he advanced 60,000 francs in gold,**

1360.
Decemb. 28.

1361.
January
and
February.

---

* Lord of Savoy and ancestor of the royal family of Italy. — (*Translator.*)

** It must be specified that in ancient times two kinds of francs were used in France: the silver one of twenty soldi, and the golden one of six Flo- rentine lire. The Florentine florin of that epoch had an intrinsic value of about eleven of the modern francs.

1361.   of which 10,000 were paid to Hawkwood's brigade. Baluzio talks of 30,000, Matteo Villani of 100,000 florins :
but Martene's document proves only one of the payments,
— that of 14,500 florins to be consigned to the Marquis
et per eumdem marchionem armigeris qui MAGNA SOCIETAS
June 6.   *dicebantur.*

Here then we behold the great English band marching
towards the sea ; attempting in vain to take Marseilles,
they set fire to her suburbs, and pass by the Riviera to
Nice ; cross the Maritime Alps by the feudal estates of
Malaspina, favored by Simon Boccanegra doge of Genoa,
and enemy to the Visconti ; and thus descend into the
valley of the Po.

And did Hawkwood go with them ? It seems that he
did like the Countess of Harcourt, who after conducting
her brigade into Piedmont, returned directly into France,
for Froissart assures us that our Condottiere was one of
the chiefs in command of the English bands, who under
Jacques de Bourbon at Brignais vanquished the troops of
the French King.

The battle of Brignais, which was a pitched battle,
1362.   took place on April 6, 1362.*

The English, superior in number, had the extra advantage of prudence. They dissimulated the real extent
of their forces so as to mislead Bourbon's spies, and they
also occupied the best positions.

The French troops attempted an assault by an open
march, but they were first thrown into confusion by a
storm of large stones aimed with singular vigour and
precision (the English were expert slingsmen as well as
archers), then they were shaken in the flank by a compact

---

* Froissart, it is true, gives the date April 12, 1361, but Simeon Luce, the
learned editor of the famous French chronicler, has shown this to be a
chronological error.

mass, bristling with lances six feet long, and finally, routed and disbanded with great loss, they left many important prisoners on the field. Bourbon, mortally wounded, hardly succeeded in flying to Lyons to die, consoled as well as may be, by the tears of the Lyonese dames and maidens.

In fact we perceive by this combat that the French had learned little from the terrible lessons of Cressy and Poitiers, and that the English were possessed of very ripened tactics for those times; even in brigandage they were artists of war.

After this signal victory the companies diffused themselves without obstacles, — some stayed in France, some turned towards the Rhenish provinces, to such effect that Rudolph of Hapsburg had to league eleven imperial cities, to oppose the damages and devices of " those villains vulgarly called English; " a good many more passed or repassed into Italy and among these John Hawkwood.

> Va; raccogli ove arato non hai,
> Spiega l' ugne: l' Italia ti do.
>
> (Go, reap where thou hast not sowed,
> Spread thy claws: Italy I give thee.)

The maritime Alps passed, the English left behind them in France their name of *Tards-venus.* It is not certain, however, that they formed immediately, as is generally believed, that single " White Company," or *Compagnia Bianca,* as Matteo Villani calls the largest of the English bands in 1360.

The ancient " Chronique de Savoie " speaks of *aucunes compagnies d'Anglois* which had for leaders Robert *Canolle,* John *Auguth,* and Annechin de Bongarden.

As to the last name it is equivocal: Bongarden came with Count Conrad Lando (or Landau) bringing from Apulia two troops of Hungarians and Germans, who were first in the pay of the Marquis of Montferrat, and then hired

1362.   by the Conte Verde : finally they passed into the service
of the Visconti, Lando first, and Bongarden after a new
expedition into Apulia.

On the other hand, Azario, a most valuable contemporaneous eye and ear witness, certifies that the English companies took as general leader a german, Albert Sterz, a man
so valorous in the field, as to inspire others with courage
(*qui virtuosus ad pugnam omnes alios facit virtuosos*). It was
necessary to have a captain, who knew the country, which
was new to themselves, and Sterz suited them, not only for his
military qualities, but especially because he spoke English.

The fact remains that Piedmont was devastated by the
Hungarians, the Germans, and lastly by the newly arrived
English, and it is difficult to say which were the worst,
the cruel horrors of the slaughter at Savigliano by the
first, or the equal horrors perpetrated by the others, in
proof of which Azario gives the names of many witnesses.
It is not true that the English brought from beyond
the Alps the plague, of which 77,000 people died in Milan
alone (?) ; the pest was already in Piedmont, as it was in
Provence, — but they brought violation, burning, extortion,
rapine, murder, and torture, illusing women in the presence
of their husbands, and fathers, and then demanding ransom ;
putting men into irons, and drowning those who were not
prompt to pay the money demanded.

The only thing in which the English were less brutal
than the Hungarians and Germans was in not roasting or
mutilating their victims. Azario, however, does not omit
to call them *perfidi* and *scelleratissimi* (perfidious and villanous), and from their entrance into Italy they justified
the old proverb *Inglese italianato è un diavolo incarnato.**
(An Englishman italianized is an incarnate devil.)

---

* The origin of this proverb is not known, it dates from before the
XVI century when Serdonati registers it in his MS. collection with a note

The " Chronique de Savoie " says coldly almost excusing them, that being many they could not live in Piedmont, without spoiling the country, so that Conte Verde, who had imprudently counselled the Marquis of Montferrat to employ the English, repented, and took arms to defend himself.

1362.

They could indeed boast of an illustrious adversary, but nevertheless under Robert Canolles * they held their own against him, and after having taken, with other places, the town of Lanzo, obliged him to shut himself up in the castle, which they held in siege, till he was reduced to such extremities that he had to make terms through the mediation of Sir William de Grandson, knight of " the Annunziata, " and agreed to pay an indemnity. By forfeiting the sum of 180,000 florins, Conte Verde obtained the restitution of his lands, and the English passed on to fight the Milanese, under the Marquis of Montferrat, making their head quarters at Sicciano near Novara. Count Landau was then serving Galeazzo Visconti, who being weak in the field tried to defend himself by fire. He burnt twelve castles and villages, thinking thus to cut off the enemy's provisions; but the English answered by fire, burning fifty-two places, destroying hundreds of others, and sacking all the territory as far as the rivers Ticino and Trebbia.

---

* English Proverb." It has some analogy with another saying *Inglesi hanno coda di serpe* (The English have serpent's tails), referred to by Landino in his commentary on canto XXVII of Dante's ' Paradise.' Strange contrast between this proverb and Gregory the Great's *Non angli sed angeli si christiani forent*. Which play on words it is curious to find some centuries later in a Turkish poet-Fazilbeg, who speaking of the English in his ' book of women, ' says: *Not anglica, but an angelic creature*. But in the XIV century they were any thing but angels! The Italians of that age could no more say *Gesta Dei per Francos* but *Gesta diaboli per Anglos*.

* This Roberto Canolles or Knolles, a german of low origin, knight and leader of brigands, had as his motto :

Qui Robert Canolle prendra
Cent mille moutons gagnera.

1362.

In fact the English preliminaries in Italy were terrible, and that first campaign was enough to give them the reputation of being invincible.

They easily occupied Castelnuovo at Scrivia for the Marquis, and then Galeazzo Visconti sent the counts Landau and Nicholas, to Tortona against them with several Germans, and 500 Hungarians, and eventually dispatched Giovanni de' Pepoli to treat with the English. They remained faithful to the Marquis, and the enemy not daring, even with double their forces, to emerge from Tortona, they devastated the surrounding country up to Pavia.

September.

Only Luchino dal Verme opposed them with five hundred *barbute*,* and obliged them to return to the Novara district, where they occupied Romagnano, and five hundred of them died of the plague.

It appears that they were wanting in cross-bow men, a weapon very important in those days, because when the Doge of Genoa placed 30 bands at their disposal, they again took the offensive, and were able to attack with success several places on the right of the Po.

Decemb. 26.

Conte Verde proposed an alliance with Galeazzo Visconti, with the object of driving out the English from their states, and dividing Montferrat, between them, but it must be admitted that the undertaking to rout the English seemed very difficult to Visconti, for he was at the same time attempting to make a treaty of peace with them.

Albert Sterz feigned to consent, by which means the English succeeded in making a fierce incursion, passing the Ticino, and pushing on to within six miles of Milan. It was night, and people in the castles and villages were keeping the New Year's festivities; while the Milanese nobles were having a merry time, playing at *tabulas et*

1363.
January 4.

---

* Barbute, the German name for ' lances.' A barbuta consisted of two men, a lance of three. — (*Translator.*)

scaccos (draughts and chess) unsuspecting and undefended,
so that they were unable to prevent the robbers from
taking anything and everything they chose. Luckily for
the ladies and maidens they were in a hurry, and contented themselves with goods and chattels, abstaining from
their usual incendiary proceedings. They made prisoners
of over 600 nobles, and would have taken more if ropes
and time had not failed them. Some of the gang dragged
behind them as many as ten nobles, together with their
cattle; they could not save them all because they were
attacked by Visconti's boats in recrossing the Ticino, but
it is said that with the money paid for ransoms, they
pocketed about 100,000 florins.

Having returned to their nest in Romagnano they made
fresh efforts to treat with Count Landau, but after their
having sacked Briona, the Count lost patience, and met
them at the bridge at Canturino, where leaving their horses   April 22.
they came to a hand to hand encounter. It appears that
the Hungarians having quarelled with their German comrades deserted the field, and the Count, mingling in the
mêlée, had the nose-piece of his helmet broken, and then
with a lance-thrust in his face and another under the
arm-pit, he was taken prisoner in a dying state.

His death was deplored even by the English leaders
who hoped by his means to come to terms with the Visconti, when their contract with Montferrat should be
fulfilled, but they made good the occasion by crossing the
Apennines and carrying their arms into Tuscany.

There were already Pisan Ambassadors at Novara offering
to hire the English Company, which was certainly called
at that time *Compagnia Bianca* on account of their white
flags, white vests, and shining arms. They numbered
3500 horse and 2000 foot, and were still commanded
by Sterz.

III.

ENTRY INTO TUSCANY.
AGAINST FLORENCE WITH THE PISANS.

[RANIERI SARDO, *Cronica Pisana* — *Consulte e pratiche fiorentine*, of February 29 1353 cited by PERRENS in *History of Florence* — ANTONIO PUCCI, *La guerra di Pisa*, poem — MATTEO and FILIPPO VILLANI, *Cronache* — DONATO VELLUTI, *Cronaca* — *Cronaca pisana*, by the anonymous author in MURATORI — *Pisan state archives*, provisions for the forced loan in 1363 and provisions of the Anziani for the guard of the Captain general, December 1363 — LUCA DI TOTTO DA PANZANO, fragment of *Chronicle* in the *Giornale storico degli Archivi Toscani*, V — SOZOMENO, *Istorie* — GINO CAPPONI, *Storia della Repubblica di Firenze*.]

The city of Pisa was engaged in one of her usual wars with Florence. The Pisans had formerly availed themselves of English adventurers, as in 1314 when they took " Messer Folco " of England into their pay, with his 1500 knights; and now wishing to come to some decisive result, they had recourse to the White Company, in which Galeazzo Visconti, who was only too willing to be rid of the scourge, willingly aided them. They therefore hired them for six months at the stipend of 40,000 florins, and to this end a forced loan of 30,000 florins was imposed on the Pisans in June 1363, which was re-imbursed in September.*

1363.

Florence too had former experiences of the English mercenaries (as we find in the *Consulte e pratiche* of 1353), and again at this time might easily have had them on her own side. Friendly commercial and banking relations had existed for some centuries between Florence and England, and the traffic in English wool, — indeed, almost the monopoly, — had survived after the famous bank failure of the Bardi and Peruzzi. Giovanni Boglietti, a Floren-

* See Document n° I, Pisan Archives. The treasury had other expenses for the Company besides the stipends; for example in September 1363 the council of the Anziani absolved the Municipality of Sarzana from a debt of 10 florins, their part of a second tax of 8500 florins levied on the Pisan territories, " to compensate the damages suffered by many private persons on the coming of the English Company. "

tine, had been taken as guide to the White Company, who knew as yet very little of Italian geography, and the Company willing to conclude the suspended treaty with Florence, would have been contented to take from her 30,000 florins.

Galeazzo Visconti favored, and would have facilitated these negociations : and Piero Farnese, the Florentine captain of war, and an expert soldier, insisted on having the assistance of the English whom he considered spirited, brave and clever.

But the policy of economy, suggested by the Gonfaloniere Ridolfi, prevailed.

> Or vi dirò; siccome è di ragione,
> Seppe la volpe qui più del leone.

(Now I will tell you how as it might be expected, the fox in this case was wiser than the lion.)

Thus sang Antonio Pucci, a Florentine of that period, when he put into verse the story of the war between the Florentines and the Pisans, which the two Villani recount in prose. And the chronicler Velluti writes: " To save the evil of present expenses we to our shame and loss spent in the end six times as much, while if we had only engaged the Englishmen for our side we Florentines would have been lords and victors in the war."

Touching at Arona, to which place they were escorted by Giovanni de' Pepoli, on Galeazzo Visconti's account, the English stopped at Pontenure in the vicinity of Piacenza, to supply themselves with arms and horses and then pushed on to Pisa.

Up to this time the war had been going badly with the Pisan " fox," — the Florentine " lion " was hitherto triumphant, but the arrival of the English suffced to secure to Pisa a decided superiority.

They even enjoyed the fame in anticipation by a ruse, for they secretly despatched a company of their own soldiers from Pisa by night, and causing them to enter next morning covered with dust as from a long march, gave them a grand reception as though they were the Englishmen, which so intimidated the Florentines that they forthwith raised the seige of Montecalvoli (a neighbouring fort), and retreated.

The real English having reached Lucca by way of Lunigiana, rode at once through the Florentine territory by the Pistoia road : and with them was the " Pisan host," making altogether a force of 6000 horse, besides infantry and archers. There were also about a hundred itinerant salesmen, provided with tinder and *acciaiuolo* (flint and steel) to set fire to the houses, as municipal enmity in those days demanded.

The Captain general of the Pisans was a Florentine exile, Ghisello Ubaldini ; but on his death a few weeks later Manetti da Jesi succeeded to the command. The general of the English Company was the German Albert Sterz. Some contemporary chroniclers do not mention this, nor does the name of Acuto (Hawkwood) appear in that year, but they all accord in saying that the very backbone of the war was the English contingent.

It was only an heroi-comic skirmish after all, — *tediosa, di scaramucce e badalucchi.*

In the first incursion, lasting a fortnight, the English assembled under Pistoia, and threw into it lances, arrows, and *bombarde ;* " they ran races according to their custom " (a far off prelude to the modern prevalence of English sport in Italy) and then they advanced on Florence. When hearing the bells and trumpets ring out for war, and believing that the people were about to make a sally, they retired, but the Florentines remained secure within their walls. Albert Sterz dubbed general Ubaldini and others 1363. knights; the Pisans might have boasted of flinging into the city arrows with the tickets " Pisa sends you this " and of striking Pisan and Florentine money ; of hanging a donkey and a dog, while as to burning, " If the English had not forbidden them (perhaps they wished by clemency to keep open a way to future contracts with Florence) there would not have remained a house unconsumed, nor a palace which they would not have set fire to."

The " host " having returned to Pisa, the English were sent to the Chianti to reconnoitre. The Florentine poet chronicler thus characterises the rapidity and caution of their nocturnal marches:

> E prima a Poggibonizi venuti
> Fûr, che di lor si sentisse niente
> E poichè i passi tutti ebber veduti
> Di notte si partir subitamente.

(They reached Poggibonsi before any one had heard of them, and after having reconnoitred the country, they went away quickly by night.)

Exploring the roads and finding the right one, they reached the upper part of Val d' Arno where they took Figline. Septemb. 16.

Pandolfo Malatesta, the accepted friend and counsellor of war to the Florentines, placed the captain general Ranuccio Farnese at Incisa, for its defence, with some peasant bands and 2000 German men at arms under his command. They were brave but youthful and badly armed, — besides which he so enlarged his lines of battle, that 500 of the best horsemen were lost sight of and returned to Florence. The English, under pretext of sending un-armed witnesses to a duel between one of their knights and a Florentine, obtained exact information about the enemy, and the following day gave the assault, in two or three places at once, thus gaining possession of the field. October 3.

1363. Ranuccio was taken and Messer Luca di Totto de' Firidolfi da Panzano, knight, succeeded him as lieutenant; he gives the following account of the action: " In the morning after the *mezza-terza* (half-tierce, a canonical hour) Incisa was assaulted and conquered, — all day the people were flying without striking a blow, and I was attacked, wounded in the face and taken, — being dragged by the neck, and bound head and foot. On the day that I was taken, I lost my horses, arms, silver belts, and gold rings." The general flight continued as far as Florence.

The barbarous treatment of the prisoners must not however be laid to the English. " The Commune of Pisa," he says, " spoiled me to dishonour and disgrace our Republic."

Having given out that they intended to attack Florence at the Porta S. Niccolò, they got the Florentines to shut themselves up in the city to wait for them, and in that way secured a free march along the Arno, encountering no opposition except a heavy rain, wich rendered the road so bad that the horses lost their shoes. At night they

October 22. dispersed to sack and pillage in the plain of Ripoli, taking, as prisoners, some four hundred people warm from their beds, and nearly a thousand heads of cattle, fresh from their stalls; then raising their standard on the parish church they saluted it with a grand blowing of trumpets and the flames of incendiarism. Malatesta, the new captain general, shut himself up within the walls, allowing the enemy to return, joyful and gorged with prey to Figline, where they kept in their quarters undisturbed for two months, since the Sienese had themselves undertaken to fight the Company of the " Cappelletto," just then hired by the Florentines in the Maremma.

There were altogether (so Messer Luca di Totto says) 600 horse, and 3000 infantry who formed the garrison at Figline, whence they made sallies as far as the Casentino.

Several castles fell, into their hands more or less easily; but they fought two days in vain, against the fortress of Tre Vigne, " leaving several killed and wounded by stones and other missiles, while the moat was full of ladders, and the ground strewn with bows and arrows."

Having amassed an enormous quantity of spoil, they thought it time to return to winter quarters in Pisa. They spread the report however that on November 11, they would pass under the walls of Florence to consecrate a priest at San Salvi, and in fact that morning almost as if they would fulfil the impudent menace, they raised their camp and feigned to take the road to Florence.

The Florentine spies fled at once to the city with the terrifying news, but the English halted directly, and burning field and town passed on by the Chianti and Val di Pesa, arriving safely at Pisa, while the Florentines ringing their bells to call their men to arms, put themselves on the defensive at San Salvi and waited to see the enemy descend the heights of Rovezzano.

There was certainly work to be done in the service of Pisa; the town of Barga for some time past blockaded, rather than besieged, by the Pisans, still obstinately resisted, but the English considered that they were brought there to fight in Florentine territory and would not undertake the enterprise to Barga, except perhaps a few who had as yet got little prey. The greater part well provided for, preferred to winter in Pisa and amuse themselves to " the harm and discomfort of the citizens whom they outraged so much, that many sent their women to Genoa and other places for safety."

So says Filippo Villani, and Sozomeno emphasizes it still more strongly in Latin; indeed so strongly we refrain from quoting: it is however possible that Villani, . a Florentine, and Sozomeno, a Pistoiese, painted in vivid

colours, so as to vituperate the hated Pisans through
their wives. It is certain that the part of the city assigned as quarters to the soldiers did not suffice them,
nor did they respect the barriers beyond which the Pisans had prohibited them from penetrating or molesting
the inhabitants.

They had no fear of cold, " in the middle of the winter,
those hardy men did not desist from running about and
plundering," but this they did at their own will, without
heeding the wishes of the Pisans, who endeavoured to
send the bands out under pretext of defending them from
imaginary incursions of the enemy.

The Pisans were obliged to tolerate every exorbitance
of the English, who were so necessary to them in the
field, that with their aid they were certain of victory; so
they made a new treaty for six months at the price of
150,000 florins, with the compact that all other stipendiaries
were to be dismissed (perhaps this was because the
English desired all the spoil for themselves), and that they
should have the faculty of marching wherever they chose
outside the territories allied to, or protected by Pisa.

The Company also obliged the Pisans to accept as
Captain general the man of their choice, — John Hawkwood, — whose name the Pisan chroniclers italianise as
Giovanni Auti, which choice proves that he had distinguished himself as much during the last year's campaign,
as he had previously done in Piedmont and France. From
this time forth till his death, we almost always see him
as general in chief, in which character he takes a prominent part in the annals of Italy.

This superior rank must have been conferred before
December 1363, for a document of that date determines the
monthly pay of the foot soldiers (*famulis stipendiariis a
pede*) " lately received into the service of the Pisan Repu-

1364.

blic, and forming the guard of Signor Giovanni Acuto, captain general of war for Pisa."

The pay consisted of 20 lire in Pisan money, to the two constables (conestabili) Simone de' Gangalandi and Lodovico di Bernardo da Micciano: 10 lire to the constables' two pages (ragazzi) and to 38 foot soldiers and their 6 boys (all Italian). In fact a sufficient and honorable bodyguard.

The highest in command of the White Company under Hawkwood were the German Albert Sterz, and an Englishman named Andrew De Belmonte (styled *Dubramonte* in Italian);* some chroniclers say the latter was of royal race, and that he was distinguished from the other *cruel and ferocious* English by his gentle manners. He fell in love at Figline, with Monna Tancia wife of Guido lord of the Forest, and served her with such knightly devotion that he managed to make even his enterprising comrades respect her castle.

The important office of treasurer was filled by Guglielmo Toreton ** (William Turton?).

---

* It is often difficult to guess the authentic ultramontane names, so curiously are they travestied in the Italian documents of the time.

** The Pisan archives contain the order of the ˆAnziani ˆ to the chamberlain Pellario Griffo, dated October 1364, to pay Guglielmo Toreton, treasurer of the Grand English Company, 5000 gold florins of 3 lire 10 soldi in Pisan money, and 6000 of 3 lire 15 soldi, on account of the sum which the Company is entitled to receive from the Republic of Pisa. The accounts of the Chamberlain with the Company were complicated by frequent anticipatory payments to this and that official; for instance, in the same month we find ˆ 100 florins to John Onselos (Onslow?) and Conrad Schonechen *ultramontani*, who are now entering the English Company on the Florentine territory and will remain with it as long as the said Company is in the Pisan service ˆ — with promise to repay it within two months (here follow signatures of witnesses). Another entry has 150 florins to Robert, 100 to Dughino (Duggan?), 10 to William Prestim Englishmen, — small sums between 20 and 2 florins to 108 men, English and Teutons — and 2 florins to Marcuccio and Marco trumpeters, and to Antonio *naccarino* (kettle drummer).

IV.

FLORENCE MENACED. — HAWKWOOD FAITHFUL TO THE PISANS.

[Sozomeno, *Istoria* — Leonardo Aretino, *Storia fiorentina* — Monaldi, *Diary* — Donato Velluti, *Cronica* — Ammirato, *Storia* — Antonio Pucci, *La guerra di Pisa* — Roncioni, *Storie Pisane* — *Archivio storico Italiano* — Canestrini's documents concerning the mercenary companies — Anonymous Pisan Chronicle in Muratori.]

1364.
February. In February 1364 the English, in spite of heavy snows, made a sally from Pisa attempting several places, but they found unexpected resistance from the peasants in every part, and the Pistoiese at Seravalle even attacked them with some success.

Many of their men died of the intense cold, so they retired with decided losses, and certainly no gains.

Soon after this a considerable reinforcement arrived at Pisa. Annechin Bongarden, who had gone to Lombardy in the service of Galeazzo Visconti, with the permission **March.** of that prince conducted his 3000 German *barbute* * to Pisa to share the pay of that Republic, — the Pisan army thus amounted to about 6500 horse, besides a great number of pioneers and native infantry.

April. In the spring the campaign was resumed in earnest.

In three marches the Pisan soldiers reached Prato, where they had the temerity to occupy the drawbridge. They passed close to Florence, so near that three or four of the boldest rode on and knocked at the Port' a Prato, but the body of the forces pressed on at once to the Mugello.

Here however they encountered the German bands which were in the Florentine pay, led by Pandolfo Malatesta and Count Henri de Montfort, and in a skirmish of

---

* The English introduced the manner of reckoning their forces by ' lances ' instead of the older name ' barbute. ' A lance consisted of three men, a barbuta of two.

the vanguards forty Florentines defeated a hundred Pisans;
one good strong German named Heinrich Paer, with his
own lance unhorsed ten Englishmen, killing two of them.

Hawkwood and Bongarden finding some backbone of
resistance here, pretended to pass on, but retiring instead,
reapproached Florence by the slopes of Monte Morello,
where they penetrated into the woody folds of the mountain, leading their horses by the most difficult passes, and
sacking and burning.... But from this time forth we may
spare ourselves the mention of plunder and incendiarism :
they were the rule, and are understood as part of the
business in a march of the mercenaries, being always
practised in an enemy's country, and often in that of their
friends. " There was nothing more terrible than to hear
even the name of the English."

It should be noted that the spirited Brunelleschi family
victoriously defended their castle at Petraia against three
assaults.

Meanwhile Malatesta finding he was not so much master
of the situation in Florence, as he had flattered himself
he would be, retired, and the sword of command of the
German legion was given to the brave Montfort.

Hawkwood and Bongarden occupied the hills of Fiesole
while Montfort fortified the suburbs of Florence outside
Porta San Gallo, with hastily erected barricades and fences.

A fierce battle was fought on the 1st of May, a day
which Florence usually gave to popular merry making,
and auguries of love. The priors who had to enter office
that very day, did so without any of the usual solemnities, — they did not appear on the *ringhiera* outside the
palace, no bells were rung, or trumpets blown, because
there was fighting at San Gallo. Hawkwood's Englishmen
and Bongarden's Germans made a fierce attack on the barricades and breaking them, penetrated as far as the city

1364. gates, where the fray became bloody. Grimaldi's Genoese cross-bow men on the walls made a great noise and did a little damage; while the English archers, from the houses in the suburb, did a great deal of damage with very little noise; the Count of Montfort paid dearly in his own person, fighting hand to hand with Averard the German.*

In the heat of combat amid smoke, fires, and the ruins of falling houses, Bongarden was created knight and then he conferred the spurs on Averard, and an Englishman named Cook, besides others who distinguished themselves for their valour.

But the brilliant action had little result, the assailants ended* by retreating to the hills; and when night came, they celebrated the new-made knights with processions of coloured lamps, with games, song and music on the piazza of Fiesole. Then they took a fancy to send some drummers and trumpeters down to the Port' alla Croce at Florence, who made such a warlike noise that the city was in a tumult, so that the screeching women put lights in the windows, and got heaps of stones ready on the towers as if the enemies had already entered.

The mercenaries employed three days in burning houses on the Fiesole hills, ** and on the plain to the right of the Arno, and then crossed the river at a place still called

---

* Count of Landau, son of Count Conrad who was killed two years before in Lombardy, and brother of Count Lucius, all three dauntless soldiers, and perfect brigands.

** Tradition says that among the castles ruined by the English one was Vincigliata, which belonged successively to the Bisdomini, and to the Albizi, who took the name of Alessandri; it now belongs to John Temple-Leader Esq., who has completely restored the ruins in the style of the 14th century. Cav. Gaetano Bianchi's frescoes in the loggia of the cloister at Vincigliata are entirely in artistic accordance with the medieval style of the castle. The inscriptions in old Italian beneath them would run thus: ' John Hawkwood with his company of Englishmen and the Pisan marauders, moves to the injury of the Florentines. — The English with John Hawkwood having taken the hill of Fiesole, disperse over the surrounding country and after having destroyed Vincigliata, depart in May 1364.'

˝ la Sardigna.˝ * For three more days they occupied the
hills of Arcetri and Bellosguardo, destroying the orange
trees, trampling down the green wheat and barley, robbing
farmyards, and renewing daring and useless attacks on the
barricades of the suburbs of Legnaia and Verzaia. In this
last place the English descended the hill in such a mass that
they looked like ants, and discharged a shower of arrows
over the walls into the city. The scuffle might have been
fierce, if a heavy rain had not separated the combatants.

Thus skirmishing they retreated, and ascended the
banks of the Arno to Incisa.

The city of Florence was, or rather had been well
defended, but she could not tolerate seeing her enemies
masters of all her territories, and not having forces enough
to subdue them, she resorted to that ˝ ultima ratio ˝ of
Philip of Macedon: — corruption.

The poet-chronicler Pucci, though Florentine himself,
clearly confesses it.

> Allora i Fiorentin tennon trattato
> Con gli Inghilesi e col detto Annichino,
> E que' che fanno fare ogni mercato,
> Concordia fêr tra loro e 'l Fiorentino.

(Then did the Florentines propose a treaty with the
English and with the said Annechin (Bongarden), and
some people who would get a profit out of everything,
made a peace between them and the Florentines.)

Ammirato gives a name to one of these mercenary
agents: ˝ Lapo di Fornaino de Rossi,˝ he writes, ˝ was
made Podestà of Prato in consideration of his services in
making terms with Bongarden's Company.˝

Some historians have it that the golden florins were
infused into certain flasks of wine, which were sent to those

---

* An empty space on the left of the river opposite the Cascine.

1364.   leaders whom they wanted to corrupt. This must have been a small payment on account, for the affair cost Florence more than 100,000 florins: i. e. 9000 to Bongarden, 35,000 to his Germans, and 70,000 to the English, of which 5000 were for Belmonte.

It appears that Bongarden deserted the field outright, with his Germans, while Albert Sterz with Belmonte (in spite of his royal blood), Ugo della Zecca (? — perhaps Hugh Mortimer) and the other English leaders limited themselves to agreeing to a truce of five months with Florence.

All were traitors, except John Hawkwood, who tried with bitter reproofs to keep Bongarden to his duty. The fact is certain that when Sterz and Belmonte returned to Pisa with the sanction of Florence to provoke a revolution in favour of Gambacorti who aspired to the tyranny of the city, our hero hastened to warn the "Anziani" of the treachery by a letter. It is true, that with his troops disordered by infidelity, he could no longer continue his tactics on the offensive, the English contingent therefore marched through the territories of Arezzo, Cortona, Siena, Valdinievole, and Lucca, finally halting at San Piero in Campo near Pisa, where they inspected the troops and realized a loss of 600 men.

None were allowed to enter the city except those whom Hawkwood recommended as faithful.

> Tornando a Pisa, e non possendo entrare,
> Di fuor la gente d'intorno s'attenda
> E cominciano a Pisa a domandare
> Molta pecunia di paga e di menda.
> Di che i Pisan gli tenieno in pastura
> Ed e' guastavan d'intorno alle mura.
>
> (To Pisa come, but not allowed within,
> The men wait round about the city gate
> And to demand imperiously begin
> Large sums for pay, and wrongs to compensate,
> So that the Pisans send them off in haste,
> And all around they lay the lands to waste.)

Thus perfidiously June was passed, the last month of *1364.* their engagement, when they ought to have been opposing the Count of Montfort who without let or hindrance was domineering the Pisan territories.

Hawkwood with only 800 men remained in the Pisan service, while the greater part of the English, being again free and their compact ended, openly treated with Florence, and took Albert Sterz as their captain.

A solemn act was signed in the Palazzo Vecchio between *July 28.* the "Signoria" and the representatives of the captain, the constables, and marshals (Belmonte was one of the representatives). These agreed to serve the Republic of Florence faithfully (?) for six months, fighting against Pisa and Lucca ; they besides swore that after the six months were over, they would observe the peace for six years, towards Florence and all her dependent Communes ; — the Florentines on their side promised to treat them " as dear brothers and friends." Albert Sterz reserved to himself the personal faculty of leaving the Company at his pleasure, provided that none of the troops followed him, and that the Company should elect a new captain in his stead. The witnesses on the English side were the Scotsmen Walter and Norman Leslie.

Thus the " great White Company " was divided. An anonymous Pisan chronicler observes: " It is certain that if they had not split among themselves, they would have become masters of all Tuscany and all Italy, so brave and powerful were they."

As to Sterz and his men, they might have had the good-will to serve their new masters better than the old, — but in any case they came too late, — for in those very days the final fate of war was decided near Pisa.

V.

THE DEFEAT AT CASCINA. — THE *DOGE* OF PISA.
THE WANDERING ENGLISHMEN.

[AMMIRATO — RONCIONI — RANIERI SARDO — Private Letters to the Florentine Council 1364 —
GHIRARDACCI, *Storie Bolognesi.*]

1364.
Before stretching itself across the wide and fruitful plain of Pisa, the winding Arno bathes the feet of that high and steep mountain which bears the very descriptive name of " Verruca " or " Verrucola " (a wart). This rises straight up on the right bank of the river, and was from ancient times crowned by a strong fortress, — no place could be better adapted to survey the whole of the lower Val d' Arno as far as the sea.

There was no passage then between the river and the cliffs of the Verruca, — in modern times a road has been cut in the mountain, — but on the left side of the Arno, a pleasant stretch of land lay between it and the first undulations of the distant hills, and here was the borough of Cascina, a strategic point, predestined to be the scene of several Tuscan battles.

End of July.
Galeotto Malatesta, the new Florentine captain general, was encamped there with Count Montfort's Germans, and many civic volunteers, besides the Genoese cross-bow, in fact with all the force Florence had at her disposal: 11,000 foot and 4000 horse. They encamped in disorder, and lived negligently, but this was supplemented by the zeal and vigilance of Manno Donati who took care to fortify the front of the town, towards Pisa with entrenchments, and to place Grimaldi's skilful Genoese cross-bow in the houses.

Pisa only had in her pay Hawkwood's 800 Englishmen and a few ultramontane brigades, but the approach of the Florentine army inflamed the warlike ardour of all the citizens; every body took arms who knew how to wield them, and Hawkwood was commissioned to attack the enemy's camp forthwith. He tried to make up for the inferiority of his forces by prudence, and leaving Pisa he encamped at the abbey of San Savino, four miles from Cascina. Here he waited for midday, so that the enemy might have the sun and the dust in their eyes (in the afternoon, a sea wind generally blows from the west across the plain of Pisa), and to deceive them, he preluded the action by three feigned attacks, so that Malatesta believed he did not mean to fight at all. Then he made a move in earnest, sending part of his English troops to the van, and keeping the others with him in the rear. He left his cavalry behind, so that the advance might be less noticeable, and to stir up the energies of his Englishmen he told them that in the Florentine camp they might make prisoners of three or four hundred young nobles, worth from one to two thousand florins of ransom, and besides, in the name of the Republic of Pisa, he promised double pay for a month if they were victorious.

This alluring prospect so fired the courage of the mercenary vanguard, that although they were fatigued by a march of four miles in a suffocating heat, and weighed down by their arms and armour, they did not wait a second command, nor even the reinforcement of the Pisan militia, but rushed to the assault of the trenches.

The horses were unsaddled and the men in the Florentine camp unarmed; Malatesta was asleep, and had told the bell-ringer of the Carroccio, or war chariot, that he was not to ring the bell under any pretence or he would kick him.

There was tremendous confusion, and the English could not be prevented from breaking the trenches, but Grimaldi was watching, and from the temporary loopholes in the

1364.   houses, commenced a very tempest of arrows: Count Montfort was on guard and he bore that day the standard of
the *felitori*, the most willing of the Florentine volunteers;
Manno Donati was also vigilant and with a corps of chosen
men of Florence. and Arezzo, with some mountaineers from
Casentino, he sallied unobserved from Cascina, made a
circuit and fell on the flank of the assailants, who fought
desperately to get out of the trap, but being poorly seconded by the other mercenaries, they were broken and
destroyed leaving 30 dead, and 300 wounded men, who
had to wait the Pisan doctors before they could get the
darts of the Genoese archers out of their flesh.*

The defeat of the advance troops put the Pisan militia
into such disorder that the Florentines, now victorious,
captured the waggons of wine sent from Pisa to her army.

Seeing the day irretrievably lost, Hawkwood, leaving
the citizens in the midst, withdrew with his English rear-
guard to San Savino where he gathered together his
wounded and followed up the retreat to Pisa in good order.

Malatesta took no trouble to molest him, for he gave
his mind to collecting trophies of victory, but though he
took 2000 prisoners he merely disarmed the foreigners
among them. and set them free. He carried the Pisans
·a thousand back to Florence together with an eagle which
had flown from Pisa to the camp where it probably
scented prey.

Florence long retained a memento of those Pisan prisoners in the *Loggia dei Pisani* on the Piazza della Signoria,
which was constructed by their forced labour. There is
too an altar dedicated to S. Victor in the Duomo, and
the feast of that Saint, — the patron of the Guelphs, — was
for many years celebrated with the *palio* (races) in honor
of this victory.

---

* They had indeed splendid doctors in Pisa. under the care of whom
a great many perished in a few days!

The victorious army did not neglect to celebrate the occasion by passing under the walls of Pisa, where they made reprisals, by returning the insults they had received at the gates of Florence the year before, with even greater spirit and opprobrium than the Pisans had done, after which they marched home. It was not long before peace was concluded between these two cities which were starved out to fatten the Germans and English.

But before peace was concluded, Giovanni Agnello, profiting by the misfortunes of his country, and the ensuing confusion of events, usurped the Lordship of Pisa and took the title of Doge ; Hawkwood in his character of Captain being his principal assistant.

It is probable that he consented to aid Agnello's arrogant ambition, because he, being a rich merchant, guaranteed the payment of the 30,000 florins required for the stipend of the martial company. To the soldier of fortune everything gave way to the question of pay.

It is certain that Agnello, as the chronicler tells us, had " tuned the lyre " (temprato la cetera) with Hawkwood, for having lulled the vigilance of the citizens to sleep, by means of the most absurd dissimulations, he bravely struck his blow by night, while the English soldiers occupied the palace and Piazza for him ; and as universal suffrage was unnecessary in those days he declared that the Blessed Virgin had revealed to him in a dream that he must assume the dogeship of Pisa for a year. As soon as the 30,000 florins were paid to the English, and peace concluded with the Florentines, he got himself elected doge for life ; moreover in the following year he nominated his sons as his successors, Francesco the second was named *Auti* or *Aukud* after his godfather, the English *condottiere,* so intimate was the friendship between him and the usurper.

1364.   Florence was meanwhile suffering from an *embarras de richesses* in the way of stipendiaries, having engaged a multitude just as the need of them ceased. She sent them into the Lucchese territory where the English White Company, and the German "Company of the Flower" encamped separately. For the good luck of the Florentines, there was an old hostility between these two bands, who were in their ill humour constantly menacing each other.

The Florentines had the wit to keep them on such terms, with each other, that they had neither long truce nor time to quarrel, and when things became serious between English and Germans, Malatesta interfered to pacify them.

September.   Peace assured, the great object was to get them out of the way, — the English were sent to encamp on the Cecina, but they would not stay there. Belmonte and his leaders (Sterz according to his clause in the compact had resigned) complained that their horses suffered in the cold nights of the coming autumn, and they wanted covered quarters.

For the rest they protested their devotion and willingness to fight, saying they would rather take 100,000 florins in war than 300,000 in peace. But it was just peace that was being stipulated.

Nothing could prevent them from coming to encamp near San Miniato. Here they behaved courteously, paying their way and doing no damage ; very likely they were afraid of Florence favouring the Germans, and setting them upon them, and so they respected the Florentine territory, and unfurled her standard together with that of their own Captain.

But as to departing, they put it off as long as possible, waiting « their people and things » (*lor gente e cose*) —

probably the women and spoil they left behind when they went away in the spring. — At the end of September they were still on the lower Val d' Elsa, not without some struggles with the peasants of San Miniato, nor losses on each side; it seems in fact that the populace knew so well how to return blow for blow, that the Florentine authorities had to interfere and make them return the horses and other things taken from the mercenaries.

To complicate the situation Belmonte, the Captain, was absent.

Florence at last managed to send Bongarden southward with his Germans. Albert Sterz united with him and they formed a strong band called the " Star Company," which turned towards the Reame (Kingdom of Naples). As to the White Company, just at that moment Cardinal Albornoz received the commission to engage 6000 men for 200,000 florins to fight for the League against Bernabò Visconti, but the project was not carried out; the Florentines had great difficulty in inducing them to go to the Maremma, and to smooth matters with Siena, but all their efforts could not prevent the English from sacking the land. It was of this that Antonio Pucci sang:

> Avieno una brigata, che la ferza
> Per insegna portavano, e d'intorno
> Facien più mal dalla mattina a terza
> Che gli altri non facieno in tutto il giorno.
> Veggendo come cotal gente scherza,
> I Sanesi pregâr senza soggiorno
> Il Fiorentin che per Dio gli piacesse
> Di metter quivi accordo, se potesse.
>   E' Fiorentini allor dimenticando
> Le 'ngiurie ricevute dal Sanese,
> Tosto mandâr gli Ambasciadori e quando
> Si ritrovâr colla gente Inghilese
> Trattaro il concio sì, ch' a posto stando,
> Fecion, che quel Comun fu lor cortese
> Di ventisei migliaja di fiorini,
> Co' quali andaron sopr' a' Perugini.

I' non intendo più di seguitare
Degl' Inghilesi, nè di loro andata;
Ma prego Iddio, che ogni loro andare
Possa essere e sia senza tornata.

Which may be thus rendered into English rhyme:

A fine brigade they had, the which a scourge
For ensign bore, and wrought about its way
More damage in the three first hours of dawn
Than other armies worked the live-long day.
Now when the Sienese perceived their freaks
The Florentines for love of God they pray
To draw them off, — to offer terms or pact
To procure peace at any price in fact.
The men of Florence straightway did forget
Old injuries which Siena them had wrought
And sent ambassadors who soon did meet
And parley with the English host they sought.
A treaty they arranged, so prompt, that soon
Siena courteously her peace had bought.
Twenty six thousand florins did she pay
And to Perugia rode the bands away.
No more do I intend to follow up
These Englishmen, nor where they went that day.
But please the Lord where'er they go or stop
They'll go and never more return, I pray.

VI.

THE ORGANISM OF MERCENARY COMPANIES.

[Codex of the stipendiaries in the service of the Republic of Florence — FILIPPO VILLANI — AZARIO — MATTEO VILLANI — CANESTRINI, Documents etc. in the Archivio Storico Ita- : ano — RICOTTI, History of mercenary companies — GREGOROVIUS, Hist. of medieval Rome — Letter of John Swiler to Hawkwood — State Archives of Florence, Riforma- gioni cl. XIII. dist II — GATARO, Paduan chronicle in MURATORI [R. I. S.]]

We beg the reader to excuse us if we refer at this
point to some particulars, which if not directly connected
with Hawkwood, are neccessary to show with what kind
of soldiery he had to deal, and what was the general
aspect of war in his days.

The White Company, like other bands of free-booters, consisted of both horse and foot soldiers. The infantry were chiefly archers armed with long and strong bows made of yew, which they carried on their backs when marching, and rested the point on the ground when taking aim ; they had long arrows and were besides armed with swords and knives. For defence these famous bowmen, who had subdued the French army, wore an iron helmet, a cuirass, or rather breast piece, and iron gloves. The " lances " were mounted soldiers; the name lance was imported by the English, for the hired cavalry used to be called *barbute,* from the shape of their helmets. Each " lance " consisted of three men, the *caporale* (knight),* the *piatta* (squire) and the *ragazzo* (page). The two first rode chargers, and the page had a pony or nag. Five lances usually made a *posta* (post), and five posts made a *bandiera* (standard) ; there was generally a decurial leader for every ten lances.

With the exception of the Hungarian cavalry, — which were rather archers on horseback, being only armed with bow and arrows, — the English cavalry was lighter than that of other nations. The German, Burgundian, and Italian lances armed their squires lightly, with only sword and knife (*coltello*), but their knights were much more heavily accoutred than the English. As a rule they carried helmet, breastplate with iron framework, cuirass and

---

* It is rather difficult to translate this word by a just equivalent in English. The nearest approach to it is ˙knight˙ or ˙cavalier.˙ He was a gentleman of independent means who gave or sold his services, together with those of his followers or servants ; sometimes one leader furnished several lances, in which case all the *caporali* may not have been knights, until they had distinguished themselves. Sometimes, as Chaucer has represented it, the squire was the son of the knight, and became knight in his turn when he had won his spurs by any great deed of valour. Froissart and other old chroniclers speak of five or six hundred *knights* fighting in Edward the Black Prince's army at Cressy and Poitiers, where Hawkwood himself was a squire and probably won his spurs. The general name for the whole troop was ˙men-at-arms.˙ — (*Translator.*)

pancerone, greaves. armlets. gauntlets. iron gloves, sword,
knife and lance. The English had no *pancerone,* and wore
a cuirass, instead of a breastplate. with sleeves of mail and
a gorget.

The English horses were also more lightly caparisoned
than the others: in fact the "Codex of the stipendiaries
of the Florentine service" which was modified in 1369,
conceded permission for men of other nationalities to wear
armour in the English style. but not so for the horses.

The English cavaliers generally fought on foot, their
horses served more to expedite and facilitate their marches; in fact they corresponded more to the modern dra-
goons, who were originally mounted infantry, and in most
countries only became exclusively cavalry about the latter
half of the last century. In Russia they still retain their
mixed character. The Hungarians were a fair represen-
tative of modern light cavalry, and the German and Italian
lances of the cuirassiers.

Filippo Villani and Azario minutely describe the tactics
of the White Company and explicitly tell us they almost
always fought on foot, leaving their horses in charge of
their pages, who retired to ambush during action in some
wood or fold of a hill. When fighting, the knights and
squires formed themselves into a circular mass, with their
long and tough lances lowered closely and compactly, each
lance being held by both knight and squire. The attack
was made by slow steps, and with fierce shouts. It is
true, they had not the advantage of a sudden rush or
onslaught, but they gained that of solidity, and were formidable in thus opposing great difficulty to the enemy
who should attempt to disorder this species of porcupine.

These tactics, analogous to those of the Swiss in the
16th century, — being more defensive than offensive even
in an attack, — explain the relative incolumity of the

White Company even in a defeat, as well as its indecisive victories. It was a convenient method to those who made warfare a mere trade, for they had every reason to prolong hostilities without uselessly exposing themselves.

In consequence of this style of fighting, they carried neither shields nor bucklers, they had no firearms (except now and then a *bombarda* (mortar?) and were very well disciplined in file and duty, but they were disorderly in quarters, and the difficulty of finding provision and forage obliged them to frequently change their camp.

As to their appearance, they were a splendid troop, were it only for the diligence of the squires, who polished the arms till they shone like mirrors.*

That which made them formidable was their custom of nocturnal marches (*de die plerumque dormiunt et de nocte vigilant*) and still more the cowardice of the Italians, who were unused to arms. They were insuperable in a " sacking " (*furatores excellentiores quibusque aliis prædatoribus*), for plunder was their ordinary method of provisioning, — and in the constant menaces with which they obtained heavy ransoms and large stipends from the Italian cities. For purposes of plunder they carried a great many scaling ladders made of separate pieces fitting into each other, " *studia et artificia ad terras capiendas quod nusquam aliqui visi fuerunt similes vel æquales*," that is to say, to take exposed or ill defended places. Where they found vigilance or valid resistance, they did not attempt to attack a fortress. In the 14ᵗʰ century, when artillery had scarcely begun to be known, a castle or walled town presented almost an impregnable obstacle, because the besiegers had usually exhausted the resources of the country before the besieged

---

* Here is a recipe of the year 1402 to prevent arms from ever getting rusty : " Cut off all the legs of a goat from the knee downwards, let them stay in the smoke for a day, then keep them 15 or 25 days. When you require them, break the legs and take out the marrow from the bones, and grease the arms with it and they will always keep bright even when wet."

had consumed the provisions stored in the city; hence in wars of that time, there was always great devastation of the country, while the occupation of the cities by the enemy was rare, and as the towns sheltered the inhabitants and their wealth, the battles were very inconclusive.

The funds of the mercenary company then chiefly depended on depredation and extortion, and the squires who made a business of it, were not at all accustomed to save their earnings : play, women, luxury, in short a gay life, consumed quickly, often in anticipation, such ill gained money, which often passed, together with arms and horses, into the hands of usurers.

This was a serious inconvenience to the republics that hired the companies. Their equipage lost, the soldiers could no longer serve, and reduced to their last shifts, they had more temptation to break their agreements, to sell themselves elsewhere, or to demand more than was in the compact.

To relieve them from the risks of usury was sometimes a wise provision, and consequently, in 1362, Florence opened a bank for Loans to the stipendiaries * which was reformed on a very simple basis in 1367.

They opened operations by allowing a credit up to 1000 lire to each company of 25 lances; a constable might borrow as much as 600 lire, an ordinary knight up to 100, and it remained with the officials to determine what sums they should allow to the subordinates. No interest was extorted, but every loan must be backed by

---

* MATTEO VILLANI XI. c. 88 : ' The greedy and dishonest usurers, under cover of lending help to the soldiers of their republic, took away their money, arms, and horses, so that they could no longer be of use to their employers, for this the commune was moved to form a bank which with the public money should assist the soldiers. In the month of February 1362 it was organized with all its officials, and the republic placed 15,000 florins at the disposal of the bank with which to commence operations.'

the security of two *conestabili* (superiors officers, of very
high grade). This last condition and the incurable impro-
vidence of the adventurers left still a large field to the
usurers, so that at the same time severe laws were
promulgated against procurators and money lenders, pro-
hibiting exchanges, or the negotiation of credits with the
stipendiaries: laws which implicated even the loss of political rights, and remained in force till 1431.

In the banking books numberless names of constables
and knights of every nation are to be found, dating
from 1367 to the end of the 15th century and even later.
There are however few English names after the end
of the 14th century.

The mode of living of the mercenary militia in Italy
during that century, their internal relations, and those
with the States employing them, are completely explained
by Ricotti and Canestrini, who quote from undeniable documents, such as contracts stipulating their stipends, and
the special laws of some Tuscan Republics. The numerous
contracts with English Constables up to 1395 which exist
in the Florentine Archives of the " Riformagioni " and
correspond with those already published, are all made on
the same scheme. They frequently contain a clause " not
to fight against the King of England " and another " that
the leaders of companies are responsible for the crimes
committed by the soldiers in camp, while the Commune
shall judge those committed in the city, or to the damage
of subjects of the Republic."

That important, curious, and complete codex of the
Florentine militia in 1337 with its fifty three chapters,
containing the rules, and various conditions for the troops,
are referred to and illustrated by the aforesaid authors (Ricotti and Canestrini). On his side Gregorovius has given
what we might almost call the philosophy of mercenaries.

He considers the system as an organic social disease, like the degeneracy of chivalry, or the rising of the lower classes, massing themselves together against the higher; it would perhaps be easier and more exact to define them as " military brigands under command." On the other hand his observation is true that the condition especially favorable to mercenaries in Italy was, that the republics, with their democratic mania for exiling their nobles, had lost their military virtue; but he is silent as to the chief reason, which was that there was much more to plunder in Italy than in other lands, and the hunter chooses the ground that most abounds in sport.

Their organization favored by circumstances was so complete, that they might almost be qualified as " Nomad Military States:" they elected their captain or freely accepted him if entering a company already formed; the captain had great power, but it was limited by the council of constables and marshals, while in the most important decisions the cavaliers or *caporali* were called into the deliberations.

The decisions were not enrolled until they had been accurately debated, and the conditions fixed by the captains: they often demanded pay in anticipation, and security against preceding enmities with soldiers of other nationalities whom they might find in the company. In treaties they required a written reply, or if it were a case of parley, they demanded a safeconduct for themselves and their embassy. This is evident from a curious letter from constable Swiler to our John Hawkwood.*

They had a numerous following of women (even nuns carried off by force) and of voluntary courtesans,** and

---

* See Document II.

** In the battle of Brentelle, June 25, 1386, the Paduans took 211 of them, and crowning them with flowers and putting bouquets in their hands, they conducted them in triumph to Padua, where they were invited to breakfast in the palace of the ruling Lord Francesco Carrara.

when the soldiers thought it wiser to keep on friendly terms with a district they honestly purchased their provisions.

They employed usurers and bankers in every city to lend them money or to keep it for them: they had able ambassadors and eloquent orators to conduct their diplomatic treaties: treasurers to regulate their financial affairs, and attorneys for their private ones, secretaries, notaries and registrars for their correspondence and the due preparations of legal acts and documents.

" The sole reason they did not establish lordship in Italy," observes Gregorovius, " is because the leaders lacked the political idea, and the adventurers the bonds of nationality." It is a fact that natives of so many different countries were enrolled in every company that they were called from the majority of the men composing them, English, German, Burgundian, or Breton, Hungarian or lastly Italians.

As to the leaders, if ever there was one who for talent, constancy, valour, prudence, and resolution might have aspired to the highest aims, but who had the wisdom to moderate his ambition, and practically remain at his post, it was Hawkwood, as we shall see in following the history of himself and his men.

VII.

THE PERUGIAN WAR.
THE ENGLISH BEATEN BY THE GERMANS.

[GRAZIANI, *Cronache perugine* — GREGOROVIUS, *Storia di Roma nel Medio Evo* — MACHIA-VELLI, *Storie florentine* — Deliberations of the Pisan Commune in June 1365, in the *Pisan State Archives* — GHIRARDACCI, *Storie bolognesi* — BONINCONTRI, *Annali* — ' Carteggio ' of the Florentine Signory, *Miss.* XIII. 40, cited by PERRENS, *Histoire de Florence* — *Sienese Chronicle*, in MURATORI [R. I. S.] — ARIODANTE FABRETTI in the notes on GRAZIANI.]

What between contemporaneous chronicles, posterior historians, and modern commentators, together with the

1364.   equivocal dates, and doubtful names which one hears vith- out knowing to whom they belong, the history of the mercenary companies just after the Pisan war is so com- plicated that much of it is undecipherable. Let us see if we can find our bearings in this sea of difficulty.

November.   Both the English White Company and Annechin Bon- garden's German band of " the Star " marched southwards, the latter against the Kingdom of Naples and the former towards Perugia. But on the way they were set against each other as foes, for the Perugians opposed the English invaders by hiring Bongarden's troops armed with long axes and with hand grenades (*bombarde a mano bellissime che passavano ogni armatura*).

This was enough for the English, who, driven also by hunger, were soon brought to terms, stipulating peace and friendship to Perugia, promising not to injure Annechin Bongarden for a year, and to withdraw within ten days. On this compact provisions were conceded them by pur- chase. The treaty was celebrated by a banquet to which the courteous priors of Perugia invited the leaders and knights of both companies.

Then the tables were turned, for Bongarden, who ad- vanced towards Naples, devastated the Roman campagna by the way, so much that Cardinal Albornoz for the Church, and Queen Joanna of Naples made a contract with the 1365. White Company, which bound the latter for the price of January 14. 160,000 florins, to keep the peace towards the kingdom for five years, and expressly to fight for it against Bon- garden. This act was stipulated by Hugh de Mortimer, Captain General, by the Captain Nicholas Count of Thod (Hungarian) and Andrew Belmonte ; George Brise conesta- bile, Eugene Ecton (Acton ?) and many of the knights.

The White Company, reinforced by the Hungarians, had evidently elected a new captain to succeed Sterz, Hawkwood, and Belmont.

Hawkwood remaining in Pisa for the winter made a trip to Lombardy, perhaps sent there by the Doge Agnello, who had an understanding with Bernabò Visconti: and from this time may be dated the relations of Hawkwood with this exemplary tyrant and head of the Ghibellines, who sent the English condottiere, in his pay, into Tuscany to assist the Ghibellines. In other words, Hawkwood on Bernabò's account reassumed the command of the White Company which had now returned to menace Florence, and in spite of their treaty attacking the Perugians. He had besides the disposal of a Pisan contingent and was receiving Pisan pay.*

1365.

As soon as the English reappeared on the Perugian territory, that city recalled Bongarden from the Campagna of Rome and united the city militia with his Germans. Three thousand cavalry and infantry commanded for the Church party by the Bolognese Tommaso Obizzoni, and sent by Cardinal Albornoz also arrived in time to assist.

July 22.

The old animosity between the Germans and English, by this time had become bitter and bloody, and rendered the battle decisive. Hawkwood with the Pisan supplement had 6000 horse, but still his forces were very inferior and consequently the English were overcome.

There have been many exaggerations about this defeat especially regarding Hawkwood. Machiavelli says he was taken prisoner; Ghirardacci describes the battle as taking place between Arezzo and Cortona, and says that for four hours it was indecisive, and that finally Tommaso Obizzoni becoming victorious took *Haucud* the English captain.

---

* In June 1365 in the name of the magnificent and potent Lord Giovanni de' Conti by the grace of God Doge of Pisa, and of the Anziani, 100 florins on account were assigned to Hawkwood who authorised *Janni* (Johnny), an English sergeant, to receive them for him, and again in July 600 florins were decreed as provision for a year from August 1st by the great general Council of the Church and that of the Senate and Credenza, ratified by the Council of the people of Pisa.

1365.   Even Bonincontri in his Cæsaresque "Annals" attributes
the merit of victory to Obizzoni, and adds that "the English were all taken with their leader Giovanni *Acuto* and
put into prison." We find elsewhere that the Pope liberated
Hawkwood from prison.

These authors evidently romance. Machiavelli is
inexact enough to attribute the action to the time of Pope
Innocent VI who had then been dead three years. Ghirardacci compiled his History of Bologna from chroniclers
who were inclined to exaggerate Bolognese achievements;[*]
he besides imagines Hawkwood fighting against the Florentines, while the Signory of Florence was in fact making
offers for his services, and though he would not concede,

July 16.   was sending these instructions to its ambassadors near him:

"By the reverence of God.... and out of regard to
him whom we esteem our dear friend we intend to
use towards him and his brigade that courtesy which
should satisfy him, though by reason of wars and great
expenses we are much less wealthy and powerful than he
esteems us, etc., etc."

This imprisonment of Hawkwood then becomes very
problematical, and we had better turn to chroniclers nearer
to the place and the deed. Now the Sienese chronicle
relates that having suffered some loss in crossing the Sienese territory, Hawkwood arrived near Perugia in July,
and here he had to combat the "Stella (Star) Company
of Germans under Bongarden," — which battle was a great
and bitter strife (*aspra e grande*); — the Germans won the
day, killing many of the English, and Andrew Belmonte

---

[*] In his preface Ghirardacci boasts of diligent fidelity in having followed
the most serious authors, and collated both public and private MSS., and in
the dedication to Pope Clement VIII he says he has consulted "the public
documents of the Vatican Library, authentic MSS. in many archives, as well
as personal deeds, especially those of the Bologna Archives." And in fact
we shall frequently have occasion to refer to him as an authority; for, generally speaking, he seems trustworthy; but in this case the facts and dates
weaken his testimony, and so we must refute it.

and fifty knights were put in prison at Perugia. Hawk- 1365.
wood fled and got away towards Siena with many others.

The Perugians sent to tell Siena that John Hawkwood
and his English Company were defeated, and the Commune of Siena presented the messenger with a scarlet
vest lined with silk which cost 26 florins.

Graziani, the Perugian chronicler, does not even name
Hawkwood. He only says that Bongarden and the Perugian militia, after two sanguinary but victorious combats,
constrained the remnant of the English to retreat to
the castle of San Mariano, where after two days, weak
with thirst, and faint with heat, being deprived of water
or other liquid, they were obliged to surrender. Sixteen
hundred were taken to Perugia as prisoners to await
ransom, while of the *canaglia* some were killed and others
set free. Among the prisoners were four knights with
their respective standards, the only one of them named
being the most distinguished ; — Andrew Belmonte, " of
royal race," the four banners are however heraldically
described as,

    1. Gules, sémé of bezants, or ;

    2. Argent, a chevron gules, starred of the field at point;

    3. Quartered, dexter argent, charged with griffon,
gules, and sinister gules with lion argent;

    4. Gules, a bend or, charged with a crescent of
the field.

This last must have belonged to the bastard Belmonte.
Neither of them corresponds to that of John Hawkwood,
which may be seen to this day in Paolo Uccello's fresco,
in the Duomo at Florence, and which has for its blazon,
" Argent a chevron sable, charged with three escallop
shells of the field," nor is there the motto " al falco "
which we find on his seal as allusive to his name.

Andrew Belmonte easily regained his liberty on swearing
to respect the Perugian territory for five years, and leaving

1365.　as hostages three captains, viz Hugh Mortimer, John *di Breccia* (Brise) and Thod the Count of Hungary, who were most probably the proprietors of the three other standards.

From all this it appears that Hawkwood was defeated but saved himself with part of his men, while the rest were shut up with Belmonte in San Mariano; and that he was still in a condition to keep the field, for, on August 3rd, the Commune of Perugia sent part of the August 3. German forces to help Siena *contro Messer Giovanni Aguto inghilese*. Thus says the Perugian chronicler and he of Siena confirms it, even saying that the Sienese did not think it superfluous to send both the German leaders, Bongarden and Sterz, against Hawkwood; and that it was only then that Hawkwood had to beat a retreat, and fighting his way through the Maremma, he passed thence, along the sea shore to Liguria, the Genoese territory.

———

VIII.

A HAWKWOOD, A VISCONTI, AND A HAPSBURG IN THE *COMPANY OF ST. GEORGE*.

[Brief of Pope Urban V, 17 February 1364 — RAYNALDI, *Annals* — "Carteggio" of the Florentine Signory, *Miss.* XII, 34 — Private pontifical letters, vol. 3, cited by RAYNALDI — AMMIRATO — CANESTRINI, Documents, etc. — *Sienese Chronicle* — Pisan State Archives, Registro 68, carte 61 tergo — TSCHUDI, *Swiss songs* — Deliberations of the Council of the "Campana" March and April, 1366, Sienese State Archives — Deliberations etc., Florentine State Archives, 29 June 1366 — GREGOROVIUS, *Hist. of medieval Rome.*]

The mercenary companies, as we see, were a hydra of a hundred heads, and their captains each like "Antaeus," who, defeated and overthrown, rose up from the earth more enterprising than before. Matteo Villani, in one of his eloquent outbursts, tells us how the Italian people suffered under them: astrologers tried to explain the scourge by the movement of the heavens, and conjunc-

tion of planets; other folks attributed it to the anger of
God. Urban V gave ecclesiastical subsidies to princes, and 1364.
indulgences to the people who would take arms against
" that multitude of villains of divers nations, associated
in arms by avidity in appropriating to themselves the
fruit of the labours of innocent and defenceless people;
unbridled in every kind of cruelty, extorting money;
methodically devastating the country, and the open towns,
burning houses and barns, destroying trees and vines,
obliging poor peasants to fly; assaulting, besieging, invading, spoiling, and ruining even fortresses and walled
cities; torturing and maiming those from whom they expected to obtain ransom, without regard to ecclesiastical
dignity, or sex or age; violating wives, virgins, and nuns,
and constraining even gentlewomen to follow their camp,
to do their pleasure and carry arms and baggage." February 17.

Soon after this, it entered the Pope's head to persuade May 15.
the English to take up the cross like Christ, and to follow
the King of Cyprus to fight the Turks, — so he wrote to
the captain and leaders, — but Hawkwood who was not
a " Conte Verde " remained unconvinced.

Seeing they were not to be persuaded, the Pope again
began to thunder out excommunications against them, and
to publish indulgences to those who would fight them.
Seeing that neither excommunications nor indulgences had
any effect, he thought to entice all the bands on both
sides of the Alps, to pass into the East by land or by
sea; and for this he formed an alliance with the Emperor
Charles IV, the Pope promising money and benedictions, 1365.
May.
and the Emperor undertaking to pay the expenses of the
journey, — he who never had a penny to call his own!

Cardinal Albornoz was commissioned to attempt the
metamorphosis of brigands into crusaders, but the captains
naturally laughed him to scorn. The Cardinal was then
set to form a league against Hawkwood, who was the most

formidable of the lot. He treated with Florence, but nothing was concluded, for to destroy the companies it would be necessary to hire more foreigners and thus increase the evil.

In the mean time, the English and Germans being left without pay, wandered about Tuscany sacking wherever they went. Florence could do nothing but send ambassadors to one, and then to the other, to smooth them down, and keep them to their word, to find out their intentions and possibly also to edge them on to fight with each other. The Pope, as we find from his secret correspondence, followed the same tactics.

Bongarden was in the Lucchese, and intended to pass into Lombardy, but Hawkwood prevented him. The latter had become the effective leader of a new Anglo-Italian Company (one of several which bore the name of St. George) which had been hastily formed in Lunigiana, and was commanded by Ambrogio Visconti bastard son of Bernabò Visconti ; — he acting Telemachus, and Hawkwood doing Mentor.

The Florentines sent out six ambassadors to the different belligerents: there were Lapo de' Rossi and Giorgio Scali who went to grant Bongarden free and friendly passage across their territory ; Piero Canigiani and Niccolò Rimbaldeschi to congratulate Bernabò on the promotion of his son to the Generalship ; and Doffo de' Bardi and Giovanni Cambi, to treat with the Company of St. George, which was already on Pisan ground.

The compact was soon concluded and signed at Florence, on October 12, 1365, the Company binding itself for the sum of 6000 florins, not to injure Florence or her allies for five years, even though it should change captains. They were besides granted passes, guides, and provisions, (by payment) with permission to hire 300 horsemen from either Siena or Perugia.

The relative document is mutilated. In the heading,
figure the names of Ambrogio Visconti, captain general;
Giovanni Ubaldini, Italian; Aymond de Rundell, and William
Boson, Englishmen; Luca di Valco, Hungarian; Lodovico
delle Spade of Parma, counsellers; Hugh Ethon, English
constable; Thomas Merezal (Marshal ?), marshal of the
English; Bartolommeo da Gaggio, marshal of the Italians.
In the context frequent mention is made of a certain
Signor Giovanni (Sir John) who can be no other than
Hawkwood, for at the end we read " For the observation
of the which things, all and single.... in the name of the
above, do oblige and pledge themselves, to the above named
Signor Ambrogio Captain, and Signor Giovanni Acud...."

Among the signatures are the names and seals of Visconti, Ubaldini, Hawkwood, and forty two others, amongst
captains and constables.

Having pocketed the florins, the Company lost not a
day : " time is money ! " so they immediately (on October 15)
encamped at the Abbey of Isola near Siena. The Sienese
sent a few fruitless embassies to offer terms, while they
were seeking soldiers to fight them, and kept two sentinels
night and day on their tower called *del Mangia*. They
found eleven companies (bandiere) of Germans at Orvièto,
and finally having got together a good many troops sallied
forth to battle.

But the Company of St. George did not stop to fight!
riding rapidly night and day, they halted only at Sarzana
and then went on to the vicinity of Genoa. The terror
they spread everywhere is expressed in a document in
the Pisan Archives where a certain Francesco Bellebuono
explains to the Anziani " that he cannot bring the goods
to Pisa, for fear of John Hawkwood."

The speed of transport of those adventurers is incredible, as in a search for spoil, or pay, they rushed
continually over the length and breadth of the peninsula.

1364
and 1365.

Among the *condottieri* then living at the expense of Italy, were a count Johann of the illustrious and imperial house of Hapsburg, and his brother Rudolf.

On the other side of the Alps Johann had sustained evil fortunes, and had let himself be captured by the burghers of Zurich, and kept prisoner for three years in the little island (now so lovely in its cool and pleasant shades) where the limpid waters of the Limmat leave the Lake to flow through the city: and where at that time there rose on a rock a dark fortress tower called the *Wellemberg*. While in prison here he composed an elegiac song to the forget-me-not, which began

So di un piccolo fiore azzurro.

(I know a tiny blue flower.)

He found brighter fortunes in Italy, where he and his brother at first followed the banner of Florence. Rudolf, being an effeminate looking man, was called by the Florentines *il Conte Menno* (the beardless Count); he belied his face however at the battle of Cascina, where he performed incredible prodigies of valour, — *cose da tacerle, perchè hanno faccia di menzogna* — as Filippo Villani has it. Johann finally allied himself with Hawkwood and Visconti, who had returned from Liguria, to the misfortune of Siena.

1366.
March.

The Sienese tried to conciliate them by presents of poultry and sweets, providing victuals, and sending to treat with them, but finding the two captains intractable, they tried the tactics of the soldiery, and set fire to the hay all over the country, so that the enemy could not lodge there. At the same time they had recourse to Hawkwood's old friend the Doge of Pisa, to beg him at least to mediate with the English brigade.

March 20.

But the Company held out, and at length the Sienese were persuaded to put their hands in their purses, — *doven-*

dosi riparare alla cattiva Compagnia di San Giorgio they
made a forced loan, and stipulated on April 20 the " conventions and accords " between the Commune of Siena on
the one part; and Ambrogio Visconti captain, Hawkwood,
the Count of Hapsburg and Giovanni da Buda, constables
of the Company of St. George, on the other. The price
paid by the Sienese was 10,500 florins, of which the first
instalment of 4000 was to be paid within fifteen days, besides
which the Company was to be allowed to pass over the
Sienese territory once a year for five years, provided they
did no damage nor annoyed the inhabitants. The contract
was stipulated by the representatives and attorneys of
the two parts, all knights or marshals in the respective
brigades. John Quartery, Englishman, sealed it with Hawkwood's arms, a *chevron* and three shells, legend indeci-
pherable.

The compact made, it was not easy to get it kept:
many of the Company's soldiers entered Siena to celebrate
the occasion, and Visconti's men behaved so badly that
the city rose against them, and several were killed or
wounded.

Having taken the money, Hawkwoord and his good
scholar Ambrogio took the road to Pisa, greatly damaging
Florentine lands by the way. Florence sent ambassadors
to accompany them and keep them in order, one of whom,
Doffo de' Bardi got Hawkwood to promise to move on in
an amicable manner. This probably meant only a day's
march which cost Florence 350 florins paid to Hawkwood,
and 55 more for indemnity to Bardi for horses lost (*per-*
duti) on the occasion. Then there was always the fear
of worse things, so much so that Giovanni di Porcellino
was sent to the Company as a spy under pretext of finding
certain boys who were said to have run away from Florence, and when Visconti wanted to return to the Florentine states, he (Porcellino) persuaded Hawkwood to pass

1366. wide of the city, sending warnings to all the places on the chosen route.

These particulars are necessary to comprehend what a terrible scourge these adventurers were, and why Italian potentates, both great and small, were impatient to find a remedy against them.

April 13.   Pope Urban V had hurled a bull from Avignon beginning *Clamat ad nos de terra multorum fidelium effusus sanguis innoxius,* and following up with a highly coloured description of the brigandish achievements of the companies, and invocations to Heaven for their extermination: then he excommunicated the captains who did not disband their armies, and restore the lands they occupied: the princes and republics, who hired them, and the lords and people who served them; he stained with infamy every one who should take their part, and then with the attraction of plenary absolution invited every body to fight against them.

After this thundering prelude, the Pope returned to his favourite nostrum, of forming a general league against the companies to expel them from Italy, and oblige them to take up the cross against the Turks. The Emperor Charles IV and nearly all the Italian princes and republics adhered to it. Florence sent to Avignon, as ambassadors for the treaty, personages no less than Francesco Bruni and Giovanni Boccaccio, thus beginning to absolve herself from the censure of having wished to employ the Company of St. George. Even Bernabò Visconti seemed disposed to withdraw his son Ambrogio from that career, and received the approval of the Pope, who offered to annul all the compacts made by different republics with the Condottieri.

But it was very difficult to come to any practical conclusion, for at that same time Florence was sending to make excuses to Ambrogio, who had asked a loan of money, and was also excusing herself to the Pope for her inability to enter the league against the existing companies.

They had then to limit themselves to the more modest
object of preventing new bands from descending into Italy
or staying there, and they perforce resigned themselves
to the ones already existing, almost recognising that they
had acquired a right to, or even monopoly of the military
stipendiary.

This admitted, the act of the league stipulated in Florence on September 19, 1366 added :

" The Companies which are at present in Italy are the Septemb. 19.
undermentioned and no others :

> The Company of Signor Ambrogio (Visconti);
>
> The Company of Signor Giovanni Acuto (Hawkwood);
>
> The Company of Signor Annechino (Bongarden);
>
> The Company of Signor Conte Giovanni (Johann of
> Hapsburg)."

But even with this limited scope the league did not
last long. It was dissolved in December of the following
year, because Florence would have nothing to do with the
Emperor.

The Company of St. George lasted even less than the
league. It was completely defeated in the Kingdom of
Naples, and Ambrogio Visconti taken and kept as prisoner
by Queen Joanna : while the remains of his band went to
reinforce Hawkwood, who had reappeared before Siena.
For eight days he had been amicably furnished with provisions, and was then obliged to take the usual refuge at
Pisa, the base of his operations. Here he was joined by his
old comrade the royal bastard Belmonte, who on his libe-
ration from prison in Perugia had got together a great
troop and refurnished them with arms. Thus strengthened,
the two Englishmen marched against the Perugians with
whom they had to settle an old account, the defeat they
suffered two years before.

At Montalcinello they encountered the Sienese who were
reinforced by the Perugians, and provided with Hungarian

and many other soldiers. The Sienese were completely
routed, and their captain, the *conservadore* Ugolino, was
taken prisoner and obliged to pay ten thousand florins of
ransom. Then the Perugians and Sienese were wholly
defeated at Ponte San Giovanni, where 1500 of their men
were killed, besides a great many horses. Their captain
(that German Paer who had signalized himself in the Florentine service, fighting against the English in the Mugello)
and the Podestà of Perugia remained prisoners.

Hawkwood and Belmonte were revenged to the full;
so much so that the Hall in which the Perugian magistrates had decided to give Belmonte his liberty, was called
the Hall of bad counsel (*del mal consiglio*).

IX.

THE DEFENCE OF BORGOFORTE. — DEFEAT AT AREZZO.
VICTORY AT CASCINA.

[*Carteggio della Signoria fiorentina, Miss.* XIII. 38; XIV. 44, 42, 43 — *Archivio Storico Italiano.* Appendix VII. 429 — Raniери Sardo, *Cronica pisana* — *Cronica pisana* in
Muratori [*R. I. S.*] — Giovio, *Elogia virorum bellica virtute illustrium* — Litta, *Famiglie celebri,* Visconti — Sampson Lennard Bluemantle, Heraldic book in the *Harleyan MSS.* 1178. 49 — Corio, *Storia di Milano* — Ghirardacci, *Storia bolognese* in
Muratori [*R. I. S.*] — Manni, *Biografia dell' Acuto* in Muratori [*R. I. S.*], Appendix
v. II — Giulini, *Memorie di Milano* — Donato Velluti, *Cronaca.*]

The successes of the English caused great apprehension
to the Florentines, who had already sent the usual Doffo
di Bardi to hear whether Hawkwood would enter their
service, and to the captain himself they wrote: "Although
we have urgent need of soldiers, we are disposed to wait even
a month for you." He refused, pledging himself instead
to an agreement with Cardinal Albornoz, the Pope's legate,
on which the Signoria wrote to the Cardinal and sent
instructions to Bardi, and to their Ambassadors at Perugia,

for they were afraid that the English after having drained   1867.
the territory of Perugia should turn their attention to the
Val d' Arno ; they feared also " the annoyances which such
people occasion even against the will of their captain."
For these reasons they were unwilling to grant them a
passage, even when they promised to make good the damages. " Manage," so run the instructions, " that they
shall not pass over our territory as M. Giovanni has more
than once promised to do, to show the great love which
he says he bears us.... At least get them to pass by the
route which will do us the least harm, and at every place
where they encamp send us a messenger, that we may know
their movements."

After all, as soon as the Pisan war was finished, rather
friendly relations were maintained, between Hawkwood and
Florence ; we have seen that the Florentines addressed
themselves especially to him in treating with the Company
of St. George ; it would seem as though he foresaw that
some day or other it would be to his interest to serve
Florence.

On the other hand the Sienese perceiving that the affair   April 28.
was dragging on, decided to offer him money provided he
would quit the country, and as their treasury was empty
they contracted a loan on the wine duties.*

In fact he returned peacefully to Pisa where he was
accustomed to live at the " Inn of Martino " at Campe-
ronesi, an honorable house, apparently, as the daughter
of the Emperor Charles IV also lodged there, in 1369.   1369.

Here they were preparing great things in honor of   1867.
Pope Urban V, who was coming to Italy by sea from
Avignon. Pisa being Catholic wished to pay its respects to
the Pope — but being also Ghibelline, she took precautions
against the head of the Guelph faction, who was to touch

---

* See Documents III, IV, V, VI.

1367.   at the port of Pisa and land at Leghorn. The doge
Agnello therefore went to Leghorn with more than a
thousand cavaliers, led by Hawkwood; and the Pope, who
had persecuted the *condottieri* with excommunications and
treaties, was so afraid, that he would not disembark.

A little while after he had stopped the Pope, it fell to
Hawkwood's lot to stop the Emperor.

In 1368 he had returned to the pay of Bernabò Visconti together with William Boson, conducting four thousand Englishmen. His passage into Lombardy was probably connected with the arrival there of Lionel Duke
of Clarence, son of Edward III. of England: who came
to celebrate his marriage with Violante, daughter of Galeazzo Visconti and niece of Bernabò * and it is very likely
that he went to pay homage at the court of his own
Royal Prince; for we already know that all the English
adventurers in Italy stipulated a clause in all their contracts affirming their loyalty to the King of England.

The ceremonials of this marriage, and the rich gifts to
the guests, with all other particulars, are amply described
by the Milanese chroniclers.

It was a splendid wedding — Petrarch and the Conte
Verde were there — but to the Duke of Clarence it was
an ill-omened day, for by reason of a malady contracted
by the change of climate, or intemperance in the too
sumptuous nuptial banquets, or by other excesses, within
three months he had passed into the other world.

Then arose a contest between the English nobles of the
Duke's suite and Galeazzo Visconti, who demanded the
restitution of the marriage portion (Alba, Mondovi, Che-

---

* The Milanese annals say in general terms that Lionel was accompanied
by about 2000 English, amongst whom were many archers. Giovio and Litta
positively affirm that Hawkwood was in the Duke's party, and the heraldic
book of Sampson Lennard Bluemantle confirms the fact.

rasco, Cuneo, and Demonte). There is no sign that Hawkwood was mixed up in this, indeed such a thing would
have been both imprudent and useless.

Besides he was otherwise employed on Bernabò's account.
This prince had erected a new bastion at Borgoforte on
the Po and stationed an Italian garrison, there, which by
reason of old rancours, had disagreed with the German mercenaries in Visconti's pay, and was reduced to evil case,
so that Bernabò had to ride in great haste to the place,
where — order being restored — he placed the bastion under the charge of Hawkwood's Englishmen.

Then the Emperor Charles IV came down from the
Alps and made common cause with the d' Estes and other
Italian princes against the Visconti, persuading them to
attack Borgoforte. It must be noted that what between
the Imperials (Bohemians, Sclavonians, Poles, Grisons and
Swiss) d' Este's Italians, those of Malatesta, and of Queen
Joanna; and the Church party which consisted of Bretons,
Gascons, and Provençals; as many as twenty thousand
combatants presented themselves before that fortress.

In the army of Visconti were Germans, English, Italians, Burgundians, all with the firm determination to
defend the bulwarks; in those days a small place, well
provisioned and manned with a spirited garrison, might
defy even " an army sufficient to subjugate Italy." To
intercept succour, the d' Este party had launched on the
Po a fleet of galleys and other boats, and the river being
much swollen by the melting of the snows, the Imperia-
lists bethought themselves of breaking the banks above
Borgoforte, but the garrison knew how to save itself from
the inundation, and returned it by breaking the banks
towards the valley by night, thus flooding the plains of
Mantua, and the entrenchments of the Imperial camp.
Charles IV was obliged to raise his camp, and shut himself
up in Mantua, after which, on account of the damage he

1868. had suffered, and of the scarcity of provisions, he hastened to agree to Bernabò's terms.

This brilliant operation completed, Hawkwood was commissioned to conduct a large force in aid of the Perugians, who had obtained the alliance of the Visconti in a war with Arezzo and the Pope. He crossed the Bolognese territory and the Romagna, without difficulty, giving it out that he was a captain on his adventures; and pretending that he was dismissed by Visconti and desirous of hiring himself to the Church, he comported himself " honestly, modestly, and quietly." Guided by a certain Monaldi, the Perugian ambassador, he arrived under Arezzo, but there he was completely defeated.

Ser Gorello of Arezzo celebrated this rout in endeca-syllabic triplets, but it will be better for us to hear the official report which the commune of Arezzo sent to the June 15. Pope,* from which it results :

That the English were encamped in the plain near the city, about a mile from the *Porta Buja,* that they were attacked by all the Aretian army both foot and horse, by the soldiers of the Church commanded by Simone di Spoleto, and by two German bands, led by Flaxen von Riesach and Johann von Rieten. The combat was long and fierce, the deaths many, even among the higher grades, and finally the English were defeated and almost all taken prisoners including their captain " Signor Giovanni Haud " (Hawkwood), and many cavaliers, together with the unfortunate Dinolo di Bindo Monaldi, the Perugian ambassador.

The honours of the day, according to the popular poet, were given to the saints Vito and Modesto, whose feast it chanced to be ; but, according to the official relation, they were principally rendered to the German " Rieten "

* See Document VII.

who was knighted, " as was proper to his most excellent valour."

The poet Ser Gorello says that " Messer Giovanni *Agudo* " (Hawkwood)

> Sconfitto fu, e tutta sua brigata
> Con grande mio onor allor fu presa. .
>
> (Was defeated, and all his brigade
> To my great honor was then taken.)

This would leave the imprisonment of Hawkwood doubtful, but the aforesaid official report is too explicit not to be admitted as truth.* In fact for some time the chronicles and histories are silent about him. Had he been free, he would not have been so long with his hands in his waistbelt.

We do not find him mounted again till a year afterwards; without doubt he was ransomed, and in the meantime had been reconstructing his Company. English mercenaries were everywhere, the Pope had some troops of them, and the republic of Pisa had a great many lances.**

And here it must be told how the Patriarch of Aquileja, who had come to Pisa as the vicar of the Emperor, demanded the oath of fealty from the horse troops, and how all gave it except the English, from whom the Pa-

---

* Ghirardacci, Buonincontri and others refer the pretended imprisonment of Hawkwood to his battle against the Perugians in 1365; they were probably drawn into error by this real captivity following the defeat in 1368 when he marched to the succour of Perugia.

** In fact in March 1869 a ' Ser Piero notary and public writer to the administration of the cavalry of the Commune of Pisa ' was, by order of the Anziani, paid the fees and salary due to him from the English mercenary horse troops for his fees on the occasion of the ' mostre ' (show) at Cascina. He was reimbursed 30 lire and 8 soldi, at the rate of one soldo a month for every ' posta ' (five lances) and the payments were made for two months. They therefore amounted to 15 lire and 4 soldi a month, which would mean a considerable number of ' poste ' and brigades. In another Pisan document of the same year, for the usual anticipation of pay on account, there are many English names among the 46 leaders of brigades specified.

1368.   triarch had to content himself with a simple promise of
obedience. Italians and ultramontanes recognized the direct
or indirect sovereignty of the Emperor, the English on the
other hand kept their insular independent nationality, loyal
only to their own king.

Hawkwood's faithful sponsor the Doge Agnello had
been exiled from Pisa, and so our hero had to seek elsewhere the elements to reconstitute his band.

When the troops were in order, by the commission of
Bernabò Visconti, whose pay he pretended to accept, he
actually moved again to aid the Perugians who rebelled
1369.   against the Pope, and rode into the Papal States.
June.

The Emperor, on hearing this news, wrote bitterly to
Galeazzo Visconti, complaining that he was opposing the
Church " *nephandam illam Sathane congregationem societatis
Anglicæ, cuius capitaneus Iohannes de Acuto dicitur ;* " and
he wrote desiring Bernabò to recall the Company.

Fruitless words.

The Pope after having been blockaded for some time
in Montefiascone, where the English arrows reached him
even in the Palace, was able to retire to Viterbo publishing solemn condemnations against the Perugians : who
August 8.   under the guidance of Hawkwood responded by encamping
at Viterbo, where they occupied Montalto, and burned the
vines of the surrounding country under the very eyes of
the Pope.

The Pontiff promised indulgences to whoever would
fight for him, and gave the Byzantine Emperor John Pa-
læologus the faculty to call the Company into the East,
absolving them from the oaths which bound them to their
employers in the West.

Hawkwood preferred to follow his career in Italy and
remained faithful to Bernabò who recalled him into Tu-
End of   scany to assist San Miniato which was besieged by the
November.   Florentines.

The plan of Bernabò was on a vast scale : he intended 1369. to take Leghorn, to attempt Pisa, to make war against the Ubaldini in the Casentino, so as to cut off the Florentines from all their commercial roads by mountain, and by sea, and thus to starve her out, while they scoured the country. This scheme was discovered by means of an intercepted letter. For the rest, Bernabò would have scrupulously respected the Sienese territory.* The war was thus restricted to the neighbourhood of San Miniato.

San Miniato " al Tedesco, " the usual seat of the Imperial vicars in Tuscany, was a place as important to the Ghibellines as it was to the Guelphs. To put himself within range of it and await an occasion to provide provisions, Hawkwood took up his position at Cascina on the Arno. Here he had been beaten by the Florentines in 1364, and here he now had a chance of obtaining a brilliant revenge.

Although reinforced by Flaxen and by *Messer Anisi di Natene* or Rieten (the two German conquerers at Arezzo), up to two thousand horse, he only had at his own disposal five hundred men-at-arms. These were however the " finest and the best-armed men that ever existed and they would fight against a thousand men." The Florentines also had a very fine army under San Miniato, — three thousand in all, between cavalry and infantry, and four hundred cross-bowmen. They flattered themselves that they would win a second victory at Cascina, and their commissary at the camp, a certain Cavicciuli, constrained the captain Giovanni Malatacca of Reggio, reluctantly to attack Hawkwood ; — the priors at Florence talked of sending to Malatacca the heart of an ox (*bue*) ** " as a reproof for so much prudence."

The English had got up a great many boats from Pisa, Decemb. 1st.

---

* See Document VIII.
** The word ' bue ' is used for ' ox ' and ' dunce.' — (*Translator.*)

to forage on the other side of the Arno, and they were tranquilly preparing their rations, when the alarm was given by the bells of Pontedera ringing *a stormo* to signify the passage of troops. They were scarcely in time to barricade the trench and place themselves on foot with lances in hand, when the Florentine vanguard of four hundred horse was upon them. They too dismounted and began to use their hands. More than five hundred lances having been broken and about five and twenty men killed, Hawkwood had recourse to one of his favourite statagems to decide the affair. He made believe to retreat and appeared to be fording the Arno at any cost, while he had placed his best troops in ambush with orders not to move till the Florentines had crossed. The pages of the English "lances" went down to the river with the horses as if to seek the ford; this being observed by some cavaliers, was reported to the Florentines, who were thereby persuaded that the enemy were flying as vanquished. The unlucky Cavicciuli obliged Malatacca to "follow up the victory," that is, to fall into the trap; eight hundred horse which were sent along the river to take the English in the flank, sank in the soft earth; and to make the story short, the Florentines over zealous, over tired, and disordered, attacked on both sides, remained in the claws of the pincers. Their captain was wounded, and Cavicciuli with many knights of rank, two thousand horses and two thousand men were all taken prisoners. It was said that to give himself courage Malatacca had drunk too much wine at the beginning of the fray and then went through the battle intoxicated, wherefore he vowed an oath and kept it, never to drink another drop — but this was Florentine gossip.

The state banner of Florence was sent as a trophy to Bernabò who had gone to Sarzana, and who from thence reinforced his troops encamped on the Arno, with a thousand men commanded by Federigo Gonzaga, sending also the pay due to the troops in action.

In spite of the victory and reinforcements, the Visconti obtained no conclusive results. They sold their spoil at Pisa and then having equipped themselves anew, indulged in their favorite occupations of sacking the land, stealing fodder and cattle, and putting the peasants to flight, destroying, cutting, and burning. "At my place," sighs the old chronicler Sardi, " they pulled the portico at Oratoio down to the ground, set fire to the woodwork and cut the poles; they burned a great deal of my stores, with beams, benches, and cupboards, bedsteads, stools, and wardrobes, which were worth altogether more than two hundred lire. The Lord destroy them all."

It was the end of December, the English were making fires to warm themselves !

X.

CAMPAIGN IN LOMBARDY FOR AND AGAINST BERNABÒ VISCONTI.

[*Letter of* Urban V, December 7, in RAYNALDI'S *Annals* — MARCHIONNE DI COPPO STEFANI, *Chronicle* — LUIGI OSIO, *Milanese diplomatic documents* — RANIERI SARDO, *Pisan chronicle* — *Annales mediolanensis* in MURATORI [R. I. S] — GHIRARDACCI, *Storie bolognesi* — *Chronicon placentinum* in MURATORI [R. I. S.] — Vatican archives, *Introitus et expensæ Cameræ apostolicæ* 1373 and *Regesti* of Gregory XI.]

The victory of Cascina had been no doubt a great achievement for Hawkwood: he had terrified the Pope and other enemies of Bernabò, but the principal object of the campaign had failed: the English managed to get two convoys of provisions into San Miniato, but nevertheless they could not prevent Roberto dei Conti Guidi (the new Florentine captain) from reinforcing the camp which surrounded the town; this inaction was attributed by some to a lack of forage, by a few to want of money, and by

1370. others to bad weather and worse roads; the fact remains that the Florentines, coming to an understanding with the inhabitants, regained San Miniato, town and castle.

Hence Franco Sacchetti, storyteller and popular poet, sang in one of his sonnets:

> L'alto rimedio di Fiorenza magna
> Ognor si vede quando è poi perduto:
> Biscia, nè serpe, nè Giovanni Aguto
> Per suo oprar non gli darà magagna.[*]

> (Grand remedies has Florence! for more great
> Does she become, the more that all seems lost:
> No viper, snake,[**] nor e'en great Hawkwood's host
> Can, by their deeds, work ruin to her high state.)

Nothing remained to Hawkwood except the satisfaction of riding on under the walls of Florence as far as the banks of the Mugnone, and the pleasure of running races and creating knights, one of whom, a Milanese named Pusterla, had no sooner won his spurs, than he must needs venture rashly beneath the very walls, and was taken. In Florence it was believed that Hawkwood was endeavouring to produce some rising or insurrection among the citizens of Florence, a thing possible enough, if Bernabò had been a tolerant person instead of a hateful tyrant.

January 16. Many of the English were taken prisoners at Prato whither they had ventured hoping to find favour.

January 10. Meanwhile in San Miniato, which was again in the hands of the Guelphs, — the Pope, the Florentines, Pisans, Venetians, Genoese, Bolognese, and Perugians, were stipulating one of their usual platonic leagues, to prohibit mercenary companies in Tuscany.

---

[*] For these lines from the autograph poem, we are indebted to the courtesy of Doctor Salomone Morpurgo who is about to publish a complete edition of ' Franco Sacchetti.'

[**] The viper was the ensign of the Visconti. — (*Translator.*)

In any way Bernabò's army put itself in readiness to recross the Apennines, and Visconti notified to Lodovico Gonzaga Lord of Mantua, that his captains Federigo Gonzaga, Achud (Hawkwood), Rieten and Rod, being unwilling to remain longer in Tuscany for lack of provisions, had demanded and obtained permission to transfer themselves with their brigades into Lombardy, where Signor Guidosavina of Fogliano, once their comrade, had promised them supplies ; — from this we gather that they were to have paid a " visit " to Signor Guidosavina and his territory.

Bernabò liked a jest and delighted in ironical language even in diplomacy, but it is certain that the Lord of Fogliano would willingly have done without that visit so politely announced. However this might be the visit was put off. Hawkwood lingered by the way, to make a useless attempt at a " coup de main " on Lucca, and on Pisa (this was certainly on account of the exiled doge Agnello) requiting himself by capturing prisoners both male and female, and damaging the country to the worth of 10,000 florins.

Giovanni Agnello was obstinate in determining to regain his lost dominion in Pisa, and to re-attempt this, he made an agreement with his friend Bernabò, taking into his pay a thousand horse, and twelve thousand foot-soldiers conducted by Johann Rieten and Andrea di Rod, under the supreme command of Hawkwood, who with these forces recrossed the Apennines in the spring, and encamped under Pisa, where he tried to scale the walls but in vain. The Pisans even took, quartered and hung on the battlements of the walls a " slave of an Englishman " (*uno schiavo degli Inghilesi*).

As a slight recompense, Hawkwood took Leghorn instead of Pisa, and went on as far as Piombino, but having heard that six thousand horse under Rodolfo Varano were concentrated at Empoli (on the part of the Guelphic league) he recrossed the mountains with the greatest solicitude.

1370.

February 6.

February 15.

May 19.

June 13.

1370.
July 18.

Visconti was preparing new work for him in Lombardy, and with his usual hypocrisy wrote to Lodovico Gonzaga that " Hawkwood, Rieten and Rod, with their comrades, without either his wish or command had entered the states of Parma ; hence and in as much as Cardinal Albanese,[*] and his colleagues of the Church, were opposing him in his pretences to the territory of Reggio, he had decided to make terms with the said companies, giving them money enough to induce them instead of damaging his lands, to aid his captain Wulf von Grovenich. " He concluded with " We then will go to Parma, so that if our enemies want to fight, we may induce them to make a " good fat war " (una buona e pingue guerra). He had blockaded Reggio, where his three thousand pioneers had rapidly constructed two strong bastions or ramparts, a mile away (according

August 1st.

to the measurement of the time). These were Hawkwood's chief support, and he displayed his resolution to take the city ; but he let himself be drawn off by riding with two thousand cavalry to the gates of Bologna. The garrison of Reggio and the members of the league — who, conducted by Manno Donati (the hero of the first battle of Cascina) and by Feltrino Gonzaga, had taken the field to help her — profited by this error ; they attacked and took posses-

---

* Called *Cardinal Albanese* because he was bishop of Albano — he is known also as *Cardinal Anglico* or *Angelico*, and as *Egidio Grimaldi* or *Girimoardi ;* he was a certain Grimoaldo of Grisant, of English origin, and he resided in Bologna as vice-regent of the Romagna for Urban V. He had risen because he was related to Pope Innocent VI, who created him bishop of Avignon, but was not liked in his office as we perceive from two epigrams which we have read on the frontispiece of the *Regestum Litterarum Camerariis aposto- licis*, 1364-69, in the Vatican archives :

Anglicus a tergo caudam gerit, est pecus ergo ;
Cum tibi dicit are, sicut ab hoste cave.

Anglicus angelus est
Cui numquam credere fas est.

a parody on Gregory the Great's famous play on words.

sion of the bastions, conducting into the city two hundred pair of oxen with their respective herdsmen, taken from among the baggage. Hawkwood returned too late for the success of the action, he fought with valour but only just succeeded in retreating and enclosing himself in the fortresses of the Parmigiano. All this occasioned Bernabò immense regret. Hawkwood was unable to regain a victory till the winter, when Rosso dei Ricci and the Conte Lupo, captains for the league, retreated after a vain attack of Mirandola. He surprised and routed them when fatigued by marching through the snow, and took Ricci prisoner; and this time Bernabò could keep the feast with fires of joy.

1370.

The Florentines next sent the Conte Lucius Landau against Hawkwood with five thousand " barbute " (lances of two men each) and he held his own with success, so that Bernabò was quite content to reconfirm those stout Englishmen in his pay, and was yet more content the following year when Hawkwood, together with Ambrogio Visconti, who had finally been released from his Neapolitan dungeon, at length routed the army of the league at Rubiera.

1371.
February.

1372.
June 2.

After this victory the two condottieri had gone with four hundred lances to reinforce Galeazzo Visconti at the siege of Asti, and they fought in various bloody frays against Count Verde's followers, who took the field in aid of the town, — in this way they had taken one bastion erected to damage the camp, and had completed two, which placed Asti in great peril.

Hawkwood had always distinguished himself amongst adventurers for his fidelity; the astonishment was consequently universal when it was understood that he had struck his tents and deserted with all his band. The cause of this defection is not very clear. According to the *Annali*

September.

1372. *Milanesi,* Hawkwood withdrew because he was not allowed
to make a serious attack on the Conte Verde, even though
he felt certain of victory. This was probably because the
youthful Conte di Virtù was among the troops with many
other young Lombard nobles, and his mother Donna Bianca
Visconti had commanded Stefano Porro and Cavallino
de' Cavalli his chancellor or notary, not to allow these
young sprigs of nobility to run the risk of an engagement.
It must have been in this way that the advice of " those
scribbling notaries " prevailed, and possibly for this reason
Hawkwood protested that " he did not choose to regulate
himself in military matters according to the counsel of
scriveners " (*de escrivans*). We may observe that Bianca
Visconti was, the sister of Conte Verde, and hence it was
most natural that she sought to prevent decisive battles,
in which either her son or her brother might be much
injured. That the siege failed on account of the departure
of the Conte di Virtù is confirmed by many other sources.
They add also that Hawkwood just then received orders
from Bernabò to ride towards Reggio with his three hundred lances and his two hundred archers, and that Galeazzo
Visconti complained to his brother that the Englishman
had not done his duty before the walls of Asti, not having
obeyed orders, and having spoiled the country.

It seemed to Bernabò a good reason to diminish the
pay of his captain. Hawkwood wanted nothing better:
he came to an understanding with the Legate of Bologna
and passed straightway into the pay of the " shepherds
of the Church " and under the orders of Aymero di Pommerio and Dondacio Malvicino, captains of the league. By
his aid the Visconti were prevented from erecting two new
fortresses as they had intended to do near Modena. Borgo-
novo was taken, and after a fierce battle Broni also capi-
tulated, and all the territory was laid waste between the
rivers Panaro and Trebbia.

Winter quarters were not necessary to ultramontane adventurers: they made campaigns in all seasons, and Bologna being menaced by Giannotto Visconti's eight hundred lances, Hawkwood hastened thither, where the mere announcement of his vicinity was sufficient to induce the Visconti to retreat. Seconded by the Bolognese, Hawkwood confronted them on the Panaro and after a fierce engagement of one hour, Visconti was completely discomfited, losing two thousand out of his three thousand men, some being killed and others drowned; he himself found difficulty in fleeing with only three hundred lances. The victors triumphed at Bologna, on account of the many knights they had taken prisoners, and the abundant spoil, but they did not long remain idle.

At that time John Brise,* one of Hawkwood's comrades, being dispatched as ambassador of the Company to Pope Gregory XI, returned from Avignon with two letters from the Pontiff to his captain.

In one (the ostensible one) the Pope asserted that he had listened benignly to all that Brise had explained in the interest of the Company, and that his reply would be given by Brise *viva voce*, adding a warm exhortation to fight the villanous Bernabò (*lo scellerato Bernabò*); he prayed the English to have patience in the matter of stipends, promising that they should be carefully provided by the Cardinal of St. Angelo.

The other letter (private) gave notice that the Abbot Berengarius, legate at Piacenza, was planning some schemes there, for the execution of which he would require Hawkwood's men; he therefore prayed him that, on the

1373.
Beginning
of January.

January 15.

* In the documents at Avignon the name is written *Britz*, the Perugian chronicler has it *Breccia*, elsewhere it is *Birche*, but in the Lucchese *Bris* and *Briz*; therefore we write *Brise*, a name still known in the county of Essex where Hawkwood lived. — (It might be also one of the more common names of Brice or Birch. — *Translator*.)

request of the Abbot, he would mount quickly and secretly, with all or a part of his brigade: "in fact it is needful as you know, that this should be kept secret and performed with rapidity." *

The Abbot had bribed several of the nobles of the district of Piacenza against Bernabò — they talked of occupying the forts and ruling them for the Church. The Pontifical instructions were precisely followed out in spite of very bad weather, and although the Pope did not pay the stipends either punctually or in full.

Some little money was sent from Avignon — we have a curious document respecting it — the order of the Papal treasurer to pay to Issarmida the Jew the small sum due "*pro certa tela empta per eam et pro cotone ad faciendum garnichones per portandum pecunias necessarias pro stipendiariis Domini Papæ ad guerram Romanæ Ecclesiæ per partes Italiæ.*"

Hawkwood therefore remained creditor for a large sum, but he resigned himself, well knowing that means would not be wanting wherewith to reimburse himself on the States of the Church, as we shall see.

XI.

A BATTLE REGAINED.
CORRESPONDENCE WITH GREGORY XI.

[*Letter of Bernabò Visconti to Lodorico Gonzaga* in the *Milanese diplomatic documents* published by LUIGI OSIO — Vatican archives, *Regesti di Gregorio XI* and *Introitus et expensæ Cameræ apostolicæ* 1373 — MATTEO DE' GRIFONI, *Memoriale storico* — FROISSART, *Chronicles* — *Chronicon placentinum, Chronicon rhegiense, Chronicon estense* — GHIRARDACCI, *Storie bolognesi* in MURATORI [R. I. S.] — GUICHENON, *Histoire généalogique de la maison de Savoie* — *Annales mediolanenses* in MURATORI [R. I. S.]]

To ensure the success of the Guelphic League, a French *corps* led by the Lord of Coucy was added to their forces.

---

* See Documents IX and X.

Bernabò Visconti however did not lose courage, on the contrary he borrowed some troops from his brother Galeazzo, and disposed himself to " requite in good earnest the Lord of Cossi ". (*Coucy*) and Sir John Hawkwood, as well as the Count of Savoy.

The Conte Verde was just at that time rashly employed in throwing a bridge across the Adda at Brivio; it was of great importance to the league to disengage their ally; consequently, at the solicitation of the Papal Legate and the Pope's letters,* Hawkwood, Coucy, and Aymer de Pommerio, captains for the Church, left Ferrara and crossed the Po by the bridge of Stellata. Visconti's army marched against them led by the Conte di Virtù and Annechin Bongarden, and the opposing ranks confronted each other on the river Chiese.

The ranks of the Visconti numbered a thousand five hundred lances chiefly Germans and Hungarians, and four thousand foot. Hawkwood and de Coucy only had six hundred lances and seven hundred archers besides the *provvisionati* ** infantry, and some civic volunteers under a certain Malatesta; nevertheless Coucy with his French impetuosity did not hesitate to make the attack, and Hawkwood was constrained to support him; indeed if we may believe Froissart, he willingly did so " because Coucy had married a daughter of the King of England." After a short conflict of an hour, the army of the league being discomfited began to flee, and that of the Visconti, stipendiaries and plunderers, dedicated their attention to spoil. Hawkwood, taking refuge on the heights of Montechiaro, saw that they might make an attempt to retrieve their defeat and though he only had the *provvisionati,* the volunteers, and very few mercenaries under his standard, he reorganized

---

* See Document XI.
** The *provvisionati* were peasant infantry recruited in haste, and poorly paid.

them, and with Malatesta fell unexpectedly on the enemy while they were intent on spoil. His quick glance and resolution changed defeat into victory. Bongarden's Germans gave themselves to flight on the instant; the Lombards made a long and useless resistance.

Not only the camp remained in the English possession, but two hundred prisoners besides, amongst whom were Francesco d' Este, Gabriotto di Canossa, Francesco di Sassuolo, and about thirty of the best nobility of Lombardy who had to disburse great ransoms. The Conte di Virtù left his helmet and lance, he was thrown to the ground, and he too would have been in the enemy's hands, if a good many of his faithful followers had not defended him and found him another horse. The maternal presentiments of Donna Bianca were thus fulfilled.

Hawkwood however was not intoxicated with success; he, coolly considering the superior forces of which the Visconti could yet dispose, the many dead and wounded which the battle had cost the conquerors, the difficulty of finding provisions, and the hostility of the peasants, feared he might be cut off from his base of operations if he advanced. He thought it would be rash to attempt to join Conte Verde, though that would have been the total ruin of the Visconti; so riding day and night he retreated to Bologna to recover his strength and dragged to prison there all the captives who had been unable to pay their ransoms. He justly considered that the effect of the defeat would be enough to prevent the Visconti from attacking the Count of Savoy who was able to rejoin Hawkwood at Bologna, and concert a plan to lay siege to Piacenza, which was not carried out, solely because the Conte Verde fell ill.

The knowledge of these successes did not reach Avignon very rapidly: a certain Francesco, messenger of the Lord of Mantua, was the first who carried the news of victory,

and he got a present of twenty five florins. Then there
came the official report, brought by the noble *donzello* Pietro di Murles, who had been sent to the camp with a letter
from the Pope to exhort Hawkwood to join Conte Verde.*
Being an employé of the court and of noble birth, Murles
had a present of thirty florins; and Hawkwood received
an eloquent Papal letter which exalted the triumph " of
the few over the many, of the invaded over the invaders "(?).

The Pope also added that he had heard of the retreat
to Bologna, but he limited himself to expressing his opinion that it would have been better to continue the onward
march, and besought Hawkwood that he would effect as
soon as possible the junction with Amedeo Count of Savoy,
captain general of the war, on the upper Milanese territory; so as " not to give the defeated enemy time to take
breath."

He sent no money for the arrears of pay; he promised
however to provide against these, as well as other arrears,
assuring Hawkwood that he and the Cardinal legate were
engaged on the subject and he recommended the English
meanwhile to have filial patience ** (*figliale pazienza*). He
could hope for little while paying nothing, — besides the
victory of the Chiese had cost Hawkwood's Company very
dear, and therefore in a successive letter, while expressing
his astonishment that " Bernabò, that son of Belial, should
have lost neither city, fortress or town of any sort," the
Pope enlarged into most tender expressions towards the
English condottiere: " We have in our own heart to regard
with serene countenance and to anticipate at all times
with our best favors your most amiable person, who rests
nearest to our heart." ***

This last letter served as a letter of recommendation
to the noble Ugo di Rupe, cavalier and master of the

---

* See Document XI.   ** See Document XII.
*** See Document XIII.

1373.   *sacro ospizio* (knights hospitaller) who was sent to Hawkwood with verbal instructions, and then the campaign was
recommenced.

July 17.   Bernabò wrote to Gonzaga : " We have heard that Hawkwood and his brigade are reformed and all united together."
In fact the English provided for the defence of the territory of Piacenza, and entered into the lower Milanese province thus rendering possible a rebellion of peasants in
the Bergamasco, which cost Ambrogiuolo Visconti his life.

It cannot be said that Hawkwood failed in his duty;
1374.   for, as in the preceding winter, he repeated an incursion
January.
in which Castel San Giovanni was taken for the Cardinal legate, and finding that the Visconti, profiting by
his withdrawal, had marched to menace Bologna, he rapidly retraced his steps falling on the flank of the invaders. They attempted to fly, but having found a broken
bridge, they were constrained to fight with the English,
and with the populace who had emerged from Bologna,
and thus being taken in the midst they sustained a complete defeat.

The Pope on the other hand continued to pay the English with fine words. Hawkwood therefore first sent the
noble knight Sir John Brise, then he wrote, and not receiving anything but vague promises * by message or
letter he sent his secretary, with instructions to propose
some formal agreement. Amongst other things he demanded that the number of lances should be augmented,
which would only have served to increase the amount of
arrears. Perhaps this was exactly what he would have
liked, hoping to get himself paid in landed possessions, but
it was denied. On the other point we only know that the
secretary had to give him verbal answers conveying the

---

* See Documents XIV and XV.

good intentions of the Pontiff.* We may believe that 1374. these were sufficiently satisfactory, as Hawkwood continued in his service.

A little while after the Pope sent his *donzello* (usher) Giovanni de Canis with ample letters of recommendation and orders to follow out the commissions which this gentleman should communicate either verbally or in writing.**

Meanwhile the Visconti had laid siege to Vercelli : every day the besieging forces increased, and the city suffered greatly from famine. On this account the Pope, who had at first commissioned Hawkwood to keep in the vicinity of Parma and Piacenza, finding that the enemies in those parts had withdrawn, begged him to fly to the succour of the besieged town, leaving a sufficient garrison at Bologna, in agreement with Cardinal Sant'Angelo, vicar general ; and he assured him that "the prince of the apostles in person would accompany him in his march." *** The Pope wrote a separate letter in the same tenor to John Thornbury marshal, praying him to exhort Hawkwood to the enterprise, he recommended his *donzello* De Canis to Thornbury as well as to Hawkwood. He had given Pietro de Murles recommendations to several of the other marshals, — Brise for example ; and he had written letters like the one to Hawkwood, to both the above, as well as to Cook, constable, and *Thomelino de Bellomonte* marshal and Guglielmo *Martedonis* (?) captain, to beg them to be patient in regard to pay, which serves to show that in the English Company, the autority of the captain general was tempered by the counsel and consent of the officers. The march to Vercelli was not effected after all. Hawkwood continued to encamp near Piacenza and the lower Parmese territory, spoiling the land " so that the corn could not be sown in the fields, which proved a great injury for the follow-

---

* See Document XVI.   ** See Document XVII.
*** See Document XVIII.

ing year." Then, having nothing to do when a truce was concluded between the Church and the Visconti, he passed into Tuscany.

XII.

THE EXHORTATION OF SAINT CATHERINE.
THE *HOLY COMPANY.*

[*Letters* of SAINT CATHERINE OF SIENA, TOMMASEO'S edition, v. II — D. M. MANNI, *Biografia dell' Acuto* in MURATORI [*R. I. S*], v. II of the Appendix — PADRE GAZZATA, *Cronica* in MURATORI [*R. I. S.*] — GRAZIANI, *Perugian chronicle* — ALESSANDRO GHERARDI, *La guerra degli otto santi* (The war of the eight saints), *Archivio storico italiano* — RANIERI SARDO, *Pisan chronicle* — *Ottave* (poem in lines of eight) inserted in the *Chronicle* of the ANONYMOUS FLORENTINE in MURATORI [*R. I. S.*]]

And here at length the long account of the incessant wars with which the foreign mercenaries outraged Italy is interrupted by a few words of peace. She who pronounces them is a humble nun, but a worthy woman both in mind and heart, — Catherine of Siena.

Gregory XI had inherited from his predecessor the idea of liberating the peninsula and the ultramontane countries from the adventurers, by inducing them to go across the sea to fight for the Holy Sepulchre. He thus deemed that in any case, whether they were victorious there, or better still were destroyed by the Turks, Christianity would thereby derive either great benefit, or a great relief. For this object he sent a brief to the Dominican and Franciscan provincials, and especially to Fra Raimondo of Capua, in order that they should prepare the ground for the Crusade. The influence of the monks was at that time immense, both with the nobles and the populace. Raimondo of Capua enjoyed an universal reputation, and was not less appreciated for his preaching than Catherine of Siena was for her writings. The nun and the monk often worked together for the Church and for the peace of the world; and by the sole means of moral persuasion, sometimes succeeded in moderating events, in an age when brute force seemed to have absolute reign. It appears then that in 1374 Catherine of Siena sent to Hawkwood, by means of Fra Raimondo, the famous letter which is one of the most remarkable in her magnificent epistolary. It is addressed *a Messer Giovanni condottiero e capo della Compagnia che venne nel tempo della fame.* (To Messer John condottiere, and head of the Company which came in the time of famine.) The ancient manuscript collection of her letters does not contain a precise indication of the date; but the passage of Hawkwood into Tuscany in the summer of 1374 is certain. In company with Count Conrad of Hechilberg, he then appeared on Sienese ground with the pretext of wishing to fight other bands who were hostile to him, and menacing a sack, if they did not use towards him the courtesy which was his due.* The " Sienese Annals " of Piccolomini (Pope Pius III) say the same thing: *Johannes Haucutus omnium stipendiis liberatus, cum suis copiis in Etruriam ex Lombardia venit, omnium hostis futurus qui se pecunia non redimerent.... Annonæ interim caritas invalescebat.* Meaning that if they often suffered hunger, in that year the suffering was greater, it was indeed " a year of famine." For the rest the date is of little importance, we have rather to note from the context of the letter, that it appears that Hawkwood had already engaged himself to go to the Holy Land, and Catherine reminds him of it, wondering that he should now wish to make war here. If anything this engagement dated from the year 1365 when Urban V had commissioned Cardinal Albornoz ** to induce the mercenaries to take the Cross.

---

* See Document XIX.
** The most authentic biography of the celebrated Cardinal would be that of Genesio da Sepulveda printed at Bologna in 1521, and compiled from the documents preserved in the Archives of the ' College of Spain ' in Bo-

1374.   Contrary to the epistolary custom of St. Catherine the
letter is very short. Tommaseo, who is not always very
happy in his comments, supposes this to be " because it
was written to an Englishman and a hasty soldier perhaps
ignorant of the language. " Now Hawkwood, who for
thirteen years had fought in Italy, treated with Italians,
and had Italians in his Company, besides employing Italian
secretaries, attorneys, chancellors and scriveners, should
certainly by this time be familiar with the vulgar tongue.
Tommaso d' Alviano and Alberic of Barbiano were not
known as more patient soldiers than Hawkwood, and yet
to them Catherine wrote in her usual diffuse and exube-
rant style. The reason of her brevity appears rather to
be that St. Catherine sent the letter by Fra Raimondo and
begged Hawkwood to listen to him. She merely gave the
theme in her epistle, leaving to the powerful eloquence
of the Franciscan the care of developing it.

The theme lies entirely in this affectionate exhortation :
" Therefore I pray you sweetly for the sake of Jesus Christ,
that since God and also our Holy Father have ordained,
for us to go against the infidels, — you who so delight in
wars and fightings, should no longer war against Christ-

---

logna, founded by this Cardinal himself. But Sepulveda, a member of that
institution, occupied himself (as he declares) more in writing good latin than
any thing else after having loosely arranged the materials extracted in confusion from the Archives, by a Bolognese named Garzoni. There results, however,
a confirmation of the facts that in 1365 the Cardinal, availing himself of the
services of Gomez Albornoz his nephew, a soldier by profession and a friend
of some of the English, conducted long and repeated treaties with these
bands, but only the ephemeral agreement already cited (see page 46) was
concluded, so much so that not long after he had to go and defend the
Perugians against them. Sepulveda does not talk of a crusade, whilst
Raynaldi's *Annales ecclesiastici* certainly do mention one. For the rest the
biography is very concise, and not always trustworthy ; he perhaps exagge-
rated the part of the Albornoz in resisting the English near Perugia, and
he certainly errs when he says that Gomez put to death the leaders of
the English who were defeated and taken prisoners in that engagement,
leaving the others free on giving their word to abandon Italy. We have
already seen the very different facts given, even to the most minute particulars, by the Perugian chroniclers (see page 49).

ians; because that is an offence to God, but go and   1374.
oppose them (the Turks), for it is a great cruelty that we
who are christians should persecute one another."

The holy woman prayed that he "from being the servant and soldier of the devil, might become a manly and
true knight."

Hawkwood might have answered that that same Holy
Father had paid him to fight Christians, and that hence
it was the Pope who acted the part of the devil in the
Christian republic. However in the Aldine edition of the
" Letters of St. Catherine of Siena " it is said (we do not
know on what foundation) that Hawkwood and his *caporali*
promised Fra Raimondo to go to the Holy Land, and that
the promise was inscribed in a document furnished with
their seals.* It was in any case a mere repetition of preceding promises, which bound them to nothing and were
only made out of courtesy.

As the Saint shewed between the parentheses of her
letter, thorns were not lacking in the career of an adventurer. Hawkwood had experienced both defeats and captivity, though on the whole, he beheld his fortunes increase,
and could still hope much in carrying arms at the expense
of the Italians.

There was another Englishman in Tuscany at that
time, William Flete (Fleet?) B. A. who dedicated himself
to study in the penitential solitude of the hermitage of

---

* Canonico Luigi Balduzzi acutely observes that ' perhaps the arms of
Hawkwood — which are a *chevron sable* charged with three scallop shells
surmounted by a cross, as we see in his effigy in the Duomo, — may have
some relation to this affair " (*Atti e Memorie della R. Deputazione di Storia
Patria per la provincia di Romagna*, 8rd series, vol. II. fasc. I). Hawkwood
however did not use this seal only, which is really the arms of his family,
and though we cannot always distinguish the seals still adhering to his documents, on account of the old custom of covering the wax with a piece of
paper, across which the name was written, yet one can sometimes distinguish on a seal the figure of a hawk, which would have been a rebus to
his name, and which we also see repeated in the parish church of Sible
Hedingham his native home and burial place.

1374. Lecceto, and was a great admirer and devoted disciple of
Catherine of Siena ; but Hawkwood no more felt the vocation to make a holy war for ascetic enthusiasm, than
he did to drink vinegar and water to follow the example
of his hermit compatriot.*

Even supposing that St. Catherine and Fra Raimondo
had touched his heart, it was not long before a tempest
burst over Italy, provoked by the infamous misgovernment
and tyranny which oppressed the people subjected to the
temporal power of the Pope ; a misrule and tyranny in
proof of which we have eloquent documents in these same
letters of St. Catherine of Siena.

The prelates who governed the provinces and cities of
the Church, chosen by the nepotism of the Avignonese Popes
to be proconsuls in Italy, being covetous of riches, given up
to every excess, and daring to practise the most systematic
injustice, were a scourge worse than the mercenaries. With
the latter, one might find ground for a compact, — but
against the former nothing remained but rebellion.

Hawkwood having increased his Company to one thousand five hundred lances, five hundred archers, and a great
number of infantry, and taken as his lieutenant his countryman John Thornbury (which Italian documents vulga-
rise as *Tornabarile*), had gone to winter on the Perugian
territory, where they robbed towns and villages, hardly
permitting provisions to be supplied even to the city. But
the citizens suffered a worse torment within.

---

* We do not wish to say by this that the condottieri and soldiers of
that time were incredulous, or that they laughed at indulgences as the Lu-
theran bands of ' lanzenknechts ' did in later days. When the remains of
Cardinal Albornoz were transferred from Assisi to Toledo, and Pope Urban V
granted jubilee indulgences to all who had gratuitously carried him on their
shoulders from one place to another, many adventurers (says Cardella in his
biography of the Cardinal) willingly profited by the occasion to cancel a great
part of their sins ; but to demand that they should entirely renounce their
calling would have been too much.

The Benedictine almoner Gherardo de Puy, abbot of   1374.
Montemaggiore, was a relative of the Pope and governor
of Perugia; the learned and pious brother in Christ, Gazzata, thus speaks, in his description of him: " He did many
detestable things, this among others. One of his kindred,
enamoured of the wife of a noble, entered her house during
her husband's absence and made infamous overtures to her;
she replied: 'Noble signore, as you desire it and lest my
husband should discover anything, enter this room, I will
send away the servants and come to you.'" It was a stra-
tagem to preserve her honour; " she closed the outer door
and tried to pass by the window into the house of a neighbour, but fell and was killed." The case becoming known,
the citizens complained to the Abbot who contented himself with saying: " Do you Italians suppose perhaps that
all the French are eunuchs?" and he sent them away.

The same kinsman, thus encouraged, three days after
carried off the wife of another citizen, which being denounced
to the Abbot, he interrogated his nephew who confessed.
Then the Abbot in the presence of all, condemned him " to
restore to the citizen his wife under pain of death.... within
fifty days."

Other possessions of the Church were not more fortunate than Perugia; — now, " he who sows the wind must
reap the storm," the exasperated people only waited a
propitious occasion. And the occasion came when Cardinal
Guillaume de Noellet, pontifical legate, attacked Florence
without any plausible motive, and provoked the famous
" war of the eight saints " (*guerra degli otto santi*).*

The Cardinal had the English Company which had returned to Lombardy in his stipend, but he had neither
the means wherewith to pay them, nor a fair excuse to
dismiss them.

---

* The history of this war has been recently well told by Gherardi; it is
enough for us to extract and fill up that which refers to Hawkwood's part in it.

1375.

He asked a loan from the Florentines, but could not obtain it, and by reason of the truce with the Visconti, he was unable to throw off the troops across the Po, so he thought to get rid of them in Tuscany.

Florence had for some time suspected this peril; when she foresaw the truce which was afterwards concluded, she thought of sending Ambassadors to find out the designs

Spring.

of Hawkwood. He having received the pontifical instructions from the Legate, and from Biagio of Arezzo, the Church official at Piacenza, in a few days reunited to his own soldiers a great many of the troops of the Church and the Visconti, and forming them into a great Holy Company (*Compagnia Santa*) manned the fortresses around Piacenza; and as the Gonzaga had not been willing to put his hand into his pocket, he ravaged the Mantuan territory along the Po.

June 18.

Bernabò Visconti wrote to Gonzaga promising to inferfere and added : " We hear that the English are waiting to receive a certain sum of money from the " pastors," — that is the officials of the Church, — and they assert that they cannot depart until they have received it."

Hawkwood, instead, had transferred his general quarters to Bologna, and in Tuscany people were trembling at his approach which had now become evident. The Florentines sent men-at-arms to the passes of the Pistoiese Apennines, but they had much more confidence in their florins, and also sent two orators to Hawkwood. These were Simone Peruzzi and Spinello di Luca Alberti,* named *della Camera* (of the chamber) on account of his office of Treasurer, and hence he was the most appropriate person for the occasion. At the same time the commune of Pisa sent Ranieri Sardo

---

* Simone Peruzzi, as following events will shew, was one of the most prudent among the political men of Florence. Spinello belonged to the noble family of the Alberti, a very rich commercial company who then possessed, and long preserved, important factories also in England.

(the chronicler we have often cited), Oddo Maccaione, and Lippo Agliata on the same errand of offering money, if he would spare the land. All the gold of Tuscany was thrown at the feet of the Englishmen.

To the Pisans, Hawkwood and his leaders responded that they must first arrange with Florence; to the Florentines they replied amicably, but made them understand that the florins must be many; and then they continued their march without breaking off the negotiations.

Was the Cardinal Legate cognisant of this or not? A popular Florentine poet answers:

> Dissesi, poi che furono accordati
> Che 'l Cardinale ne fu poco lieto:
> Ma biasmar non poteva il Capitano,
> Perchè gliel' avea scritto di sua mano.

> (They said when all the terms were fully signed
> Small pleasure was there in the Cardinal's mind:
> He could not blame the Captain in command,
> For he wrote the order with his own right hand.)

A significant comment on this is found in a letter of the Signoria to Messer Carlo di Durazzo, saying that " by advice of the Ecclesiastics, Hawkwood had demanded a sum which it was believed the Florentines would be unable to pay. Then seeing they consented, they tried to break off the agreement." There was a credible rumour that the Legate and Hawkwood had an understanding that half the money extorted from the Tuscan communes should go towards the pay which the Church owed to Hawkwood, and the other half to the advantage of the Condottiere and his soldiers.

XIII.

TWO MILLIONS AND HALF IN THREE MONTHS.

[*Letters of Florentine envoys to the Signoria* published by IODOCO DEL BADIA in the *Miscellanea fiorentina — Archivio storico italiano*, documents relating to the *Mercenary companies* published by CANESTRINI, *Processo dei traditori di Prato*, in series 3rd, vol. X, part 1st — In MURATORI [*R. I S.*] anonymous *Pisan chronicle* — D. M. MANNI, *Biografia dell' Acuto* — RANIERI SARDO, *Cronica pisana* — Lucca State Archives, *Contract of the Commune with the Holy Company* — *Documents* in the State Archives of Siena.]

1375.
June 21.

The Florentine ambassadors wrote from Bologna, *before sunrise in the morning* (the urgency of the affair did not let them sleep) a letter to the Signoria, of which a copy, like many other intercepted epistles, went to repose in the archives of Siena.* Very interesting circumstances result from this.

The Company was encamped near Imola; it was very numerous, and well provided with *bombarde* and with iron implements for use in war against walled towns; the soldiers threatened to take the Italian cities of whose internal discords they were aware, and foretold new invasions of companies as soon as peace should be concluded between France and England, then belligerent: they would not specify precisely the object of their imminent march, but the envoys suspected that once the Company had penetrated into Tuscany, they would take the Pisan road or that of Montepulciano where it was thought they had an understanding with the inhabitants.

The Florentine ambassadors acted in accordance with those of Pisa, and kept them informed how the negotiations were going, and the Pisans on their part, knowing that Hawkwood was not willing to come to terms with

---

* For precaution two copies of important letters were sent, one by the direct route and the other by way of Vernia and the Casentino.

all Tuscany at once (for he shewed himself especially ill disposed towards Pisa on account of arrears of pay and because they had not kept their promise of giving him a fortress), advised the Florentines to make their own agreement, reserving the right to aid Pisa, — which aid it appeared they could not deny, because if Pisa were conquered, Florence and other Tuscan cities would be lost.

In respect to Florence, the Company had already formulated its pretensions, viz: 130 thousand florins in four rates between June and September: and yet they seemed to repent having asked too little, in comparison with what they might have gained by taking prisoners for ransom.

The personal opinion of the ambassadors was not very favorable to the agreement. According to them, the citizens ought to have shut themselves up in Florence and let the Company burn up the country as they chose, because " that which did not take place to-day, would very soon happen " (quello che non è oggi sarà tosto). In fact some good men had forewarned them that the Company kept its promises but badly, and would not abstain from plundering on the way. At least the ambassadors wished to make the first rate of payment to the English, as small as possible.

But they had instructions to conclude the compact at any cost, and that same morning went to the camp accompanied by Pietro di Murles agent of the Cardinal Legate, by Ruggiero Cane * and by the Viscount of Savoy " captain of Piedmont," which three persons were to take the part of mediators.

The agreement was concluded, drawn up, and signed

---

* As we shall see, this Cane took part in many successive negotiations during the war of the ' eight saints,' because he was a man much trusted by Bernabò Visconti, and familiar with Hawkwood. He was the son *nobilis viri Adoazzi Canis de Casali de Luagij Pedemontium* (see Document XXIV) and perhaps of the same house as De Canis, the Pope's usher.

at the camp near an old bridge on the via Emilia, built by the Countess Matilda. The signatures on the part of the Company were those of Hawkwood captain general, the two marshals, the constable, and twelve more between councilors and *caporali* (knights).

This deed is important as a type of those *condotte* which we might call " guaranteed " or ' reserved ; " it will be sufficient to cite the principal clauses:

" That neither the Company nor any of its men shall for five years injure the commune, the city, the country, or district of Florence, nor her dependent towns unless the Company should be regularly engaged by some lord or commune, and even if legally hired, it shall abstain from hostilities for three months, excepting only in case that the Republic of Florence should make war on the Pope, Bernabò Visconti, or the Count of Savoy (because the Pope had an alliance with the one, and a truce with the other).

" All those who enter into the Company shall be bound to take the above oath.

" The Commune gives in recompense 130,000 florins in gold, of just weight and of the Florentine mint, of which 40,000 shall be paid in June, 30,000 in July, 30,000 in August, and 30,000 in September.

" Moreover in case the Communes of Pisa, Siena, Lucca, or Arezzo should come to terms with the Company, the latter may pass over the Florentine territory, on the condition of giving four days notice to the Priors and Gonfaloniere, and of marching by reasonable and fit roads, according to their destination, and under the guidance of those deputed by the Commune for that office : and that they shall pass by amicably, paying the price of provisions and doing no damage, — nevertheless they may take without payment wine, poultry, and litter for the horses.

" That during their march, the knights and men may

enter Florence so long as not more than one hundred are
within the walls at the same time.

" That the Commune of Florence shall have the faculty
of denying passage and provisions to the Company, if it
be not in the pay of either Pisa, Siena, Lucca or Arezzo,
and of subsidizing the said Communes her allies, with money
or troops, against the Company as against any other enemy.

" Finally that for the said term of five years, the
Commune shall not treat of taking any one or more persons
out of the Company, to engage them in her own, or other
service."

This agreement was immediately approved by the Florentine Signoria, — which in consequence deliberated, that
the chamberlains of the Commune might pay the sums
decided on, either to Hawkwood or to his procurator.

Meanwhile the Company crossed the Apennines at Firen-
zuola. Two new Florentine envoys, Doffo de' Bardi and
Giovanni Ducci, accompanied it in the quality of commissaries. Bardi on account of preceding embassies was already
intimate with the English, and Hawkwood seemed, at
least in words, to carefully regulate the march in good
faith. But in fact, the soldiers only abstained from capturing prisoners and from incendiarism, while they robbed with a free hand; " they go wherever they please by
ones, twos, or threes, finding out every crag of Apennines
and cutting down the corn." The mountaineers demanded
from the commissaries permission to fight these plunderers, but when Spinello Alberti interfered citing the terms
of the compact, the commissaries were obliged to command
the mountaineers to abstain from every hostile act, and
to sell to the English the commodities they required. It
ended of course in the English " taking the commodities
and paying no money."

The Florentine " orators " ventured to speak to Hawkwood in favour of the Sienese, but the captain loftily replied

1375.   that " the Sienese needed advice, and that he would go and reason with them so closely that they must needs hear it."

Thus menacing Tuscany, and amicable only with Florence, Hawkwood neared Prato. It appears that the Cardinal had given him the commission, not only to starve out Florence by cutting off her roads, but to occupy Prato where an act of treachery was already arranged.

At least the Signoria, in a diplomatic manner, afterwards accused the Cardinal of it, while in Prato they arrested as traitors the notary Ser Piero da Canneto, and a grey-friar priest, who, when tried in Florence, were convicted, tortured, and buried alive with their heads downwards. We may hold that Hawkwood revealed the plot, which would explain how

July 12.   the Signoria " considering the terms " ultimately concluded with Hawkwood, " and inasmuch as his nobility and the exercise of his valour might be able in many ways to work for the honour of the Commune of Florence," should have assigned him an annual pension for life of 1200 florins. At the same time, besides liquidating the expense of 77 florins, contracted by the Florentine mission of Spinello Alberti and his companions, they deliberated to give 400 florins to the nobleman Gozzo Battaglia da Rimini " for his services and expenses in treating with Hawkwood on behalf of the Commune."

The first rate of 40,000 florins was not paid at the time specified, that is in June, perhaps on account of a short absence of Hawkwood, and therefore by a deed sti-

July 3.   pulated at the monastery of Nicosia in Valle di Calci, it was agreed that the payment should be received by hand of the noblemen John Foy, knight, Bernard Rammise (Ramsay?), Robert Sever, and William Tilley as procurators of the Company and of its captain general; and it was

July 7.   paid to them in Montopoli.

Thus we see that the English had passed into Pisan territory; and as soon as they appeared on the Serchio, amidst a rush of fugitive peasants, the great bell of the Campanile of Pisa was rung for the defence, and the citizens placed strong guards at the gates, and on the walls, day and night. The inhabitants of the valley of Calci felt themselves secure amidst the folds of Monte Pisano, but a squadron of eight hundred English, passing the mountain from the North, fell upon them, and thus assailed above and below, before and behind, they were easily routed and plundered.

Stationing their general quarters at Nicosia, the English at length deigned to listen to Maccaione and Agliata, again sent by the Commune of Pisa, and they agreed for 30,500 florins, thus divided: — 3000 to Hawkwood as his pension for five years at the rate of 600 florins a year: 2500 to John Thornbury and Cook, Englishmen (the chief lieutenants), these to be paid within a day, — and to the Company 15,500 florins due within ten days, and 12,500 in September. Besides this, the entry into the city was conceded to two thousand five hundred soldiers, provided they were only armed with sword and knife, and that they would leave it again in the evening.

The Pisans were punctual in payment; the English abstained from incendiarism and from " making prisoners and slaves," — but not from other injuries, — until they passed into the territory of Volterra.

Such vast sacrifices of money weighed very heavily on the treasuries of the Tuscan cities. Florence was obliged to have recourse to several extraordinary taxes and forced loans ; for example, Piero de' Corsini was, on that occasion, obliged to expropriate certain rustic possessions, situated outside the walls in a place called *in Polverosa,* where we shall in future behold Hawkwood as peaceful proprietor.

1375.

June 28.

July 3.

1375.

Taxes not sufficing, Florence was constrained to make wretched exactions of small sums from debtors, and humiliating entreaties for subsidies to the Communes allied to her.

As it was well understood, in spite of the hypocritical protests of the Cardinal Legate, that the English had come down to Tuscany in agreement with him, — the Tuscan republics were induced to turn against the Church, thus breaking the Guelphic Confederation.

Florence was the first to decide, and to set the example, June 25. she notified to Pisa, Siena, Lucca and Arezzo that she had leagued herself with Bernabò Visconti "considering the great peril in which we are now placed owing to the sudden and unforeseen coming of the English Company, and knowing how formidable and dangerous we may yet expect its stay in Tuscany to be." She did not hesitate to impose rates on the clergy, defying ecclesiastical censure; and in this too she was imitated by the Sienese, who hearing from their ambassador, the notary Ser Iacopo di Ser Gano, how much money the English demanded, resigned themselves, only attempting to include Cortona and Montepulciano in the ransom and deliberating to raise a tax of 20,000 florins on the clergy, a forced loan of 3 florins on a thousand from the citizens, a loan of 12,000 florins from the Municipalities of the country, and the loan of a sum not determined, from the feudal lords of the Communes and their dependents.* They were even reduced to the extreme measure of putting their hands on some hereditary moneys deposited with the bankers, for example on 300 florins which had belonged to the defunct bishop of Siena.**

We perceive that Hawkwood carried out his threat of being exigent with Siena, for, besides the money, he wanted

---

* See Document XX.   ** See Document XXI.

provisions * and even wine and sweetmeats to feast merrily withal.** 1375.

Having received the money from Pisa, the Company July 31. passed to Laterina, where they drew the second rate of the Florentine contract and menaced Arezzo; the third Florentine rate was paid at Bibbiena after Arezzo had been obliged to compound for 8500 florins. August 28.

The English were inexorable in exaction, — would they have been so faithful to their contracts? They much doubted this at Florence, saying "that in mercenary soldiers there is neither faith nor pity. Their hands are venal, and they turn themselves where they can find the greater gain." *Nulla fides pietasque viris qui castra sequuntur,* — the quotation is from Filippo Villani. It was reported that Hawkwood would have taken the first opportunity to prove the truth of the intelligence, and even to treat personally with the Pope's Legate.

To keep him in good faith, the Florentine Signoria, not content with sending Giorgio Scali to him as envoy, thought of calling from Milan that Ruggiero Cane who had assisted them in the treaty of peace, and had a great influence over the English captain, who seemed to have a very reserved and inaccessible manner. "He is the only one," they wrote to Bernabò, "to whom Hawkwood is accustomed to confide his most secret designs, and who knows his weaknesses and his good moments."

And as Cane was late in starting and then was detained some days by illness at Lucca, the Signoria wrote and rewrote to Hawkwood that he should "patiently put up with the delays of his desired friend, and most faithful counselor." At length Cane arrived at the English camp, and soon understood clearly that Hawkwood expected the an-

* See Document XXII.   ** See Document XXIII.

nual pension of 1200 florins would be assured to him even if he should leave Italy. The Signoria immediately consented, only making the proviso " except that he enter the service of the Church, when we do not choose to give him anything, " and recommending Scali and Cane to persuade him to enter the service of Florence and Bernabò Visconti, or " at least keep him free from the Church."

Like their captain, the English soldiers were evidently held in great estimation at Florence, for Scali, the ambassador, received the following instructions : " In regard to the other brigade, do the best you possibly can, — especially with the English, — to bring them into the pay of ourselves and Messer Bernabò, on such terms that those who come to us, shall be obliged to serve freely against every other man in the world, otherwise we will not give them a *grosso* (a small coin)." In fact Cane procured for the league four hundred lances, and four hundred archers, who by their own stipulation must have voluntarily deserted the Company, since their compacts forbade the Florentines to treat with, or induce any soldier to leave it.

While his friend Ruggiero Cane was busying himself with Hawkwood on account of the Florentines, the Lieutenant John Thornbury was exerting his persuasions on behalf of the Cardinal Legate, Hawkwood resisted for a long time, but in the end he gave in, and Cane was able to write to the Cardinal: " It has been a serious task to bring back your captain into your service.... he would no longer remember anything he had promised. I remedied this however, and he was satisfied with promises and my word of honour." Hawkwood had found by experience that the money of the Florentines was much more certain than that of the Church; and precisely at this time the treasurer Alberti arrived at the English camp at Staggia, to effectuate the payment of the last rate.

In those same days Hawkwood exacted other large

tributes from Lucca and Siena ; the agreement with Lucca amounted to six thousand florins, against the usual promises to treat the Lucchese territory in a friendly manner.* We cannot give the exact cipher of the contract with Siena, but it cannot have been less than fifty thousand florins.

Anyhow, between Florence, Pisa, Lucca, and Arezzo, the English Company had obtained in little more than three months 174,800 florins in gold, which with those of Siena would amount to nearly two millions and a half of francs, — an enormous sum for those times, — without counting the annuity of 1200 florins, assured to Hawkwood.

Perhaps the latter was persuaded that he had drained Tuscany quite dry, and therefore he decided to treat with the Church.

XIV.

A CARDINAL AS HOSTAGE.
HAWKWOOD AS LANDED PROPRIETOR.

[GHERARDI, *La guerra degli otto santi* — PIERO BUONINSEGNI, *Cronaca* — *Chronicles of Gubbio* — *Chronicles of Rimini* — Poem in the *Chronicle* of the ANONYMOUS FLORENTINE — *Archivio storico italiano*, 1st series, v. XVI, part 2nd. Inventory of the goods restored to the Abbot of Montemaggiore.]

The Florentine Signoria finding that the greater part of the English remained with Hawkwood in the service of the Church, hastened, by calling on the troops of Bernabò Visconti, to put the Genoese, Pisans, and Lucchese on the defence against the probable movements of the Company.

But the latter marched on Siena instead, and Florence was warned directly, for Ruggiero Cane and Spinello Al-

---

* See Document XXIV.

1375. berti accompanied the English camp and kept them diligently informed of its movements.

Thus the Sienese received certain intelligence that Hawkwood had concentrated his forces at Montepulciano, intending to possess himself of that town, and they placed a garrison there, paying 200 florins to him who had revealed the design.

The Florentines still preserved some hope of seducing Hawkwood, for they had secret assurances that the Condottiere resigned himself unwillingly " to the deceit and treachery which he found in the priests;" and their agents at the camp received these instructions: " If we cannot by any means obtain the service of Hawkwood with one of his brigades, and if he wishes to stay with the Church, do not bring us any of the English, — but let the Church bear the whole burden." They calculated that the Church was not in a condition to pay the stipendiaries, in which case this would have created great embarrassment. They did not know, as we shall soon see, that Hawkwood had already provided himself a recompense for the lacking stipends.

October 18. Alberti returned to Florence with the news that the Church had engaged the English for 30,000 florins a month, the pay to begin from the middle of October, besides two loans and pay in anticipation, and that they were to be enrolled in November.

November 6. Great was the consternation, — so great that Florence hastened the march of Bernabò's men-at-arms, who had already arrived at Sarzana; although the faithful Ruggiero October 31. Cane had forewarned them that in eight days Hawkwood intended to pass into the Papal states, whereas if Bernabò's troops should come into Tuscany he would stop to fight them.

But in the meanwhile nearly all the towns dependent on the Church rebelled, invoking by their deeds that *Libertas* which they inscribed on their standards. It was necessary for the Legate to employ all his forces to repress the rebellion, and leave Tuscany in peace. Consequently no worse tribulations awaited her than the violence perpetrated by some sanguinary spirits, who on the occasion of the English invasion had seized the opportunity to join with a number of bandits from the various cities.

The Cardinal Legate had caused the English to encamp in haste under Perugia, sending a detachment to garrison Città di Castello, — but even this town rose in insurrection; November 7. about fifty of the English were killed, while the rest were blockaded on the piazza and scarcely succeeded in getting off with their arms and baggage.

The Cardinal immediately sent Hawkwood with all his Company against Città di Castello, but in those days a resolute defence sufficed for a walled town even with inferior force ; Hawkwood could do nothing ; on the contrary, two of his outworks were assaulted and taken before his eyes. Meanwhile, profiting by his withdrawal, the Perugians also rebelled, and constrained their diabolical governor the Abbot to shut himself up in the castle where they held him in a state of siege.

The English being again recalled, encamped under Perugia, but as to any decisive action, they did not even attempt it ; and as the rebellion spread over all the Papal states, they were next sent to the succour of the citadel of Decemb. 5. Viterbo. Here the people and militia fairly opposed them in open fight, the attempts of the English were vain, and, leaving many dead and wounded in the ditches and trenches, they were obliged to return to Perugia.

The affairs of the Church were going so badly, and the temporal power was so shaken, that the *Otto di balia* (the Council of eight) of the Florentines were enabled to write to Bernabò Visconti: " If they have the strength Decemb. 10. to hold out the campaign for a month, the domination of the French and other foreigners in Italy will be made an

1875. end of for ever." Moreover they were still afraid that the English not being able to do anything on the Papal territory should again turn against Tuscany.

But if the English could not attack Perugia, neither could the Perugians succeed in their assaults on the castle and so they had to treat openly with the besieged Abbot taking Hawkwood as mediator. They tacitly established a species of armistice till the end of December, during which time the English frequented the city, and the Perugians risked themselves in the camp.

In vain the *Otto* warned the Perugians that "the foreigners could not possibly be on the side of liberty," and advised them rather to bargain that Hawkwood should go away, or at least cease from hostilities.

As a consolation for the siege, the Abbot of Montemaggiore received on his birthday a fine present from his kinsman the Pope, — no less than a cardinal's hat, and the grade of pontifical Legate! his exemplary virtues could merit no less! but this did not suffice to raise the siege nor was it enough to provision the three thousand men shut up in the castle with him.

1376. On new year's day he was constrained to surrender himself to the Perugians, with the understanding that he was to be permitted to retire to Hawkwood's camp. But as soon as he entered, Hawkwood courteously placed a guard over him as a prisoner, saying, "We want our pay."

> Avendo Gianni Aguto dal suo lato
> L'Abate e altri ched eron nella rete,
> Disse: Signor, s' i' non son pagato,
> Giammai da me voi non vi partirete;
> Ch'io debbo aver del tempo valicato
> Cento migliaia o più, e voi il sapete.

> (John Hawkwood had within his net one day
> The Abbot, with some others he had caught,
> And said: "Sir, if you do not quickly pay

My dues, then you and I shall never part.   1376.
For all my time and labour lost you owe
A hundred thousand florins, as you know.")

Moreover his unlucky reverence lost a great many of his belongings, — according to the treaty, his own baggage with that of his soldiers had been retained by the Perugians, who after ten days consigned them to the Englishmen. The deed of consignment was made in the cloister of San Martino where Hawkwood had his camp, and there the delegates of Perugia met Marshal John Thornbury, the agent of Hawkwood. An incomplete inventory was hastily made, while Thornbury restored the goods to their owners, taking a note of them. " And also a great number of things were without written formalities *restored* to divers persons and men to whom they *were said to belong*, which things they were not able to describe by reason of the great haste and eagerness," which is to say that anyone who chose, took the goods. Although incomplete, the inventory is very interesting: we see for example how the mercenaries were clad, for there was returned to an Englishman " a Milanese *barbuta* (helmet) with its nose-piece, and another with three silver *cannonibus* and a steel neck-piece ; also an old red doublet, with white and green fringes." The list of objects given back to the Cardinal is most edifying, there were many sumptuous things, several women's gowns(!) and the episcopal mitre and rosary, thrust into the same valise as his shoes and hose ; the only books were a breviary and a little volume of songs.

The hurry of this operation is accounted for, by the fact that Hawkwood was hastening to raise the camp, taking the Cardinal with him as hostage for the arrears of pay. January 21. Having reached Rimini, Hawkwood on proceeding to Cesena, left the Cardinal under the efficient guardianship of Galeotto January 22. Malatesta, who conceded to the prisoner the use of the palace garden (*Orto dei Signori*), but he kept him in good

custody, having promised Hawkwood to restore him (
demand, under pain of a fine of 130,000 ducats (probab
the amount of pay for which his reverence was hostage
And Hawkwood was a man to whom one could not light
make promises without keeping them.

He had indeed received enough promises in lieu (
money from the Cardinal Legate of Bologna, to who:
Thornbury wrote that his captain hesitated to resume th
service of the Church " on account of that castle whic
had been promised him." But now that Hawkwood ha
another Cardinal in his hands, and he a kinsman of th
Pope, the Church was obliged to maintain its promise
and so gave the Condottiere the lordship of Bagnacavall
of Cotignola, and of the village of Conselice, contiguor
estates in the neighbourhood of Lugo in Romagna; impo:
tant enough to constitute almost a little principality, a gi
which though it did not entirely balance the credit, yet col
stituted a large sum on account.*

Many incorrect assertions have been made respectin
this domain of Hawkwood's. Domenico Maria Manni woul
not admit its existence, saying that " adventurers wei
paid in money and not in lands." Ricotti in one plac
speaks of Bagnacavallo and Cotignola, and in another (
Bagnacavallo and Castrocaro. Some constantly substitut
Castrocaro for Cotignola, others discuss the nature of th
dominion, holding that Hawkwood was only the Governc
of these places, which he held for the Church, all of whic
are uncertainties dependent on the various versions of th
chroniclers.

Without staying to argue the point, it will suffice to mak
everything clear if we give the historical succession (

---

* The precise date of this event is not given; it was certainly befo:
the 18th of July 1376, on which day the Cardinal left Rimini, liberated aft
his confinement. It probably took place in the early months of the year.

facts and documents; and meanwhile we will note that there is nothing to confirm the supposition of Fra Bonoli author of a History of Cotignola, according to which the Pope had conceded those places to Hawkwood as Gonfaloniere of the Holy Church (!!) with the condition of not alienating them to any one except to Niccolò II, Marquis of Ferrara.

It would seem that Bagnacavallo was consigned, as soon *February.* as the English shewed that if they were not paid, they were determined to pay themselves, by infesting several places in the Romagna, taking Castrocaro, and putting it to the sack, by way of restoring it to its rightful lord Astorre Manfredi.

These events put Bologna, where Hawkwood and his men were quartered, in a ferment. The Cardinal made the mistake of not giving heed to them, and sent Hawkwood to take the fortress of Granarolo, occupied by Manfredi. The Bolognese wished nothing better, and openly rebelled against the Church for the cause of *Liberty,* aided by a thousand infantry under Count Antonio da Bruscoli, sent to them by Florence.

Nor did the English succeed in their enterprise at *March 20.* Granarolo; the same luck fell to their share as at Perugia, and Città di Castello, — they were obliged to encamp between Granarolo and Bagnacavallo, both their captain and themselves being, as may be imagined, greatly irritated, the more so because some of them remained shut up in Bologna in the hands of the citizens; altogether they were but too ready for the worst excesses, and even decided on a reign of terror.

XV.

THE SLAUGHTER AT FAENZA. — HOSTILITY WITH BOLOGNA. OCCUPATIONS IN TIME OF TRUCE.

[*Chronicle* of the ANONYMOUS FLORENTINE in the *Documents of Italian history*, v. VI — *Sienese chronicle* by NERI DI DONATO — DELLA PUGLIOLA, *Bolognese chronicle* — GHIRARDACCI, *Storie bolognesi* — *Diary* of SER NADDO DA MONTECATINI — *Chronicle* by MARCHIONNE STEFANI — *Consulte e pratiche* of the Commune of Florence, State Archives of Florence — BONOLI, *Storia di Cotignola* — *Document concerning the fortifications of Cotignola*, copied from Prof. Domenico Vaccolini and cited by Canonico Balduzzi, *Acts and memoranda of the R. Deputation of national history for the province of Romagna*, 3rd series, v. II, fasc. I — BONINCONTRI, *Annals* — CORIO, *Storie milanesi* — GIOVIO, *Elogia*, ec.]

1376.

Here the figure of Hawkwood appears in a sinister light, and the only excuse we can make for him is that the authority of the captains over the mercenary companies was not so complete, as in a well ordered army, and so they could not always bridle the excesses of the soldiery, nor be held wholly responsible for them, as for things premeditated and commanded by themselves.[*]

The city of Faenza was governed by the bishop of Tarragona with the title of Count of Romagna. He fearing that the people of Faenza might follow the example of their neighbours at Bologna and participate in the general rebellion, called Hawkwood and the English to garrison the town ; — they came, but it was to plunder, not to man the forts.

March 24.

The bishop-count had scarcely posted them within the walls, when he went off, leaving everything to their tender mercies ; and they began to run about the streets crying : " Long live the Church." Hawkwood quickly made a pro-

---

[*] In fact it is only as an exception in some Florentine contracts with the Condottiere that we find this clause: " That at the request of the commander the notary of the troop shall dismiss those stipendiaries who are not obedient, or do not give true service."

clamation that every citizen or countryman must consign his arms whether of offence or defence, in the rooms of the fortress, under pain of fine and bodily punishment (*pena l' avere e la persona*).

And soon after, without loss of time, the Englishmen, crying this time, " Long live Sir John Hawkwood, death to the Church" (*Viva Messer Giovanni Aguto, muoia la Chiesa*), hurled themselves on the *goods and persons;* indeed to be more at their ease, they drove out the men, the old people and children, keeping in the city only young women and girls, *a loro posta e per vitupero, trattando ignominiosamente le vergini e le matrone a guisa di meretrici e di schiave vilmente vendute.*

The Sienese chronicle says that two constables fought a duel for the possession of a nun, and that Hawkwood, like a new Solomon, plunged his dagger into the unfortunate creature exclaiming: " Half for each." This is probably a fantastic embellishment, the above mentioned chronicle being very hostile to Hawkwood, from whom Siena had more than once to suffer oppression, and extortions. If we may believe Marchionne Stefani, the bishop-count was particularly greedy in the matter of this kind of spoil, for standing at the gate where the women went away (for many were spared by the knights, who were pitiful of them), he turned them back saying : *Torna addietro : questa sia buona per la masnada,* and besides he would not allow the convents to be spared, but had them put to the sack and treated just like the more worldly abodes.

Other historians and chroniclers, although deploring the excesses of the English in Faenza, do not speak of bloodshed, nor were useless cruelties habitual to those soldiers, who were more than anything avaricious of gain.

" Everything that was in Faenza was appropriated by the Company," this we can easily believe, the more so that the Company laid claim to large credits for arrears of pay, — while the captain, for his part and account, had obtained the castle and land.

When this news reached Bologna, the indignation was general, and the temptation to make reprisals was very great, since the citizens had in their hands Filippo Puer one of the principal constables, Cook the cavalier, and several other soldiers, together with the illegitimate children of Puer and two young sons of Sir John Hawkwood, who had remained there when the Company marched forth on the Granarolo expedition. But they were afraid to take strong measures, and contented themselves by treating them as hostages, confining Puer in the house of Salvuccio Bentivoglio, and putting the other soldiers in prison.

Even this was enough to excite the anger of Hawkwood, and to provoke fierce menaces. The Bolognese sent Roberto da Saliceto to try and make terms, but he wrote that " he could do nothing, because there are no worse people in the world (*perchè al mondo non v' è peggior gente*), they demanded such tremendous terms that if they had been citizens of Faenza they could not have wanted more." Saliceto returned to Bologna, terrified out of his wits, and thanking God that Hawkwood had not taken him prisoner.

The question became grave, so much so as to preoccupy also the Signoria of Florence. The Florentines were anxious that the Bolognese should enter into a decisive campaign, as their allies against the Church, and would have wished to procure an agreement between them and Hawkwood, as a preparation towards detaching that valuable captain from the ecclesiastical service; but they feared to make matters worse by interfering, and they moreover doubted whether peace between Bologna and Hawkwood might not mean war to Florence. It was therefore resolved to let Bologna alone, as best understanding her own business, and to remind her that the Florentine men-at-arms were already in the field.

This much we find from the *Consulte e pratiche*, or report of the business transacted in the councils of Florence, in which there met together with the Signoria (or in war time with the *Otto di balia* *) the Gonfalonieri,** the twelve Buonuomini *** and the Captains of the Guelph party.

They are therefore documents of great interest, because they reflect, day by day, the public opinion then prevalent in Florence, and reveal the mechanism of government from behind the scenes, and the private reasons of the events in which the Florentine Republic took part.

Hawkwood, without so many councils, passed directly on to practice. Exhorted thereto by the Cardinal Legate who had taken refuge at Ferrara, he invaded the Bolognese territory, treating it " with fire and the sword," which decided Bologna to formally enter the League of Florence against the Pope.

The English were encamped at Medicina, and Hawkwood flashed out from the camp in person, with four hundred lances, and for three days rode towards Ponte Maggiore, sacking, burning, and taking prisoners about four hundred peasants. Thus hard pressed the Bolognese took courage, and this time threw into prison all the English who were in the city, not excluding Hawkwood's two little

---

* The *Otto di balìa*, which was called in war times the *Otto di guerra* (Eight of war), was a council first created during this very war, and it took the place of the Signoria, or was added to it, in the general war council. Its office was to decide on matters of expense, and means of raising funds etc. in time of war. In peace, it was a council of eight which ruled the political economy of the city. — (*Translator.*)

** The *Gonfalonieri* were the heads of the different quarters of the city. Each quarter had four *gonfalons* or standards, the bearers of which were called into council on special occasions. — (*Translator.*)

*** The twelve *Buonuomini*, or good men, was a council formed of three elders (Anziani) from each quarter. Its sittings lasted three months, and it was called into council with the Signoria on especial occasions. — (*Translator.*)

sons. This was all that was necessary; paternal affection outweighed the fury of the captain. To regain the hostages, a truce of sixteen months was accorded — while the prisoners, and even the cattle taken as spoil, were restored.

Having got his children back, Hawkwood employed the armistice in arranging his affairs and insuring his territorial lordship.

Having by this time squeezed out of Faenza all that was worth having, he decided to cede the empty husk to Alberto d'Este Marquis of Ferrara, some say for 60,000 ducats, some 40,000, others 24,000 florins.

In agreement with the Pope who, above everything, feared the city getting into Bernabò Visconti's hands, the Marchese settled the account with the English, taking from them the pledge which they had in hand : and the cession was made the following year.

Meanwhile the affair being concluded, Hawkwood took up his abode at Bagnacavallo, a well fortified town in which nothing was lacking, and without more ado, he began to enlarge and strengthen his contiguous possession, Cotignola. In those days fortifications were of the greatest efficacy, as artillery was either not yet employed, or used in exceptional cases and rudimentary form. We might even say that Cotignola was reconstructed by him from its very foundations: — hitherto we have only seen him as the rapacious vandal, now we behold him as an architect.

A century before this the people of Faenza and Forlì had made a strong fortress at Cotignola, but in Hawkwood's time it was in a very bad state, perhaps because it no longer corresponded to good military rules, the area being very small and not capable of holding a sufficient garrison. Hawkwood enlarged it to five times the size, surrounding it with new walls a deep moat, and bulwarks. A plan is still existing in the Archives of Cotignola which minutely describes this rebuilding, and shews us that besides several small forts, and the various suburbs, he also erected a ˮ large and royal palace with dungeons like a very stronghold ” (*magnum et regale palatium cum foveis in modum fortissimi loci*).

According to Bonincontri, an historian little trustworthy in regard to facts, he had even thought how this enlarged town was to be populated, and proposed prizes to immigrants, — but in practice he seems to have done the opposite thing, seeing that to build the above-mentioned strong palace, he had to take away from Giovanni Attendolo, son of Muzio and father of the Sforza, a possession which was contiguous to his own and imposed a tribute in favour of Giovanni and his descendents on all those who wished to build houses within the new circuit.

This shews that the English captain was not a tyrant without a sense of justice, capable of expropriating possessions without recompense, and it proves besides that the tradition of the rise of the great family of the Sforza from a poor peasant was unfounded.

Hawkwood kept for some years the lordship of Bagnacavallo and Cotignola; that he had leisure to complete the works we have mentioned, which he began towards the middle of the year 1376, is placed beyond doubt by the map we have cited, in the Archives of Cotignola.*

Near Cotignola, arose in those days, the Castle of Cunio, afterwards completely destroyed in the 16th century; the ruling count was Alberico da Barbiano, whom we shall soon find in the field as condottiere of some troops (Italian

---

* Another mention of Hawkwood's dominion might be perhaps gleaned from Pietro M. Carantho, a learned man of Cotignola, who wrote of the events happening in his native place as he had heard of them from his ancestors, or seen them with his own eyes. Thus says Leandro Alberti (*Descrizione d' Italia*), but this Carantho does not appear in the *Bibliografia storica degli Stati pontifici*, by Ranghiasci, nor do we know whether his history has ever been published.

1376.   ones at last), and fighting even against the English, and against Hawkwood. In Cotignola there was also that Muzio Attendolo son of the Giovanni mentioned above, who was then a boy of seven years old; — he began the career of

1381.   arms at the earliest age (Giovio asserts without foundation that he was a pupil of Hawkwood's), and by this career the Sforza had the good fortune to found their dynasty.

Indeed some years after, when Hawkwood, as we shall see, was despoiled of his lordship, this same Muzio Atten-

1414.   dolo was created Count of Cotignola, by Pope John XXII, and the lordship passed to his descendants the Sforza, who gave to Cotignola the title and privileges of a city, amongst which privileges may be classed the ancient jocose spectacle of the *Sega vecchia* (old saw) at mid-lent, which has lingered to our own days.

It is probable that Hawkwood fortified and built also at Bagnacavallo, but no memorial of this exists except some possessions left to his heirs and a street which still has the name of *Strada Aguta* (Hawkwood street). This opens towards the east of the city and terminates in an open space marked on the old maps as *Commenda* (Commandery) *di San Giorgio;* near there was a fortress called the " Bastion of Villanova," so it must have been a military road opened by Hawkwood, to ensure communication between the capital of his feudal territory, and that rampart, which was perhaps built by himself and certainly was held by him to be important.

On the other hand, we have at Cotignola a well preserved monument of Hawkwood, especially interesting from its military character. We may therefore be permitted to linger awhile in this little city, an inheritance of two of the most celebrated condottieri who held the sword of command in Italy.

———

Setting aside objects which do not concern our history, there is a grand old building, which from its architecture might be attributed to the end of the 14th, or beginning of the 15th century, and which has the merit of preserving almost intact the internal distribution of rooms of that epoch. One might at first sight almost seem to recognise that "great and regal palace" of Sir John Hawkwood; but on the capitals of two marble columns which sustain the arches of the "Loggia" are sculptured the arms of a lion rampant bearing the quince * of Cotignola. The lion rampant was given by the Emperor Sigismund to Attendolo Sforza in 1401, and in a large terra cotta medallion on the façade at the back of the building the same arms are repeated, with the well known crest of the Sforza, — a winged dragon with a human head.

So we treat of a palace either radically modified, or entirely rebuilt by the Sforza.

Hawkwood then was domiciled in his new possessions, and restraining his English Company from spoiling the lands about Faenza, — and here ere long a letter reached him from the *Otto*, who, in Florence were directing the war against the Church. The letter, which referred to the intentions communicated by Hawkwood through his chancellor Ruggiero Cane, and Spinello Alberti, simply expressed a hope of coming to terms; and added that Ruggiero Cane, the faithful friend, and usual mediator, would explain to him the wishes of the *Otto*. ** The captain seeing that the Church and her enemies were disputing for his sword, naturally raised his demands, — he could exact the more from Florence and her allies, because a company of fierce Bretons commanded by most ferocious captains, and led by the Cardinal of Geneva who was more

1376.
June.

June 9.

---

* The Italian name of quince is *cotogna*. — (*Translator.*)
** See Document XXV.

1376. ferocious than captains and soldiers put together, had crossed the Alps on the Pope's behalf; and one of the captains, Malestroit, had boasted he would enter Florence as easily as the sun-light could get in, while the Cardinal threatened the Bolognese that he would wash his hands and feet in their blood. In fact he disposed of both Bretons and English.*

June 16. Then the *Otto* wrote to their ally Bernabò Visconti, that he should order his dependent Ruggiero Cane to obtain for the League " as many Englishmen as he could " even up to 1500 lances and 800 archers. They doubted the result " because Hawkwood had demanded impossible things, and an intolerable price," however they had sent Spinello Alberti their treasurer to begin the negotiations, and were " ready to participate in the expense, because it was important to prevent the union of the Bretons with the English." **

June 20. The fear of contracting " intolerable " expenses was very soon overcome, for the peril seemed so urgent that it was agreed in consultation that " the *Otto* should manage to obtain the English brigade at all costs; to which end they should employ every means both secret and open; that they should make the deeds and remissions, requested by Hawkwood; and it was only in case they could not possibly get him, that they were to obtain a captain of war and every other possible means of defence."

On that very day the Signoria wrote to Hawkwood that while acceding to his requests they accorded him full pardon for all past injuries and evils, praying him to reciprocate it.***

---

* Baluzio cites a codex (56 of the Colbert library in Paris) which contains a prospectus of the men-at-arms under command of the Cardinal, and the payments made to them by Domenico Francesco d'Incisa bishop of Acqui, who was lieutenant of the bishop of Bologna, and the Pope's treasurer general for Italy. In the first place is nominated *G. Acuto* captain of the English, then comes Malestroit captain of the Bretons.

** See Document XXVI.   *** See Document XXVII.

We may believe that Hawkwood and his Englishmen 1376.
did not care to measure themselves with the Bretons,
whose " ferocity " they had probably experienced in the
French wars. At Florence it was known that negotiations
were commenced for an agreement between Hawkwood
and the Church, and hence they deliberated :

 " That the *Otto,* as they have hitherto done, shall June 21.
use every means to procure that the Bretons and English
shall not injure us, providing nevertheless that there shall
be no agreement between them. That in this peril the citizens shall be called on to assist the Commune with money.
And that they shall use every effort to do this, and the
Otto shall provide how and when the companies shall
eventually leave the country.

 " That the *Otto* shall provide for the well-being, liberty
and defence of the country, and for the fortifications of
the towns."

We can feel what trepidation the Florentines were in,
we might say hour by hour ; they feared beyond everything that Hawkwood would agree with the Bretons, and
make one company out of the two.

Notice arrived that his contract with the Church was June 22.
concluded, but at the same time secret assurances to the
contrary must have been received. The captain had decided to keep both feet in the stirrups — to take money
from each side and do nothing serious for either, avoiding
the dreaded conflict with the Bretons, and having respect
to the Florentines. The latter in fact wrote to Bernabò
begging him to corrupt the Bretons at their united expense,
whilst they themselves undertook to keep the English
at bay.

And in the *Consulte,* although foreseeing that they could June 23.
hope nothing from Hawkwood's words, and agreeing with
the opinion of those who wished to fortify the passes of

1376.

the Apennines, and make every provision for war, against him, as well as the Bretons; yet Filippo Corsini advised them " nevertheless to make haste in consulting about an agreement with Hawkwood."

June 25.

It being known that the Bretons were at present aiming at Bologna, the prevailing idea was, that by closing the passes, clearing out the country, and displaying the crossbowmen, they could give efficacious aid to Bologna and " yet keep an eye " on Sir John; — but " meanwhile" (the orders ran) " try to procure a contract with Hawkwood. " To render this less difficult, the Signoria, by means of the Scaligers, persuaded the Marquis of Este not to lend the Church the 30,000 florins necessary for the stipends of the English.

Whether this were the cause, or the brave resistance of Bologna had made it clear that the Bretons were not so formidable in war as they were ferocious to the defenceless, certain it is that Hawkwood began to yield again to the golden seductions of Florence.

July 10.

In conformity to his request the Signoria assured him, that they had made arrangements, for his annuity of 1200 florins to be paid him in Venice, and continued even if he should leave Italy.* But even this was not enough to decide him: he still maintained such an ambiguous part, that in Florence they gave credence to rumours of the most insidious perfidy on his part.

July 22.

News arrived that three Genoese archers (of that troop sent to the Romagna by the Florentines, to help Bologna) had schemed to give Hawkwood the castle of Granarolo, which lay near his possessions of Bagnacavallo and Cotignola, and that Giorgio Grimaldi, the captain of the Genoese, having discovered the plan, had hanged the three archers by the neck.

---

* See Document XXVIII.

Then came notice of the discovery of a treaty made by certain men of Arezzo, to betray Arezzo to the Church, for which purpose the traitors had changed the lock of one of the gates so as to have the key; it was said that " somebody's head was cut off, " and as to the treaty, " John Hawkwood and the Bretons had a hand in it. "

But it was all empty talk, for rumours will circulate in time of war for terror. It is more probable that the Florentine Doffo de' Bardi, who had been successful on some previous missions, and was at this time sent to Faenza to confer with Hawkwood, found that the Captain had gone to Medicina to hold an interview with the Cardinal of Geneva. The Englishman prudently attended this conference with an accompanying guard of five hundred lances. The interview took place in the tower of Giovanni Isolani, and all the day was consumed in parleying, without coming to any agreement, so that when the Cardinal presented himself at Faenza with the Bretons, he was denied admittance.

Hawkwood persevered in his double game: he managed to send word to the Florentine captain of war Rodolfo da Varano,[*] requesting him to send a person of trust: the treasurer was sent, as being the most fit envoy, but he was taken by the Cardinal's men-at-arms.

Vice versa when the Florentines inflicted a defeat on the Bretons near Faenza, Hawkwood went out to help them, if not " they could not have held their own. " And then the English and Bretons together attempted Forlì and were repulsed.

---

* There is a tradition that the Varani, Lords of Camerino, were of Anglo-Norman origin, in common with the English *Warrens*. Litta however in his ' celebrated Families ' holds this theory to be unfounded,— it may perhaps have arisen from the fact that towards the year 1260, Gentile da Varano obtained assistance from Pope Alexander IV, and was put in command of an English brigade, which had either stopped in Italy after the Crusades, or came when the Pope offered the crown of Naples to the Duke of Lancaster, son of Henry III.

1376.

Hawkwood, though enriched by the sale of Faenza, and well furnished with provisions, yet received very tempting proposals from the Bretons: he might even have schemed to have the overtures made to him, as he was not at that time content with his men, nor were they with him. Then the Florentines, Bernabò, and Bologna agreed to make the attempt to break up the English Company and take into their pay as many as seven hundred lances, and three hundred archers. They made a secret understanding with Philip Puer (Power), John Berwick and with another " Messer Giovanni " to bring their men, promising the high pay of from 22 to 24 florins a lance, but these knights only succeeded in bringing two hundred and fifteen lances and ninety two archers. " And this I know, for I enrolled them, being employed in Bologna on behalf of the Commune," says Marchionne Stefani.

To sum up, the Florentines had reason in encouraging the Bolognese to resist, for they sent them as captain the expert Rodolfo da Varano; but they could also persevere with good hope of success in the attempts to deprive the Church of Hawkwood and the English, its best leader, and finest soldiers.

XVII.

THE SLAUGHTER OF CESENA.
HAWKWOOD AGAINST THE CHURCH.

[Sozomeno — Poggio Bracciolini — St. Antoninus, bishop of Florence — G. Gori, in the *Archivio storico italiano*, new series, v. VIII — Ricotti, *History of the mercenary companies* — Sienese chronicle in Muratori [*R. I. S.*] — Coluccio Salutati's *Letter* written to the *King of France for the Florentines*, quoted in the *Annales mediolanenses* published by Muratori [*R. I. S.*], t. XVI — *Chronicles of Bologna, Estense, and of Rimini* — Diary of the Anonymous Florentine — Ammirato — Salutati *Epistolæ*.]

If the English Condottiere had more promptly decided to abandon the Pope's service, he would have saved himself the shame of figuring as an actor, although repugnantly, in one of the most atrociously bloody deeds recorded in history. It is too true that on this occasion he was still under the orders of Roberto Count of Geneva, a Cardinal-priest of the order of the "Holy Apostles," ugly and deformed of body, whilst in character he could rank first among those Avignonese bishops, who scandalized the world with injustice, simony, avarice, gluttony, lust, luxury, pride, and all the cardinal vices; adding to these, as an especial characteristic, bestial ferocity, so much so, that catholic ecclesiastical history is pleased to be able to classify him amongst the *antipopes,* though it cannot cancel the fact that he was first the legate of the legitimate High Pontiff Gregory XI, and commissioned to restore the temporal power.

The Cardinal had failed to enter Bologna, and he revenged himself by putting all the country under the horror of fire or bloodshed; rewarding, and absolving with great rejoicings such of his Bretons as recounted to him the murders they had perpetrated, he even blessed and consecrated their bloodstained swords.

Then he took up his winter quarters with these unbridled soldiers at Cesena, the only city in the Romagna which would receive him with "a joyful and reverent spirit," the only one which "benevolently favored" the head of the ecclesiastics; but the Bretons illtreated the unfortunate Cesena in such a manner as to reduce the citizens to despair. The Cardinal gave no heed to their remonstrances, while the captain-general, Galeotto Malatesta, told them to take justice into their own hands.

The leaders of the Bretons in their turn complained that provisions were dear, so the Cardinal gave them leave to procure them without payment; the soldiers then fell to and plundered the butchers' shops;— the measure was full, the Cesenese armed themselves and killed a good many of the brigands. The Cardinal then matured and carried out an unparalleled scheme of revenge. He made a solemn promise of pardon to those citizens who turned to him with repentance for their rebellion, and for that almost excusable man-slaughter on the sole condition that they should consign their arms ; this he swore by his cardinal's hat, and to inspire them with more faith, he asked, and obtained fifty hostages, whom he immediately released again with benign words. Having thus rendered them defenceless (whilst he had called Hawkwood and his Englishmen from Faenza, secretly causing them to enter the fortress known as *la Murata*), as soon as night came he gave orders, for the captain to fall on the city and "administer justice." Hawkwood attempted to lead him to milder measures, declaring himself ready to constrain the citizens to disarm, and to promise obedience, but the Cardinal had already attained this, and wanted quite a different thing : — he explained that by *justice* he meant *blood and more blood*. Hawkwood insisted, showing the Cardinal that he ought to look to the result, but he finished by resigning himself to the reiterated commands.

His repugnance may possibly help to diminish our horror of the part he took in the affair. It arose perhaps from his intention not to compromise the already advanced understanding with the Florentine League, any way it showed that he did not approve of useless ferocities.

On the other hand was he certain of securing the obedience of his Englishmen, if he denied them the chance of a sack ? And did not Alberico da Barbiano himself, whose praises are sung by generous spirits and Italian sentiment, take part in the fierce repression of Cesena together with his two hundred lances ? In fact, both Bretons and English threw themselves on the defenceless and trusting city. For three days and nights, they made such horrible slaughter of the citizens that the pen refuses to describe the particulars. It may be admitted perhaps that authors have related it with some exaggeration, — for example how are we to believe the Sienese chronicle which calculates that the little town contained 40,000 inhabitants? But on the whole there is a formidable array of chroniclers, historians, diplomatic documents, and popular poets, all agreeing in describing the slaughter of Cesena as an outburst of insuperable barbarity.

The letter of the Florentines to the King of France written by Coluccio Salutati, chancellor of the Commune, is a circular *manifesto* sent to the different powers, denouncing the horrors committed in the name and defence of the Papal dominion, by two bands of robbers. Even if we doubt the interested eloquence of this witness, we may believe Poggio Bracciolini, the secretary of eight Popes, and we may trust the archbishop St. Antonino. The latter without reserve compares the Cardinal to Herod and Nero, and the Bolognese chronicle says: " People no longer believe either in the Pope or Cardinals, for these are things to crush one's faith."

There is a short latin comedy in four scenes which has been erroneously attributed first to Petrarch, and then to Salutati, the subject of which is a description of " the slaughter of the unhappy city of Cesena." It agrees with many of the chronicles, and asserts that five thousand inhabitants were killed in one day; — the most moderate reports say " about two thousand five hundred Christians." Naturally the men did not let themselves be butchered like lambs: three hundred of the murderers were killed, a few in the town and more disbanded about the country, but the mass of the citizens, being unarmed, were only able to seek safety by flight. Those who did not flee in haste, or were overtaken, found no quarter.

The chronicler of Rimini, who is especially trustworthy from his vicinity, says more than all: " As many men, women, and nurselings as they found, they slaughtered, all the squares were full of dead. A thousand drowned themselves in trying to cross the moats — some fled by the gates with the *Bretons* pursuing, who murdered and robbed and committed outrages, and would not let the handsomest women escape, but kept them as spoil; they put a ransom on a thousand little boys and girls, neither man nor woman remained in Cesena.

" Then they methodically began to plunder — sending the best things in cars to Faenza, and selling the rest of the furniture to the people of the neighbouring towns.

" By the 15th of April neither corn, nor wine, nor oil, remained, except what the mountaineers supplied them with, and even they took away a load of blankets or clothes, whenever they brought a load of straw, and so the city was undone.

" About eight thousand between great and small came to Rimini, all begging for alms, save a few artisans who found work, and thus the said *Bretons* consumed Cesena inside and out till the 13th of August."

It seems then that the worst was done by the Bretons, who, being naturally fierce, were rendered more so by revenge for their lost comrades. St. Antonino specifies that the English preferred plunder above everything, and on this account they urged to flight the people of Cesena. Ammirato confirms this, and the *Cronaca estense* says : " Sir John Hawkwood, not to be held entirely infamous, sent about a thousand of the Cesenese women to Rimini." But even his men did not entirely relinquish atrocities in search of prey. " All the survivors left in the city were constrained by the English to ransom themselves; they barbarously illtreated men and women, to make them reveal where real or supposed treasures were to be found."

To conclude, the slaughter was such that the following year when means were taken for the restoration of the city, many deep trenches for the conservation of corn, and two large cisterns were found full of corpses. Hawkwood had hastened to inter the dead in that manner, because his Company was quartered at Cesena.

Remembering his reluctance to execute the Cardinal's orders, it may not be out of place to suppose that disgust at these doings contributed to his resolution to leave the service of such rulers.

It is certain that very soon after this, the negotiations which were already begun, to employ him on the part of the League, were brought to a conclusion. This news April 10. seemed to the Florentines " good news, for you have disarmed the power of the Pope and strengthened yourselves."

The Pope was so bitter, that he revenged himself by excommunicating and interdicting Florence, and the Florentines replied by obliging their priests to officiate notwithstanding.

We have a rhyming echo of the Florentine joy on the *conversione* of Hawkwood, in a verse of a song composed after the war, by Franco Sacchetti, in which he magnifies twelve great enterprises, achieved by Florence in his days, by comparing them to the labours of the mythic hero, Hercules: *

> Hercole arse il feroce serpente
> Che, per natura avendo teste molte,
> Ne rimettea tre, tagliandon' una :
> Chi combattea con esso era perdente,
> Ma con fuoco e con stipe assai ricolte
> Fu morto senza aver potenza alcuna.
> Fiorenza vaga, quante volte ad una
> *L'anglico serpentel* s'è mosso ad arme
> Con molte teste, radoppiando sempre :
> E tu, con dolci tempre,
> Sanza alcun fuoco, a te l'ài sì rivolto
> Che sotto il tuo vexillo s'è raccolto.

---

* Communicated by Sig. Salomone Morpurgo from his monograph on the poet story-teller.— (Hercules was the patron of the Florentine Republic, whose seal bears his figure. — *Translator*.)

(Brave Hercules doth burn the fearful snake
Which nature has endowed with num'rous heads,
So that for one cut off, three more awake
And he who dares to combat it is dead.
But on a fire of gathered sticks he flings
That Hydra dread, which dies and no more stings.
Fair Florence, ah! how oft thou hast to one —
The English serpent — turned thine arms to fight
Whose heads increase the oftener they're cut down:
But ah! in warm sweet words, how great thy might!
Altough no fatal fire for him doth burn
Beneath thy standard doth the dread one turn.)

Bernabò Visconti, whose influence had been the principal means of gaining Hawkwood, so disposed, that his brigade should be placed at the service of the League between
Cesena and Forlì; its stipend was fixed for a year beginning on the 1ˢᵗ of May, and it was to be composed of eight
hundred lances and five hundred archers (of these two hundred with two horses each, and three hundred with one),
at the monthly rate of 21 florins each lance, 14 florins for
the archers with two horses, and 8 florins for the others,
which with 3200 florins for the *provvisioni* and *premi-
nenze* of Hawkwood, of the leaders etc. etc. made a sum of
25,200 florins a month. Of this sum a third was at the
cost of Bernabò Visconti, the other two thirds were divided
between the Florentines and the other allies; and these
were apportioned in the following manner by Florence, who
kept the accounts for all, advanced the money, and had, it is
said, some trouble in getting it reimbursed: Bologna had to
pay 9000 florins, Perugia 4000, Siena 3000, Arezzo 2250, the
Prefect of Viterbo 2250, Ascoli 600, Forlì 1500, Urbino 1340,
Fermo 1800, Città di Castello 600, Guido da Polenta lord
of Ravenna 1200, Bartolomeo di Sanseverino 300, Bertrando
Alidosi lord of Imola 450, Rodolfo Varano lord of Camerino 600 florins.

This last, who had been until now captain of the
League, took offence at being required to cede the supreme

command to Hawkwood, and went over to the Church * not returning to his alliance with Florence till after the death of his rival. In any case half Italy was tributary to Hawkwood, and it being an affair of gold, Florence paid for everybody; it was a lucky day for him when he arrived at Bologna to assume the baton of command.

Together with his magnificent pay Bernabò Visconti had adopted another means of seduction; and to make sure of his brave captain, he gave him one of his daughters in marriage — it is true she was illegitimate, but in those times, even the bastard child of the lord of Milan was considered an honorable match for the son of the modest landowner and tanner of Sible Hedingham.

A famous Condottiere, rich in pay, lord of feudal estates, and now become also the son-in-law of the most potent of Italian princes, Sir John Hawkwood here reached the climax of his fortunate career.

XVIII.

MARRIAGE TO DONNINA VISCONTI.
IN THE ROMAGNA AGAINST THE BRETONS.

[Suit entered by GALEAZZO Conte di Virtù to the memory of Bernabò Visconti in the *Annales mediolanenses* — LITTA, *Famiglie celebri*. Visconti — BALDUZZI, *Bagnacavallo e Giovanni Hawkwood* in the *Documents and Memorials for the state history of the provinces of the Romagna*, 3rd series, v. II, p. I — MORANT's *History of Essex* — BRAYLEY and BRITTON's *Beauties of England and Wales* — WRIGHT's *History of Essex* — OSIO, *Diplomatic documents of the Milanese Archives* — RAWDON BROWN, *Venetian Calendar*, etc., *Letters of Hawkwood to Gonzaga* lord of Mantua — SALUTATI *Epistolæ* — Carteggio of the Florentine Signory, *Missive*.]

Bernabò Visconti's prolificacy was proportionate to his extremely energetic temperament. His wife Beatrice Scali-

---

* On account of the defection of Rodolfo, the Florentines deprived him of the citizenship, and in several places painted infamous effigies of him with a mitre of devils and with figures of the vices on his face. They sent Count Landau to fight him, but Hawkwood did not go with him, as Litta asserts in his *Famiglie celebri*.

1377. ger, called Regina, bore him fourteen sons, and he had many
others by less legitimate mothers, amongst which his favorite was "Donnina," daughter of Leone Porro, a lawyer
and Milanese noble.

*Quadam vice numerati fuerunt Bernabovi quod habebat
36 filios vivos et 18 mulieres pregnantes. — Quum esset in
senili etate constitutus, ut notorium est, tenebat duodenarium
vel vicenarium numerum meretricum, inter quas erat una* DEA
AMORIS, *videlicet Donnina, quam una cum sorore sua et ambas sorores in concubinas publice et notorie detinebat.*

This favorite "Donnina" had by him two sons, Lancellotto and Palamede (who is indicated as a counsellor);
her daughters were Ginevra and Soprana, who were unmarried at their father's death, and Donnina who espoused
Hawkwood, and who by the error of some genealogist has
been named as daughter of Montanaria Lazzari, another
of Bernabo's "favorites."

That Hawkwood's mother-in-law was the favorite of Bernabò, is proved by his donation of towns and castles to her,
and we shall find other proofs to follow; but, however this
be, the wife of the Condottiere was only a natural child. It
would appear that Hawkwood was at the time a widower;
as from the manner in which the chroniclers speak of his
1376. two sons at Bologna, it would seem they were legitimate; —
1379. there is besides a document in which he himself speaks
of a "son-in-law"* hardly two years after his marriage
with Visconti's daughter; and some memorial, relating to
his monument in England (now destroyed),** shews that he
was there represented in effigy with his two wives. Still
we cannot absolutely affirm that those sons may not have
been less lawfully born in the course of camp life, and the
more so that there is no mention of such offspring after his
marriage with the Visconti. The only mention of children

---

* See Chapter XXI.   ** See last Chapter.

is in the deeds of the Brandolini family at Bagnacavallo, where *the heirs of the late John Hawkwood* are cited: he had perhaps, on his legal marriage, made provisions for his sons whether natural, or born of more humble wedlock.

Following this wedding, we hear of several matrimonial alliances with the Visconti which served to insure to the interest of that family the most famous condottieri. Filippo Maria Visconti married Beatrice di Tenda, widow of Facino Cane, so as to get her men-at-arms under his banner, and he gave his relative Antonietta Visconti to the Conte di Carmagnola; Bianca Visconti espoused Francesco Sforza: but Bernabò, reserving his legal daughters for princes, made bargains for the others with the condottieri: thus he gave Riccarda to Bertrand de la Sale, one of the leaders of the " ferocious Bretons; " Enrica to Franchino Rusca da Como, Isotta to Carlo son of Guidosavina of Fogliano, and Elizabeth to Count Lucius Landau.

According to the *Annali Milanesi,* the last mentioned marriage was contemporaneous with that of Donnina to Hawkwood.

Bernabos comiti Lucio Lando theutonico Elisabetham et domino Johanni Aguto anglico capitaneo anglicorum aliam, ambas ejus filias naturales pulcherrimas, tradidit in uxores in civitate Mediolani. Fortunately Hawkwood obtained a most beautiful woman for his wife. Some English authors call her *Domitia,* and want to specify even her *dote,* which they give as an annual income of 10,000 florins. The extreme improbability of this cipher, enormous for those times, releases us from the necessity of seeking the origin of information so evidently unfounded. In his will, Bernabò left 6000 florins to his unmarried daughters by Beltramola de' Grassi, and 20,000 to those by Donnina Porro. To Elizabeth, who married Count Lucius Landau, he gave a *dote* of 12,000 florins and many *jocalia* (bride's dress). We may then argue that the wedd-

1377. May.

ing portion and trousseau of Donnina would have been equal, or not much superior to those of the last mentioned.

As to the marriage, the following letter from the ambassador of Lodovico Gonzaga at Milan, gives us plenty of information :

" ..... Last Sunday, Sir John Hawkwood conducted a bride with all honors to the house where he was living, that is to say to the house once belonging to Gasparo del Conte, in which the late bishop of Parma lived, and the wedding was honored by the presence of the lady Duchess, and all the daughters of Signor Bernabò. After the dinner the said lord Signor Bernabò with his Porina* went to the house of Sir John, where there was jousting going on all day. They tell me that after dinner the lady Regina** made a present to the bride of a thousand gold ducats in a vase. The Signor Marco gave her a *zardino* of pearls, worth three hundred ducats, and the Signor Luigi,*** a gift of pearls of the same value, and in like manner did many of the nobles. So much silver was offered in *largesse* to the Englishmen, that it is estimated at the value of a thousand ducats. They had no dancing, in respect for the late lady Taddea.**** I have heard that Sir John was near Parma on Thursday, and according to what Signor Bernabò told me amongst other things, he will soon be starting towards Modena with his English soldiers; and when I was in Cremona, there came some *provvisionati* (country militia) from Signor Bernabò's towns, who they say are

---

* Donnina Porro, the mother of the bride.

** The legitimate wife of Bernabò had enough superiority of mind to treat the children of her rivals well; this might contribute to explain the great ascendancy she always maintained over that terrible man.

*** Marco and Luigi (or Lodovico) were two of the legitimate sons of Bernabò: at that epoch they held Parma as an appanage, in common with their brothers, Rodolfo and Carlo.

**** We do not know what Taddea this can refer to, unless it be that daughter of Bernabò's who married Stephen duke of Bavaria: if this is the case, Litta erroneously assigns her death to the year 1381.

to be quartered there in place of those who were ordered
off. I also understood that they were preparing a great
many projectiles and gunpowder (*pulvis a sclopis*)."

Other sources also confirm the fact that Hawkwood
passed his honeymoon at Cremona, where, besides being occupied by his bride, he was making preparations for war.

He had for instance to provide for the defence of his
possessions, in Romagna, now that he had broken with the
Church. For this purpose he asked Lodovico Gonzaga to
grant a pass free of tolls through the Mantuan territory,
as he had to send by way of the Po a quantity of battle
axes, crossbows, and many other things necessary to garrison
his castle at Bagnacavallo.

He also prepared to resume his place at the head of
the troops, and therefore requested the same privilege of
a free pass for his secretary of war, Giovanni da Cingoli,
who brought his servant Giovanni da Napoli, with his at-
tendants and furniture from Ferrara.

Everything spoke of an imminent renewal of hostilities.
The Florentines reinforced themselves by hiring the English
constable Philip *Puer* (Power) with a hundred and two
lances and thirty nine archers, the German Heinrich Paer
with seventy five lances, and several other German and
English captains of ten and thirty lances, and some
Italian *caporali* with two or four lances; in fact they took
anybody, in spite of the trouble they had in getting their
allies to refund the part which they had advanced * towards
the Englishmen's stipends.

Although the Bolognese had profited the most by the
agreement with Hawkwood — seeing that after the slaugh-
ters of Faenza and Cesena, both the English and Bretons
were menacing them more than Tuscany — they yet re-

---

* Amongst the others, the Sienese and the Perugians were in arrears.
SALUTATI *Epistles,* July 81 and August 6 1377 and June 2 1378.

1377.

fused assistance on the ground that Hawkwood had only been engaged in the name of Bernabò Visconti. At this " the Florentines * marvelled and Visconti was indignant."

June 19.

But he soon found a remedy for it by signifying to the Bolognese that they must contribute 30,000 florins or give Hawkwood's Company passage and provisions. In fact the English did pass through that friendly country, committing serious injuries which the two Florentine ambassadors at the English camp were quite unable to prevent. Such was the oppression of the country that the

July 12.

Signoria of Florence wrote to Hawkwood, begging him " for pity's sake to have some compassion on the poor Bolognese, who had been so illtreated the previous year, and that he would at least leave the Bolognese territory as soon as possible, and pass into the Romagna against the enemy."

The letter arrived too late; on that very day Hawkwood left the neighborhood of Bologna, and encamped that night at Faenza. Here he helped Astorre Manfredi to recover the dominion of his hereditary city (the English thus wresting from the Marquis of Este the pledge consigned to him). The following day he constrained the Bretons, who wanted to enter Faenza, to retire towards Cesena; he was then reinforced by the Company of Astorre Manfredi, and by some infantry from Forlì, and finally to

August 25.

deprive the Bretons of their provisions, he rode towards the rich salt-springs of Cervia.

There the territory of Ravenna had to suffer. Guido da Polenta complained to Florence very resentfully, and the Florentines answered him that " they had recommended all respect to his land, writing with as much earnestness as though Guido himself held the pen, and not content

Septemb. 1st.

with writing they added the authority of Bernabò, by sending his kinsman Ruggiero Cane."

---

* Letters of 2 and 4 of July 1377. *Sign. Cart. Miss.* XVII, State Archives of Florence.

Remonstrances were of little importance to Hawkwood who fulfilled his intentions in spite of them; the Bretons were compelled to evacuate the Romagna and pass into Umbria; Hawkwood surrounded them, and wrote to Florence demanding archers, because being only four miles behind the enemy he had stopped them from crossing the Tiber, and intended to fight them if they came near him: but instead of archers Florence sent advice.

It is the celebrated Coluccio Salutati, chancellor of the Commune, *cor et mens curiæ,* who in his almost Ciceronian letters shows himself the guiding genius of the war against the Church.* He, writing to Hawkwood in the name of the Signoria, prays him to avoid fighting, so as not to give the enemy a chance of victory, — " curb the generous impatience of your men, so near the discouraged enemy, who being already reduced and enraged might fight desperately, — wait till they are more demoralised, or till they rashly risk themselves in an insecure position. — For the rest we trust in your prudence and well-known capacity."

In the postscript he adds:

" If you see that the enemy turns towards our territory, then at once with all your energy take the surest and shortest paths as may seem most convenient, and make every effort to precede them."

These suggestions were reasonable enough, for Hawkwood did not disdain them as he did those of the *escrivans* of Bianca Visconti at Alexandria, nor did he reply as he once did to Andrea Vettori: " Go you and weave your cloth and leave me to guide soldiers." In fact for that time he evaded a battle.

---

* The Italian Historical Institute promises at length a complete edition of Salutati's ' Epistolary,' and the programme which Signor Novati has announced in the ' Bulletin ' of the Institute (n° 6) assures us that the undertaking will prove worthy of that learned man, and confer great benefit on literature and history.

XIX.

HAWKWOOD AS A MEDIATOR FOR PEACE.
GROSSETO LIBERATED. — WINTER QUARTERS.

[SALUTATI's *Epistles* — *Sienese chronicle* — *Consulte e pratiche* of the Commune of Florence — *Diary* of the ANONYMOUS FLORENTINE published by GHERARDI in the *Documents for Italian History*, v. VI.]

1377.

Still following up the Bretons in the valley of the Tiber, the English Condottiere descended into the Perugian territory, where he spoiled the towns which sided with the Church. As to Perugia, although one of the League, it did not lend itself to the requirements of the captain with the expected zeal. This he complained of, writing to Florence that the Perugians "would not furnish him with mounted guides who knew the country, as it was necessary to take fresh ones from one place to another, because they are thus familiar with the district, and are able to spy out the intentions and movements of the enemy," * and he said that the Perugians had also refused to proclaim a recruitment of archers, and that they would not even send some musicians to the camp for a few days *cum*

Septemb. 13. *timpanorum et classicorum fremitu in ostentationem solam.*"

And therefore the Florentine chancellor besought the Perugians to reinforce Hawkwood with foot soldiers, horses, and archers: or at least, as it would cost them nothing, that they would oblige him *de ostentationis pompa,* to terrify their enemies withal.

End of September.

These enemies took the road through the Sienese Maremma, and with a thousand eight hundred lances blockaded Grosseto. Hawkwood, who had but few forces to dispose of, was encamped in observation, on the narrow table-land

---

* *Chi è povero di spie, è ricco di vituperio;* ' Those who are poor in spies are rich in shame,' an old proverb praised by Matteo Villani.

which forms almost a bastion from Montepulciano to 1877.
San Quirico.

Here he remained almost two months " as a friend, and
the Sienese ambassadors with many of the citizens were
constantly in his camp. The Sienese sent him a horse with
caparisons worth a hundred and fifty florins, much confectionery and corn, amounting in all to the value of three
hundred florins." Whilst here the Florentines sent him Septemb. 25
and 26.
commissions to reassure Siena — which he did — and to
assist Grosseto, which was not at that moment convenient
to him ; for one reason he did not feel strong enough to
attack the Bretons, and for another, because by his means
the Church was attempting to commence negotiations with
the League.

This is the only occasion in the career of Hawkwood
in which we see him as a mediator for peace — but even
this mediation was unheeded. The Signoria answered with
badly concealed ill humour, recalling him to his duty of
vigorously conducting the war:

" We have understood the request made by you on behalf of the High Pontiff, about a contract of peace and
concord with our ' magnificent' brother Signor Bernabò, or
with him and ourselves on one part, and the Roman Church
on the other.... We recognise that you have undertaken
to establish peace on worthy conditions and that you are
moved by sincere and pure intentions ; we thank you for
your counsels, but we pray you to pursue the war in the
manly way you have commenced it, because this is, — or
at least we believe it to be, — the only path which will
lead us with honor to the wished for peace." Septemb. 27.

The same kind of " bitter-sweet" was repeated more con- Septemb. 30.
cisely three days later, with the addition that they had
written to Bernabò for advice.

They informed him besides that his brother-in-law October 1st.

Count Lucius Landau, who was also in the pay of the League, had returned from the March of Ancona and was at Perugia; and that he should hold a conference with him, and arrange to give a decisive blow to the enemy, who infested all the Sienese Maremma, and was threatening Florence.

In spite of this it appears that Hawkwood still pursued his negotiations. He went to San Quirico to meet as a friend " certain commissaries of the Church, who were coming to make peace, " but who at the moment had a good reason for not coming. Anyhow the negotiations were broken off, the Bretons besieging Grosseto were obliged to retreat ; indeed in the following year a certain number of them passed into the service of the League.

On this account the campaign closed in a manner favorable enough, and Florence could joyfully send the treasurer Spinello to the English camp with the usual pay; but he returned bringing very unwelcome news, which was that Hawkwood's brigade intended to winter on Florentine territory under certain given conditions, and that they were making their preparations. In plain terms this was equivalent to having the enemy at their gates.

Without even waiting for Spinello to explain the propositions, the Signoria sent a dispatch to Hawkwood, regretting he had such intentions, as " a thing very displeasing to Bernabò as it would be a cause of exultation to the enemy, and dishonorable to him. What would he say to the invincible English flying the foe, and seeking repose afar from the war? And what will happen when the enemy occupy the confines of the League, as they will lose no time in doing? And would not the Bretons boast of having forced him to retreat? — Dispose then your Company to honorable deeds with your usual prudence, either return to the Papal States to help the allies, or go to the Marches where you could stay very comfortably in the territory of Camerino or other places. Whenever you make your decision, the Florentines will immediately remove from thence the Germans (of Count Landau) and other troops, so that in those opulent and rich places the English Company may fight alone with great slaughtering of enemies, to their glory and advantage."

The following day Spinello had the opportunity of explaining himself better to the Signoria, and he made it clear that Hawkwood had done all he could to persuade his troops to remain where they were, but that the Englishmen would not listen to reason, and had obliged him to seek winter quarters where they were sure of finding every convenience, — that is, on Florentine ground: — that the captain had still tried to move them, and in any case he gave the best advice to the Signoria how to manage things with the least possible injury to themselves.

A general counsel was held on this elucidation. The Signoria sustained that the coming of the English would be perilous to the towns, on account of strife and depredations, *and for words which are often spoken, and many others which might be said, against Bernabò* (it would appear that the alliance with the Visconti was not very popular) it would be even profitable to spend something to send them elsewhere.

The Gonfalonieri resigned themselves with heavy hearts to the wish of the English, trusting in the opportune precautions of the *Otto di balia* (Eight of war) recommending them to keep their eye on San Miniato and other towns in the Val d'Arno, besides placing soldiers in towns of proved fidelity and, *if possible, to arrange that Sir John and others should stay in Florence,* almost like hostages.

On this last point the twelve *Buonomini* also insisted, saying: *make sure that Hawkwood remains in the city with as many of his Company as possible;* they also advised that the fortresses should be well garrisoned.

1377.   It was deliberated to write again to Hawkwood immediately, reiterating the desire that he should march into the Papal States or the March of Ancona; if that were not possible, they would be content to follow out his counsels and the plan he had made : they advised however " that he should arrange to preserve from injury the territories of Florence and her allies, providing that each brigade should quarter in the place destined to receive it, and where such order was established that all should be content." He was also recommended to provide against any scandals, either on the entry of the English, or after it, and to place the smallest possible number in each town, and that one of the *Otto* should go to Hawkwood in person

Novemb. 24. to make the required arrangements.

The fact was, the Florentines were in great distress at the near vicinity of those dangerous mercenaries, and they made a last attempt to pass them on to Siena.

Novemb. 26.   They wrote to Siena that they had heard from Filippo Bastari, envoy at the camp, that Hawkwood would willingly quarter his troops in the territory of Montepulciano, observing that during the winter, the country could not be injured by this, and it would be a very useful position enabling him to oppose the enemy, and to protect the Sienese and Perugian territories.

For the rest Hawkwood himself must have conferred with the Sienese ambassadors: they ought therefore to take immediate steps, and if need be, Florence would decide the campaign according to " that wise counsel " (*a tal salutare consiglio*).

However they hoped so little from this, that the same day they discussed the benefit of making the English return towards the enemy, even if it entailed expense (*magari spendendo*), and whether they should not send one or two of the *Otto* to Val d'Arno to collocate the English there, and arrange for the fortifications and garrisoning of the strongholds, placing the fewest number possible in fortified places, and in any case to keep about three hundred lances *of our troops* in the city.

The next day brought the definite resolutions of the Condottiere. Wherefore it was written to Gioannello di Vico Mercato, commissary at the quarters:

" Bastari on his exit from the interwiew with Hawkwood informs us that the captain is content that the English shall be stationed in our territories of Val di Nievole, Val d'Arno, Pistoia and Prato, and that they will personally swear to the preservation of the towns which are in the hands of our officials. Over and above which Hawkwood himself would write to him and the other officials placing every thing in his and their hands." The Florentines were now obliged to take ill luck with a good grace. Some still wanted to try and get the English away as soon as possible, giving Hawkwood every satisfaction, for he did not seem quite content with the Commune, but Giovanni Dini, one of the *Otto,* was of the opinion that " with the English it is needful to proceed prudently so that no scandal shall ensue. And as they must remain a long time in our service, we must treat them, and act with them in such a way as not to enrage them, because if they are made to march against their will, they will do things to the Commune which we shall not like — indeed quite the contrary. Here they have to be stationed for the present; and we must try and manage that they shall leave spontaneously."

Decemb. 1ˢᵗ.

His troops being thus on their way to winter quarters, regaled by the Pisans with barrels of white wine, confectionery and other gifts, Hawkwood celebrated his triumph.

" To-day Sir John Hawkwood entered Florence with his Company at the twenty third hour (hour before sunset) and dismounted at the Palace of the Archbishop of Flo-

December 7.
.

ged him also to confirm, even on his own responsibility, the 1378. January 5. explanations which were given to Bernabò, *circa factum Rogyeri et sociorum.* Perhaps this referred to Ruggiero Cane and to some suspected relations with the enemy. Lastly they entreated him to return quickly to Tuscany, " otherwise the management of the English will be rendered very difficult, and without a leader many things are in disorder." As he delayed, they thus insisted :

" Come and command your troops as soon as you can, January 21. especially as the Ecclesiastics have become very strong in the Sienese district, and are doing some injury every day. And as to the English, they were, as you are aware, placed in such narrow quarters that it is now necessary to change them on account of scarcity of fodder and other things ; without you we can neither control them, nor send them to the help of the allies, which may be the cause of consequences displeasing both to you and to us."

He was to come then, to arrange, consult, and effect all that was necessary to the honor of Florence and all the League.

This letter crossed Hawkwood on the way, and as soon as he returned to Florence he again started to his sol- January 25 and 27. diers' quarters. The soldiers were behaving very badly : fifty plunderers of the brigade commanded by that Cook who had won his spurs under the walls of Florence, rode February 7. to Corliano, insulting and even wounding the peasants ; sacking all the houses, carrying away the cattle large and small, clothes, and everything, just as though they were the enemies' belongings. The Signoria claimed compensation from Cook for damages, and warned him that such an occurrence must not be repeated : they also wrote to Hawkwood adding, " that similar things were happening every day, which they were sure would displease him, and Bernabò would be more sorry than if the men were his own subjects. It was the captain's office to imme-

1378.   diately repress this scandal, going at once to the place
where his presence and prudence would be sufficient to
re-establish order."

Hawkwood had other affairs to see to; he was at San
Quirico in close contact with the ecclesiastical camp, and
requested of the Florentines a pass for himself, and of the
Sienese a safe conduct for two months, for the Papal am-
February 3. bassadors and for their escort of two hundred horse.* The
Florentines delaying to send the required permission, he
February 8. insisted and obtained it.

Then the schemes for which he had journeyed between
Milan and Florence became clear; Bernabò having other
projects of war in view wanted to propose negotiations
with the Church by means of Hawkwood, and demanded
that the League should give leave to all, or to part of
the English to serve him. As to the safe conduct, the
Florentines dared not refuse it, indeed they consented that
Hawkwood " should go with other commissaries of Bernabò
February 12. to the camp of the Church party."

There were serious apprehensions about dismissing the
English; according to what Piero Canigiani, one of the
Buonomini, explained, " this dismissal is very perilous;
firstly, because if Bernabò wishes to invade the Genoese
territory with the English troops, that would set the
Genoese at enmity with us, and in the same way if he
wants to invade the Marquis of Mantua or act against the
Veronese, — his aggrandizement is perilous to us. Besides
it might be that he has a secret understanding with the
Pope and may set the army of the Church on us, or the
Sienese. If we really are forced to dismiss the English,
February 15. we must recall our own troops from all parts."

It was besides considered that the Ecclesiastics menaced

---

* See Document XXIX.

the territories of Perugia and Siena, the latter of which *1378.* was ill adapted for defence. To ensure himself on that side, Hawkwood proposed to take up his position at San Quirico with a hundred lances (the position was in fact very well chosen, and he thought he could thus leave the rest of the Company at Bernabò's disposal). But the English refused to move till they had received their pay for February; and yet by reason of their continual depredations, their presence on Florentine ground was very annoying.

To resolve all these difficulties, the *Otto,* the *Buonomini,* and the *Gonfalonieri* were unanimous in deciding that the English must be paid without ado, anticipating also Bernabò's share, and thus making sure of their marching against the enemy without delay.

Hawkwood having returned to Florence was given to *February 24.* understand this decision, and about the 18th hour (which, *February 26.* according to Florentine astrology, was the propitious hour to begin a military enterprise) he rode off without delay to take command of his troops.

According to the plan adopted by the Florentines, Hawkwood was to go to the defence of Perugia, with all, or at least the greater part of the English. The Perugians were therefore written to, that they should prepare quarters and provisions, and send a commissary to conduct the English as soon as possible to the quarters designed for them.

But to go to Perugia it was necessary to cross the Sienese territory, and the people of Siena, although allies, would not hear of giving them a pass. On this the Florentines wrote to Siena, greatly marvelling, and reminding them how they had, *even with importunity,* entreated for the *invincible hand* of the English, and exhorting them, shewing them the need they had of it; this dispatch was communicated to Hawkwood, who, if he made difficulties in *February 25.* starting, was perfectly justified. In any case he would not

1376.   have moved. and had in fact scarcely reached the quarters
of his troops. when he began to open treaties for a truce
with the Ecclesiastics, going himself to meet the Pope's
March 2. ambassadors.* This being known at Florence, there was
a clash of opposite opinions such as frequently happens at
critical moments.

" That as soon as possible an upright and honorable
man shall undertake an embassy to Hawkwood, advising
him to leave the negotiation in the hands of Bernabò,"
was Andrea Salviati's advice.

" That we send to say that in peace or war the Commune intends to do that which pleases Bernabò, — let the
captain abstain then from concluding an armistice, but if
after all he should have orders from Bernabò, let it be
made for a month," proposed Simone Ranieri.

The Gonfalonieri wanted to " boldly continue the war "
allowing no truce, which is dangerous, because capable of
being prorogued. Let a bold envoy be sent to Hawkwood
and to the other commissaries of Bernabò, who would
explain the great astonishment of the Signoria ; and at
the same time dispatch an embassy to Parma (where Bernabò was) so that the intentions of the Commune should not
be thwarted.

The *Dodici* and the *Otto* put forth a more complex
counsel: " Let us signify to the commissaries of Bernabò by means of an envoy, that we do not consent to a
truce, or at least that the negotiations for it must rest
entirely with Bernabò. If they already have his command
for it, the truce should be for fifteen days rather than a
month. At the same time let Hawwood have orders to go
to the frontier on the Perugian side with his men, which
will prove whether or not he is free to act," — this was
to measure better the projects of Bernabò.

---

* See Document XXX.

Almost as if foreseeing this request, there arrived a letter in which Hawkwood explained his inaction; he wrote that the Perugians had no need of troops, because they had received security from the Pope's ambassadors and that his Englishmen would not mount till they had received their pay.

To which the Signoria replied with resentful wonderment :

" How can you possibly make treaties without our knowledge or that of Bernabò ? We admit that you have acted with a good object ; but we warn you it was never our intention to suspend hostilities till peace was concluded, nor to lose time which we can never regain. Let us have no truce ; now that the Pope is unfurnished with means, on account of his discords with the Romans, is just the time to leave the confines of the League and carry the war into the enemy's country, if your men will only mount according to the orders given. Go then at once with your men to Perugia, where all is ready to receive them. Spinello is in Val d' Arno ready to pay the troops as soon as they are in marching order. Every day we are having complaints of homicide, violence, and rapine, at which the people already begin to murmur. This is another reason for hastening your departure."

In confirmation of this letter Filippo Alamanni, a keen man, was sent as envoy ; but Hawkwood had already gone to meet the Pontifical ambassadors (the cardinal of Amiens, the archbishop of Pampeluna, and the archbishop of Narbonne), who were on their way to Pisa. He es- corted them with Ruggiero Cane and some other cavalry soldiers, dismounting at the house of Ser Jacopo d' Appiano, the next morning he continued his journey with Cane to Lucca, thence to Sarzana where the ambassadors found Bernabò and began the negotiations.

1378.   " The English had promised the treasurer Spinello to commence action as soon as the stipends for February were paid; but when they had received the money, they again refused; meanwhile the towns they occupy, are entirely destitute of forage, and the enemy is still domi-

March 16. neering in the Perugian territory greatly to its injury." These were the Florentine last and still ineffectual remonstrances to Hawkwood, who certainly would make no move now that Bernabò in person was negotiating a peace with the Church, and to render it more easy the death of the Pope took place just at that time.

Nothing was now left to Florence but to liberate herself from the disobedient Englishmen: the peril of keeping them in San Miniato and other towns in the lower Val d' Arno had increased, because it was necessary to quarter there some other stipendiaries of Florence, — the German Company of the " Stella " commanded by Count Lucius Landau. If they united, they might put the state in danger, therefore it would be worth while even to give the English their pay for March, on condition that they would go elsewhere, and immediately arrange to remove them from the towns on which they were quartered.

In one of these towns the English captain Tomellino was dying, and without doubt all the cavaliers would come to his funeral; this seemed a very good opportunity, so it was proposed to commission Sig. Lotterio to shut the gates upon them everywhere when they had gone away, and to advise the country people not to let themselves be caught in the open country, where the Englishmen might take revenge on them, for the trick.

But it does not appear that this practical joke, which was suggested by Ghino Bernardi, was put into practice. A better idea was to keep Count Landau's Germans in the service as a guard against the English, but first to endeavour, by peaceable means, to send them to serve Bernabò, in which case they would be contented with an assurance from them, " not to oppose the Commune in the form of a Company, and for this the proper price would be paid." This was done; Hawkwood came to Florence for the necessary understanding, and then returned to Lombardy where he was preceded, or soon followed by his troops.

XXI.

A FATHER-IN-LAW BADLY TREATED BY HIS SONS-IN-LAW.

[*Consulte e pratiche* of the Commune, in the Stato Archives of Florence — *Venetian Calendars of State papers*, edited by RAWDON BROWN, taken from the State Archives of Mantua — SALUTATI'S *Epistles* — GATARO (father and son), *Paduan chronicles* in MURATORI [*R. I. S.*] — VERCI, *Storia della Marca Trevigiana* — GHIRARDACCI, *Storie bolognesi* in MURATORI [*R. I. S.*] — *Annales mediolanenses*, ibid — RICOTTI, *Storia delle compagnie di ventura* — CANESTRINI, *Documents* etc. in the *Archivio storico italiano*.]

Florence could congratulate herself but little on Hawkwood and his services. But this frequently occurs when one is the servant of two masters. In comparison with any other condottiere he might yet pass as a pearl of fidelity, and if there were still much to fear from him, something could also be hoped; hence we do not wonder that the Florentines deliberated to " keep the promises made to Hawkwood, " that is to continue his life-annuity.

Besides, while campaigning in Lombardy he might favor Florentine interests with Bernabò: in fact they wrote to remind him that the latter with Ruggiero Cane had made an agreement with Florence, about the payment of the Germans, of Hawkwood's own brigade, and of the Bretons, that is, of all the mercenaries who fought for the League during the preceding campaign. Now Bernabò, — the truce being concluded, and he treating for peace with the Church, — made a show of knowing nothing about it, and therefore Florence applied to Hawkwood " that he should, as it were, cultivate the alliance between Florence and Bernabò, availing himself of the influence of the illustrious lady Regina or any other personage."

Bernabò was at that very moment making war, with Hawkwood's help, against the Scaligers of Verona, his wife's family; and his consort the *illustre Signora Regina* herself was, in fact, the one who most violently urged her husband against them; but although the Visconti had hired the new and exclusively Italian Company of *San Giorgio,* formed by Alberico da Barbiano, it was a long drawn war.

In the archives of Mantua there exist several letters from Hawkwood, written to the Marquis Lodovico Gonzaga during this campaign: they are severally dated from the " *Entrenchments of the camp under Verona,*" from " Piadena," from the " *camp of Villafranca,*" from the " *camp of Monzambano* " and other places between the Mincio, the Adige, and the Po, but none of them refer to military events of any importance.

We find that Hawkwood had orders from Bernabò to respect the Mantuan territory, but notwithstanding this, frequent violations occurred, which were inevitable, as the Mantuan land lay between that of Milan and Verona. We learn that the Mantuan soldiers sometimes ventured to steal some horses or baggage belonging to the English, or to intercept letters and dispatches, that every now and then skirmishes took place with Veronese freebooters, — the letters therefore treat of excuses, protests, restitutions, indemnifications, and punishments.

Generally it is Hawkwood himself who writes to explain these " little incidents ; " sometimes it is William Gold, constable-general of the Company.

There being very good-will on both sides, the relations between Visconti's army and the Lord of Mantua continued to be amicable in spite of the " little incidents," so much so that Gold did not hesitate to ask for special favors. For instance, he requested that the custom-house officials at Mantua would arrest three servants, who had fled from the camp after stealing two horses, with their respective breastplates, and a silver flagon; and also a certain Janet his domestic, who had taken the road to Venice with 500 of his master's florins. Then finding himself ill provided with forage, he also begged that some might be provided by the captains of the Marquis.

Amidst his numerous occupations as captain, Sir John Hawkwood did not lose sight either of his possessions in Romagna, or of interesting events in general politics.

One of his letters demands a free pass on the Po for six boats going to Ferrara laden with arms, woodwork, tools, corn, and other supplies, all destined for Bagnacavallo; and in the postscript he informs the Marquis of Mantua that he had received notice of the election of the Cardinal di San Pietro (*in Vinculis*) as Pope (Urban VI).

At Bagnacavallo some English brigades doubtless held the garrison. In fact Nicholas Clifton, Englishman from Bagnacavallo, treated of entering with his brigade into the service of the Signoria of Florence, which promised him the same terms as those made with another of his compatriots named Berwick.

And thus it is confirmed that many of the English fought on their own account in Italy, after having formed part of Hawkwood's Company, and even when secure of returning to it.

Each leader, even of two or four lances, constituted a small independent atom, which disintegrated itself from, or united with the brigade under a *conestabile;* and each brigade either separated from, or joined with the permanent nucleus, according to reciprocal convenience, or to the course of events.

For example, that John Thornbury who had often acted

as lieutenant to Hawkwood, had passed into the service of
the Scaligers; was taken prisoner by his old comrades and
fellow-country-men, and obliged to pay a ransom: this we
find from a letter in which he begs Gonzaga to allow him
to live quietly in Mantua, and pay expenses at the inn.

Such extreme mobility in the elements constituting the
companies explains how little dependence could be placed
on their discipline, and might excuse the frequent breaches
of trust, for which history usually holds the captains responsible. And this renders the habitual fidelity of Hawkwood yet more meritorious.

It is said that he gave a brilliant proof of rectitude
during this very campaign. The " Ten " of Venice, offered him a large sum if he would devastate the Paduan
territory, and he refused because he was a friend of Carrara,
Lord of Padua. Such delicate regard for friendship seems
doubtful, because it is not known that before this there
were any relations between the Carraras and Hawkwood.

The Paduan chroniclers substantially confirm the fact
which they also attribute to 1378, but they recount it thus:

Lucius Landau and Hawkwood being dismissed by Bernabò Visconti, the Signoria of Venice wrote officially to
them proposing to give them 30,000 ducats to harry the
Paduan territory for fifteen days, and 1000 ducats, for
every day over that time. They communicated this to the
Carrarese, who with " good means " (which is to say money) so arranged that Hawkwood should go across the Po
without touching the Paduan soil. Now since Landau and
Hawkwood did not leave Bernabò's service till 1379, the
date would contradict this; in any way the two condottieri, honestly and without risk, gained as much, as it had
been offered them to gain dishonestly and sword in hand.

Without doubt the Florentines were in great distress,
fearing a new visit from the English Company, and the
Signoria wrote in confidence to its annuitant, the captain:

" We understand that Bernabò wishes speedily to send
the English brigade to another destination, asking for
transit either by our territory or wherever it is most convenient to him. We earnestly pray that you will take
the road through Romagna, where there are frequent cities
and towns, and where abundant provisions and forage will
not be wanting ; while on our lands it would cause great
injury to the country and also serious scandals."

1378.

August 7.

The Florentines were not ill-informed : Hawkwood himself writing to Gonzaga from the camp of Monzambano,
on account of the usual damages, confirms the fact of his
having to march elsewhere " for certain services required
by his masters."

August 8.

It seems he replied to Florence with a variation of the
usual song, alleging that the English were their creditors
to the sum of 10,000 florins. And whether this credit
existed or not, the motion was carried in the Florentine
councils, to " take this measure to content them : " while the
proposal to hire them for the city was negatived.

August 15.
September 4
and 16.

The usual contract for six months between Bernabò
and the Company having run out, it was renewed, and the
forces increased by the German Company of Count Lucius
Landau who also passed into Lombardy, uniting with his
brother-in-law Hawkwood in the service of their father-
in-law Bernabò.

End of
September.

A considerable force was indeed necessary, for the King
of Hungary had sent, first against the Venetians, and then
in aid of the Scaligers, five thousand Hungarians conducted
by the " Vaivode " of Transylvania and the " Ban " of Bo-
snia, and these had already entered Verona.

August 15.

Neither Hawkwood nor Landau prevented the Hungarians from domineering as they chose in the Brescian territory, whence they pushed their way on to Cremona, they
were even defeated and put to flight under Brescia, so

Septemb. 1st.

1378.

that Bartolommeo Scaliger was able to attack Brescia and take several outworks.

Middle
of October.

Bernabò immediately agreed to a truce for forty-five days, and Hawkwood tranquilly placed himself in his autumn quarters at Cremona. From thence he sent his domestic *Pierino della Latta,* to provide ten cart-loads of Gazzoldo wine for his own use and that of his household.

Middle
of Novemb.

The truce expired, the lady Regina in person left Milan with her eldest son Marco, to take part in the war, with a thousand four hundred lances, and numerous infantry. She took with her the companies of both Hawkwood and Landau, then rode on to Brescia and urged all the troops to devastate the Veronese country between the lake of Garda and the river Adige.

The Hungarians disputed the passage of the river with Hawkwood and Landau ; — there were some killed and drowned on both sides, but the two brothers-in-law crossed safely, and giving themselves to plunder, penetrated as far as Valdagno.

Meanwhile the Hungarians and the Scaligers in revenge, pushed on across the river Oglio, returning with six hundred prisoners, and twenty thousand head of large cattle.

1379.
January 29.

Hawkwood and Landau were at Caldiero when the news of the enemy's return with such immense spoil reached them. The temptation was too great, they crossed the Adige by night, lay in wait for the enemy near the river, fell upon them while they in their turn attempted to pass over, and, cutting up their forces greatly, they recovered a good many prisoners.

In spite of this, rumours were circulated that they allowed themselves to be corrupted by the Scaligers; at least, it appeared to Bernabò that they did not conduct the war with a zeal proportioned to their immense salaries *

---

* The two Companies cost at the rate of 250,000 florins a year.

nor yet as behoved two sons to their father-in-law, and 1879.
hence arose ill humour and discord, which the vehement
lady Regina certainly contrived to fan.

This explains why Count Landau and Hawkwood wrote February 18.
to Gonzaga, that Bernabò denied a pass through his territory
to the recently made prisoners. The time to present them
at Verona and receive their ransom thus expired; the captains however, with the agreement of their soldiers, determined to prorogue it, sending the noble and prudent Ulrich
Ofsteten, and praying that he might be received at Mantua,
and that it might be conceded to him to go and return from
Verona with the prisoners, under the necessary escort.

The next day they wrote again to Gonzaga informing
him that " a *little misunderstanding* had arisen between
themselves and Bernabò, but that, with the help of God,
they hoped to regain the favor of the Visconti, and that
whatever should be the result they would keep him informed." They sent an analagous communication to Florence on which the Florentines " deliberated " to send an
envoy to their camp with the mission of procuring concord,
for " it grieved them not to be in harmony with Bernabò: "
but also to fathom their intentions. March 2.

If free of engagements those two condottieri might take
a course of action which would be perilous to Tuscany; —
indeed the Visconti had hastened to secure the concourse of
the Florentines against his sons-in-law, but they replied by
showing him the danger that would accrue if Hawkwood and
Landau should unite themselves with the Italian Company
of *San Giorgio,* brought to the Po by Alberico da Barbiano.

Marchionne Stefani, the chronicler, was sent to them, but
he could conclude nothing, and the rupture became com- Beginning
of March.
plete; a son-in-law of Hawkwood * left Milan where he had

---

* Perhaps that Lancellotto del Maino who according to Corio had married
Fiorentina, a daughter of Hawkwood, by his first unnamed wife. See the
last Chapter.

1379.

lived a long time, and took refuge in the camp of his father-in-law, who sent him to Bagnacavallo with an escort of sixty horse, for whom he demanded a safe conduct from Gonzaga. And the Visconti's two sons-in-law, Hawkwood and Landau, considering themselves dismissed, provided for themselves by forming an Anglo-German Company of a thousand two hundred lances.

Which party was in the right? Some chroniclers say that Bernabò did not pay the two condottieri, perhaps calculating that the bond of relationship was strong enough to make them patient creditors. Others would make us believe that the whole was an understood game with Bernabò, and that he hoped by the aid of his sons-in-law to subjugate Tuscany, but successive facts do not justify the supposition: and later, Bernabò though silent about Hawkwood, who was not a subject of the Empire, made a formal accusation to the King of the Romans, that Count Lucius, his brother Eberhard Landau, and other German captains had betrayed him in the enterprise of Verona; indeed at the time of the rupture the fury of Visconti was so great that he published a reward of 30 florins for every adventurer whether taken or killed.

1380.
October 25.

XXII.

THE COMPANY OF THE TWO BROTHERS-IN-LAW. — HAWKWOOD FIGHTING FOR HIS POSSESSIONS. — A REVOLUTION PREVENTED.

[Consulte e pratiche of the Commune in the State Archives of Florence — Diary of the ANONYMOUS FLORENTINE — GRAZIANI, Perugian chronicle — Carteggio of the Signoria, Missive, XVIII, 15 e 16[bis] — Diplomatic documents, Riformagioni, Atti pubblici, treaty of Torrita, June 10 1379 and Provvigione August 4, which ratifies it — NERI DI DONATO, Sienese chronicle — Letters fom Hawkwood to Gonzaga in the Archives of Mantua, collected in the Venetian Calendars by RAWDON BROWN — Chronicle of MARCHIONNE STEFANI — GATARO, Chronicles of Padua — IACOPO ZENO, Life of Carlo Zeno.]

1379.

The brothers-in-law Hawkwood and Landau, with their respective Englishmen and Germans, only stayed a few days

to spoil the territory of their father-in-law; then having
crossed the Po they encamped in the Bolognese district
certain of finding good employment ere long. Meanwhile
Bologna, to obtain quiet, disbursed them 2500 ducats; and
Peracchino (of Padua), just then made Cardinal of Santa
Cecilia by Urban VI, proposed to the Florentines that
they should engage them.

Florence would willingly have done without this new
burden, especially as the two condottieri were bound for
two years more to respect Florentine property; however
while protesting their own loyalty to this contract, the
two captains gave them to understand that there was a
danger of Count Eberhard, brother of Count Lucius,
moving his brigade against Florence on his own account.
Wherefore the good Marchionne Stefani observes: "Thus
they broke faith with the city; which thing though not done
openly, was yet more than evident. I don't oblige you
to buy us again, but, even if you don't want us, you have
got to give us money, whether you will or not. (*Così rup-
pono fede al Comune: che non fu palese, e fu più che palese. Io non ti fo ricomprare, ma tu mi dai soldo, e non
hai bisogno, o vogli tu o non voglia.*)" At the same time
they sought a pretext for litigation, addressing veiled and
polite menaces to the Sienese, and to all the cities in
Tuscany. On account of this Florence sent a notary to
Bologna, together with the Cardinal's envoy, with the
mission of verifying the adventurers' intentions, " secretly,
and through the medium of trustworthy persons who
have access to the Company." * To the Cardinal, they
declared themselves disposed to make a treaty if the money
were not required immediately, and if he himself would
undertake the negotiations, stipulating that the Company
should not touch on the Florentine territory. At the same

1879.

March 19.

---

* See Document XXXI.

1379.
17, 18 and 20
of March.
time debates took place in the *Consulte* (Councils), how they could be hindered from passing the Apennines.

Having received the required information, the Florentines resigned themselves to sending commissioners to attempt an agreement, but as a precaution they disposed that the peasants should evacuate the open country and the district, taking refuge within the walled towns, and that the fortresses should be garrisoned and manned by archers. By this time the Tuscans were quite accustomed

March 31. to measures of this kind.

The Cardinal of Padua opened negotiations on the base of 250,000 florins a year; but one fine day he unexpectedly departed, leaving everything uncompleted, and the Signoria, who had already disbursed some money, had the trouble

April 22. of finishing the treaties. This office was given, as usual, to the treasurer Spinello Alberti, but this time he did not so easily bring affairs to a conclusion, perhaps because Landau was harder or more particular than Hawkwood.

End of May. Germans and English had passed into the Perugian territory, nominally as friends, but in reality they comported themselves more like enemies, not keeping their contracts, even after having extorted 8000 florins from Perugia, and molesting Montepulciano, and Val di Chiana. Much ill humour fermented amongst the people in Florence, which often degenerated into tumults; outside the city several companies of disbanded adventurers and rebels were raging, so it was urgent that the Signoria should make sure of the two captains.

May 22. They therefore sent couriers to Spinello Alberti, to make the contract at all cost, then they sent a man on

May 27. horseback with "full powers" (*ampia balia*) in a dispatch in cypher, and orders not to move from the camp till

May 28. the matter was concluded; together with other instructions, to the effect that after having signed the agreement with the condottieri, they should form a defensive league between the Tuscan Communes, and those of Bologna; that the companies should be hired in the name of this league, dividing the expense of the pay between the allies.

At the same time they wrote longwinded thanks to Hawkwood for all the good "which they hoped from him."

The diplomatic energy of Spinello resulted in the contract concluded at Torrita, between Hawkwood and the two brothers Landau (Lucius and Eberhard), on the one part; Florence, Perugia, Siena, Arezzo, and Città di Castello, on the other.

The agreement was to the effect that each of the cities should take a certain number of lances into their service and at an exorbitant price not including extras. Florence had 450 of them.

We are minutely informed of the sums paid by the Sienese: — to the two Landaus and to Hawkwood a royalty of 6000 florins promised by Spinello, besides a remuneration of 1600 florins; to Count Lucius 2000 florins for "damages before time *suffered* (!) by him on Sienese ground;" to Count Eberhard 100 florins for a palfrey, and 500 for his registrars and procurators; to the Sienese commissioners 200 florins; besides 32,000 florins, for the pay of 200 English and German lances which fell to the share of Siena at the rate of 20 florins a month each lance, from June 4 to February 4, that is to say 100 German lances, 77 English ones under Giovanni *Gulione* (?) and *di Monte*, and 23 of Hawkwood's. The latter as usual showed himself relatively discreet. During the hostilities preceding the agreement, a Sienese gentleman, Stefano Maconi, had been taken by Gulione and had bound himself to pay a ransom of 100 scudi in gold, but this was remitted by the solicitation of the Senate to Hawkwood.* The Com-

---

* From a letter dated November 6 1879, written by Francesco Casini of Siena, doctor to Pope Urban VI, and cited by Tommaseo in his comments

1379.
June 26.

pany dissolved at Grecciano near Montepulciano, and every one went to his destination.

Hawkwood had left (or reconducted thither) the greater part of his brigade in his possessions of Romagna, where his neighbors Manfredi Lord of Faenza, and Polenta Lord of Ravenna, were both hostile to him. He himself writing from Bagnacavallo to Gonzaga, said he had gone there to reside, and added that he had 300 lances without pay on the Faentine territory, and that Count Lucius had gone to the March of Ancona with 500 lances: the rest of his troops, that is to say 600 German lances and 500 English, were engaged at service in Tuscany.

July 3.

In the same letter Hawkwood recommended one of his men Nicholas Tanfield, who had gone to Mantua to obtain the consignment, or the ransom of a prisoner who had escaped from Astolfo, one of Hawkwood's officers, — the said prisoner had been taken in " our territory at Gazzolo" (*terra nostra Gazoli*).

We have thus an indication that, besides his possesions in Romagna, Hawkwood had land also on the Po; but we do not know at what time, or on what title he had acquired this land at Gazzolo, nor indeed how long he kept it. We cannot even decide which it was of two places, both called Gazzolo, nor can we say it may not have been that Gazzuolo which at the end of the 15th century belonged to the Gonzaghi, by whom it was adorned with a noble fortress (destroyed by the Austrians in 1772) and with beautiful porticoes which still exist.

The possession of Gazzolo explains the care with which Hawkwood cultivated friendly relations with the Marquis of Mantua, and of which we also have an interesting document in a courteous letter of thanks and compliments

on the letters of St. Catherine of Siena. He might in error have mistaken the *Britons* for Bretons.

written to Gonzaga by *Donnina Visconti of Milan, consort of Sir John Hawkwood.*

Hawkwood was in open hostility with his neighbours in Romagna, especially with Astorre Manfredi; so that Florence, who judged that this did not conduce to her interests, sent an envoy to attempt making peace between them. By this time Florence had the opinion that Hawkwood was the best, and the least false of the condottieri, and as she continued to pay his annuity she wished to have him always at her disposal; therefore the Signoria wrote also to Bernabò Visconti, to try to reconcile him to his son-in-law.

For his own safety Hawkwood took care to reinforce himself against his hostile neighbours, and to excite other enemies against them. He himself informed his friend Gonzaga * that he had called up a considerable force from the Marches, of which 100 lances entered the service of Bologna, and the remainder consisting of 250 or more, comprising archers, under the command of constable Gold, had gone towards Forlì " to certain barons of the Romagna ** who were waiting to make an attack on Guido di Ravenna, and Astorre Manfredi." He stayed at Bagnacavallo with about 60 lances, and there he provided himself with provisions and arms, ordering from Gazzolo 500 battle axes and 100 head of cattle, large and small.

While attending to his own business he did not lose sight of the affairs of Florence, for his bonds of interest with this city were strengthening daily. The government was at present in the hands of the conservative party, but it was menaced by the chief burghers *(popolani grassi)* and by the low populace *(ciompi)*. It chanced to

1879.
September 7.

July 2.

July 30.

July 7.

August 28.

---

* In this letter Hawkwood signs himself ' English knight ' *(miles anglicus)*.

** From other sources we find that Galeotto Malatesta, Lord of Rimini, was at the head of these barons.

1379.   come to light, that the Florentine opposition was plotting
nothing less than a revolution, and that the leaders of the
conspiracy were some exiles at Bologna; the agitation of
Decemb. 10. the Signoria was great when a letter arrived from Hawkwood saying it had been revealed to him in confidence by
a citizen, that there were *great plots going on in Florence.*

He added that he was in relation with a person who
knew the whole scheme, and would explain it to him in
full, in the presence of an emissary of the Commune ; that
he was ready to serve Florence in such a serious emer-
gency, but if they wanted the complete revelation of the
plans, and of the conspirators he would demand 50,000 florins and the faculty of saving six men — " their lives
and property, excepting only exile *(per la vita e l'avere,
eccetto il confino)."* If they were satisfied in knowing the
plot without the names of the conspirators, he would be
content with 20,000 florins, — the money to be taken to
Bagnacavallo where the revelation was to take place.

The prevailing idea was to spend as little as possible,
and the delicate mission was confided to Guccio Gucci.
He was a wise man, wealthy and loyal, who would not
allow himself either to be deceived or corrupted.

They thought that Hawkwood wanted too much profit,
first on the Commune, and then on those citizens to whom
he reserved the right to sell their impunity. Consequently
Gucci haggled about the price, although the Signoria in
its anxiety sent a man every day to Bagnacavallo for news.
It ending by obtaining a reduction of terms : 20,000 florins and impunity for six persons, if everything were revealed with the names of the conspirators ; and 12,000 florins if the names were kept back. The last proposal being
accepted, and the necessary understanding arrived at with
Hawkwood, the Florentine emissary was introduced by night
into Sir John's room, where there was no light except a
little charcoal in a brazier, and where the unknown infor-

mer, who did not even remain unknown, was admitted :
Hawkwood had already him tracked several times in vain,
but that night, after the colloquy, with success.

The Signoria now knew all that was necessary to coun-
teract the plot, and did not regret the 12,000 florins,
especially as it was afterwards confirmed from Count Antonio da Bruscoli and many other sources, that a very serious rebellion was treated of. The Commune was thus
able to take precautions, secure proofs, and discover and
condemn those who were culpable.

After this secret and profitable service against the internal enemies of Florence, Hawkwood had soon occasion
to lend other service more open and not less lucrative,
against the external enemies of the same Republic. To
complicate the troubles of Italy a new element was
added. Carlo di Durazzo of Anjou came from Hungary
to sustain his pretensions to the crown of the Kingdom
of Naples, and, in agreement with the Pope Urban VI,*
threatened the Tuscan cities who were hostile to the
Pope. The prince of Anjou had large forces at his disposal, and the chief of them was that Italian Company
of *San Giorgio*, with which Alberico da Barbiano had become quite an important military power after his famous
victory over the Bretons near Rome.

To provide for their own defence, the Florentines immediately turned to Hawkwood, whose sword was at present disposable, his hostilities with the Lords of Faenza
and Ravenna being for a time suspended. Venice too, who
found herself involved in the critical war of Chioggia,
wanted him for her captain, but he refused, for he had
a better understanding with the Florentines ; so the Ve-

---

* Buonincontri (*Annali*) says, we do not know with what foundation,
that the Pope called the Hungarian prince of Anjou into Italy, after having
held counsel with John Hawkwood.

1380. netians gave the command to Carlo Zeno instead, and then took into their pay Gold, Cook, and some others of Hawkwood's tried comrades and compatriots.

He lent a much more willing ear to the proposals of the Florentines, because his brother-in-law Lucius Landau had also accepted them.

XXIII.

AGAINST THE COMPANY *OF ST. GEORGE.*
THE CONTEST WITH ASTORRE MANFREDI.

[*Consulte e pratiche, Provvisioni* of the Commune of Florence — MARCHIONNE STEFANI, *Chronicle* — *Diary* of the ANONYMOUS FLORENTINE — *Chronicle* of PIERO BUONINSEGNI — *Register* of the Deliberations of the Signoria and Councils from 1378 to 1390, carte 38 et seq. — NERI DI DONATO, *Sienese chronicle* — D. M. MANNI, *Biography of Hawkwood* in v. 2nd of the Appendix to MURATORI [*R. I. S*] — Carteggio of the Florentine Signoria, *Missive,* XIX. from 87 to 170: letters of December 23rd 1380; January 15th and 26th; February 24th and 27th; March 24th; April 27th and 30th; May 3rd, 16th and 19th, and August 1st 1381, on the subject of Astorre Manfredi.]

Beginning of March.

The Company *of St. George,* being masters of Arezzo, were menacing the neighbourhood of Florence: it was therefore provided to bring the corn into the city, and arm the people, but there were dissentions in the Florentine councils as to the choice of a captain.

7, 9 and 18 of March.

The *Otto di balia* proposed Hawkwood, and would even have received him into the League as a potentate, engaging to induce the Bolognese and Perugians to accept him; but many others wanted a man of noble birth, faithful, honest, and "not of too much weight" (*non di troppo gran peso*); some resigned themselves to take Hawkwood, but were diffident about it, they did not want him "in the city, nor to distribute the garrisons in the fortresses, elsewhere they might make use of him as long as it was necessary." Marchionne Stefani thus explains the

case : " Those who were suspected, or had been *ammoniti,* *   1380.
and their friends wanted him, and they made the people
believe he was necessary to them. Others did not want
him, some because he should not favor the above-mentioned, and others because they did not want to spend
more than they were obliged."

They were doubtful, in fact, of his interfering with
the sword, in the civic questions which were continually
arising in Florence. Meanwhile they sent him a messenger
with proposals, reserving his nomination to the captaincy,
until they had received replies from their allies.

The approach of the enemy cut short all delays and
hesitation. The Signoria passed a motion that they should   20, 21 and 22
of March.
themselves conduct the election of a captain, together with
the councils, and other officials and the *capitudini* (that
is a consul elected from each of the twenty three *Arti*).
The *capitudini* being elected, Hawkwood was unanimously   March 26.
proclaimed captain without loss of time; the only dispute
was that some were disposed to take him with the 300
lances offered by him, and others only wished for 200, but
they begged him to make the best terms he could for
them. There was no time to lose, they had already come   April 1st.
to blows. Eberhard Landau repulsed an attack of the
Company *of St. George* taking 70 horses, together with Count
Giovanni brother of Alberico da Barbiano (in which action
John of Berwick, *a brave Englishman,* was wounded); but
this little success was not enough to reassure them.

The following day Hawkwood's election as captain-general for six months was announced to him, and he "en-   April 6.
tered into Florence at the 22nd hour of the day (about 4 p.m.)
with the Signoria and a large company of citizens. The
great bell was rung, and he entered with great honor, and

---

* To be admonished or *ammonito* under the Republic of Florence was to
be excluded from the power of holding public office; it was a punishment
a degree less severe than exile for the disaffected. — (*Translator.*)

1380.

April 14.

sounding of trumpets, and ringing of bells, as our captain of war in the name of God and of good fortune. In the morning he received the *bâton* in the name of God, at the palace of our Signoria, as our captain-general of the war, to the undoing and death of our citizens (exiles) who had come back, and were with that cursed Company (*of St. George*). At *tierce* he rode forth from Florence with all the men-at-arms and they were considered fine and grand troops."

The fame of his name was enough for the exiles and the Company *of St. George* who had approached Lucca, with a demand for 20,000 florins, for they hastily compounded for half the sum, and took the road into the Maremma.

April 20.

Having made the first defensive preparations in the upper Val d'Arno, Hawkwood with many of his men returned to Florence to regulate the conditions of the *condotta*. Now the Florentines were in an economical mood, especially as they had made some proposals towards a compromise with Barbiano, and wanted to await his reply. They desired Hawkwood to be content with 130 lances,

April 27, 28.

but rather than let him go away they preferred to grant him the 300 he wanted, dismissing the other stipendiaries. They had the prudence not to let him guess how much they depended on his services; it was not without good reason that they had become the most astute merchants in the world. Thus Hawkwood was induced to accept only

April 29.

200 lances, and 1000 florins a month for his salary; and on these conditions he was nominated captain-general till

April 30.

All Saints' day, accepting the office by a public attestation.

The Florentines did not wish to attack the army of Carlo di Durazzo now made master of Arezzo. Hawkwood always said to the Florentines: *Se voi volete vi darò rotta questa gente* (If you wish, I will conquer those troops for you); and they would not let him on account of the bad condi-

tion of Florence, and out of regard to the King of Hungary 1380.
(a kinsman of Carlo).

The "Eight of war" provided for the defence, the
"Eight of peace" for making negotiations with the enemy.

It has however been noticed in preceding campaigns
that Hawkwood always showed a great wish to fight when
he knew his masters would not give him the means of
doing so, and liked to drag out a slow war when they
wanted decisive action; such little hypocrisies were useful
to the reputation of adventurers and served their interests.

It is probable that in his own mind Hawkwood was
very well content that the wishes of the Florentines did
not go beyond the defensive, and in providing for this he
displayed his undeniable abilities.

He placed a camp of observation at Montevarchi, where
on all sides, wherever the enemy appeared, he opposed
an efficacious resistance, so that Carlo of Anjou was induced to make those terms in earnest, which he had at first
only proposed to blind the Florentines.

With this kind of plan of campaign the immediate
presence of the captain is not always necessary. Hawkwood
was sometimes able to demand and obtain leave of absence,
perhaps to run up and glance at his estates in Romagna. May 19.
He had finished by gaining the entire trust of the Florentines, who chose him as arbiter in a question (probably
that of an armistice for the treaties already begun) with
the hostile Company *of St. George;* they tried to wean June 1st.
him from the project of entering the service of the Duke July 16.
of Bavaria; they recalled his troops into the city and followed minutely his advice to be as cautious and carry
arms, exactly the same as if they were not treating for
peace, or as though the Hungarians with whom they
treated were their enemies. They accorded him extensions
of time in the execution of their orders, nominated him
and another Englishman William *Chorsal* (Kursel?) con-

stable of a small brigade, on the same conditions as though they were actually fighting, granting them the usual benefits of toleration about the supply of better horses and ponies, and absolving them from the obligation of regi-

August 22.
Sept. 10, 12.
October 24.

stering the names of pages (with all which little extras every captain made considerable profit on the pay).

Septemb. 24.

Hawkwood returned to Florence when the troops of Durazzo moved away towards Siena and Montepulciano, and notwithstanding this retreat of the enemy he was on All Saints' day re-elected captain-general for another six months. He sent verbal instructions to the *Defenders* of Siena through his comrade the noble Antonio di Porcaria,* but during the winter, having nothing to do for the Florentines he returned against Astorre Manfredi, his own particular enemy, and occupied some towns over which the Commune of Florence asserted a right (they were probably in the upper valley of Lamone). The Commune discreetly deliberated to provide that *those towns should not pass into other hands,* unless restored to Manfredi, but above every thing else to *extinguish that fire,* by hastening to procure

1381.
January 8.
February 6.

peace between the two combatents.

The Florentines were anxious to suppress this contest, for, although they disputed how many lances should be paid for, all with one accord wanted Hawkwood as captain, renouncing, if necessary, the services of Eberhard Landau, who had also served them faithfully. They so firmly believed that, he " would have observed and maintained his written word," that in their Councils they absolved the *Otto* in anticipation from all responsibility, in case

January
10, 30, 31.

things fell out differently.

By force of diplomacy, they succeeded in concluding a

March 20.

truce as the *Anonymous* diarist informs us: " John Hawk-

---

* See Document XXXII.

wood and Astorre Manfredi are coming to Florence; it is
said that the Signoria have procured peace between them,
for the honor of the Commune. And if I had anything
to do with it, I should pay them off and have done with
it, and we needs must have a truce for two years. And
so goes the affair. God send peace to all the world."

This done, the captainship of Hawkwood was immediately renewed by the *Otto,* and because stipulated without
the full powers necessary, it was revised and confirmed
with an official commission, in which the form is as remark-   April 10.
able as the substance. It solemnly begins thus:

" The Priors and Gonfaloniere, principally because the
men-at-arms of the Commune should be led when occasion
requires by a good captain, with sound judgment, also one
approved in valour, and circumspect in military arts,
especially in feats of arms, of wide experience, and self-
confidence, cast their eyes on the magnificent cavalier John
Haukcuod Englishman."

He was nominated captain for seven months with
thirty lances at the expense of the Commune. He was
not required to serve immediately, it was enough if he
placed himself at their disposal, but he could not without
leave absent himself more than eighty miles from Florence. He might however enroll the thirty lances even
at Bagnacavallo, where he resided.

Consequently the pay was less than usual, being fixed
at 333 florins, 6 soldi, and 8 danari for Hawkwood himself,
— 10 florins and 10 soldi for the lances of three horsemen
each, — 6 florins, 10 soldi for the lances and archers of
two horses each, — and 4 florins for the archers with one
horse.

If it should afterwards be deliberated that Hawkwood
and his brigade were to be wholly at the orders of the
Signoria, his stipend was to be tripled and that of the
brigade doubled.

And here we have an additional proof of the especial consideration shown to Hawkwood, for at the same time William Gold (called Coccho), whom we already know as a brave veteran, was hired with fifteen lances on the same terms, except that to him personally the pay was only to be doubled in case of active service.   The terms made with another Englishman Richard *Romise* (? Romsey) were even less liberal.

Every proposition made by Hawkwood was listened to with the greatest deference, — hence they promised him 600 florins " for those Englishmen of whom he had written."

Hostilities were very soon renewed with Astorre Manfredi ; the truce was not observed ; so Florentine envoys were sent into Romagna, to enjoin the two parties to " do nothing new " (*non far novità*), and in accord with the Bolognese commissaries, they were to give sentence as arbiters in the litigation.

Then they made efforts to arrive at a good treaty of peace, to be stipulated at Bologna or on her territory, inviting the Bolognese to summon the two litigants — proroguing, if necessary, the date of the umpirage.   It was the opinion at Florence, that Manfredi was in the right, but they recommended that justice should be rendered if it were possible, and they were also inclined to maintain the truce, leaving the disputed question in abeyance.   Not coming to any conclusion in Romagna, Manfredi and Hawkwood had repeated invitations to come to Florence, and *with good reasons,* leave of absence was refused to Hawkwood, who, foreseeing that the arbitrator's sentence would be unfavorable, intended to protest by going farther away.

The arbitration was conciliative, although when it came to the execution, the Bolognese had orders to punish

Astorre if he rebelled, and to reassure him if he obeyed.
The Florentines then took on themselves to write to Hawkwood reproving him for his attempts against his neighbour.

Any way this long litigation, and the hostility which
had embittered it, convinced Hawkwood that it did not
suit him to keep his estates in Romagna among such perilous neighbours, and that he could not with advantage
be at the same time a feudal lord and hired captain. He
must choose between the two positions, and he with practical English sense preferred to continue his lucrative and
now honorable career as a soldier, rather than waste himself
with his few forces in the poor little principality of Bagnacavallo and Cotignola. He liked better to be the first
of the condottieri, than the last of the lords of Italy.

XXIV.

HAWKWOOD SELLS HIS POSSESSIONS IN ROMAGNA
AND HAS FLORENCE AT HIS FEET.

[Contract between Sir John Hawkwood and the Marquises d'Este, published by Canon Bal-
    duzzi in the *Atti e Memorie della R. Deputazione di Storia patria per le provincie di
    Romagna*, 3ᵃ serie, v. II, fasc. I — BONÒLI, *Storia di Cotignola* — CANESTRINI, *Docu-
    ments*, etc. in the *Archivio storico italiano*.]

Just beyond the ford of the river near Bagnacavallo August 10.
in the territory of Lugo (either in the open fields or at
an hostelry near the ford) the two contracting parties met
on the 10ᵗʰ of August 1381. They were Hawkwood on the
one side; and on the other Tommaso de' Gilli di Terdona,
proxy, and the noble Paolo di Lendinara, a confidential
friend, both procurators of Niccolò and Alberto Marquises
d'Este. There were present the chamberlain, the captain
of Lugo, the Englishman John Rayner, and others as
witnesses to the legal act which was there stipulated
between them, and drawn up as a public document.

In it Hawkwood acknowledged the receipt of 60,000 gold ducats from the Marquises d' Este, and promised to restitute the said sum, at any time and before any court the said Marquises shall be pleased to require it. As a guarantee he pledged all his possessions present and future, but especially the estates of Bagnacavallo and Cotignola, with the fortresses, palaces, towers, gates, bastions, and their respective buildings and lands, together with every jurisdiction, and every right which had belonged to him ; besides all and every stronghold which at present was held by him, or by others in his name, in the province of Romagna, except the bastion of Sezada.

Further, Hawkwood rendered all the aforesaid possessions responsible for the expenses which the Marquises d' Este should sustain for restorations, repairs, and custody of the same, whenever the expenses should outweigh the receipts, in which case the Marquises d' Este might retain and demand legal compensation from any person holding the goods so pledged. We conclude then that Hawkwood declared that he possessed those estates on a precarious title, and promised to restore them to the Marquises d' Este or their agents, in their charge and absolute free power, just as above specified, excepting always the single bastion of Sezada.

" And this in consideration that the said Sir John is not himself powerful enough to defend the said territories with honor to the Church, from the enemies' incursions and from their persistent machinations; and observing that the said Marquises have been, and will be, faithful sons and servants of the Pope our Lord, and most true defenders of the Roman Church, and its rights; and being thus powerful, they know how to defend the said lands to the honor of the Church, and the Pope our Lord."

Hawkwood besides solemnly renounced all his rights to these possessions in favor of Pope Urban VI, or his successors and their commissaries; to the effect that the Marquises d' Este might be invested with those rights in his place, and for this object, he nominated the procurators of the Marquises d' Este as his procurators in the contract, pledging himself never to revoke the nomination. And this under penalty of 1000 ducats without prejudice to the validity of the contract.

All which, according to this faithful summary, would at first sight appear to be a contract of mortgage, but containing certain clauses by which Hawkwood on one part takes 60,000 ducats, and on the other he cedes to the d'Estes all his possessions in Romagna, excepting the bastion of Sezada, which doubtless served as a military precaution against Astorre Manfredi.

If we do not style it a sale, it is a loan against a cession of property, and interesting to us not so much from its legal singularity, as because it renders the fact evident that Hawkwood was in Romagna a true territorial Lord of feudal character, under the high domination of the Pope; and it also shows that he resigned this principality because the trouble of defending it was not convenient to him, the expense exceeding the income. The Marquises d' Este, being rich and ambitious, endeavoured to extend their dominion between the Po and the Adriatic by eyery possible means, and for this they had bought from Hawkwood the possession of Faenza, and although they did not long retain that place, yet they now risked spending 60,000 ducats for Bagnacavallo and Cotignola, where their lordship was less precarious. It was they who brought the Jews into Cotignola, allowing them a *ghetto* with a synagogue, and a bank for usury, which lasted till 1598, in that part named *Castellina* where Hawkwood's ancient tower still rises.

The d' Estes sent as their commissary to take possession of Bagnacavallo, Cotignola and the annexed village

1381.   of Conselice, Filippo Guazilotti of Prato, brother of one
Alberto Guazilotti, commissary general in Lugo, now deputed to the government of Faenza.*

Having sold all his estates Hawkwood was still irritated at the little favorable interference of the Florentines
in his dispute with Astorre; they besides delayed in
granting him a sum of money to buy a house at Florence,
as he intended to do, now that he no longer had a residence at Bagnacavallo, and they were rigorous in the
liquidation of his pay. Hence he formed a league between
his Company, that of Eberhard Landau and that of the
Ban Johann of Hungary, lieutenant and captain-general of
Carlo Durazzo, which he was free to do, as in October he
ceased to be at the disposal of the Florentines, and was in
every way free from active service.

End
of August.   He sent an embassy to the Florentines, to obtain an
absolute dismissal; but by this time they could no longer
do without him, and deliberated that it would be well to
give him a verbal reply, sending Spinello Alberti, a pleasing
person who was well acquainted with him. They did not
wish to dismiss him without knowing his intentions, so
they would proffer him " sweet and good words " accepting
him as a friend and servant. As to the affair with Astorre,
they would justify the rights of the Commune in such a
manner as to satisfy him, and in agreement with the
Bolognese, they would clear him of every reproach. They
would arrange the account of his stipends so as to content
him, respond graciously to his good wishes, offer him the

---

* Bonòli, *Storia di Cotignola*. This author says that Hawkwood was
induced to sell the estate for lack of money, after having spent too freely
in the fortifications of Cotignola, and not being able to pay his soldiers, who
had now for some months been his creditors. But although he cites an ancient
MS. in the library of the Duke of Modena and another MS. of the Signori
Trotti, one can put little trust in a writer who makes one affair of the two
sales, that of Faenza in 1376-77 and this of 1381, giving the date as 1380.

house he required, rather than pay out the price of it, and 1381.
endeavour to re-nominate him as captain, or at least to
bind him not to injure the Commune, her allies, or the
Lord of Milan.

In fact Florence threw herself at his feet; and yet as
a precaution she prepared men-at-arms and defences as
though Hawkwood's Company was to be her enemy.

But on hearing of the league with Landau and the Ban, Sept. 2, 3, and following days.
and that they threatened to ask a *loan* (!), they sent Spi-
nello at once with secret instructions to break the league,
and bring away Hawkwood, taking him into their pay as
captain, and to quiet Count Landau with smooth speeches.

Spinello did better, he succeeded in making an agree- October 3.
ment, concluded at Isola Romanesca near Assisi, where
Landau and Hawkwood were encamped. They stipulated,
also in the name of the Ban, to keep the peace with
Florence, taking the oath for three months as stipendiaries *(in modum stipendii)* and for eighteen months as
good friends *(in modum societatis)*. Five thousand florins
were paid them (which proves they had not a large brigade)
and they were granted a pass on the aforesaid conditions.

A little after this, Siena and Florence were obliged to Novemb. 18.
disburse 30,000 florins to the great bands *of St. George,*
of the *Uncino* (Hook) etc., who were encamped near Arezzo.
This was enough to convince Florence that she must *by all* Decemb. 19.
means have Hawkwood as her captain, and he was re-elected
captain-general for six months, but this time it was for
active service, and consequently with the more favorable
conditions contemplated in the " provvisione " of April 10
(see page 165) and besides with the faculty of taking as
many as ninety lances as his brigade, and with the
extraordinary power of dismissing them.

For the time during which he delayed presenting
himself in Florence he was to receive the third of his

1381.   pay and his men the half. Moreover he was accorded ten per cent on all which was gained in war by the stipendiaries of the Commune under his command.

No condottiere had ever obtained like favors; he was at the same time drawing more money from the Sienese, on his own account, and that of Count Landau and the Ban.* Nevertheless there flashed across him the longing for his native country, since he had expressly reserved the faculty of returning to England, or to cross the seas, even during his engagement with Florence.

In truth the 60,000 ducats recently received from the Estes must have rounded into a very respectable fortune in his hands, and the prospect smiled upon him of peaceful enjoyment in his own country, if it should please God, after he had been purged from his sins by fighting his last fight against the infidels beyond the seas, thus accomplishing the vow and promises sealed by him in answer to the exhortations of St. Catherine of Siena.

But habit and circumstances are often stronger than our resolutions, and always more so than our intentions. One who has a business well started cannot easily decide to leave it. Moreover Donnina Visconti had already made him the father of several children both sons and daughters, without counting his other offspring legitimate or otherwise preceding that marriage. Nobody ever seems to have enough means when there are children.

Hawkwood therefore stayed in Italy, and at Florence he had a part to sustain in the service of the public order; the part of a man-at-arms in the tumults which too frequently afflicted that democracy. It was his office to provide for the internal peace, as well as the external defence of the Commune, and this was the reason the Signoria had made such efforts to have him in Florence and quickly.

---

* See Document XXXIII.

XXV.

HAWKWOOD MAINTAINS ORDER AND CHECKS THE COMPANY OF ST. GEORGE. — ENTERS THE PAY OF THE POPE.

[GINO CAPPONI, *History of the Republic of Florence* — *Diary* of the ANONYMOUS FLORENTINE — AMMIRATO, *Storie fiorentine* — Ser NADDO DA MONTECATINI, Fragments of *Chronicle* — RICOTTI, *History of the mercenary companies* — *Consulte e pratiche* of the Commune of Florence, and the *Provvisioni*.]

Serious disturbances broke out in Florence, provoked by the rebellion of Giorgio Scali, Scatizza, and their companions. To assist the captain of the people in arresting the rebels, Hawkwood appeared on the Piazza of the Signoria with his ninety lances. The sight of those three hundred veterans on horseback was enough to intimidate the mob.

The tumults were renewed at night; and in the morning, behold Hawhwood fully armed again arrived on the Piazza with a great many soldiers and the seven consuls of the greater "Arti." Unable to maintain order, the captain of the people threw away the *bâton,* and said " he resigned his office ; " on which Hawkwood with his men-at-arms " went all round the city shewing themselves " so as to reestablish peace, and if nothing else, he managed to make an end of the excesses of that brutalized mob. He met a brigade who had mortally wounded Simone di Biagio, and with a halter were dragging him to execution and he said : " Lead him away " (*menatelo via*).

The enemy profited by these disorders : the Company of the *Uncino,* commanded by Villanozzo at Roccafranca, which formed the avant-guard to *St. George,* had approached as far as Marcialla, a few miles from the city. It was quickly decided that Hawkwood should defend it if possible ; if not, that he should come to terms, taking care not to compromise the State ; that he should fight only if he

1382.
January.

January 16.

January 24.

were certain of success, and in any case they would hear his opinion before negotiating.

With these instructions, with 800 lances, 200 archers, and 600 infantry, Hawkwood immediately left the city, attempted in vain and with some loss to make himself master of the hill of Marcialla, and encamped at Santa Maria Nuova where he fortified his position and awaited reinforcements. The two camps entrenched and fenced, faced each other as though they would come to action. At the end of three days the Company of the *Uncino* was obliged to commence a retreat, which they continued, masking it by skirmishes of the rearguard. Hawkwood followed them as far as Berardinga where he had orders to retire to Val d' Arno.

The report of Piero Buoninsegni " that Hawkwood had had speech with the corporals of the *Uncino*" does not seem to be justified, neither does that which Marchionne di Coppo Stefani wrote " it was thought he did not do as much as he could in the service of the Republic." On the contrary we have numerous documents, showing his activity in organising and conducting the defence, bringing forward also the Sienese forces, and procuring good soldiers for the united service, and watching that their pay was adequate,* and if the *Uncino* Company was able to retreat with spoil and prisoners, while it seemed to the good Florentine citizens that they had them in a trap, Hawkwood, it must be remembered, had instructions not to run any risk. It was the Signoria who, seeing the internal condition of the city, wanted to have him at hand.

In fact, when the burghers and populace again invaded the Piazza, they were once more stopped by the " halt there " of Hawkwood with many soldiers both horse and foot. Then at the sound of the hammer-struck bell,

---

* See Documents XXXIV to XLV.

every man took arms. " Moscone with the other misguided
men, ready to do evil," led on by the aristocratic party,
" made a rendez-vous at St. George," intending to increase
their numbers and fortify themselves on that hill, " but
finally Sir John Hawkwood managed to get them into the
Piazza." The rebels being thus hunted down, they were
soon brought back to their duty.

These experiences persuaded the Signoria that the
stipendiaries might render invaluable service to them in
maintaining public peace, and therefore in a contract with
two English constables of sixty lances, is this unusual clause
inserted :

" *Item,* if the aforesaid constables or any of their company shall be informed of anything which treats of, or is
designed to, the prejudice, injury, or offence of the Commune, or of its peaceful condition, he shall immediately
by letter or messenger notify the same in good faith, as
soon and as fully as possible, to the Priors and Gonfaloniere etc."

Relative peace being established in the city, the Signoria desired Hawkwood to march into the Arezzo territory with one or two hundred lances; he had also some
infantry, but with such poor forces he could accomplish nothing. The " Anonymous Florentine " explains the secret :
Hawkwood was only to place himself on guard at the
frontier, and the treasurer Spinello went with him to
buy the Company *of St. George* if it were possible.

What a quantity of florins had by this time passed
by means of Spinello, from the pockets of the Florentines,
into the hands of the mercenaries ! Stefani exclaimed with
reason : " This is the blessing of Florence, the money of
the Florentines is so sweet that everybody wants it."

St. George wanted too much of it, so Hawkwood and
Spinello returned to Florence without having concluded

1382. anything, and now the Florentines burned with unusual ardor and wanted to make every effort at the frontier. If Hawkwood felt secure in doing so, he might exterminate the Company without coming to any terms; 1500 lances were to be put together against it, and if Hawkwood May 2 and 4. approved, he could also attack Wilhelm Filibach, a German, who among the many mercenaries, had made himself a nest at Arezzo.

And in fact from his camp at Civitella, Hawkwood anxiously asked the Sienese to join him in the attack on their common enemy, and to send all their troops to Lucignano, where he would meet them and thus attempt some decisive action.* But the warlike fit was of short duration, even a few hours sufficed to change the wind, May 5. and then the Signoria wrote to Hawkwood to do nothing fresh, nor to take the field, but limit himself to resisting if Filibach attacked him; finally they adopted a middle May 8. course, and gave him faculty to make an attack, informing him of the enemy's numbers.

Amidst these uncertainties, an event happened which carried the war elsewhere. Louis duc d'Anjou, a formidable rival to Carlo Durazzo, came down into Italy, with doubtful claims but strong forces, to wrest from him the crown of Naples. Hence all the troops which were warring in Tuscany for Durazzo, were recalled to the defence of the Kingdom of Naples, — the Tuscan cities could breathe again, and Hawkwood might sheath his sword.

But new openings for war were offered to the Condottiere, this time by the Pope, who, as High Sovereign, had espoused the cause of Durazzo regarding the crown of Naples.

The Florentines were informed that Urban VI intended to ask for their captain and his soldiers, and they had

---

* See Document XLVI.

1382.

some trouble in deciding whether to let him go: they were so well satisfied with Hawkwood that they had accorded him the benefit of "ten dead lances," *dieci lance morte* (i. e. pay in the same proportion as though they were effective lances), for as long as the price of the house which he desired, — and which had been promised him in Florence, — remained unpaid; but on the other hand they did not want to offend the Duke of Anjou; they would, if possible, only have given leave to Hawkwood when the Duke had passed Romagna on his march towards the Kingdom of Naples, and then on condition of his promising to return in case of need.

Meanwhile they consulted on the eternal dispute with Manfredi, endeavouring to make an end of it once for all, and to induce Hawkwood to purchase a certain bastion which was the cause of the litigation (probably that Sezada which he had kept back in the cession to the d' Estes). They even offered him 4000 florins if he would leave it to Astorre, who would in return guarantee to furnish the Commune with 1000 moggia of corn.

July 23 and 31. August 28.

The uncertainty lasted till the middle of August. In the Councils they wanted first to know whether the Pope were in Rome, and if the Romans would give a good reception to Hawkwood. There were some who maintained that to dismiss him would prove *the destruction of Florence:* in any case such a grave affair as this ought not to be discussed except in a full Council, at which all the Consuls of the Arts and many citizens and artisans would intervene, forming almost an universal suffrage.

August 13 and 14.

At length the ambassadors arrived from Rome bringing the following brief from Pope Urban VI:

August 20. July 31.

"For a long time we have desired that our beloved son the noble John Hawkwood knight should with six hundred lances militate in the service of ourselves and of the Roman Church. And inasmuch as it conduces no less to our benefit, honor, state and well-being than to that of your city, whether the said knight fights in your service or in ours, we pray most urgently, that as soon as the time shall come to prove the sincerity of your devotion and to display it in your deeds, you will efficaciously and without delay arrange that he shall enter our service, and every thing which you shall pay as stipend to him shall be deducted from the debt which you owe to us and the Church."

The war of the " Eight Saints " being ended, the Pope had remained creditor of the Florentines for an indemnity, and thus suggested to them the mode of paying the debt, for which they were still under an interdict.

There were great discussions in the Councils, and seeing there was not money enough to pay the Pope, the general opinion was that his request should be granted.

There were besides a great many merchants decidedly partial to entering into a league with King Carlo Durazzo, but they wished to do so in a manner not to compromise themselves with the Duke of Anjou, *ita honeste quod nemini displiceatur*.

The following wary subtilty was suggested by Simone Peruzzi — that they should give the Pope's envoys a written reply, refusing the dismissal of Hawkwood requested of them, but if Hawkwood himself should demand it, in another written document, alleging the contracts of the *condotta* (which in fact did not exist), the resignation should be accepted. When once Hawkwood was placed in a condition to act as he chose, and to go where he pleased, who could blame the Florentines if he passed into the service of the Pope?

It was so decided, and Bernabò Visconti, as soon as he heard a rumour of the affair, wrote protesting against the Condottiere hired by the Florentines, passing into the service of an enemy to himself — their ally; they answered

him immediately that on their own account they had re-
peatedly refused Hawkwood to the Pope and the King of
Naples, but that according to the contract he had a right
to go. And when Bernabò again attempted to raise the
same objection, he received the same answer.

1382.
August 30.

The affair being arranged, Urban VI authorised Cosi-
mo Gentili, clerk of the chambers, to give the Florentines
a receipt for the sum which they would in succession pay
to Hawkwood, up to the amount of the 40,000 florins,
they owed.

1383.
February 13.
1382.
September 6.

But before leaving for the camp Hawkwood wished
to arrange his affairs in Florence and settle his wife
there.

October 2.

Such was the devotion of himself and Donnina his
consort to the Commune, that they intended to reside in
the city and its neighbourhood, and to possess property
there, which they could leave to their heirs, demanding
as foreigners the necessary privileges, and subjecting
themselves to the taxes on the contract they were about
to make.

The Englishman Richard Romsey (hired together with
Tyliman and 333 lances) made the same petition, alleging
that he had contracted marriage in Florence, although
with an Englishwoman, and that he wished to collocate
there the greater part of his property.

The general Council of the Captain and People consented with 211 affirmative notes against a minority of
only 12. Hawkwood requested a loan of money on interest,
from the Commune, but it was not granted, nevertheless
it is probable that the purchase of the houses outside
Port' al Prato may be dated at this time.

October 3.

Everything being in order, he took the road to Rome
with 2200 horsemen, stopping a moment at the Abbey
of Isola to demand from the Sienese 14,000 florins, of
which he declared himself their creditor from the preceding

October 22.

1382. year, when in league with the Ban of Hungary.* The Sienese complained to Florence, but they ought to have applied to the Pope by whom he was now engaged.

XXVI.

DEEDS AND AFFAIRS OF HAWKWOOD IN THE KINGDOM OF NAPLES.

[*Chronicon siculum vaticanum — Diurnali* of the Duke of Monteleone in Muratori [*R. I. S.*] — Capponi, *History of the Republic of Florence* — Bonincontri, *Annali — Historical Archives for the Neapolitan provinces*, 12th year, extracts from the *Anjou Registers of the Chancellor's office* — D. M. Manni, *Life of Hawkwood* in Muratori [*R. I. S*], v. II, Appendix — *Consulte e pratiche* of the Commune of Florence — Summonte, *History of the city and kingdom of Naples* — Marchionne Stefani, *Chronicle.*]

October. With a rapid march Hawkwood, accompanied by Carluccio Brancaccio and Andrea Carafa, arrived at Naples,** bringing a brief from Urban VI to the archbishops of Naples and Capua which presented *dilectum filium nobilem virum Joanni Agut militem Anglicanum*, as condottiere in the pay of the Church.

His intervention in the war seemed of such serious injury to the French Anjou party, that the Duke of Anjou,

---

* See Document XXXIII.

** In fact the Florentine chronicler Marchionne Stefani says that Hawkwood stayed in Rome some days, that the Pope gave signs of going to the crusade of Naples with him, or of returning to Corneto, for greater security from the Duke of Anjou : that then the Roman populace went to the house of ' Messer Giovanni Acuto ' and because he was taking away the Pope, they threatened him that if he did not go away at once, they would do him some injury. So on the 6th of November Sir John Hawkwood left Rome and went to Naples.

But the authority of the chronicler loses much of its value by treating of things which happened so far from his own sight, and it would seem wiser to believe rather the Neapolitan Diarist, the Duke of Monteleone, who determines the date and the company of Hawkwood on his arrival at Naples. This would exclude the possibility of his stay in Rome, and the hostility of the people there, which Stefani was willing to believe, as he was of the opposite opinion when the Council discussed the question of favouring the Pope and King Carlo, by giving the leave to Hawkwood.

without much heeding the subtle distinctions of Simone Peruzzi, wrote orders to France that reprisals should be made on the goods and persons of the numerous rich Florentine merchants in that Kingdom.

With his concourse the army of King Carlo reached the number of 14,000 horse. The Duke of Anjou only had 7000, concentrated at Maddaloni, whence the superiority of the enemy, together with cold and hunger, compelled him to move into Apulia, losing on the road a good half of his forces.

It is to be supposed that in this retreat Hawkwood followed obstinately at the heels of the Anjou army, and made not a few prisoners of rank, for he afterwards boasted of being the creditor of Iacopo di Capri, Ugo di San- December. severino, and Antonio Carracciolo, for 1000 florins each; of two others for 500; seven more for 400 each; of twenty-one for 300; and finally four more for 200 florins each. The greater number of the debtors bore the most distinguished names of the Anjou faction, and were qualified as *militi* (knights). These circumstances, together with the round numbers attributed to each debtor, and the gradation of the sums in proportion to the importance of each, whether military, political, or economical, leave no doubt that taxes under the form of ransoms are treated of.

Hawkwood had granted liberty to the prisoners on receipt of promissory notes. When these fell due there was a deficiency of an aggregate sum of 10,900 florins; and he appealed to the King against his thirty-seven debtors, and in fact obtained from King Carlo a mandate to Do- Decemb. 24. nato d'Arezzo, judge of the Supreme Court, that the debtors should be constrained to pay.

Here then we see our Condottiere involved in the difficulties of the forum, and in the tedious delays of a lawsuit. But for him Themis and Astraea showed themselves . resolute and solicitous, thanks to the personal intervention

1382. of the sovereign. The jurisdiction of the civil causes did not pertain to the judge of the *Magna Curia* (Supreme Court), but the King's mandate gave Donato d'Arezzo the necessary competence and special jurisdiction. It was necessary to cite the debtors, but it was not possible to administer the summonses to all of them. The Neapolitan ushers could not reach Ugo Sanseverino who was out of the Kingdom, nor Iacopo da Capri, who was imprisoned at Nocera, nor Aserello da Capri among the rebels at Ischia, nor Andrea da Messina in the army of Louis of Anjou. Hawkwood again appealed to the King, who commanded
1383.
January 14. the judges to cite them by public edict.

Hawkwood succeeded in getting a great part of the 10,900 florins if not all, for the same year he sent his savings to Tuscany where he invested them in landed property, buying from Raimondo Tolomei of Siena a possession, composed of house, tower, and a palace, with several *poderi* (farms) in a place called *la Rocchetta* in the parish of Santa Maddalena, in the Commune of Poggibonsi near the river Elsa.

Although it is said " out of sight out of mind," Florence showed the same regard to him as if he had been near ; it was discussed whether he should be called on to pay the property tax, and by common consent it was decided that if he were not a citizen he was exempt by right, but if they considered him a citizen (on account of
January 7. his purchases), they should exempt him by favor.*

---

* Like the captain, the other Englishmen were always the mercenaries preferred by the Florentines. We find that on February 12th 1383 they engaged the constables John Berwick with 30 lances; John Beltoft with 65 lances, 3 fifers and a trumpeter ; and Johnny (Gianichino) Swin, Johnny Boutillier (Butler), and Ozochino (Hoskyn or Hodgekin?) Norton with 37 lances. On October 3rd 1384 John Gulion, John Cokum, Thomas Ball, and Richard Sticklet were engaged as constables with 100 lances and 4 trumpeters. Robin Corbeck, and Johnny Barry with 50 lances, John Liverpool with 10 ; and on the 6th of October, John Trickell with 100 lances, and 2 trumpeters.

The winter being over, the King wished to advance to 1383. meet the enemy, and left Naples with all the troops now April 4. increased to 16,000 horse and a great number of foot. After the Count Alberico of Barbiano, the commander in chief, the chroniclers give the first place amongst the foreign captains to Hawkwood who had the official title of *captain general of the Church;* but none of them had to fight in earnest. The King having arrived at Barletta sent the April 12. gauntlet of battle to the Duke of Anjou, who accepted the challenge; the two armies were displayed in battle array, but by the advice of Otho of Brunswick the King let prudence prevail, and it all ended in an insignificant skirmish of a few cavaliers.

There was a battle at Pietracatella instead, but it is not stated whether Hawkwood took part in it.

Moreover while in these troubled waters the Duke of Anjou was taken away by a natural death; and King Carlo, who had garrisoned Apulia, returned towards the capital. He employed his men-at-arms to keep his ally October 4. Pope Urban VI almost as a prisoner at Aversa, for five days, while he imposed his will on that Pontiff, who had thus unluckily arrived on the scene of action; he then re-entered Naples, and Hawkwood seeing that there was no- Novemb. 10. thing conclusive to be done down there, again drew near to the beloved and fruitful Tuscany, accepting in his company two first-rate soldiers, the Italian Giovanni Azzo degli Ubaldini, and the Englishman Richard Romsey.

His first menaces were for the Sienese, who sent three December 7. ambassadors to him hoping to escape for 3000 or 5000 or at most 8000 florins,* but they had besides to resign themselves to giving him a year's pay, at the rate of Decemb. 12. 100 florins a month, and thank him into the bargain for

---

* See Document XLVII.

his services.* The Florentines had paid him on account of the Pope, first 12,000 florins, then 8000, but the captain asked for another ten thousand. At first they wished to refuse, but afterwards they thought better of it, and while they maintained that he could not demand any of the *King's money,*** they judged it wise to pay him, still on the Pope's account, provided that he should obtain absolution from the interdict which the Pontiff still kept suspended over the Florentines since the war of the " Eight Saints, " and that he should ensure Florence from injury by his Company.

From all this it results that Hawkwood, serving King Carlo directly, and the Pope indirectly, was not content with holding out his right hand for the pay of the Church, but he extended also the left for the pay of the Kingdom.

King Carlo had ordered the immediate exaction of the new tax called the *tarì**** in the *Principato Citeriore* and in *Basilicata*****declaring it to be necessary for the pay of John Hawkwood's Company. We must suppose that as Hawkwood tried to make the Florentines pay him with the *King's money,* the *tarì* of those two provinces was insufficient, and in making up the accounts he remained creditor, so much so that in exchange for his credit the feudal village of Carinaro in Aversa and other properties in Capua and Naples were conceded to him.

In leaving the Kingdom, he left the administration of these rural lordships to his procurator the Sienese Recu-

---

* See Document XLVIII.

** What this *King's money* was is explained by Marchionne Stefani. It was a sum of 38,000 florins deposited with the Commune at Florence, by the Duchess of Durazzo, when she found herself in the enemy's power, with orders not to dispose of it in favor of any person, as long as she were not free and in safety, or dead. And therefore although King Carlo's ambassadors alleged new and different orders from the Duchess, the Commune would not infringe the primitive conditions of the deposit.

*** *Tarì* or *Tarena* was the name of a small Sicilian coin worth about fourpence. — (*Translator.*)

**** Two of the Neapolitan provinces. — (*Translator.*)

pido Lazzari; *Recupido!* — an ill-omened name for an agent! Nevertheless Lazzari showed himself zealous. Rumours having been circulated that Hawkwood had been murdered in Florence, these feudal estates were without delay assigned to three of the great functionaries of the Kingdom, viz: the *Almirante* (admiral) Giovanni Stendardo, and Giacomo Gaetano. The new lords soon hastened to disturb Lazzaro in possession, and he appealed to the Queen Margherita di Durazzo (King Carlo being deceased, his widow became regent for her son King Ladislao a minor), showing that his master was alive, and declaring him to be always ready for loyal service. The Queen accepted the petition, and ordered that Lazzari should be kept in possession.

1384.

1385.
January 4.

XXVII.

THE CATASTROPHE OF BERNABÒ VISCONTI.

[*Consulte e pratiche* of the Commune of Florence — *Sienese chronicle* in MURATORI [*R. I. S.*] — RICOTTI, *History of mercenary companies* — GIULINI, *Memorie di Milano* — SER NADDO DA MONTECATINI, *Fragments of a chronicle* — *Diary* of the ANONYMOUS FLORENTINE — OSIO, *Diplomatic documents*, taken from the Milanese Archives — *Annales mediolanenses* in MURATORI [*R. I. S.*]

The inquietude of the Perugians, on the reappearance of Hawkwood in central Italy, was very great; they invoked the good offices of Florence, and got the Signoria to deliberate on recommending them to his mercy by letter, or, if necessary, by means of an embassy. Nor was the intervention in vain. The Florentines had reason to send and thank him for *his doings towards the Perugians and to Assisi.* In growing older Hawkwood became somewhat more humane and tractable, as about the same time the Florentines dared to excuse themselves for being unable to disburse money, and to neglect to give an answer about some certain places which he had taken, and which he probably offered for sale.

1384.

May 18.

June 1st.

1884.   It is nearly certain that this referred to the castle of Montecchio, the fortresses of Migliari in the valley of the Ambra, and of the Abbey at Pino, which we shall see later were possessed and sold by Hawkwood, though there is no documentary evidence of the epoch, or probable occasion of the acquisition.

But if he were tractable towards Florence where he now considered himself almost as a citizen, he was not equally so with others. This time the blows fell on Siena, which refused to pay new extortions, and wanted to hinder him from spoiling the land; Hawkwood reinforced by the Prefetto of Viterbo, and a new band formed by his col-

June 12.   league Giovanni Ubaldini, routed and completely defeated the Sienese troops, taking prisoner the captain *Niccolò di Messer Galeotto* (Malatesta?) whom, to the astonishment of every one, he released a few days afterwards.

On their side the Florentines deliberated to continue the promised payments to Hawkwood, and also to interpose between Sir John, who declared himself creditor, and the Bolognese, who denied the debt, so that they should not come to a rupture.

July 9.   He having arrived at Florence, and being well received by the Signoria, they again took up the discussion on the still smouldering question with Astorre Manfredi, procuring

July 29.   a truce for two years and arranging things in his favor, also replying graciously to Bernabò Visconti, who protected Manfredi with the ardor of a father-in-law at discord with his son-in-law.

These councils kept him some time in Florence, whence being pacified towards the Sienese, he wrote to

Septemb. 3.   recommend to them Pietro Boncompagni, doctor of laws and his *protégé,* as candidate for the office of Syndic.*

Then he joined the camp above Cortona, forming

---

* See Document XLIX.

there together with Richard Romsey, and Giovanni Ubaldini, the Company of the *Rose** with the money drawn from Siena.** 1384.

Septemb. 23.

With this then he must have gone into Romagna, where, as some historians say, he united with Lucius Landau, and was able to take Ravenna and put it to the sack, selling it afterwards to the Malatesta. October.

But the Florentines did not lose sight of him; indeed they thought of hiring him together with Romsey, and before negotiating with others, they wanted his advice, and asked him to give information about the men-at-arms, trusting entirely in his judgment; they acquiesced in his counsels, and begged him to come soon. Moreover they dreamed of stipulating a league between Hawkwood, Florence and Perugia, thus considering him almost as a potentate.***

Meanwhile a very serious event took place in Tuscany; the Sire de Coucy, that French adventurer and great baron **** whom we have already seen fighting with Hawkwood for the Church, had returned to Italy for the Anjouvine wars, and had taken Arezzo. It was a case for action on the part of Florence: a number of men-at-arms were immediately engaged, and Hawkwood, though still receiving his pay, being employed beyond the Apennines, Giovanni degli Septemb. 28.

---

* This title of ' the Rose ' appears several times in the mercenary companies: there was one in Provence in 1357; another of 300 lances, lasted from 1398 to 1410, it extorted money from Siena in 1404, and is cited as the last company which had a name of its own, not taken from its captain.

** See Document L.

*** A note from the Signoria to Donato Acciaioli, Bartolommeo Ridolfi, and Jacopo de' Medici, ambassadors, perhaps refers to this. See Document LI.

**** The castle of Coucy still exists in French Flanders (near St. Gobain', and among the noble armorial ensigns, similar to that noted in Rohan, is recorded

> *Roi ne suis*
> *Prince ni comte aussi*
> *Je suis le Sire de Coucy.*

Obizi was taken as captain of war. But as Coucy let himself be persuaded to sell Arezzo to the Florentines for " ready money," the worst was over; — all that remained was to assure their possession of the new territories, to wrest from the Signori Tarlati the places they held on the confines between Arezzo and Florence, for which slight duty it did not seem necessary to take a captain of such valour and expense as Hawkwood.

The Florentines contented themselves with his counsels, and confided the execution thereof to Giovanni degli Obizi and Vanni di Michele di Vanni.

On the other hand the fall of Arezzo left Hawkwood undisputed Lord of Montecchio and other towns recently occupied by him in the Aretian territory, of which the Florentines did not even dream of contesting his possession. He had a little leisure to see to his own affairs, to liquidate his debts and credits * and he was reposing in the bosom of his family, in Florence, when there reached him the most astounding news, which was of the greatest importance to him, his family and also to Florence. This was, that Gian Galeazzo Visconti, the Conte di Virtù, nephew of Bernabò, had disloyally overcome his uncle and ruling lord, and shut him up in the castle of Trezzo, and was now over-running Milan on his own account, usurping the lordship ** without opposition, and that one of Bernabò's sons, the young Carlo Visconti, had fled to Crema and thence to Cremona. The other young men and Donnina Porro (just now married or about to be married to Bernabò, whose wife Regina Scaliger had died a year before) shared the prison with their father and consort.

Together with this serious intelligence Hawkwood received entreaties to assist his father, mother, and brothers-

1385.

Between
January
and May.

May 9.

---

* See Document LII.
** The official announcement of this dynastic coup d'état was received by the Signoria in a letter from Gian Galeazzo on May 13.

1885.

in-law in this catastrophe. Among the brothers-in-law, Carlo especially wrote that he held the citadel of Crema in his own hands, as well as the fortress of Porta Romana at Milan, and was ready to pay him well, beseeching him to come in person as soon as possible, with as many men-at-arms as he could collect.*

In this urgent case it is easy to conceive that Hawkwood's wife Donnina exerted herself warmly to send her husband to the succour of her relatives, but nothing prevailed, and Bernabò very soon died at Trezzo of rage or poison, while no one dared move a finger to help him.

In the first place Hawkwood, as we know, was in absolute discord with his father-in-law; next, although a brave soldier and a famous condottiere, he never could have held his own against the new Lord of Milan; and finally, we must allow, that besides resentment and caution, the very vulgar reasons of self-interest appeared to rule his mind.

July 1st.

Papers will speak! from the contracts stipulated at Villa di Cavazzo near Modena, in the house where Hawkwood was then residing, we find that he had before that time promised and sworn fidelity and homage to Gian Galeazzo for 1000 florins!

Now that shameful contract was to be improved upon, and Hawkwood *recognising his oath already sworn* and qualifying himself as *the most beloved kinsman of the illustrious lord Signor Galeazzo Visconti, with solemn oath on the holy Gospels, corporeally touching the holy scriptures with his hand* promised and agreed:

"That if the Count should request his personal service, he would hold himself obliged to go to him, excepting that he should be in the pay of any other Commune, lord or

---

* See Document LIII.

1385. prince, to whom he were so bound that he could not with honor leave his service; but as soon as the time for this contract should be completed, he would feel himself bound to personally serve the Count whensoever he pleased.

" The Count on his side should give him a salary of 300 florins a month, and the faculty of leading 30 lances, to which the Count should give the same stipend as his other lances.

" By order of the Count, Hawkwood might also conduct a greater number of lances, who in that case would be paid, and bound like the others who were in the Count's pay.

" If Hawkwood — his service being required and he being free of other engagements — should not present himself for the Count's active service within four months, the Count shall not be obliged to pay the 1000 florins offered by his procurator in the preceding act of fidelity...."

The accessories in this contract are very interesting: for example, among the usual concluding formulæ, the following is noteworthy: " the tenor of the clauses written herein has been read and vulgarized in the common tongue, to the full understanding of Sir John." He therefore knew no latin, but could speak italian perfectly. Besides this the act was not only written by Martino, *quondam* Giacomo de Robbis di Città di Castello, Hawkwood's notary and secretary, but also signed by the same notary at the request and order of Hawkwood, whose usual seal was appended to the deed — a sign that Sir John Hawkwood did not know how to write.

But it is the subject of such a stipulation that most astonishes us. It seems impossible that Hawkwood, who was accustomed to put quite a different price on his sword, should needlessly and for mediocre gain sell himself to one who so seriously compromised his own interests, and even his family peace, since Gian Galeazzo, to justify his usurpation, made a kind of legal process *de vita et moribus,* and sent out into the world a formal act of accusation against Bernabò, alleging in it a curious species of *incesto concubinario,* pretending that the marriage of Bernabò and Donnina de' Porri was null and void :

1385.

> *Cognovit carnaliter Donninam de Porros et Johannam ejus Donnine sororem; de qua Donnina plures habuit natos: postea ipsam Donninam desponsavit que nihilominus non potest esse uxor sua.*

Thus the legitimacy of Hawkwood's wife, ensured by subsequent marriage, became impugned. It might be that Hawkwood, being a most astute man, wished in this surrender to lull the natural suspicions of Gian Galeazzo, reserving to himself to act as an enemy against him on a better occasion; and the fact remains that he never was in the effective service of Gian Galeazzo, and it was against him that he schemed so long and, as we shall see, conducted the last and most brilliant of all his campaigns.

<hr />

XXVIII.

WAR BETWEEN THE CARRARAS OF PADUA AND THE SCALIGERS OF VERONA.

[*Provvisioni* of the Commune of Florence — RAWDON BROWN, *Venetian Calendars of State papers* — Paduan *chronicles* by GALEAZZO and ANDREA GATARO in MURATORI [*R. I. S.*] — Diary of the ANONYMOUS FLORENTINE edited by ALESSANDRO GHERARDI — *Deliberations and Condotte* of the Commune of Florence — *Chronicon Estense* in MURATORI [*R. I. S.*] — MINERBETTI, *Chronicle* — VERCI, *Storia della Marca Trevigiana.*]

In the spring the Florentines, having ensured the acquisition of Arezzo, were undecided whether or not, to hire their favorite captain (so that in the summer he began negotiations with Siena*); but in the autumn they adopted

---

* See Document LIV.

the more economical course of satisfying him with words and with some favors.

We know that he was exempted from the *estimo* (property tax) which was an ordinary tax, but he was not so from the extraordinary rates, and it is not to be wondered at, that he belonged to the category of backward payers, so that fines and penalties would have fallen to his share, had not the government exempted him from its usual rigorous rules, thus tempering it's fiscal refinement:

"Considering that Sir John Hawkwood is registered in the *prestanze* and *prestanzoni* (forced loans) of the city in the gonfalon of the Golden Lion (quarter of San Giovanni) and that, whatsoever the cause, he has not paid up to this date, but declares himself ready to pay, if the penalty shall be condoned; we hereby concede this, on con- dition that he pay within 15 days."

Following this, in Hawkwood's absence, Donnina explained to the Signoria that her husband had made two loans, lending 400 florins to the Englishman William Boson, and 1000 to Wilhelm of Corbrich, and that now his property was charged with the payment of the duty relative to the said contracts and that he as a foreigner had nothing to do with such a tax, that neither to him, nor to others for him, was any notification given until the last few days; she supplicated therefore that without being required to prove her statement, it may be conceded to her to effect the payment within 15 days without the aggravation of a penalty. And this was graciously granted.

Whether Hawkwood were fighting, or where he stayed during the early months of 1386, is not clearly shown. According to Bonincontri (whom we have seen however that we cannot trust at all), he went as far as Hungary; according to the Paduan chroniclers he was in the service of the Pope.

We must look for him where there was fighting, and precisely at that time war broke out between the Carraras of Padua and the Scaligers of Verona, and numerous condottieri took part in it, on one side or the other, amongst whom there was in the Veronese camp a half brother of the Black Prince, exiled from England for assassination.* 1386.

In fact the *Anonymous* and diligent *Florentine* diarist registers that Antonio Scaliger was defeated by the Carraras who had also Hawkwood in their camp. The latter could not have taken an important part in that campaign which was commanded for the Carraras by Giovanni degli Ubaldini, and decided by the battle of Brentelle,** since at that time the Commune of Florence was endeavouring as usual to conclude a general league, — and equally as usual concluding nothing, — against the mercenary companies; and hired Hawkwood as chief constable of eighty-two lances, who were paid at the rate of 18 florins each a month, with ten days *benvenuta* *** on entering the service. May 11. June 25. May 28.

Florence negotiated the league foreseeing that the war in Upper Italy would not last long, and that then the three thousand or more lances engaged in it would soon return to their usual brigandish proceedings. In fact

---

* English adventurers continued to pass one by one into Italy, for many years after the first comers, up to the 15th century, but we need not believe that all those styled *Anglici* in documents of the time were really of English birth. The phrase means, merely, that they were in the rank of lances *all' Inglese* or organised on the English system. In fact in 1397 Bologna had in her pay about 1100 men qualified as English, and yet not an English name is to be found amongst the constables and *caporali* of these troops at the general review held at Mantua.

** To speak correctly, Galeazzo Gataro in his Paduan chronicles makes Hawkwood take part also in the battle of Brentelle, but we must note that this chronicle, which is in Muratori, presents a great confusion of dates and of places, and an evidently erroneous repetition of facts. On the other hand the chronicle of Andrea Gataro, who completed and rectified his father's work, does not mention Hawkwood in the campaign of 1386.

*** *Benvenuta* (welcome) was a kind of bounty money given to soldiers on entering service. — (*Translator.*)

1386.
September. Hawkwood, leaving the honest Florentine pay, had again moved to menace the Sienese, as before making the noble Antonio di Porcaria the bearer of his intentions. They first sent a certain Monaldi with soothing words,* then a man named Coltini to see if Sir John would be content with 500 florins and the liquidation of his credit with Niccolò Piccolomini.** At the same time they hastily recalled an embassy from Cortona, perhaps fearing it might be taken in hostage,*** and demanded succours of troops from Florence, from Perugia, Pisa, and Lucca;**** but foreseeing too well the replies they were likely to get, they accorded at once 800 out of the 1000 florins demanded by the captain.***** Things being thus arranged, Hawkwood paid an amicable visit to Siena with an escort of 40 or 50 horse-December. men,****** thence he passed into Romagna, but some of his men still remained to molest the Val d'Ambra, obliging the Sienese to apply for Florentine intervention.*******

However, before the year was over, the Lord of Verona engaged Lucius Landau; and the Lord of Padua on his side hastened to hire Hawkwood, with five hundred lances, and six hundred archers. We are inclined to believe that he had provided himself with this considerable brigade in the service of Queen Margherita of Naples, as we find that the Signoria had refused a loan of 4000 florins asked by July 16. the Queen for Hawkwood.

Carrara first wrote, and then sent Giovanni Ubaldini his captain-general in person, to stipulate the contract with Hawkwood, who was then in Faenza. The best relations existed between these two leaders: they had together beaten the Sienese, and Hawkwood looked on Ubaldini as the most experienced captain of the times; but yet he,

---

* See Document LV.   ** See Document LVI.
*** See Document LVII.   **** See Document LVIII.
***** See Documents LIX and LX.   ****** See Document LXI.
******* See Document LXII.

who without doubt ranked first among the condottieri in
Italy, would not easily have consented to serve under the
orders of another; on the other hand he could not expect
that after the recent brilliant victory of Brentelle, Ubaldini should cede him the command. We believe it was
to regulate these difficulties that Ubaldini undertook the
journey, and that he found a way to arrange it by attributing the honor of supreme command to the prince, i. e.
Francesco Novello, the brave and youthful son of the Lord
of Padua; and in reality reserving the effective direction
of operations to Hawkwood and himself, he nominally
holding the *bâton* as captain-general; — in fact they understood each other. Besides Hawkwood, Ubaldini hired in
Romagna Giovanni di Pietramala with 1000 horse, hastening his march, because they wished to follow up the
campaign vigorously during the winter.

The body of the Paduan army had already crossed the
Adige, and taken up its position at Cerea; soon after, Pietramala and Hawkwood arrived, and posted their men at
Montagnana; they, with the principal persons of the band,
stayed at Padua, where they were honorably received,
loaded with gifts, and lodged by the lord, Francesco the
elder; between whom and Hawkwood many colloquies took
place to concert the plan of the campaign.

All being arranged, Hawkwood and Pietramala returned
to the camp, escorted by Messer Rigo Galletto; between
Este and Monselice, Francesco Novello came to meet them,
and taking up the troops at Montagnana, they all together
directed their steps to Castelbaldo, where a chain bridge
spanned the Adige. Finding the bridge broken, they crossed
the river at another place, and concentrated themselves at
the camp of Cerea.

A council of war was held immediately, in which Ubaldini (perhaps it had been already concerted) spontaneously

ceded the *biton* as captain to Hawkwood. The army was of a strength of 7500 horse, besides 1000 foot; they then resolved to march boldly into the Veronese territory and in fact pressed on to close under the city, spoiling everything without hindrance.

Antonio della Scala on his side, although he had lost Lucius Landau, who had been corrupted by the Carraras, had put together 9000 horse, 1000 foot, and 1600 between archers and crossbowmen, without counting a great mass of peasants, — who in reality counted for nothing. He had also some artillery, that is to say, three machines which we might call *mitrailleuses,* composed of 402 *bombarde* (small mortars) disposed at different levels on each car, and which threw " great stones as large as hen's eggs." The Scaligers' captain-general was Giovanni degli Ordelaffi, but the effective condottieri were Ugolino and Taddeo dal Verme.

While the Carrarese army rashly pressed forwards, that of the Scaligers took a long round, and descending along the right bank of the Adige, ended by finding itself on the enemy's line of communication, thus threatening to cut them out, and without delay cutting off their means of provisioning.

Very soon the Carraras found themselves unprovided with bread and wine, and reduced to meat and turnips; finally they had to eat their horses. This lasted some days, and then they retreated in good order of battle, towards the Adige, where they would have found abundance.

The situation was critical. Hawkwood however was expert enough to evade a disaster.

Antonio della Scala sent to him and Ubaldini a certain man named Pulliano, with the apparent office of inducing them to persuade Francesco Novello to propose that his father should make negotiations of peace. Hawkwood discovered the spy under the disguise of envoy, and there-

fore kept him closely shut up in his tent the whole day, 1387.
not allowing him to speak with anyone, and when night
came he dismissed him with his answer, and sent him away.

Indeed if we may believe the Paduan chroniclers, Hawkwood must literally have worked miracles in that retreat.
Galeazzo Gataro says that when at length the army again
reached Cerea, they found that all the wine had been
poisoned, but Sir John Hawkwood *with his ring* put it
right again. " Andrea Gataro even embellishes the fable
recounting that the water of the wells was poisoned and
many died of it. "Hearing this, Hawkwood who had with
him an *unicorn five feet long, which I saw and touched with
my own hands,* had it let down into the wells, and cutting
it in many portions, he gave it as a drink to those injured,
and thus remedied the cursed scheme of the enemy." *

Continuing to retreat, the Carraras found themselves March 11.
at the longed-for banks of the Adige, before Castelbaldo,
where by the care of the Lord of Padua a great quantity
of provisions were amassed, and the bridge rebuilt.

But the Veronese army also arrived still intact, and
we may believe the chroniclers when they tell us, the force
was four times that of the Paduans, if we choose to reckon
as combatants the 16,000 peasants who formed a rear-guard

---

* It is not to be wondered at that people in those days believed in the
marvelous virtue of. the unicorn, as a test and antidote for any kind of
poison. Another condottiere less antique than Hawkwood, i. e. Bartolommeo Alviano, took as his device an unicorn in the act of bending his head
and putting the horn in the water with the motto *Venena pello.* Two centuries after Hawkwood's time, the unicorn still enjoyed the greatest credit;
princes disputed for the rare specimens of it at their weight in gold. Pope
Julius III paid 12,000 scudi for the headless body of one, hence it is credible that the unicorn used by Hawkwood belonged to the treasure of the
Carraresi, and that Francesco Novello had carried it to the camp, for amongst
its other virtues is attributed that of preserving its possessor from mortal
wounds.

(From *L'Alicorno,* a discourse by the excellent doctor and philosopher
M. Andrea Bacci, in which he treats of the nature of the unicorn and of its
most excellent virtues to the most serene Don Francesco de' Medici, *grand-
prince* of Tuscany. Florence, 1573 and 1582.)

1387.   of plunderers to the real army. They certainly had the advantage of arriving fresh to the attack of an enemy who were in the last straits after a long and difficult retreat, and they were moreover strongly entrenched in a good position.

To cross the Adige under such circumstances was a serious risk for the army of Carrara. Hawkwood perceived immediately that it would result in a disaster; it would be better to fight, but on the other hand, to attack the enemy within its strong entrenchments seemed a desperate measure.

However it was necessary to decide; several brigades, having arrived in sight of the river and bridge, deserted their standards to hasten to the provisions prepared at Castelbaldo. Novello, not having succeeded in retaining them, crossed the river himself to try and get them to return to their posts, and to bring provisions back to the camp. Meanwhile Hawkwood and Ubaldini, badly seconded, remained steady round the standards, discussing with the other captains the best mode of acting. Novello having returned, he found that the council of war had decided to come to an engagement, and in this he honorably wished to take part himself, although Hawkwood exhorted him to retire to a distance and not in his own person to risk the state.

XXIX.

THE BATTLE OF CASTAGNARO.

[Paduan chronicles of GALEAZZO and ANDREA GATARO in MURATORI [R. I. S.] — Chronicon estense, ditto — MINERBETTI, Chronicle — VERCI, Storia della Marca Trevigiana — Cronica di Treviso — RICOTTI, History of the mercenary companies — Consulte e pratiche of the Commune of Florence — BONINCONTRI, Annals — State Archives of Florence, Dieci di balia, Legazioni, v. I.]

Having assumed the responsibility of giving the orders of combat, Hawkwood commanded that every man should first eat and drink; and then armed at all points, should go each to his repective standard. Then he arranged the men-at-arms in eight battalions, of different strength according to the number of the contingent which each condottiere had at his command. Some numbered as many as 1500 horse, some did not exceed 500. Hawkwood kept in the front lines with his 500 lances and 600 archers; then followed in succession: Ubaldini, Pietramala, Ugolotto Biancardo, Francesco Novello, Broglia and Brandolino, Biordo and Balestrazzo, and Filippo da Pisa.

The two last battalions remained mounted, forming a reserve of 1600 horse, placed at a distance and commanded to guard the *Carroccio,** the Carrarese ensign of the *Car,* the other standards, and the council of the camp. The other six dismounted, forming two lines of about 3000 men each, distant about two arrows' flight the one from the other; the pages were sent under cover with the horses, at a considerable distance.

Hawkwood also placed in reserve the thousand native foot soldiers (*provvisionati*) commanded by Cermisone of Parma, extending them in two long squadrons along a bank from which a moat was dug out, and over the bank he had improvised a *pavesata ** which could oppose a solid resistance, and was garrisoned by 600 cross-bowmen.

Mounting a Thessalian charger (*destriero tessalico*) he did not fail to invoke St. Prosdocimus, St. Anthony, St. Justina, and St. Daniel, the protectors of Padua; and to incite every man to his duty, he gave the golden spurs to five Paduans whom Francesco Novello then created cavaliers, and on his own side he knighted some Englishmen.

---

* The *Carroccio* was a species of war chariot with the bell on it.—(*Translator.*)

** *Pavesata,* a temporary palisade formed of the large shields or *pavese* used by foot soldiers in the 14th century. They were of a square form with the upper corners cut off, and so high as to almost entirely cover the soldiers who used them. — (*Translator.*) ·

All this was quite easy; the difficulty lay in making
the Veronese army abandon its excellent position, and in
this he succeeded by sending to the attack the *saccomanni*
and other light militia, mounted on horseback for the occasion: those, allowing themselves to be overcome and
yielding their ground, drew the Veronese first outside, and
then far away from the entrenchments, so that little by
little their flank was exposed to the Carraras.

The manœuvres commenced, Hawkwood with Ubaldini
and Ugolotto Biancardo proceeded to survey the ground
towards the enemy, and perceiving that this lent itself
very well to the plan, with a rapid march moved the camp
beyond the canal of Castagnaro, which is derived from
the Adige, supporting his troops with its banks. He thus
inverted the position, and the Carraras gained the advantage
so lightly lost by the Scaligers. He had calculated so well,
that the new position was scarcely taken when the Scaligers attacked them with the cry of *Scala! Scala!*

The enemy was already fatigued and disordered by
chasing the *saccomanni*. It was still much superior in
force, amounting in fact to twelve battalions of cavalry,
besides a superiority of number, in archers and cross-
bowmen. The *mêlée* having begun, Hawkwood confided
the lieutenancy of his own battalion to Pietramala, and
followed by his page rode rapidly round the field to give
another general glance and see how the affair was going.

The moment had come " to close the pincers: " he
caused the band of Francesco Novello to change its position, for as this prince persisted in fighting, Hawkwood
did not wish him to be too much exposed, he would at
least leave a way of escape open to him. Then throwing
his *bâton* amongst the enemy, drawing his sword and
crying to his men not the usual *Carro! Carro!* (Car), but
the ferocious *Carne! Carne!* (Flesh), fell with his men-

at-arms and infantry on the flank of the Scaligers, already engaged too far forward, whilst his clever archers showered their arrows from the bank, till it seemed to be raining. Ordelaffi and Ostasio da Polenta, who with 2500 horse constituted the reserve of the Veronese, made an effort to come to the rescue, but found the road already closed by Hawkwood's interposition.

The action was rapid in the extreme and the effect instantaneous ; the enemy was driven back upon its standards which were thrown to the ground. Francesco Visconti, who guarded them, lost his own flag and was unhorsed. Ordelaffi captain-general, Ostasio da Polenta, the two dal Verme, Facino Cane, many other captains, and about eighty cavaliers of rank, were nearly all taken prisoners. A thousand nine hundred of the cavalry took to flight, but being energetically followed up they were nearly all taken.

1387.

A corps of infantry and Veronese peasants commanded by Giovanni da Isola remained intact on the field. Hawkwood ordered them to yield, but they answered that they would resist, and so they were cut to pieces.

Relatively to the success there was but little bloodshed in that battle (716 dead and 846 wounded), but the number of prisoners was extraordinary : in all there were 4620, of whom 2620 were soldiers forming part of mercenary companies, and 284 men-at-arms ; besides the three famous *mitrailleuses* cars with their respective *bombarde* which had not had occasion to throw their *hen's eggs*.

We have a proof that the conflict was as short as it was decisive : in the dispatch sent to Treviso by Francesco Novello, and dated " from Castagnaro, in my fortunate army on March 11 ; an hour after sunset " (*a un' ora di notte*), which says that " the fight began an hour before sunset " (*alle ore 23*).

The Paduan chronicler says:

" Thus by the skill of the knight Sir John Hawkwood was Messer Francesco da Carrara victorious over 14,000 men, horse and foot."

The victorious army returned triumphantly to Padua; the old Lord Francesco da Carrara went to the gate of the city to embrace the captains, and re-entered with Hawkwood on one side, and Ubaldini on the other, their ensigns being very much applauded.* There was a great feasting of the people on the Prato della Valle, a great supper at Court, fires of joy and martial noises all night. It had indeed been a great victory, all the more valuable as it remedied a very critical military situation. Hawkwood had shown the finest qualities of a first-rate captain: — constancy in peril, rapidity in conceiving a good solution to a problem, and in modifying the plan chosen according to circumstances, resolution in action, a judicious use of the different arms, an exact valuation of the opposing forces, above all things a conscientious study of the ground, and knowing how to make use of it to attain his object, together with the personal courage to lead his men-at-arms at the decisive moment.

Hawkwood was at that time nearly seventy years of age, and yet he thought and acted with the vigour of the most spendid youth.

Having rendered such signal service to the Lord of Padua, he had a perfect right to expect some recognition, but things turned out differently. In his own interest

---

* The chronicler describes them in this manner: ' a white and blue striped standard, in which is the device of cockle-shells (which pilgrims wear round their hats) and a blue flag with two white deer's horns with a golden star in the centre.' He attributes both these to Hawkwood, but the latter notoriously belongs to the Ubaldini; we may then question the exactness of the colors in the standards which should have corresponded to the arms of the English Condottiere (see note, page 83).

Francesco da Carrara did not fail to ask Hawkwood's best   1387.
advice how to carry on the campaign, and by following
his instructions the Veronese territory again passed into
the power of the Paduans; while Francesco Novello who
would insist, contrary to his opinion, in passing the fortified moat of San Bonifacio, suffered considerable losses.

There were however serious dissentions between Carrara and his captain. The *Chronicle of Treviso* goes so
far as to assert that if the Florentines had not intervened,
Hawkwood would have been beheaded by Carrara, — an
incredible statement.

According to Ricotti, the disgust of Hawkwood was
occasioned by an alliance of Carrara with Visconti, towards
whom, Sir John maintained rancour, — a doubtful statement.*

The Paduan chroniclers, instead, simply say, that the
contract of Hawkwood terminated at the end of April and
that he was obliged to return to Florence where he was
made captain-general, — an incomplete statement.

During that campaign the Florentines had not forgot-
ten their favorite captain: they endeavoured to show in
many ways that they preserved their faith in him and
cultivated his friendship, having a care for his private
interests besides punctually handing him the pay contracted
for. They wrote to him not to make another contract
with the Carraras without first giving them notice, so that   January 10.
they might take the necessary measures, and at the expi-
ration of the term he did not fail to place himself at their
disposal.

Then some would have preferred to dismiss him with
thanks, promising to give him the first choice whenever

---

* In fact, in consequence of the alliance the captains Ubaldini and Ugolotto Biancardo must have come to the aid of Carrara, but we know that
they were in his service from 1386. Hawkwood had already left Padua when
the alliance took place, by means of which the Conte di Virtù was enabled
to cheat the Carrara family out of the state, and wrest their power from them.

1387.
May 1st.

they should need a captain : but as the necessity might unexpectedly arise, the decision to elect him for six months prevailed.

This was pleasing to Hawkwood, for he was disgusted with the Carraras. That he was not duly paid his salary we cannot believe: in such a case he was not the man to go away without obtaining it by force. It was more probable that he was displeased about the ransoms of the numerous prisoners of rank made at Castagnaro ; for three days after the battle Carrara had published an edict that the mercenaries were to give the names of all the prisoners, and not to dispose of them without his permission ; then Carrara wanted them all at his own disposal, paying the ransoms it is true, but perhaps not so high as those demanded by the captor to whom they belonged.

It is certain that Hawkwood left the service of Carrara, feeling himself in some manner defrauded of his right.

June 16.

In fact the " Ten " of the Florentine *balia* wrote to the Lord of Padua recommending, with trust in his justice, the rights of Hawkwood, whom they had always found an upright and faithful man.

On its own account the Commune of Florence lent itself very willingly to favor the interests of Hawkwood,

January 10.

by facilitating the sale of his possessions, after having however verified that his title as proprietor was a just one ; but the relative proceedings are too interesting not to be made the subject of a special chapter.

XXX.

LIQUIDATION OF PROPERTY.
THE ENGLISH IN THE SERVICE OF THE POPE.

[*Provvigioni* of the Commune of Florence in the State Archives — *Historical Archives for the Neapolitan provinces.* 12th year, extracted from the registers of the Anjou chancery — *Consulte e pratiche, Deliberazioni e condotte* of the Commune of Florence — GREGOROVIUS, *History of Rome in the Middle Ages* — State Archives of Florence. *Dieci di balìa, Legazioni,* v. 1.]

During so many years of war, between stipends, fees, annuities, profits on the pay of the soldiers, tithes on spoil, and direct plunder, ransoms of prisoners, with every kind of means * (some of which would not be edifying, and besides it would be useless to discuss their legitimacy), Hawkwood must have made a fortune more than sufficient for the needs of his family. He had thus been able to invest considerable sums in landed property, without counting Montecchio and other fortresses taken and held by him on the territory of Arezzo.

But if we may believe the declarations made before the Priors of Florence in an authentic document, he found himself hampered by a considerable debt. Nor do we wonder at his pecuniary embarrassments: for a man of his stamp it was easier to make much money, than to keep that which had been gained, whether it were ill gained or well. We know that adventurers after having made extortions, from city and country, generally fell easily into the net of the usurer. Now there were in Florence usurers with a capacity to spirit away from Hawkwood those glittering florins which Spinello the treasurer had so often counted out to him on the part of the Commune.

We will sum up the tenor of the document according

1387.

February 5.

---

* We do not know for what especial merit a certain Guglielmo di Andrea of Avignon left Hawkwood a legacy of 20 gold florins in his will dated August 16 138....

1387.   to the text preserved amongst the *Provvigioni* of the Florentine Commune :

John Hawkwood and his wife Donnina Visconti represent to the Priors, that John being in debt for a very large sum of money to several Florentine citizens, whom he desires to pay according to honor and duty, but is unable to do so without selling the undermentioned property, which they cannot sell because they can find no one who will guarantee the sale, by standing bail for them (as strangers); they therefore supplicate that the officers of the diminution of debts on the *monti* of the Commune * shall be retained in the quality of syndics of the Commune for selling and alienating; — that the said official syndics — or even two parts of them whenever the others shall be absent or not forthcoming — may proceed to the sale in the manner and form which seems best to them, and receive the price, or cause it to be received; and that they shall charge John, his wife, and heirs, and the respective possessions, for the expenses of evictions and defence; — that with the price received they may be able to pay the creditors of the said John (with his consent however), and those shall be considered creditors and to the amount which shall be declared by the aforesaid officials, and the residue, if any, shall be given to the said John ; — that if the latter should not consent to the payment of the creditors declared as such by the syndics, these shall keep the money in hand until they shall agree together; — that the sales so effected shall enjoy all the privileges and advantages of other sales hitherto made by the officials or syndics deputed by the Commune to superintend the affairs of absent and fugitive persons; — that thus the property sold shall not on any plea be taken away from the purchasers nor shall they be evicted or their right be in

---

* The *monti* was a communal debt like our national debt, of which the capital was not paid back, but interest paid to the shareholders.— (*Translator.*)

any manner contested, and that they shall not be molested in the proprietorship or possession of the said property; — that the magistrates shall not admit or lend ear to any one who dares to act contrary to this, but shall absolutely repulse the action under penalty of 500 lire of small florins, besides the nullification of the act.

Excepting that any one who considers himself wronged by the said sales may have recourse to, and get redress at the office of the Mercanzia, provided that he make the appeal within 15 days from the sale publicly announced by the herald of the Commune. The counselors of the Mercanzia, within three days from the appeal shall elect and add to themselves two merchants, citizens and Guelphs at pleasure, for each of the five greater arts, under penalty of 50 lire of small florins.

The which counselors and adjuncts, or even two parts of them, together in concert, shall under penalty of 1000 lire of small florins, examine and decide within one month from the appeal. And that the decision shall not be delayed by their absence, the official Judge of the Mercanzia, on the petition of the appellants, shall assemble in his own house the counselors and their adjuncts until the decision be made, under penalty of 100 lire of small florins. But the aforesaid 15 days having elapsed, all appeal shall be inadmissible.

Here follows the description of the property:

" A *podere* (farm) with houses both high and low, courtyards, *loggia,* dove-cot, garden, and walled stables for the master, with two separate houses for the workmen; together with arable land, vineyards and cane plantation, with trees, fruit trees and others, in the parish of San Donato di Torre near Florence, in the place called *in Polverosa,* bounded by moats the first and second on the Via di Polverosa, the third on the high road.

1387.

" A piece of arable land with a house facing the aforesaid *podere,* with the Via Polverosa between them, — the *podere* and the bit of ground together is said to be of a hundred and fifteen *sestari* (an ancient Roman measure) or nearly so by line.

" A *podere* with houses, tower, and arable land, vineyards, and plantations in the place called *la Rocchetta,* in the parish of Santa Maria Maddalena, in the Commune of Poggibonsi, near the river Elsa.

" Two other *poderi* with houses and trees in the same parish and Commune, in the place called *Castiglioni.*

" Another palace, with vineyards and other *poderi,* together with pieces of wooded land in the *Piano di Campi,* parish of San Lorenzo; these other *poderi* are seven in number; one with a house in the place called *Migliarino,* another in Petriccio, two near the river Elsa, and one in a place called *Caselle* or *Maltraversi.*"

From this it appears that all these lots formed dependencies of the farm and residence of Rocchetta.

They were in fact two considerable possesions, that of San Donato near Florence * and that of Rocchetta in the Commune of Poggibonzi in the Val d' Elsa.

In conformity to the dispositions of the Signoria already affirmed, the Priors consented to the request, probably already agreed to with the procurators of Hawkwood and Donnina, adding only that the consent of the conjugal couple should precede, concur with, and succeed the sales.

From ulterior documents it results that the sale was not effectuated. Hawkwood must have made an arrangement, and have silenced the creditors with the considerable gains of successive campaigns, or perhaps he found it sufficient to realise the urban lordships he possessed at

---

* It is very near the locality on the right of the Mugnone which in our days forms the princely suburban residence of Demidoff.

Naples, Capua and Aversa; for almost at this same time
he demanded of the Crown there the license to sell some
beni burgensatici to the Admiral Giacomo di Marzano, to
be able to pay a debt of 2930 florins which he had borrowed from the Admiral: this license was granted to him.

1387.

October 17.

From this Florentine " deed " we gather that part of
the property was in the name of Donnina Visconti, perhaps
acquired with her wedding portion.

No house is cited within the walls of Florence; which
would lead us to suppose that Hawkwood had no property
in the city, and that he was inscribed in the gonfalon of the
Golden Lion only for the payment of extraordinary personal
taxes; * of which we shall find a confirmation later.**

After the victory on the Adige, Hawkwood returned
to the banks of the Arno where he wielded his captain's
bâton in peace; there was a thought of giving him something to do, to make use of him as it were, by sending him
with Rinaldo Orsini and a few troops to conquer the city
of Naples for their ally Queen Margherita of Durazzo, who
asked for money, but nothing was done.

July 6.

Septemb. 18.

He was instead paid 1200 florins for the fourteenth
year of his life annuity, and another 1200 for *the new
contracts* of the present *condotta,* and it is noteworthy that
in the analogous warrant he is designated *olim capitaneo
compagniæ anglicorum in Italia militantium.*

Thus we have the official confirmation of a fact verified some time since, that from an English condottiere
Hawkwood had become captain of war to the Florentines.

The veterans of the White Company were dispersed,
and served in this field or that, either individually or in
small brigades.

The Englishman Beltoft had gathered together several

---

* See pages 182 and 192.   ** See pages 274 and 275.

of his countrymen in the service of the Pope, and these were totally defeated by Rinaldo Orsini and Bertrand de la Sale, the Gascon (the former leader of the Bretons), so that the Englishmen John Guernock, Johnny *Boutillier* (Butler?), Johnny *Trichil* (?), John Liverpool, Richard *Gus* (Goss?) and others, abandoning Beltoft, passed for the consideration of 7800 florins into the service of Florence, and under the command of their glorious old countryman; and another Englishman Nicholas Payton followed them.

The Florentines now began to discuss another arrangement in hiring Hawkwood; they would have liked to augment his salary, and only pay it when they needed his services, but once more prudence overcame parsimony, and he was engaged for another year as captain of war. Successive commissions established the monthly stipend at 500 florins, without prejudice to other higher sums which might be accorded to him, and without any obli- gation to find men or horses.

It was a wise course, for Bertrand de la Sale came plundering on the Pisan territory, and Hawkwood had the charge of keeping him at bay and not allowing him to treat Florentine territory in the same way, which charge he fulfilled.

His personal brigade was small and not in good order: it only numbered eighty two lances, and for defects and fines, resulting from the review (which was held periodi- cally for the stipendiaries), 104 florins, 16 soldi, and 8 danari were confiscated from the pay. As captain of war however he had the disposal of sufficient forces, so that he was able to concede a hundred lances to the Pisans who were menaced by Beltoft.

With the new year the latter had put together a strong company in which Germans predominated, and having made a league with Bertrand de la Sale and the German Averard (Landau?) *della Campana,* they extorted 34,000 florins from Siena, Lucca, and Pisa: then encamping on Perugian ground, they were making negotiations to enter the pay of Pope Urban VI, who had come through Genoa from Avignon, with a numerous escort in which the five hundred horse furnished by Beltoft soon figured.

This constituted a peril to the Florentines, who sent Hawkwood to encamp between Cortona and Perugia with orders to hold all the men-at-arms equipped and ready to march, and at the same time they dispatched Vieri di Pepo, ambassador at Perugia, to see if he could come to an understanding with Beltoft and take him into their pay. But by order of the Pope the Florentine ambassador was arrested and ill-treated.

The Signoria then sent the commissary Vanni Vecchietti to Hawkwood with instructions to beg him to write to Beltoft communicating the event, showing the blame which would be attributed to him, and urging him to seek satisfaction.

Then Vecchietti was to make Hawkwood give him an escort of thirty horse to Perugia, where he should seek Beltoft, and speak to him to the same effect, and thus fulfil the mission which Vieri di Pepo had been unable to execute.

The scheme had its effect; the Company of Beltoft was hired by the Pope, who wanted to attempt that enterprise at Naples which for centuries was the cause of so many Italian wars and foreign invasions, but he held himself bound also to the Florentines in certain circumstances.

CARLO VISCONTI AND THE POPE'S ENGLISHMEN
UNDER HAWKWOOD'S ORDERS.

[MINERBETTI, *Chronicle* — *Consulte e pratiche* of the Commune of Florence — *Deliberazioni e condotte* — *Chronicon siculum italicunum* — GRAZIANI, *Perugian chronicle* — Diary of the ANONYMOUS FLORENTINE — GHIRARDACCI, *Storie bolognesi* — AMMIRATO, *Florentine history* — Florentine State Archives, *Dieci di balia, Legazioni*, vol. I.]

1388. Whilst Hawkwood was in camp near Cortona, his brother-in-law Carlo Visconti, the son of Bernabò, was advancing in that direction, on his return from Germany where he had attempted to get together some soldiers for an attack upon the usurper the Conte di Virtù.

At the time he only had sixty mounted soldiers with him and on his way he had stayed a few days in Florence in an hostelry where he acquired a character of *being a stupid and low kind of man,* and the Florentines with their usual prudence, not wishing to compromise themselves with the Lord of Milan, for the sake of a pretender who had not very high prospects in view, had not associated much with him : on the contrary they had given the commissaries instructions to draw him away.

At Cortona he doubtless tried to ingratiate himself with his brother-in-law, and to plan out the revenge which they shared in common, and it is probable that Uguccione de' Casali, Lord of Cortona, in entertaining him so kindly did so more in respect for the condottiere, than pity for the exile. Besides being a condottiere, Hawkwood was moreover a formidable neighbour, and owned the Castle of Montecchio near Cortona.

The Florentines themselves thought that Hawkwood would yield to Carlo's arguments ; for at the end of May he asked for leave of absence, but although there was no longer danger from Beltoft's Company, they would not grant it, because *it seemed he wanted to insult the Conte di Virtù, which would be dangerous.* In fact the Count, might have held the Florentines responsible if they had granted him leave. On the other hand, not to offend Hawkwood, they determined not to inform the Count of what they were doing on his behalf, and to ask Hawkwood how long he wished to continue his engagement as captain at 500 florins a month, and what guarantee he desired.

Now where subtilty and subterfuge were concerned they were in their element; still they did not know precisely what the captain's ideas were, only they began to doubt whether he intended to go into Apulia against the French Anjou party for Queen Margherita.

Some wished to dismiss him, because his troops were doing all kinds of damage, besides which it was very expensive.* Others feared the enmity of the King of France if he should go into Apulia, and the hostility of the Count di Virtù, if he went into Lombardy. But the majority were inclined to let him go, provided that the Commune should make sure of having a captain in case of need.

Not being able to acquire this assurance in any other manner, he was for the time being refused leave of absence by the *Requisiti.*

Later on this matter was again discussed, and it was decided to let him go, but *secretly,* so that he should seem to be making use of his rights, as he had done before.

Meanwhile a very numerous company was gathering around Hawkwood. Urban VI had started from Perugia towards Tivoli with Beltoft's stipendiaries, declaring his intention of marching upon Naples. There were a thousand

1388.

May 30.

June.

July.

1382.

1388.

August 2.

---

* 5600 florins were paid to Hawkwood for the month of June, and on the 1ˢᵗ of July he received 12,000 more for three months, as the pay of 400 lances and 500 between foot soldiers and cross-bowmen, without bringing into account 1200 florins paid him on July 9ᵗʰ, for the 15ᵗʰ year of his annuity.

1388.

lances, many of them veterans of the " White Company," and the Pope, in order to flatter them, rode with them, armed, in a white coat, with his *bâton* in his hand, just as if he were their real captain.

But scarcely had they reached Narni, when discord broke out amongst the Englishmen : either through a sentiment of loyalty for their engagements, or because they mistrusted the Pope's promises of payment, all the *caporali* (commanders) refused to follow Beltoft and the Pope, alleging as their reason that the Company had agreed to be at the service of the Florentines, under certain circumstances. Now if they passed into the Kingdom of Naples, they would not have been able to fulfil this eventual obligation, for this reason more than two thousand of them set out to Perugia : Beltoft and his brigade, consisting of two hundred men, alone remaining with the Pope.

From Perugia they passed on to Cortona, where they proclaimed as their captain Sir John Hawkwood, who was already captain of war to the Florentines. He however was not pleased at seeing his Company increase in this way, for after he had accepted the *bâton* of command, many Italians and Germans had joined it.

August 18.

Therefore the " Ten of war " commissioned Biliotto Biliotti to go and tell Hawkwood that the number of English brigades being excessive, they preferred to obtain permission from the Signoria and Councils for Hawkwood to go and perform the services already discussed with him. And if they should not be able to obtain permission, they would send another commissary with orders, which would satisfy the brigades.

Meanwhile Biliotti was to be sure and flatter the knights, " to keep them amiable with fair speaking," and to inform the Signoria how he found them disposed, and how many,

August 21.

and who, they were. The Councils and Signoria were unanimous in wishing to grant the dismissal proposed

by the " Ten " ; the only condition they made was, that
Hawkwood should promise not to injure the allies of Florence, and to obtain the same pledge from as many as he
could of the highest officers.

1888.

The adventurers had no difficulty in making these
promises, but as for keeping them, that was quite another
thing.

In fact while the " Ten " were sending detailed instructions to Biliotti, concerning the payment of 3000 florins to Hawkwood and his brigade, so that they could
pass from the district of Cortona, and Città di Castello,
suggesting to him minute precautions so that the *procure* *
of the knights, or of whoever was to receive the pay for
them, should be according to rule, they added : " Reprove
Hawkwood, because by means of letters and also personally, he had requested 4000 florins ** from Siena, thus
breaking his word, and tell him that he may now do
whatever he likes with his brigade as we can make no
further use of it." And in fact, whilst Hawkwood was
passing Città di Castello, and was on Perugian territory,
the Florentines prepared to dismiss him, always however,
doing it in such a manner as to evade the enmity of the
King of France, and of the Count of Virtù. The latter was
very suspicious of Carlo Visconti's doings at Cortona, and
it seems he attempted to remove his cousin by one of his
favorite practices — poison.

September 6.

Septemb. 16.

They relate that having promised and deposited 30,000
florins, Maestro Gioioso, the physician of Casali, Lord of
Cortona, let himself be induced to put some poison into
certain figs which were brought to Carlo for breakfast.
At the moment when he was preparing to eat them, a
letter was brought to him from Hawkwood which put him

* Power of Attorney. — (*Translator.*)
** See Documents LXIII and LXIV.

1388.

on his guard against poison for himself, and for the Lord of Cortona, without naming the traitor.*

Maestro Gioioso being discovered and convicted, was put to the torture on a car all through Cortona and then quartered.

August 8.

Carlo Visconti having put together a numerous brigade had united with Hawkwood, so that the latter had more than 4000 cavalry at his disposal, but the hour was not yet come for revenge on the Conte di Virtù, and those 4000 horsemen dispersed, damaging Tuscany, the Papal States, Umbria, and the Marches.**

In spite of reproofs the Florentines could not resolve to do without a man whom they judged to be most capable of defending them in any eventuality, and they were less disposed than ever since the proceedings of the Conte di

---

* From this and other facts already known to the reader, it results that Hawkwood had a well organized police. From his castle at Montecchio he could easily superintend all that was going on at Cortona.

** Here, according to the learned Rawdon Brown, should be recorded the exploit of 800 Englishmen, between men-at-arms and archers, who calling themselves the ˙brigade of St. George˙ sent Sir Robert Felton (a nobleman in the suite of the reigning Queen of England) from the camp at Serra near Fabriano, to offer their services a long way off to John of Moravia patriarch of Aquileja, knowing that he had to fight with his rebels (in truth he too wanted to wrest something from the Carraras of Padua, already reduced to great straits by the hostile coalition of the Count of Virtù and the Venetians). Felton passing by Venice procured recommendations from Pietro Morosini. The letter of proposal is signed by Sir John Armsthorp, John Barry, Robert Lock, Roger Baker, and Richard Swinford; and Brown wonders that no mention is made of Hawkwood who had been lately elected captain general of the English.

But Brown seems to have mistaken the facts. There still exist in the Archives of the Chapter-house at Cividale the above mentioned letter of August 28th, and that of Morosini dated September 17th, as usual with no indication of the year. It cannot however be 1388, because Morosini's letter refers to relations already established in several affairs with the patriarch, and he did not come to Italy till September 23rd of that year. With more foundation, the Abbé Bianchi, a well-known historian of Friuli, assigns the date 1393 to both letters; hence those 800 Englishmen had nothing to do with Hawkwood, but belonged to the great Company of St. George which was formed in April and dissolved in September 1392.

Virtù, whose unbridled ambition it was easy to imagine, 1388. after his having caused the total ruin of the Carraras of Padua. On account of these fears and in accord with the Bolognese (to whom Hawkwood had given the good counsel not to come to fighting with Ubaldini's Company, but rather to make a composition in money), they paid 3764 florins October 30. for a month's stipend for 1800 horses and 10,000 florins for their pledge not to injure, — in the form of a company, — either the Commune or its allies for two years.

At the end of the month the danger of hostility on Visconti's part seemed to increase, and in the Florentine councils very few could now have preferred sending Hawkwood to Naples by giving him money. Most of them insisted warmly on the expedience of retaining him at their disposal; preferably at a low price, then a *fair stipend,* but finally *at any price.* Rinaldo Gianfigliazzi said: " Don't dismiss him or the Lord of Padua will be discouraged; " and Franceschino degli Albizi used evangelical language saying : " Be vigilant because ye know not the hour, and take care that ye have oil in your lamps ; " in other terms the famous admonition of Oliver Cromwell.

Meanwhile Hawkwood moved slowly towards the Kingdom of Naples, where Queen Margherita, regent for her son Ladislao, offered him high terms. He was near Trevi Novemb. 10. and was making negotiations to take Beltoft under him, with two hundred lances of his brigade, for which he asked 5000 florins from the Florentines. They sent Boccaccio Alamanni to tell him that 1000 florins had already been paid to his procurators Johnny Trekell and Pierotto Fedini ; and that the other 4000 were ready at Perugia and would be paid as soon as it was made clear to them that Beltoft was effectually under his orders.

Alamanni was also commissioned to make Hawkwood restore a load of skins and the mules seized by the English from certain Florentine muleteers.

1388.   He must have received oral instructions to search out
the Condottiere's intentions: and it is certain that Ghino
Early   di Ruberto was sent to Hawkwood's camp with written
in December.
instructions of great importance, besides the order for the
restitution of a mule belonging to Donato Acciaioli which
was taken by Carlo Visconti's soldiers now included in his
brother-in-law's Company with his brigade.

XXXII.

THE NEAPOLITAN ENTERPRISE.

[*Consulte e pratiche* of the Commune of Florence — D. MARIA MANNI, Biography of Hawk-
wood in MURATORI [*R. I. S.*], v. II of the *Appendix* — SUMMONTE, *History of Naples* —
MINERBETTI, *Chronicle* — *Chronicon siculum vaticanum* — State Archives of Florence,
Duci di balia, Legazioni, v. I.]

The instructions to Ghino di Ruberto were to the effect
that he should with the opportune information "confirm
Hawkwood *in his good resolution* not to pass into the Kingdom of Naples." The Signoria had in truth reason to doubt
him, but they dissimulated; in any case the orator had to
touch a very delicate note in intimating to the Condottiere
that the events in Lombardy and Tuscany were entangling
themselves in such a form that, *the event which he had long
desired, would soon happen, and if he stayed in this country,
good would accrue to himself and to his friends.* They showed
by this their knowledge of the profound hatred against
Gian Galeazzo cherished by Hawkwood and that he now
intended to make common cause with his brother-in-law
Carlo, who had entered into his Company and that his
day-dream was a great war against the Conte di Virtù.

Ghino di Ruberto was besides instructed to suggest to
Hawkwood that instead of going into the Kingdom of
Naples, he should send to Otho of Brunswick (who was

already fighting there against the Anjou party) to withdraw him from thence and take him into his company: *they two together would do great things, considering the valour of Messer Otho and his enmity to the Conte di Virtù.*

And he was to inform him that without going elsewhere, he might winter in the March of Romagna, where *there was good living,* and that the Count of Urbino had promised to receive them amicably and find them provisions.

If Hawkwood displayed a wish to follow up the march towards Naples, he was to try and frustrate it, discouraging the English knights by alleging the famine and discords down there. On his return he was to bring news whether Beltoft had entered the Company, and all kinds of information as to the state of the troops.

The impressions brought back by Ghino were that " the Englishman was inclined to go into the Kingdom; indeed he made no mystery of it," saying " that in the affairs of Lombardy *one must act and not merely make a show* (in truth he spoke wisely) alleging that we might always have him back again, and that he would return stronger and with a better brigade."

Therefore the Signoria dispatched Giovanni Orlandi, who to distract Hawkwood from his projects was to give amongst other reasons " that little honor would accrue to him from it, and considering how much he had talked of going into Lombardy in past times, it would seem he was postponing it from cowardice or some other cause."

If Hawkwood demanded money in return for his consent he was to politely decline the request, observing that in the preceding month the Commune had lent him 5000 florins merely to oblige him, and strengthen his troops; so he must now be obliging in his turn.

But the mission of Orlandi was fruitless, so much so
that Niccolò Ricoveri deplored that it had become difficult to retain Hawkwood, as every one desired.

They made still another attempt: Pera Baldovinetti was sent, with instructions minutely mercantile. If Hawkwood insisted on having money, Pera was to endeavour cautiously to find out how much he expected, and to reduce it to the lowest possible figure, rather lending than giving it, and thus to extract a promise from him not to act until he had received an answer. If he hold out, then promise him 5000 florins as a loan, — and if he be not content with a loan, then offer 3000 florins as a gift; but oh Pera! take great care! "before you offer him money, hear from himself what he wants, and do not offer the said sum all at once." If in spite of all this he persists in wanting to go, stop him by asking time to hear from Florence, whether she wants to hire him for herself.

These were the instructions dictated at the Palazzo Vecchio, but thought out in Calimala;* there was however one added of a secret-police character: "shew him the letters which we give you, and which are written by an English person, so that no one may cause him to break up his brigade. And tell him that Beltoft was here, and wanted to be released from his obligations to us, saying he wished to go with the other Englishmen. And that then he went to the Conte di Virtù, offering to draw away from Hawkwood the greater part of the English troops now with him;" which information was not best adapted to persuade Hawkwood to bring his men, where he ran a risk of seeing them bribed to leave him.

Any way with two thousand lances hired by Queen Margherita till May, he marched rapidly towards Naples to help Alberico da Barbiano, and Otho of Brunswick in conquering that capital.

---

* A street in Florence where the 'Arte' of the Wool Staplers had its head quarters. — (*Translator.*)

He arrived at Capua with 1300 horse, Otho of Brunswick was at Aversa with another 3000. By orders given in the Queen's letters they concentrated at Caivano and marched with 5000 combatants towards Naples. 1389. Beginning of March.

The capital was held for Louis d'Anjou by the viceroy Montjoye, a man resolute to defend himself, although the garrison (for the most part composed of the Gascons of Bernard de la Sale) did not exceed 1100 horse, and had to blockade Castel Capuano, where the flag of the Durazzo had been raised. The citizens however were well disposed to resist, so Montjoye was able to make a sally from Porta Nolana and menaced the flank of the enemy as they marched, having now reached as far as a place called Liburna; here they halted two or three hours, sending forward a recognition: when seeing the danger from Montjoye's offensive movement Brunswick sounded the retreat, and they drew back to encamp between Afragola and Aversa. March 14.

The identical advance and the identical retreat were repeated, perhaps they calculated on a sally of the little garrison shut up in Castel Capuano. March 23.

Then the fleet of Durazzo (four galleys and five brigantines) conducted by Luigi di Capua appeared in the gulf, and took up its position behind Posilipo: the following night it approached Ponte Guizzardo and was placed in communication with the army. At the hour of *tierce* next morning, there were Otho and Hawkwood again at Liburna scouring the plain of Casanova up to Naples. Two hundred horse and as many foot came out of the city, and a glorious skirmish took place (*pulcerrimum badaluctum*). The troops of Durazzo left two knights prisoners, and re-entered the camp at Afragola without honor. March 31. April 2.

The garrison at Castel Capuano meanwhile was in great straits: they engaged to surrender if no succour arrived within five days. At dawn on the day before this time April 8. April 12.

1389.   was fulfilled the Durazzo party attempted a general action, and the army menacingly approached; Otho and Hawkwood attacked the city at Casanova, at San Pietro ad Ara, and in Borgo Nuovo. About forty of the bravest men risked a sally from Castel Capuano, but some of them were killed, others taken prisoners, and the rest had the good fortune to be able to re-enter the fortress. The infantry, crossbowmen, and *saccomanni*, came out of Naples against the assailing forces, and they came to blows in a skirmish, in which the troops of Otho and Hawkwood were repulsed with sensible loss on all the line, and constrained to make a fourth fruitless retreat to Afragola. The army on its side could do nothing, and the attack on the town having failed, they placed themselves further back at a distance of two arrows' flight from the city. To sum up, it was a decisive failure, so much so that Castel Capuano surrendered to the Anjou party next day.

Meanwhile the Florentines recommended " Madame's state " (*lo stato di Madama*) to Hawkwood, for they favoured Queen Margherita rather than the French Anjou branch. A certain Benedetto di Nicola, to whom this mission was confided, was told also to insist, in praying Hawkwood to come to an understanding and unite with Otho of Brunswick, saying clearly when he could come to Florence and with how large a brigade.

February 25.

The rupture with the Conte di Virtù was felt now to be inevitable, so the *Requisiti* recommended the " Ten " to recall Hawkwood by all means, sending him orders and money so that he could bring with him other troops besides his own. Donato Strada was sent to him on the following embassy : " for reasons which regard his honor, utility and state, he (Sir John Hawkwood) must come to this country without delay, *to do those things which he has always desired.* As he has promised, sworn, and sealed (without

March 6.

March 15.

doubt in answer to Benedetto di Nicola), we wish him to be
in our service with a company, for four months, commencing
from the day he arrives in the plain of Viterbo and Montefiascone (the Tuscan frontier), when the contract will
be given, and sworn, and the review held. Let him be
in the aforesaid place on the 1st of May with troops up
to 1000 lances, with foot soldiers and cross-bowmen, in all
amounting to 5000."

If Strada could not see him before the 11th of April,
he was to give Hawkwood twenty days to arrive at the
place assigned. The money would be brought by a commissary to Viterbo.

He was to recommend him to accept in the brigade
Messer Piero della Corona, Ivon Giovanni Brigante, Pansart
and some other knights " who are great friends of his,
and have sent a confidential messenger from Naples to
say they would willingly enter the service of Florence."
Excepting Corona, all those who thus offered to pass into
the service of the enemy were Bretons hired by the Anjou
party for the defence of Naples.

Finally Strada must agree with Hawkwood on the
best method of hiring also Otho of Brunswick, trying meanwhile to procure from the latter the release of a Florentine named Iacopo di Zanobi, who had been taken by his
brigade. He was not to speak of his commissions *to any
person in the world,* and the paper of demands to Hawkwood must be drawn up by a notary. Taking into consideration that, owing to the distance and the war, the
messenger might meet with misfortunes, an identical commission was given also to Ghino di Ruberto, only he was
authorised to name another meeting place instead of
Viterbo.

Although the enterprise of the conquest of Naples
might by this time be considered a failure, Hawkwood did

1389.   not hurry to move at the request of the Florentines. He
sent envoys to excuse himself, and as to *Della Corona* and
the Bretons from Naples, he proposed that Florence should
treat directly with them, and hire them into her own service.

April 21.   Then Guido Cavalcanti was dispatched to renew, by a
legal act, the recall of Hawkwood within twenty days:
and agree that the Bretons should be comprised in the
thousand lances granted to him. In this he ought to find
no difficulty as he had only five hundred at present : if he
wanted money, he would find a month's pay at Rome (less
if possible), but he must be made to start without delay.

    In fact, after receiving 3000 florins he took leave of
May 16.   Queen Margherita, and moving his brigade slowly and reluctantly to Aversa and Rome, he then took the Orvieto road.
not without promising Urban VI to respect the territory
June 1 and 3. of the Church and especially that of the Perugians.* Cavalcanti was in a letter desired to complain to Hawkwood of his dilatoriness, which was not in conformity
with his contracts, and by way of hastening the captain's
movements he was told to say that the rest of the money
would be paid after the review of the troops, because before that " they could not decide how many they would
have to pay for," and that the review must be held in
the plain of Trevi or at Borgo San Sepolcro. " And take
great care how you have given, or will give the money."

June 8.   An ample comment followed these recommendations in
minute instructions to the commissaries Vettori and Ia-
copi ** about the hiring and inspecting of the soldiers, above

---

* The pontifical brief relating to this pledge was published by Ghizzi
in his *Historical notes on the castle of Montecchio;* the last sentence is noteworthy : *Ita velis attendere cum effectu proinde facturus quod finem tuam decet,
sed et nobis non mediocriter placiturus;* in these words Urban VI seems to
allude to Hawkwood's projects against Gian Galeazzo Visconti, and in a measure to approve of them. The address is also interesting : *Dilecto filio, nobili
viro Joanni Haukendwod dicto* Acut *nonnullarum gentium armorum capitaneo.*

** We report them entire in Document LXV, as they serve to give an
exact idea of the usual proceedings in such circumstances.

all insisting that the commissaries should in all these operations make a point of the personal presence of Sir John
Hawkwood, Johnny Butler, Liverpool, and several other
worthy knights.

The inspection over, Hawkwood was requested to come
to Florence and consult with the Signoria: and in fact
he came, since it was to treat of hiring him (for four   June 10.
months, in *form of a company*), or at least to detain him
on Florentine territory in such a manner as not to provoke the enmity of other Tuscan cities, which otherwise
his soldiers might have injured.

They soon came to an understanding and " provided "   June 15.
to take 10,000 florins of the imposts on the *Distrettuali*
(i. e. the inhabitants of the Florentine district) and to put it
into the fund of the *condotta* to satisfy the engagement
made with Hawkwood.

The contract was the engagement of the Company for
six months, at the rate of 500 florins a month for the
captain; 9 florins for each of the 400 lances; 3 florins
for each of the 500 between foot soldiers and cross-bowmen.
None of the Company shall, during the term of contract
and the month succeeding it, be in any way molested for
debts contracted or misdemeanours committed before the
term (civil and criminal privileges in fact). Each one shall
have the faculty to obtain his dismissal within fifteen days,
on condition that he swear to return to his native country
or go beyond the seas. Hawkwood and his officers shall
be obliged to inform the Signoria of all that might come
to their knowledge, which is injurious to the Commune,
and, at Hawkwood's requisition, those who are disobedient
or do not serve dutifully, shall be expelled the ranks.

This concluded, the captain left Florence to join his   July 7.
troops between Cortona and Perugia.

XXXIII.

WAR IN TIME OF PEACE.

[VERCI, *Storia della Marca Trevigiana* — State Archives of Florence, *Dieci di balia, Legazioni*, v. I — *Consulte e pratiche* of the Commune of Florence — GREGOROVIUS, *History of Rome in Middle-ages* — MINERBETTI, *Chronic's*.]

1389.   Gian Galeazzo Visconti Count of *Virtù* could not have borne a title more inappropriate to his merits. Pretending an alliance with the Carraras and to aid them against the Scaligers, he had possessed himself of Verona and Vicenza, and had treasonably wrested from them their dominions, and the hereditary lordship of Padua. Old Francesco da Carrara, after having abdicated in favor of his son Francesco Novello, had become more the prisoner than the guest of Visconti; and Francesco Novello in his turn had been obliged to renounce in favor of Visconti the dominions usurped by him. He was thus able to save his life and by dissimulating prepare his revenge.

Francesco Novello experienced the most romantic vicissitudes in that hazardous journey from Lombardy to Florence, where he hoped to obtain valid support in attempting the recuperation of the State, but they do not enter into our subject; it is enough to say that he arrived safely in Florence with his wife, children and all his family, End of April. and with money and jewels to the amount of 140,000 ducats.

Here he was joined by his brother Conte Carrara and they remained a long time, fomenting in the Florentines their hostility to Gian Galeazzo; but although Florence was justly suspicious of the aggrandizement and ambition of the latter, they were not yet disposed to become open partizans of the Carraras, — that is to say to wage a war with Visconti.

Francesco Novello comprehended that he must bide his

time, and meanwhile he thought of passing into Croatia to secure the concurrence of his brother-in-law Stefano Count of Segna, but first of all he wished to take counsel with two famous enemies of the Conte di Virtù, — Carlo Visconti, and John Hawkwood, the former of whom was at Cortona, and the latter in his camp near there, or at his neighbouring castle of Montecchio; so Carrara with his brothers Conte and Rodolfo, and twenty horsemen went to Cortona.

Carlo Casali lord of Cortona, and Carlo Visconti not only received him well, but they also invited him to enter Hawkwood's Company with 200 lances. He excused himself on the score of wishing to travel to Croatia, and proposed instead that his brother Conte, also a good knight, should be engaged with 100 lances if Hawkwood were content. They were to give 50 ducats a lance, and he would find the remainder of their pay. Hawkwood, being called to Cortona, came at once from his castle at Montecchio, paying great respect to the Carraras; indeed he promised to Conte the *bâton* of Marshal, not only of the Company, but of all the field, when they should fight against the Conte di Virtù.

Thus the insolent career of Gian Galeazzo was secretly being undermined by many who had suffered from him, and who were already preparing arms while waiting their opportunity. Francesco Novello, resuming his perilous wanderings, passed into Germany, and to his sister the Countess of Segna at Modrussa in Croatia; from there he wrote to his brother Conte, to Carlo Visconti, and Hawkwood, recounting the progress of his schemes against their common enemy.

Meanwhile it was necessary that Hawkwood's Company should live at some one's expense. By means of 13,764 florins disbursed to him and Count Landau, the English

1389.   captain was bound not to molest either Florence or Perugia nor any other commune, and they were earnestly re-
July.   minded of this compact by the " Ten " (*Dieci di balia*).

It was therefore inevitable that he should inflict himself
on the Sienese, the more so as the soldiers of Count Conrad
Landau were added to his own troops. The Florentines
themselves had managed that this brigade should unite
July 25.   with Hawkwood, and the two proceed together; they were
in all 3000 horse and 1000 foot, and the Commune paid
them 20,000 florins for six months.

But the Florentines wished, at least in appearance, to
preserve good relations with Siena, and could not openly
consent to allow their condottieri to injure the inhabitants;
August 2. Simone Altoviti was therefore sent to Landau and Hawkwood with the embassy of preventing them from overriding
the territory of the Sienese, " who might impute the action
to Florence; " but they added " at least spread the report
that they were asked to do so by the Count of Soana (who
was in open hostility with Siena) or else that the Sienese
are collecting men-at-arms of the Conte di Virtù to do them
injury, and that they will not tamely wait to be beaten."

Matteo Arrighi and Lorenzo Machiavelli were sent with
August 3. analogous instructions.

The two condottieri, although ultramontanes and illite-
rate, easily comprehended the machiavelican Italian, and
without ado fell upon the people right up to the walls of
Siena,* replying to the Signoria that " they did not intend
to oppose the Sienese, but to go *against the troops of the
Conte di Virtù, who had offended them by their insolent vi-
tuperation.* It seems true that the Sienese, knowing the
feeling of Florence and Hawkwood towards Gian Galeazzo,
took as their war-cry in the skirmish "*Long live the Count
of Virtù, Count of Siena!*" And Hawkwood's men responded,

---

* They attempted, says Malevolti, to set fire to the gate of San Marco
and to penetrate into the city.

crying " *Long live the Count of Florence and Messer Carlo* "
(Visconti !).

The Florentines, who always wished to keep up appearances with the Sienese, insisted on openly reproving Hawkwood and Landau for these cries, denying that their men had a right to call themselves Florentine " seeing that they do so with the bad object of making mischief between us and our neighbours." Then they asked them, " *since they had avenged their honor* against the said people to respect the territory of Siena, as well as to desist from menaces to gain money from Pisa and Lucca." In short, Florence made a display of having nothing in common with the enterprise of those bands against Siena, and even blamed them publicly ; i. e. in the official instructions which passed through Siena to inform the Priors.

With extreme duplicity they gave Ormanno Foraboschi that same day the following secret commission : " When you are with Sir John Hawkwood and the Count (Landau), say to them alone and in secret, that as they are on Sienese ground and the people are so ill-disposed, we beg them to stay on the territory for a month, doing as much damage as possible." For this they offered a *backsheesh* of 1000 florins, reinforcements, provisions, and precise information respecting the Sienese forces, from whom the companies should gain some towns and not come to terms without first giving notice. Only they were to respect Pisa and Lucca.

To the commissary Francesco Rucellai they added " that the Company might by payment have provisions on the Florentine territory, although he must make a show of only conceding this by force, and if it should come to a fight and Hawkwood's army should get beaten, *which God forbid!* then he (the commissary) was to aid and assist them, by hastening the work of an hydraulic engineer (*maestro*), who had gone to Hawkwood to *cut off the water from the*

1389.   *city of Siena,* where corn and bread were already wanting."
That was how Italian communes treated each other in time
of peace ! *

Beginning   The difficulty was in making the troops respect the
of Septemb.   Florentine territory while devastating the Sienese. Complaints, either mild or severe, were of no use, nor were
the efforts of the commissaries Matteo Arrighi, Guido di
Tommaso, Biliotto Biliotti, and Lorenzo Machiavelli, to
keep them at least six or eight miles from the confines
of Florence ; some of the adventurers seemed disposed
to pass into the Maremma, but the English knights would
not hear of it, and it finished by consenting that the troops
might approach Florentine land when they needed provi-
Septemb. 26. sions, as long as they kept the camp on that of the Sienese.

The truth is that between Florence and Siena the marauders stole so much that they were able to sell 1500 oxen
by auction.

The two condottieri had commenced some mysterious
and delicate affair with the Florentine Signoria, a business
concerning which Guido di Tommaso and Lorenzo Machiavelli had secret instructions, both oral and written, for
Hawkwood and Landau had asked for a *citizen to whom
they wished to confide certain things;* we only know that
Machiavelli was sent to hear them, endeavouring to extract
the truth and sometimes holding separate interviews with
each in turn.

We know on the other hand that those famous brigands
were not all good fighting soldiers, and it required great
October 1st. caution in those who hired them to get them equipped
according to their compacts.**

While the Val d'Elsa was thus being devastated, another
company of English, Germans, and Italians led by Beltoft,

----

* See also Document LXVI.   ** See Document LXVII.

after having damaged the territory of Pisa for thirty   1389.
thousand florins, extorted thirteen thousand more to retire;
then Gambacorti lord of Pisa proposed the usual useless
remedy — a general league against the companies. To this
the Conte di Virtù, the Florentines, Sienese, and Bolognese
adhered, and amongst the compacts it was decided to dissolve
the great Company which was then under the orders of
Hawkwood and Landau. The Bolognese took 500 lances
at their expense, and the Florentines 300 with Count Landau and other knights.

As to Hawkwood, the following proposal was made in October 17.
the Florentine councils, by Alessio Franceschi in the name
of the "Ten of war," and the other ambassadors from
the congress of Pisa: "Considering the fame of Sir John
Hawkwood, the Signoria will to-morrow convoke the
councils (*collegi*) to deliberate on his *condotta,* and if the
Signoria deem it well, they will also call some citizens
into council, and the "Ten" (*Dieci di balia*) will also
assist."

His presence was not judged to be necessary, — on the
contrary they officially proclaimed the league against the
companies, so that he again went towards Apulia to re-enter
the service of the house of Durazzo.   October 19.

But 'ere long the relations of Florence with the Conte
di Virtù became so strained that no objection was made
to the proposal of Alessandro Niccolai: "Let us provide December 9.
ourselves a captain, and let him be one in whom the Commune can trust, — and the Commune has faith in Sir John
Hawkwood."

He was at Gaeta when the Florentine proposal reached
him; the moment he had so long desired had come: the
war with Gian Galeazzo now seemed inevitable, and the
Florentines turned to him to conduct their army, knowing
him to be the greatest leader of the times, and besides a
special enemy of the Count, and they entreated him to

bring with him his brother-in-law Carlo Visconti, hoping
that he would be of service in exciting rebellion among
the subjects of Gian Galeazzo.

XXXIV.

FIRST OPERATIONS AGAINST GIAN GALEAZZO.

[AMMIRATO. *History of Florence* — D. MARIA MANNI, Biography of Hawkwood in MURA-
TORI [*R. I. S.*], v. II of the *Appendix* — Dicci di balía, *Deliberazioni e condotte*, State
Archives of Florence — *Consulte e pratiche* of the Commune of Florence, ibid. —
POGGIO BRACCIOLINI, *History* — DELLA PUGLIOLA, *Bolognese chronicle* — *Delizie degli
eruditi*, v. XVI, Letter of the Florentines to the Duke of Bavaria — GHIRARDACCI,
Storie bolognesi — *Provvisioni* of the Commune of Florence — *Acciaioli papers*, Ash-
burnham MSS., Laurentian Library Florence — *Letters* of PIER PAOLO VERGERIO.]

1390.   The Count of Virtù had Carlo Malatesta in his pay as
captain general, with Iacopo dal Verme, Facino Cane,
Biancardo and Ubaldini, almost all the most noted condottieri: Hawkwood only was wanting, who in his own
person was capable of outweighing all the party and this
made him not a little anxious.

April.   Hawkwood on his part, having reached Rome without
opposition, was with reason doubtful whether the Sienese
or some other partisans of Visconti might not hinder him
from arriving in Florence; he escaped the difficulty with
his usual foresight, and sent men to several places to ask
for safe conducts, while he with long marches and great
fatigue took the unusual road through the Maremma instead. He lost a good many horses by the way, but arrived safe and sound at Volterra and then at Florence,
April 30.   where he was received with great joy by the citizens.

He was engaged for a year with two hundred lances,
and on the compact that if the request were made before the last thirty days of the agreement, he should be
obliged to serve also the following year. Among the other

obligations he assumed, he was bound to supply sentinels and guards, for night or day, as should be commanded. For the two years succeeding his engagement, he pledged himself not to act against the Commune, " *come compagnia* " i. e. as the captain of a company, and for six months not even as a stipendiary or as holding any commission.

For the rest they made the same conditions as on May 3rd 1387, with the addition of fifes and trumpets, for we have already seen that Hawkwood with good reason held to these accessories of military pomp.

Altogether we perceive that the Florentines were taking precautions, as though foreseeing a long and great war, and ere long they sent Hawkwood with his brigade and 500 cross-bowmen to the aid of Bologna and Romagna, where the arms of Visconti were beginning to make themselves felt, and the " battle was imminent."

These reinforcements were followed by another English brigade which was at Volterra, and the men-at-arms were called up from Sienese — the defence of the territory and its towns being entrusted to native infantry. They reserved a more convenient time to hire Beltoft and send him against Siena.

Hawkwood however insisted that they should keep a strict guard on that side, because Giovanni Ubaldini was there, — a condottiere of whom Hawkwood had a great opinion, deeming him to be worth a thousand of the best lances in his own person,[*] and he did not leave until he had planned a very wide strategic moat from Montopoli

---

[*] Giovanni Cavalcanti, an almost contemporaneous writer, mentions the advice of Hawkwood among the anecdotes published in the Appendix of his Florentine history, in the ' Documents of Italian history ' saying : ' This excellent man went most mornings to consult with the ' Ten of war,' and more often than not it fell out that the said captain gave advice to the Ten instead of the Ten giving orders to him. His attending the meetings shewed that he especially desired the good of the city.' Cavalcanti besides confirms the fact that the English Condottiere had organised a diligent service of military spies.

1390.

to the Arno for the defence of the lower valley of the Arno.*

May 14.

He arrived at Bologna with only an escort of 15 lances and forthwith betook himself to San Giovanni in Persiceto, where under Giovanni da Barbiano 1200 lances and 3000 infantry were assembled at the expense of the Florentines and Bolognese. The rumour of his arrival was enough to make the Visconti army abandon Crevalcuore, where they were really very well fortified. He profited by this to ravage the Modenese and Reggio lands, making raids for prisoners and cattle, and when Iacopo dal Verme, taking courage, had pressed on the Visconti

June 20.

army, as far as Samoggia a few miles from Bologna, he was soon on the defensive and encamped at the bridge of the Reno on the Via Emilia.

There, still in accord with Barbiano, he did not neglect to guard himself on all points, taking the best position, and garrisoning Casalecchio, occupying the bridge and pebbly bed of the Reno : — the enemy on his side fortifying himself with banks and deep moats.

Having obtained the consent of the Bolognese senate, Hawkwood sent Zuzzo the trumpeter to Dal Verme with a blood-stained glove, challenging him to come out to battle. Dal Verme declined the challenge twice with fierce abuse; the third time he kept the trumpeter prisoner for a night, but not feeling very safe, or from want of provisions, he removed from his position.** Hawkwood quickly followed, and overtook him, constraining him to

---

* They had in those days great faith in this kind of defensive obstacle. (See Matteo Villani, book IX, c. VIII: ˙ On the many moats made by the lords of Lombardy in the defence of their territory.˙)

** The fox would not meet him, and at night on 24th he slyly went away. (˙ Non volle la volpe, anzi adì 24 di notte si partì di furto.˙) Letter of June 27th from the ˙ Ten of war ˙ to Donato Acciaioli commissary in Val d'Elsa. (Laurentian Library, Ashburnham MSS.)

fight, while Barbiano attacked him on the flank; so that within two hours Dal Verme was beaten and put to flight, leaving as prisoners Facino Cane, Anghelino da Padule, fifty men-at-arms, and two hundred and twenty horses.

Not long after this a very important and pleasing piece of news arrived at the camp — i. e. that Francesco Novello had victoriously entered into Padua, thus regaining his city; a notice which was celebrated by large bonfires, blowing of trumpets, and other signs of rejoicing. There was indeed a great desire to meet the enemy again and give him battle, to which Bologna would have consented, but Florence prudently opposed it, holding that one should only fight when one is compelled to do so, or is perfectly sure of victory.

The Florentines instead deliberated how they could diminish useless expenses, discharge those stipendiaries who did not serve as well as they ought to do, and reinforce Hawkwood with troops and money, so that he could hold the field as far as the Po, or even cross it. On the other hand the progress of Carrara's army towards Vicenza and Verona had constrained the Conte di Virtù to recall his troops from beyond the Po; so that with 1000 lances, and 500 foot soldiers, Hawkwood could freely override Lombardy (Cispadana), and he pressed on as far as Parma, regularly furnishing himself with provisions and respecting the inhabitants of the country, because he hoped by this means to induce them to shake off the tyranny of Gian Galeazzo.

Two pennons waved in Hawkwood's brigade, — the arms of the King of France, and those of the Duke of Bavaria.

The King of France was always considered as the head of the Guelph party, and had received and favored Francesco Novello da Carrara when he passed the Alps to

1390. initiate a general movement against the Visconti, who
were entirely Ghibellines. Besides this the Florentines
were already negotiating for the French army to enter
Italy and decide the war which had commenced.

The Duke Stephan of Bavaria, who had married Taddea daughter of Bernabò Visconti, and was therefore the
natural enemy of Gian Galeazzo, being solicited and well
paid by the Florentines, had come with a considerable
force to Italy aiding Carrara to besiege the fortress of
Padua, and regain his other possessions.

August 6. The Florentines wrote informing the Duke of Hawkwood's march and praying him to unite with him; but
instead of doing so, the Duke sent ambassadors to the
Florentines, to ask that Hawkwood might come to join
him; meanwhile autumn set in, and the rivers swelled
to such an extent that the operation was difficult and
the Duke of Bavaria, having pocketed the Florentine pay
for the fourth month, returned back across the mountains,
not without a suspicion of an understanding with the
Conte di Virtù.

September. Having returned from the incursion on the territory
of Parma, Hawkwood together with Barbiano sustained a
most cruel fight with 300 of Carlo Malatesta's infantry.
Contrary to the custom of war among the mercenaries,
they, this time, fought "like barbarians, and each side made
a miserable slaughter of the other." The victory was at
length gained by the two captains of the League, who
doubtless having superior forces at command were able to
take the fierce but numerically few enemies on the flank.

Then having crossed the Po, Hawkwood gave assistance
to Francesco Novello, who was fighting vigorously in Po-
lesine, where he constrained the Marquis of Ferrara to
October 3. leave the Visconti party and enter into the League. On this
the bells were with good reason merrily rung at Bologna

and Florence : for Gian Galeazzo, who at the commence-
ment of hostilities was master of all the subalpine territory as far as Friuli and also menaced Bologna, was now
reduced to defending himself on the banks of the Adige.

Florence was especially able to boast of her captain,
and in fact she treated him with every loving-kindness.

The Signoria confided to him their good reasons for
not wishing that Carlo Visconti should figure in the Staff,
indeed they begged Hawkwood to keep him at a distance
from the camp. They assigned to Sir John the lances
they had denied to that Visconti, and excused themselves
for not being able to take into their service all the
knights he had recommended ; besides which they made
him a gift of a hundred good Lucca bows to arm his
archers, and remitted his imposts.

In a letter from the " Dieci di balía " to Donato Acciaioli and Niccolò da Uzzano, ambassadors at Bologna,
we read :

" . . . . . As to Giovanni Balcano, we are content that he
shall have 30 florins a month for five months between us
and the Bolognese, but in regard to John Guernock we do
not want to give him anything at all. And tell Sir John
not to give us so many worries on other people's account,
for his own are enough for us. We are content to give
Sir John those hundred bows which he had, and will
take them off his account. We will send to Lucca for
the best kind of bows, for they are not good here, then
we will send them at once to Padua. Respecting Messer
Carlo, we must beg you to urge Sir John to try by all
means not to let Messer Carlo go to him there, for within
the last few days certain persons from Milan have come
to us secretly, telling us plainly that if Messer Luchino *
goes with the brigade the Milanese will let him enter,

---

* Luchino Visconti junior, called also *Luchino Novello* or *Luchinetto*, believed to be son of Luchino former lord of Milan.

but if Messer Carlo goes, they will not turn, but will keep steadfast to the Count. They assign their reasons for this, which are perfectly true. On this account we are content to give Messer Carlo a salary of 150 florins a month for four months, between ourselves and the Bolognese. Those twelve lances of Messer Carlo can go to serve Sir John unless Messer Carlo wishes to keep some of them with him, in which case you can cancel them. This " provvisione " is made only in case he does not go with Sir John, otherwise it is void. Sir John's forced loans and imposts shall be taken off; we have already seen the Signoria — you can tell Sir John so."

And in fact the Commune " out of regard to the brave knight, John Hawkwood, so prudent in affairs of war as to be superior to almost all those of his time in Italy, so devoted a friend and captain-general of war to the Commune — wishing to treat him with liberality, holds him free from every fine, impost or residue, and also from the great dues which are called *prestanze di libertà* or vulgarly *prestanzoni,* which he should have paid, and also from all the penalties for payments omitted." Equal privileges were accorded to his wife, his sons, and daughters.

Fearing lest Alberico da Barbiano should eventually accept Gian Galeazzo's offers, the Florentines were disposed to engage also that condottiere, and commissioned Donato Acciaioli to go and meet him at Ravenna and enter into negotiations, but in this they wanted to secure the concurrence of Hawkwood. These were his orders:

" In conclusion request Barbiano that it may please him to be our captain-general together with Sir John Hawkwood, not because we wish to keep them together, but in different camps, each with an honorable brigade of Bolognese and our own troops, saying that we will give him such *provvisione* (salary) and men-at-arms as shall be requisite, and contrive to draw out his intentions and inform us of them. If he wants to have a decisive reply, tell him at last that we are content to take him for six months, and six more at the pleasure of the Bolognese and ourselves, giving him the same pay as that to Sir John Hawkwood, i. e. 500 florins a month for himself and two hundred lances. If he be not content, and wants greater things, do not break off with him, but give him good hopes without binding yourself, signifying his last intentions to us.*

They could have managed without Barbiano, but in fact the Florentines had engaged in the war with exemplary energy, and were preparing a grand *coup,* i. e. while Hawkwood with all the army then fighting for them, and for the Bolognese, Carraras, and other allies, should attack the States of Gian Galeazzo from the east; the Comte d'Armagnac, who had been persuaded by his brother-in-law Carlo Visconti, and convinced by the good pay of the Florentines, was to descend from the Alps with 2000 lances, and 3000 infantry, and attack him on the west. Gian Galeazzo on his side had arranged to oppose d'Armagnac with the troops under Iacopo dal Verme, while Ugolotto Biancardo was sent against Hawkwood.

The latter was on his arrival at Padua lodged with all honor in the court of Francesco Novello, his men being quartered some at San Martino and the rest at Montagnana. Here the captain was met by the treasurers Messer Lotto, and Messer Niccolò, who, as we gather from the following letter to Acciaioli, brought him the money for the pay, and a handsome Christmas present.

" ..... We wish you to say to those lords of Bologna that they must recognise how useful Sir John is to us, and how much good or ill it lies in his power to do us, seeing that he carries in his hands our State and theirs too, and that

---

* The ' Ten of war ' to Donato Acciaioli and Niccolò da Uzzano, October 6th 1390, the third hour of night.

moreover it appears· expedient to us, that we should jointly make the aforesaid Sir John a Christmas gift of a thousand florins, they paying a third of it, and we two thirds. In case they consent to do so, cause their share to be sent to Padua, and write by our commission to Messers Lotto and Niccolò, that they may pay our share of it. But if the Bolognese will not agree, then write to the said Messers Lotto and Niccolò, that they give the said Sir John five hundred florins on our own part....."

During the month, at Padua the Count Giovanni da Barbiano joined them with two hundred lances, Count Conrad Landau with another two hundred, and Astorre Manfredi with fifty. (The arrival of Manfredi could not have been very welcome to Hawkwood after the interminable disputes of which we have spoken.) Add to these the troops of Carrara, and it made a fine and strong army for those times, so fine that the celebrated Pier Paolo Vergerio, Carrara's secretary, wrote with great magniloquence to his friend Doctor Giovanni da Bologna after
he had seen them reviewed in a field outside Padua, and had witnessed them manœuvering with flying banners, and executing a mock battle. As to their number, he estimated it at nine thousand horse, and five thousand foot, without counting the multitude of *saccomanni*. No one could say precisely how many they were, but the expert Galeotto Malatesta suggested this method for an approximate calculation: "take the mean between the maximum given by exaggerators, and the minimum by detractors, and deduct a third."

This is more eloquent than any discourse, to make us understand that if the very captains who led them could not calculate the number of their forces from one day to another, they must have been even less able to depend on discipline and on the obedience of the mercenaries.

As to leaders, Vergerio particularly mentions Francesco Novello lord of Padua as generalissimo, Conte da Carrara as commandant of the Paduan contingent, Astorre Manfredi and Giovanni Barbiano, while the Florentine troops are led by "Signor Giovanni Aucud, — who is so celebrated for the remembrance of his worthy achievements, and with this victory about to give the last and greatest elevation to his fame."

And in truth Hawkwood, now nearly octogenarian, prepared to undertake what was indeed the last and most splendid of all his campaigns. For more than fifty years he had been a soldier, a condottiere, and a captain, but he never displayed such energy, such promptness, such constancy, and such courage as we shall now see him do, in most difficult circumstances. One might say that before sheathing his sword for ever, he had called up at one time all his military virtues. And as in the sorry trade of a mercenary he had in comparison with others been almost an honest man, we may be allowed to contemplate him with almost reverent admiration in these his last feats of arms.

XXXV.

THE MARCH TO THE BANKS OF THE ADDA.

[*The Accinioli papers*, Ashburnham MSS. in the Laurentian Library — *Letters* of PIER PAOLO VERGERIO — ANDREA and GALEAZZO GATARO, *Paduan chronicles* in MURATORI [*R. I. S.*] — VERCI, *Storia della Marca Trevigiana* — MINERBETTI, *Chronicle* — PIETRO BIGAZZI, *Diplomatic letters* (of the Florentine Balía), edition for a marriage gift. Florence 1869 — LEONARDO ARETINO, *Florentine history* — *Chronicon bergomense*, in MURATORI [*R. I. S.*] — GIULINI, *Memorie di Milano.*]

In 1387 the Carraras began a war with the Scaligers, and to complete their ruin they allied themselves with Gian Galeazzo Visconti, who, after having taken away Verona and its state from *the men of the Ladder* (quei della

1391. Scala), wrested Padua and that state from *those of the Car* *
(quei del Carro): it was indeed with good reason that he
himself bore the ensign of the voracious serpent. Now the
old enemies were leagued together against the usurper:
Samaritana della Scala, as mother and guardian of her son,
invoked and obtained the aid of Carrara, that he, having
regained Padua, should assist her to recover Verona.

After many councils with Hawkwood and the other
captains it was decided to encamp on the Veronese territory without delay: and all preparations with regard to
provisions and other necessaries being completed, the army
January 11. made its exit from Padua two hours before sunrise, according to the advice of the astrologers. The numbers were
soon multiplied, — we will not venture to say reinforced, —
by a great many troops, Paduan, Vicentine, Veronese, citizens and countrymen, dwellers in the plains, hills, and
mountains, who altogether brought up the number of foot
soldiers to 15,000.

January 15. A part of the army marched along the lower Adige to
cross it at the usual bridge of Castelbaldo, which they
accomplished, the lady Samaritana riding amongst them
in knight's attire: thence they ascended the river banks
towards Verona: and the body of the army, with Francesco
Novello in the van-guard, took the Vicenza road, of which
movement Donato Acciaioli, then Florentine ambassador at
Padua, was informed by this note from Francesco himself:

*Magnifice frater carissime, ut viarum mearum habeatis
processus, significo vobis me hucusque cum gentibus meis et
maiori parte felicis exercitus ligæ alogiasse in villa Barberani,
et aliis villis circumstantibus Vicentiæ civitatis, ibi expectans
adventum spectabilis militis domini Johannis Augudh, qui
hodie huc applicuit, ubi invenimus gentes et habitantes locorum
bene dispositos et unde crasdoman discedentes versus Veronam*

---

* The Ladder (*Scala*) was the ensign of the Scaligers, the Car (*Carro*) that
of the Carrara family. — (*Translator.*)

procedemus, allogiaturi crasdepò iuxta Lunicum etiam de comitatu Vicentiæ, sperans in Domino quod feliciter incepta de bono in melius secundabit, nam habeo a quampluribus fidedignis hostes valde trepidare, et igni necessaria quæquæ exposuisse ad usus hominum et equorum supra territorium tam Vicentiæ quam Veronæ existentia.... Datum in villa Barberani 13 januarj hora vesperarum.

They occupied the open borough of Illasi, and having found the fortress to be impregnable, unless under a regular siege, they left in the borough only a weak garrison (which a little while after was cut to pieces by the inhabitants in concert with the garrison of the fortress), and descended towards Verona taking a hundred and fifty prisoners and killing several of the Viscontese, who shut themselves up in the city and in their fortresses.

Beneath Verona the two invading armies united, pitching their camps on the two banks of the Adige, in sight of the city, while they scoured the valleys and plains for forage (they were bound under pain of the gallows to abstain from taking any thing except hay and straw from the peasants), and trying to excite tumults by the cry of *Scala! Scala! Long live Can Francesco!* the young Scaliger.

But Ugolotto Biancardo had a few months back fiercely repressed an attempted rebellion and had wisely provided every defence : so that there was no probability of a favorable result. Therefore the Lord of Padua, Francesco Novello, at the instance of Hawkwood, left the supreme and honorary command to Conte da Carrara, and returned to Padua with an escort of three hundred horse. The old captain was unwilling to have reigning or hereditary princes in the army, for he considered them as hindrances to the operations and battles ; and would joyfully have sent to the devil even the lady Samaritana, who kept the army at making fruitless attempts on Verona and her fortresses, and who had hired his mortal enemy Astorre Manfredi.

1391.

February 10.

February 13.

February 9.

February 23.

The news of such a slow war could not be very welcome to the Florentines, who were spending so much on it. They would have liked a rapid march towards Milan, where it seems they had an understanding.

The " Ten " wrote to Donato Acciaioli and Francesco Allegri ambassadors at the court of Carrara, wondering that " our troops.... linger over such trifles, and leave the great deeds and good fortune which are prepared for them towards Milan, for he who will not when he may, cannot when he will.... Hasten the captain, our commissaries and the others, that they go to Milan without delay."

The same day duplicating the letter they said: " Hasten the brigade, and send it towards Milan, and not remain wasting time about little castles, — for the expense is great, and the hopes of success will become less if we do not act quickly."

And again : " Work day and night that the troops cross the Adige."

Hawkwood was of the same sentiment, and had forestalled the exhortations : he made his army cross the Adige, and encamp at Santa Lucia ; which rejoiced the Florentines, who wrote to Acciaioli: " We are content with the news, provided the troops follow up the march towards Milan, where from certain things of which we have had secret intelligence, we have great hopes...."

But the extraordinary rigor of the winter rendered provisioning and marching very difficult : many volunteers were already disbanding, and instead of crossing the Mincio, the camp approached to within a few miles of Mantua, plundering the farms of cattle, and intimating to Gonzaga that he must either adhere to the League, or suffer the penalty of a general sack.

The Marquis of Mantua asked for time to decide. These new delays rendered the Florentines very impatient ; they wrote again to Acciaioli: " Let the Lord of Padua proceed boldly, and hold no parleying either with Agostino Cane, or any other enemy.... We have written to the camp by two of our couriers, urging that no discussions shall be held, and that they start at once, we have scolded and abused them well, and have made the Bolognese do the same." 1391. February 24.

Meanwhile Hawkwood discovered that Astorre Manfredi had held a midnight interview with certain peasants, and suspecting treachery, he raised the camp and returned to between Verona and Vicenza, thence on the Paduan land. Therefore the following orders from Florence to Acciaioli were useless: " Exert yourself and see that the March 1st. troops do not on any account leave the enemies' country, and that they hold themselves prepared and ready to turn back towards Milan, which we intend them to do at all costs. And we have arranged to send money immediately, so that the troops have no cause for any excuses."

Hawkwood maintained that Astorre was plotting to murder both him and Francesco Novello, and said so much that Astorre was obliged to return to Faenza.

It is but too true that treachery was at that time so common a thing that it created no astonishment. The Count of Virtù by means of deceit induced Gonzaga of Mantua to order that his wife (Agnes daughter of Bernabò and thus a natural sister-in-law to Hawkwood) should be beheaded, as being implicated in the plot of Carlo Visconti, against the life of her husband.

But it might be that Hawkwood was ill-advised by reason of his old hatred. Vergerio, alluding to these reports, writes thus to his friend Giovanni da Bologna: July 19.

" In this retreat some were, as I believe, falsely accused of infamous felony; it often happens that in great things if the result does not correspond with one's hopes, that is lightly called a crime which is really only inca-

1391.

pacity, and one attributes to the few that which is a general fault."

From these words we can comprehend that at Padua the want of success of that ill-attempted winter campaign was very displeasing.

As to Florence, the chancellor Ser Benedetto Fortini

March 15. wrote to Acciaioli: " All the good people and others here, think very ill of the way in which the troops have turned back from their object, for we had hopes of great doings. I know from certain signs in many ways, that if the army had neared Milan, the city would have revolted. Great things are expected from the coming of the Count *d'Armignac.*"

News had been heard that d'Armagnac was to come down into Piedmont towards the end of May. All that was necessary then was that Hawkwood should make a move in time to attempt a conjunction, which would have been most fatal to Gian Galeazzo.

The end of that winter was employed in reinforcing the army and preparing it for the coming campaign. To keep it in exercise Hawkwood made frequent incursions into the Vicentine and Veronese provinces, inspiring the inhabitants with such respect that many of them took the trouble to buy provisions to supply his soldiers.

May 10. In May seeing the time was propitious, because the corn and oats were already high, and some, being already in ear, gave abundant forage, he issued from Padua with the army in marching order. Well provided with pay and food, he was content with the preparations, for which he gave Carrara great credit. This time he had the command-in-chief himself, Conte da Carrara, Lodovico Visconti, and Count Conrad Landau being under his orders; 1400 Florentine lances, 600 from Bologna, 200 from Padua, 1200 cross-bowmen and a great many infantry consti-

tuted a considerable force. These numbers are given by
Minerbetti. Vergerio says 5000 chosen cavalry, and 2000
foot soldiers, adding that the red lily of the Florentine
preceded all the other standards; then came the " Car " of
the Carraras, the red cross and lily of Bologna, and then
the ensign of the captain and the other condottieri.

The Adige being shallow was crossed without any
other delay than that of putting to flight an exploring
party of the enemy, consisting of 300 lances and some
infantry. Another obstacle was presented by a wide and
deep moat excavated by Antonio della Scala in 1386.
Hawkwood made his men fill up a space large enough
for the passage of the troops and rapidly marched on
towards the Mincio.

If we may believe Vergerio, the captain on that occasion
made an eloquent speech to exhort his soldiers to great
deeds, which capricious invention we will leave to the
fantastic rhetoric of the humanist. For we think it more
likely that he bid them abstain from incendiarism, and
from taking the peasants prisoners, because it was to the
interest of the League to win the friendship of the popu-
lation subject to the enemy.

The Mincio was also crossed without hindrance, and
Vergerio relates that on Brescian territory Taddeo dal
Verme opposed them with 9000 horse and 3000 foot, all
hired soldiers, with a large number of peasant troops, and
countrymen, besides a great many carts and mules. This
time Vergerio has probably neglected to follow the golden
rule of Galeotto Malatesta, for Leonardo Aretino's account
is much more probable; which is, that the greater part of
Visconti's forces had been sent towards Piedmont to oppose
the now much talked descent of d'Armagnac, and that no
troops were left in Lombardy except the garrisons alone,
leaving the country freely open to the invaders.

Taddeo dal Verme, coming out of Brescia with seven

1391.   hundred horse, placed himself on the bank, watching his opportunity to attack Hawkwood, who accelerated his march. The best moment seemed to be when he had crossed the Oglio at Rudiano, and a great part of the allied army was already on the left bank. Hawkwood had however calculated on this, and prepared his trap by placing Conrad Landau in ambush with 300 lances.

Taddeo found himself caught in the midst, and had great fortune in being able to flee, leaving about a hundred prisoners, and three hundred between killed and drowned. He returned with the mass of his army, but by that time the allies were established on the other bank, and recommenced their rapid march towards the Adda.

Hawkwood halted at Trescorre without molestation. At Colognola, under Bergamo, a fruitless attack was made on him by five hundred chosen cavalry from that garrison; but they were easily made an end of by an energetic counterattack of Conte da Carrara, who was slightly wounded, and the Count of Anguillara, who was knighted as though to seal the victory.

Then they dispersed in the valley of San Martino, always having due regard to the inhabitants, and amicably buying provisions, so that a knight of that country joined the League bringing with him a thousand men-at-arms.

Thus they safely reached the Adda, and descended for three days along the left bank vainly seeking a ford, and having arrived at Pandino and the woods of Bofalora (Bernabò Visconti's hunting ground and refuge from the plague) they pitched their camp, intending to decide on their forward march, as soon as they had notice from d'Armagnac, with whom they were to effect a conjunction on the Po, either at Pavia or Piacenza. Taddeo dal Verme was near them, having followed slowly behind, and Hawkwood did not hesitate to challenge him to a battle. After an exchange of cartels and messages, it was agreed that each army should choose four captains of note, and sixty men who were to fight in an enclosed field. This was a remnant of chivalric military customs, which the mercenary soldiers cherished by tradition, but rarely used. The champions were already chosen, the first on the part of the League was Michele da Rabatta, but Vergerio does not give the names of the others. Hawkwood moved his camp a little for better convenience of forage and provision; and the Viscontese made this a pretext for declining the combat, unless the allied army would return to their first position. Hawkwood however was not so shortsighted as to renounce a positive advantage; and hence, instead of the challenge, frequent indeed almost daily skirmishes took place : and when the Viscontese made prisoners, instead of agreeing as usual on a ransom, they deprived them of arms and horses so that they could not take the field again. In this way they tried to weaken the enemy, on which the allies took to fighting with extreme resolution, and as usual became victors freeing themselves at the same time of useless arms and mouths.

So they steadily kept their favorable position on the Adda, and on the *fête* of St. John (the patron of Florence) they triumphantly ran the *palio*,* according to Florentine usage, with festive shouts to the great shame of the enemy who were constrained to take the most extreme precautions.

Gian Galeazzo ordered that 300 Milanese citizens should go to reinforce the garrison of Lodi; being very devout, he ordered public processions for three days, and being timid and anxious to provide for his personal security, he armed another 1200 citizens, chosen among the most able men, as a body guard.

---

* It was an ancient Florentine and Tuscan custom to have races on the occurrence of civic solemnities and as an insult on the territory and under the walls of the enemy; such races were run by horses or foot soldiers or the courtezans of the army. — (*Translator*.)

XXXVI.

THE RETREAT ACROSS THE ADIGE.

[GORO DATI, *Chronicle* — MINERBETTI, *Chronicle* — *Chronicle of Gubbio* — *Letters* of PIETRO PAOLO VERGERIO — RICOTTI, *History of the mercenary companies* — POGGIO BRACCIO-LINI, *History* — *Chronicon estense* — GATARO, *Paduan chronicle* — CORIO, *Milanese history* — AMMIRATO, *Florentine history* — OSIO, *Diplomatic documents selected from the Archives of Milan* — *Deliberazioni e condotte, Consulte e pratiche of the Commune*, in the State Archives of Florence.]

1391.   Hawkwood had carried out his part in the general plan of campaign excellently: he had reached the Adda, and there had for several days awaited the right moment to bring about a juncture with d'Armagnac, who was leisurely coming from France, and was still a long way off. In vain did Hawkwood urge him on by means of letters and embassies, and advising and begging him to accelerate his march. Gian Galeazzo was therefore able to bring nearly all his forces against Hawkwood, recalling Iacopo dal Verme from Piedmont, with 1800 lances and 10,000 infantry: together with Taddeo's troops they then were nearly 26,000 men, of whom 10,000 were trained soldiers. The French condottiere's delay rescued Visconti from the danger of a simultaneous attack on both sides, and allowed him to fight the two hostile armies in turn, at his own convenience. For these reasons, and owing to the difficulty of procuring provisions, Hawkwood was positively compelled to beat a retreat. But even a retreat was a difficult matter to accomplish, in the face of an enemy much stronger than themselves, and with several large rivers to cross.

Iacopo dal Verme was so confident of turning it into a disaster, that he wrote thus to his master: " Write and tell me how you wish me to settle them." And here Hawkwood proved himself a great captain, knowing in the first place that if he wished to procure relative liberty of action for himself, he ought to instil respect into his enemy, and give him a lesson : he therefore marched in an oblique direction between the Adda and the lower Oglio, but stopped at the castle of Paterno Fasolaro, where he strongly entrenched himself, and forbade his men to leave the trenches. Visconti's army encamped a mile off, and for four consecutive days advanced beyond a small stream running between the two camps, and offered battle. Hawkwood remained ensconced in his camp, leaving them to vent their anger in making provoking demonstrations.

By way of a practical joke Dal Verme sent him a fox in a cage. Hawkwood answered the enemy's envoy who brought the cage: " I see that the animal is not dull, which means that he will discover a way out," and breaking one of the bars of the cage, he set the fox at liberty.

On the fifth day, when Visconti's soldiers were at their usual game, and thought they would follow it out, Hawkwood and all his men suddenly left their entrenchments, and fell vigorously upon the enemy whom they chased to their very camp ; twelve hundred of Visconti's men were made prisoners, and there were fifteen hundred between killed and wounded.

In his turn Hawkwood offered battle by sending to Dal Verme a blood-stained gauntlet, a challenge which was accepted for the following day, but in the evening Sir John abandoned the camp leaving the banners tied to the tops of trees, and telling the trumpeters to sound the reveille till day-light, and then to forsake the banners and to go about their own business, moreover he managed to leave several beasts of burden along the way.

In this manner, by means of victory, deceit, and with the temptation of booty, he hindered the enemy, and having procured the necessary rest, he hastened to the river Oglio, which he reached at Soncino, with the intention of ascending its right bank as far as the known ford of Rudiano.

Visconti's soldiers prudently kept them back, making entrenchments, and skirmishing in such a manner, that for two days and for two nights there was a continual marching and sharpshooting, during which days by means of an ambuscade Count Conrad Landau again distinguished himself, and Facino Cane, one of Visconti's knights, was severely wounded.

After all, if Hawkwood suffered fatigue in this most difficult retreat, it is very wearisome for us to search out the most probable details, amongst the incomplete and often contradictory narrations of the chroniclers, which offer serious discrepancies; so that it is not to be wondered at if Ricotti fell into the error of placing this retreat after the defeat of d'Armagnac, and to explain it as being the result of that rout, which took place on the 25th of July, when Hawkwood was already in safety on the left bank of the Adige. For example, if we are to believe the story of Ghirardacci, it would seem that Count of Virtù in person, leaving the territory of Bologna, came to fight the allies on the Oglio; that Hawkwood, on account of inferiority of forces, was unwilling to risk a battle, but accepted it as a point of honor; that, after a couple of hours' fierce fighting, Visconti, seeing that his men were in disorder, took to flight with a few horses and much anxiety: and when he had found and reorganised a few cavalry and infantry troops, he attempted a rescue, lying in ambush at the pass of Rudiano; that when Hawkwood and his soldiers reached that place they were attacked by Iacopo dal Verme, Ugolotto Biancardo, Carmignuola, and Guglielmo Pusterla, and that having met hand to hand, they put to the sword almost all the assailants, naming especially Carmignuola and Pusterla; that the victorious Englishman made twenty of his bravest men *cavalieri aurati* (knights of the golden spurs) on the very field of battle: they were Francesco

and Ettore Visconti, Count Hugh (of Montfort, a German),   1391.
Filiberto and Febo della Torre (who would only wear a
single gold spur), Ugo Guazzalotti, Conrad Prospergh, Count
Bolsomino, Fritz, a German, Donino, an Italian, Rapp, a
German, Berlinghiero (Beringer?), an Englishman, Count
Micatinio, Guernock, an Englishman, and Martin, a German....
These particulars of dates and names cannot be imaginary.

Still neither Bracciolini, nor the chronicles of Este, nor
those of Gubbio, or Gataro's Paduan ones, nor Corio, nor
Ammirati say anything of all this; only Minerbetti remarks
that Hawkwood, after having challenged Dal Verme to
battle, knighted ten warriors.

Pier Paolo Vergerio, in a letter, written a short while
after these events, proposing to relate them in full, *
merely says that, being attacked in the midst by Conrad
Landau, a hundred of Visconti's most imprudent soldiers
were slain; that, after two days' fighting, the army of the
League having found a ford, — difficult indeed but practicable, — near a mill *on the lower Oglio* (and therefore not
at Rudiano), they prepared to cross.   When a part of them
had crossed, Visconti's soldiers made their attack, but
Hawkwood, always on the alert, had sent forward the archers, and bowmen, with the baggage, and had placed
them in a lofty position on the bank, with orders to shoot
fiercely at the enemy whenever they came within range;
these orders were carried out, and thus a crossing was
effected without much harm being done.

There is no doubt, that the Oglio was successfully passed;   July 4.
and that Hawkwood must have maintained absolute supe-

---

* It is a great pity that Pier Paolo Vergerio, who left us some particulars of this campaign referring to the uncertain rumours which were
being circulated at Padua, did not put into effect the plan of writing a
history of it, after finding out the facts from reliable sources. If he sometimes gives way in his letters to the temptation of rhetoric, a moderate
judgment, and the analytical spirit, which are the guarantees of truth, are
generally to be observed.

riority over Dal Verme in the battles fought with him, seeing that he was able to cross even the Mincio without molestation, and reach Castagnaro and Castelbaldo on the Adige, places where in 1387 he had gained the most brilliant of all his victories, on the borders of the Paduan territory, and thence to the gates of his home. Moreover, d'Armagnac had crossed the Alps and was although somewhat tardily approaching Alexandria. Gian Galeazzo was for this reason compelled to turn his best forces against him, as well as Iacopo dal Verme.

But at the very moment when he was reaching safety, Hawkwood saw himself threatened by a most serious and unexpected danger. He and his whole army were very nearly drowned, for the Visconti's army had taken the precaution to break the embankments of the Adige, so as to submerge for several miles the plain in which the leagued armies had pitched their camp. It was night time, and the men were resting, and getting ready for their last march. Being awakened by the noise of the waters, they would probably have been seized by a panic, if Hawkwood had not kept his presence of mind; he immediately made the cavalry mount on horseback, and the foot soldiers climb up behind them, and knowing the ground, and trying to find out the fords by the tops of trees emerging from the water, he lost not a few of his men, but saved the greater part, and succeeded in reaching a point where the water was not deeper than the horses' bellies, and in this manner having advanced ten miles, he reached the banks of the Adige below the rupture, where he did not find it difficult to cross. In this almost miraculous manner he placed his troops in security at Castelbaldo near Padua, and then at Montaguana.

The retreat was accomplished, and to this day it is greatly praised by the historians of the art of war.

1391.

Count of Virtù while sending to the Pope the copy of a letter from Iacopo dal Verme, announcing his own signal victory over d'Armagnac, spoke casually of the retreat, in the following words: "Swift and precipitous flight of *signor Giovanni Acuto,* and of the forces of the League from my territory, which was of such a kind, and brought about such a massacre of people and horses, and such a loss of baggage, that it might more fitly be termed a rout than a retreat."

And truly a great part of the infantry and many of the horses were lost; but Vergerio, the Carrara's secretary, judged more accurately that a retreat carried to the end, under the conditions which we have seen, was to be considered as a victory. If the splendour of a battle won on the field were lacking, it is plain that Hawkwood, owing to the great inferiority of his forces, was not in a position to attempt it without risk; on the contrary, we cannot even blame Dal Verme for not having attempted it, although he was much stronger, because he had to reserve himself for his encounter with d'Armagnac, and content himself with getting Hawkwood's army out of the way.

In conclusion, we have here the strange case of each of the hostile parties contemporaneously attaining their own object: — Dal Verme of causing the retreat; Hawkwood of accomplishing it; and his success deserves more praise, because great difficulties were placed in his way.

And the fact that Hawkwood made twenty cavaliers, from amongst those who had greatly distinguished themselves in this glorious campaign, was no vain ostentation.

Hawkwood stopped several days at the court of Francesco Novello, where he was received with the applause due to the captain, who had carried out his part nobly, and had saved the army; and Ugolotto Biancardo, who had become captain of Visconti's soldiers on the Adige, although reinforced by Antonio Porro and Balestrazzo,

1391. did not even dare to attack the states of the Carrara as long as Hawkwood defended them.

The Florentines, before their captain undertook the expedition to the Adda (as we shall see when the account May 2. of the war is finished), besides re-electing him for a year with 220 lances and the same pay, had been munificent in their kindness to him and to his family; he had solemnly promised to fight bravely (like a man); now the Florentines themselves, judging that he had kept his word, discussed July 27. about writing him a letter of praise, and sending him the 5000 florins he had asked for.

Meanwhile d'Armagnac had been utterly routed and mortally wounded in the predestined plain of Marengo: this fact raised the fortunes of Gian Galeazzo Visconti, and permitted him to make preparations for transporting the war into Tuscany. But only vague rumours of this August 2. were heard in Florence, as it was there being determined " to take care that Hawkwood should be able to keep the field beyond the Po, and at the same time lend a helping hand to d'Armagnac's troops, to warn him not to tempt fortune, but to proceed cautiously and safely moreover to send him reinforcements in case d'Armagnac should be already beaten."

August 13. When a true statement of the case was heard, they sent him the reinforcements. And a short while after, when they saw that Iacopo dal Verme was passing into Lunigiana, they recalled him in great haste.

Septemb. 12. Hawkwood set out from Padua accompanied as far as the gates by Francesco Novello, who after many embraces took leave of him outside them. Now we shall see him again at arms with Dal Verme, conducting himself with the same prudent firmness in the Val d'Arno which he had displayed in the Valley of the Po.

XXXVII.

THE WAR IN TUSCANY.

[State Archives of Florence, *Consulte e pratiche* of the Commune —
MINERBETTI, *Chronicle* — *Chronicle of Gubbio.*]

With 1200 lances and 1000 bowmen, Hawkwood hurried   1391.
on by forced marches, crossed the Apennines by the hill
of Sambuca, and thence he hastened to San Miniato al
Tedesco by way of Pistoia. There Count Giovanni da
Barbiano joined him with 600 lances and 700 cross-bowmen
from Bologna, and then came 1500 lances and 2000 between
foot soldiers and archers, who under Luigi da Capua were
fighting for the Florentines against Siena and Perugia,
the allies of Visconti. Thus Hawkwood had 3300 lances
and 3300 infantry, while Dal Verme reinforced with Sienese and Pisans by the Visconti had 3000 lances, and
5000 infantry; the forces were nearly equal, so it was easy
to foresee that neither of the two captains would lightly
risk a great battle.

They faced each other, Dal Verme at Cascina, and
Hawkwood at Montopoli; the former passed by a march
at the flank to Casoli, the latter distributed his men in
the strongholds of Poggibonsi, Colle, and Staggia with the
understanding that a single march was to bring them all
to him, as soon as the enemy appeared.

Dal Verme ventured to the foot of the fortress of
Poggibonsi; Hawkwood, who had 1000 lances there, let
him pass, only molesting him with skirmishes, without
hindering his sacking, and incendiarism, nor the pitching
of his camp on the Elsa. Then quickly gathering all his
troops in the plain of Poggibonsi, Hawkwood encamped
in a strong position three miles in the rear of the enemy.

The Visconti army raised their camp by night, and the
next evening, after a very fatiguing day (being much mo-

1391.

lested in their march, and that not without loss), they pitched their tents on the confluence of the Elsa and Arno. And Hawkwood, aiming to cover Florence, took an opposite position between Empoli and Montelupo.

Dal Verme passed the Arno at Fucecchio, crossed the hills of Pietramarina and halted at Poggio a Caiano.

Between Septemb. 20 and 21.

Hawkwood in his turn traversed the Arno at Signa, and rounding the plain placed his camp at Tizzana. It was a game of chess played by two brave champions, but this procrastination served Hawkwood's purpose, as it gave him a better chance of being reinforced. There was naturally great anxiety in Florence, but they knew how to keep down their impatience. Filippo Corsini said in the *Consulte e pratiche:*

Septemb. 21.

" Let us take measures to save our towns and people. We must press closely on the enemy while reinforcing the camp with foot soldiers, and not oblige the captain to give battle."

And Filippo Cionetti advised: " Let us make a last effort to reinforce the camp, and end the affair honorably. We should collect all the *distrettuali,** and for this they should send one from each house."

Ranieri di Luigi Peruzzi was of the opinion that " we should reinforce the camp with citizens, peasants and *distrettuali,* and also exhort Hawkwood by reminding him of his own words, that with 500 lances, 2000 infantry, and 1000 cross-bowmen...." here the document is mutilated, but it certainly means to say that those forces would have sufficed for the undertaking.

During the two succeeding days the Florentines sent no less than 10,000 men to reinforce the camp. They were nearly all peasants, but we shall see them behave like spirited and brave soldiers.

---

* Country militia, called out from all the district of Florence in time of war. — (*Translator*.)

In the night, news was brought to Hawkwood that the enemy was making a move. He thought their march was directed towards Pistoia, and took up his position accordingly, disposing his men in three battalions in the best order, and under their respective ensigns. Day-light proved that the enemy had taken the road up Monte Albano, to pass into the Val di Nievole; so he immediately detached 1000 lances to follow and attack them in the rear; and sent all his infantry by a side route of mountain paths to get in front of them, while he followed more slowly with the main body of lances and archers, in order of battle: and as he was doubtful of some ambuscade he made the troops keep a vigilant look-out.

1391.
Septemb. 23
and 24.

Taddeo dal Verme, who commanded the rear-guard of the Visconti army, was obliged to face about and give battle; and in a very short time was routed and defeated: 2000 foot, almost all Sienese and Pisans, remained dead on the field; and 1000 were taken prisoners. Of the men-at-arms about 400 were killed, and 200 taken captive, amongst whom were Taddeo himself, Gentile Varano da Camerino, and Vanni d'Appiano.

Meanwhile the Florentine infantry reached the mass of the Visconti army at the foot of Monte Vettolini, and endeavoured to hinder them by skirmishes, but nightfall overtook them sooner than Hawkwood did; — his troops being very tired, and destitute of provisions and forage.

Dal Verme on the other hand spurred on by danger, after having repulsed a last attack of the too spirited infantry at Pieve a Nievole, hastened through the valley at the foot of Montecarlo, where he arrived four hours after sunset. There he halted a short time, and at midnight again marched on. After refreshing his troops at Lucca, he did not pitch his camp till he could fortify himself in the already strong position of Ripafratta.

As soon as day broke Hawkwood presented himself in order of battle at Montecarlo ; he found some lame and hamstrung horses, a great deal of baggage, several *bombarde* and tents, but no enemy! They had to stay two days on the Pescian territory to recover themselves, and when they reached Lucca, they found that the enemy was impregnable at Ripafratta. Then having returned into Val d' Arno, Hawkwood thought to guard against any eventuality by encamping under San Miniato, and in fact Dal Verme re-appeared, and fortified himself at Cascina.

At Florence many fires of rejoicing were lit on the palace of the Signoria and all the other prominent places, to celebrate the victory of Tizzana, and a jubilant letter was written to Pope Boniface IX ; but as "appetite comes with eating," they now wanted the total destruction of the Visconti army or nearly so.

They did not reflect that Hawkwood might with reason fear an ambush at Tizzana, and even with his extreme daring irreparably lose the day.

As to Dal Verme, after the experience of his marches and counter-marches following the defeat, he must by this time have been convinced that he could not succeed in getting the upper hand, and still wished to attempt a *coup-de-main* by surprising the town of Santa Maria a Monte. He hoped thus to mislead the adversary, and induce him to withdraw his garrison from that place ; October 11. he left Cascina, and moved towards Fabbrica. Hawkwood changed to Castel Fiorentino, but took care that a good guard should be kept on all points.

October 14. Dal Verme abandoned Fabbrica by a quick march, crossed the Arno, and vigorously attacked Santa Maria where the garrison held firm : the enemy maintained the siege for four hours, but having suffered serious losses without gaining anything, and fearing lest Hawkwood should come

on them from the rear, they left their scaling ladders on
the walls, and recrossed the Arno in haste, encamping
between Cascina and Pisa. Hawkwood had in fact returned
to San Miniato.

The chronicle of Gubbio says that Hawkwood had treated
with the Bretons who were in Visconti's army, and agreed
on a betrayal, that this treaty was discovered, and all the
Bretons put to death; but when we remember that the
chronicler estimates the Bretons at five thousand, it is time
to ask whether Dal Verme had enough faithful soldiers to
kill the traitors!

Dal Verme, it is true, could do very little good, and
the autumn being now far advanced, he retreated into
Liguria; while Sir John Hawkwood took up his quarters
in the fortress of Val di Nievole.

Hostilities however did not entirely cease: for not being
able to do anything better, Gian Galeazzo Visconti tried
to interrupt and injure the Florentine commerce, knowing
that would strike them on their most vulnerable part.
This he did by means of the Genoese galleys, which cruised
before Leghorn and the port of Pisa; and as the Florentines opposed to them, with good success, the galleys of a
certain Gargiolli, a Florentine pirate, he by favor of the
Pisans and Iacopo d'Appiano was allowed to place his
troops in the valley of Calci, in Monte Pisano, whence
he could easily intercept the road through Val d'Arno
between Florence and the sea.

It was therefore Hawkwood's business to guard the road
and protect the merchants, and in fact as a large convoy
of five hundred pack-horses laden with grain and other
merchandise was to go from Pisa to Florence, John Beltoft
was sent to escort it with two hundred lances and five
hundred foot soldiers, together with Hugh Montfort and
about a hundred horsemen.

1391.   The convoy and its escort followed the road which to
this day runs along the left of the Arno; the river was
very full, however Iacopo d'Appiano informed the Visconti's army, which was esconced beyond, of all that was
going on, and indicated to them a ford which though difficult was quite practicable.

The convoy having nearly reached the country-town
of Cascina, lo! two thousand of Visconti's cavalry plunged
in the stream, and swimming across with great difficulty
threatened an attack; and behold! Beltoft without waiting
for them, shamefully took to flight with his two hundred
English lances, leaving the convoy, infantry and Count
Hugh's hundred horsemen in the clutches of the enemy!
Montfort opposed a desperate resistance, but was at last
taken and his soldiers nearly all killed or captured. Some
five hundred loads, and two hundred mules were lost, worth
altogether 15,000 florins.

This event was very displeasing to Florence, especially
because the Sienese and Pisans rejoiced over it. The
brave Count Hugh was ransomed by the Florentines, and
received with great honors on his return, while Beltoft,
blamed and driven away by them, passed into the service
of the Pope, and soon after, being taken by the Orsini,
he was beheaded.

Hawkwood too had his share of responsibility in the
affair, either for not caring to inform himself of the forces
of the Viscontese, or for having sent an insufficient escort.
It seems he excused himself to the Signoria by letter, and
proposed to vindicate that injury by attacking the Viscontese.

Decemb. 18.   In the *Consulte* Filippo Corsini proposed: "Let us reprove
Hawkwood for the error he has committed, but incite him
to the enterprise of which he has written, which will recupe-
rate both his honor and that of the Commune; reinforcing
him as well as we can. Let him encamp near Cascina."

But Donato Acciaioli more calmly counselled: " Let us incite and even commend Hawkwood for what he has written, but moderate him, so that he proceed with caution and prudence, not to put the State of the Commune in peril."

A general peace was soon after concluded at Genoa, and solemnized in Florence, with fires of joy and illuminations, with a *Mass for peace* in Santa Maria del Fiore (the Duomo), and notice was given of a great tournament which was to come off on the calends of May.

The captains of war gave up their ensigns, and measures were taken to relieve the Florentine tax payers, now almost exhausted by the heavy weight of the 2400 lances and the 3500 infantry then in their pay. By compositions according to the time for which they were hired, the lances were reduced to less than 1000, and the infantry to about the same number.

However before Hawkwood could take his final rest, he had still to make a last expedition.

The peace left many adventurers unoccupied, and they immediately gave themselves up to brigandage. Azzo da Castello had already formed the nucleus of a company on the territory of Urbino. Broglia, Brandolini, Biordo dei Michelotti, and a great many others being dismissed by Gian Galeazzo, wished to join Azzo as he passed by Bologna from Lombardy, and they commenced their march in that direction. The Bolognese demanded help from the Florentines, who soon sent 500 lances under Hawkwood and Count Hugh. The adventurers took the road by Sarzana and the Maremma, but they hurried so much for fear Hawkwood should overtake them, that they left a great number of their horses by the way.

Thus the military fatigues of Sir John Hawkwood ended with a modest expedition on behalf of public security, and he retired to quiet life in Florence.

XXXVIII.

MARRIAGES OF JANET AND CATHERINE HAWKWOOD.

[*Capitoli* of the Commune of Florence, v. I, in the State Archives of Florence — *Inventory and Registers* of the above mentioned *Capitoli* — D. M. MANNI, Biography of Hawkwood in the II v. of the *Appendix* to the *R. I. S.* of MURATORI — GHIRARDACCI, *Bolognese history* — Books of the customs on contracts in the National Library of Florence, Strozzi Collection — *Acciaioli papers*, from the Ashburnham MSS. in the Laurentian Library — CAVALCANTI, Anecdotes, in the Appendix to *Florentine history* published among the *Documents of Italian History.*]

1391. We have said that Florence showered signal favors on Hawkwood during the campaign.

Before undertaking the dangerous expedition from Padua towards the Adda, he, with due reflection on his advanced age, obtained from the Florentines a certain and sufficient provision for the latter years of his life, together with ample wedding portions for his daughters, and a pension to his wife after his death.

April 8. These facts result from the *Capitoli* * agreed between Giacomo di Borgo della Collina, Hawkwood's procurator, and the Signoria of Florence, of which the following is a summary : **   .

" The ' Ten of *balia*,' considering the great war of Florence and her allies against Gian Galeazzo and the Sienese, and judging that the worthy and in deeds of arms most approved and valorous knight John Hawkwood, who has fought for a long time with extreme probity, prudence and good fortune, and has long been a devoted friend to the Commune of Florence, whose wars he has faithfully conducted, — recognising also the offers made on his part in negotiating for the said war against the enemies of the Commune, and chiefly considering his brave

---

* *Capitoli,* Pacts or conventions made between two States or two belligerent armies ; the word is also used for Statutes of Companies or Confraternities. — (*Translator.*)

** Manni also published an extract, which agrees with that contained in the *Inventario e Regesto dei Capitoli del Comune di Firenze.*

deeds in the said war, and above all diligently taking heed to the felicity and prudence with which for so long he has kept, conducted, and governed the men-at-arms, and to what happy and prosperous results all the warlike affairs have proceeded under his hands, — and though he be already remunerated as captain of war, they (The Ten) recognise the expediency of encouraging him still more with the under mentioned benefits, pensions, favors and privileges.

" That prudent man *Giacomo di Piero di Borgo della Collina,* having entered the presence of the ' Ten ' to say in the name and stead of Sir John Hawkwood, that the said Sir John always intends to be a devoted friend of the Commune, and that in the said war, as he has done before, he will give himself in the best manner for the defence of the Commune, and the offence of her enemies, overriding in a hostile manner the territories of the Conte di Virtù, and manfully combating against him and his adherents.

" Having taken the votes of the Signoria, the Gonfalonieri and the twelve Buonomini, they deliberate :

" That Hawkwood together with his wife and family shall be received as a perpetual friend of the Commune, and deputed its captain of war;

" That besides the pension of 1200 gold florins conceded since 1375, he shall, during his life, receive a new annual pension of 2000 gold florins, without any deduction, and the first year of this new annuity shall begin with May 1" 1392 ;

" That the annuity shall be paid every three months, without the necessity of ulterior formalities ;

" That to the first three daughters, whom Sir John at present acknowledges, and whose names are given below, shall be given as portions, when they marry, or shall be of a marriageable age (i. e. at least 14 years old),

1891.   6000 florins of gold, — that is to say 2000 for each ; — the
chamberlains shall pay these portions to their respective
husbands, or their procurators, on presentation of the matrimonial contract, and providing it be made with the
consent of Sir John, if he be alive, or his procurator ;

" And as it is asserted that one of the said daughters,
that is to say Janet, has at present completed the age of
14 years, from this time hence, whenever it shall please her
father that her marriage shall be contracted, the payment
of the portion shall be immediately made.—   Janet is the
first of the daughters, Catherine the second, Anna the third ;

" Moreover after the death of the said Sir John,—which
God grant may be a peaceful and happy one after a long life,
and meanwhile may he give him good fortune, and direct
his steps happily, — that the noble Lady Donnina, wife
of Sir John as long as she is a widow, and remains in the
city, country or district of Florence, with the son or daughters of herself, and the said Sir John, shall have every
year of her widowhood the pension and gift of 1000 gold
florins, in honor of the memory of that noble and brave
man her husband ;

" Whenever however she lives away from her son or
daughters, or out of the city and country, the pension
shall be deducted *pro rata* of the time ;

" And that the said Sir John, with his sons and descendants in the male line, born, or yet to be born, shall
enjoy the privilege of Florentine citizenship, and shall
only be excluded from the power and ability of holding
office in the commune or city."

1392.
March 14.   The war ended, these *Capitoli* were accepted and ratified by Hawkwood in a public deed.

Then he gave his attention to marrying his daughters
honorably ; Janet was fifteen years of age, and Catherine
scarcely fourteen.

He found a husband for the eldest in the very noble family of the Counts of Porcia in Friuli. This was the young Brezaglia son of Count Lodovico, formerly prœtor and captain of the people at Bologna, next podestà of Ferrara, and then captain of the people at Florence.*   1391.

1393.

The marriage was celebrated by the following deed drawn up by Ser Giovanni di Simone: 1392. September 7.

" Performed in the house inhabited by sir John Hawkwood (Sig. Giovanni Haucut) situated in the district of Florence in the *popolo* (parish) of San Donato a Torre, the witnesses present being the noble gentlemen *Guido son of the late signor Tomaso* knight, Andrea di Neri Capponi, and Ser Benedetto di Ser Lando notary of Florence, together with the citizens and others especially bidden and invited.

" The noble gentleman Brezaglia son of the magnificent lord signor Lodovico Count de' Puziliis (of Porciglia or Porcia) on the one part ; and the noble lady Janet — daughter of the magnificent and potent knight Sir John Hawkwood of England — Florentine citizeness, on the other; who with the consent of the said Sir John her father, here present, consents to be the said wife.

" The required questions and answers by word of mouth (*verba de presenti*) having been spoken, and the ring given and received, legal matrimony is contracted between them. The said Brezaglia with the said lady Janet as his spouse and legitimate wife, and the said lady Janet consenting to take the said Brezaglia as her husband and legitimate spouse."

The receipt for the 2000 florins, which was paid by Hawkwood as Janet's wedding portion, was given in a deed drawn up by Ser Lorenzo, the procurator of the Porcias, (i. e. Count Lodovico, with Iacopo and Brezaglia, his sons). Novemb. 19.

---

* In the Italian republics the offices of podestà (civil governor) and captain of the people were always held by strangers from other cities who had no kinship with the city they ruled — the offices were held yearly.— (*Translator*.)

A note of this is also to be found in the books of "customs on contracts" for the taxes which we should call "registration fees."

For his second daughter Catherine, Hawkwood chose a man of his own profession, the German Conrad Prospergh, a brave young soldier of fortune. The documents do not prove him to have been of noble family, although some chroniclers call him Count. Florence had hired him *for the League with two hundred lances, and Hawkwood himself had given him his spurs, during the retreat on the Oglio the year before.

*While Hawkwood was campaigning in Tuscany, Prospergh being detained in the pay of Bologna, commanded six hundred lances on the territory of Reggio, and showed himself a good disciple of his future father-in-law; for he was able to draw the Visconti into an ambuscade, and to capture sixty men-at-arms, a hundred *saccomanni,* and two hundred horses.

*When the war was over, a tournament was held on the public square of Bologna, on February 28th to enliven the citizens and soldiers.

"After dinner in the presence of all the people, *the famous captain* Conrad Prospergh appeared with a band of thirty four Italian soldiers, equipped in white armour with his grand white ensigns. The opposite band was of thirty three German horsemen with red doublets, who were commanded by Prendiparte della Mirandola. They tourneyed worthily with lance and sword. The senate distributed money to the soldiers, and a cap entirely covered with the finest pearls to each of the captains."

*And in Piazza Santa Croce at Florence when a tournament to celebrate the peace was held in May, Prospergh again won the highest honors. Eighty knights divided into two brigades, were armed for the joust; the red com-

manded by Prospergh, the white by Count Antonio Guidi. 1892.
The victor in each brigade was to receive as a prize a
little lion covered with pearls : Conrad Prospergh won the
prize for the " red " side.

We may suppose that Hawkwood and his ladies assisted at this tournament, and a romancer might without too much boldness imagine that the young Catherine's heart palpitated in sympathy for the victorious
knight.

The fact remains that, by a legal document, Hawk- November 5.
wood promised Catherine in marriage to Conrad Prospergh,
German knight and captain, and to assign her such a
portion and in the manner which shall be determined by
the arbiters, which are the Signoria of Florence, and that
of Bologna.

The intervention of these sovereign arbiters is a proof
of the high consideration in which Hawkwood was held,
and of the great honor shown him in the marriage of his
daughter. The rank of the witnesses contributed not a
little to this, one was Milano de' Rastrelli of Asti, formerly a Florentine stipendiary in 1376, then marshal, and
who in due time was honorably interred in Santa Croce,
in the south aisle of which might once have been seen
his banners, targets, shields, his tunic with his emblema-
tical arms, and a memorial tablet with some funereal verses ; * the second was also a marshal, named Bartolomeo
dei Gherardacci di Geri of Prato, surnamed *Boccanera* (black
mouth), formerly exiled, and then in 1382 pardoned by the
Florentines, after which he became their captain-general ;
the third was no less a personage than Messer Ugolino
de' Preti da Montechiaro of Bologna, at that time captain
of the people in Florence.

---

* We take these particulars from the monograph by D. Maria Manni.
The numerous ensigns and memorials of the soldiers of the Commune in
ancient times were removed from Santa Croce in our days.

1393.

January 20.

The marriage was celebrated some weeks after the betrothal; in fact a public act signed at Hawkwood's residence at San Donato in Polverosa (witnesses amongst others Ser Francesco da Milano, Hawkwood's chancellor, and Ermanno of Acqui his usher) declares that Hawkwood had on that day married his daughter to Conrad Prospergh; who on his side acknowledged the receipt of the wedding portion of 2000 florins disbursed for Hawkwood by the chamberlains of the Commune. The chamberlains on behalf of the bride Catherine, *quæ quidem asseritur esse ætatis annorum quatuordecim,* acknowleged the receipt from Prospergh of 50 lire of *Morgengab,* * according to the custom of German weddings. The civil laws were less strict and more easily satisfied in those days.

Nor is the relative note lacking in the book of " customs on contracts." An entry under the date of *Duomo 1392* (by the Florentine style the year 1392 ended on March 24th 1393) is thus worded: " To the noble and worthy soldier Conrad *Prospero* German, captain and stipendiary of the Commune of Bologna, 2000 florins for the *dote* of the generous lady Catherine, — daughter of the magnificent and potent knight Sir John Hawkwood, captain-general of the Commune of Florence, — and now wife of the said signor Conrad."

Hawkwood however did not intend to expend his own wealth in marrying his daughters. He might perhaps have provided the necessary *trousseau,* but gorgeous dresses and other accessories to celebrate the wedding festivities were considered by him as superfluous. The mother had to provide them, and she was obliged to turn to her son-in-law. Strange as it may appear, we have a proof of it in

---

* The *Morgengab* is a present from the bridegroom to the bride the morning after the wedding: it is an ancient Teutonic custom. — (*Translator.*)

the following letter of the bridegroom Prospergh to Donato Acciaioli.

1392.

" *Magnifico et potenti militi dño Donato de Acciaiolis de Florentia hoñ et patri car.ᵐᵒ*

" Magnificent and powerful cavalier, with due recommendations I pray you for the love of myself and the good fame of Sir John Hawkwood * that you will use your influence with the honorable Signoria of Florence

---

* Donato Acciaioli, one of the most illustrious Florentines of his age (he translated Leonardo Bruni's history of Florence from the Latin, held high magisterial offices, and fulfilled important embassies), was on good terms with several of the English knights and especially with Sir John Hawkwood.

Manni (1770) speaks of several letters from Hawkwood to Acciaioli preserved in the Archives of the Certosa (near Florence — and founded, as all know, by the Acciaioli). At the time of the French suppression the Archives of the Certosa passed to the State, and in 1853 to the State Archives of Florence. The indices of these Archives register some letters and other Acciaioli papers; but posterior annotations say ' missing " or ' other things." There are also two imposing parchment envelopes with the words: *Letters addressed to the magnificent knight Donato Acciaioli*, in a fine border in the style of the 16ᵗʰ century, illuminated in colours on the back. One contains some insignificant monastic papers of the 17ᵗʰ and 18ᵗʰ centuries; the other is connected with the Acciaioli, but contains only certain accounts relative to the feuds in the Neapolitan states; the rest of the papers being copies of papal bulls, privileges, etc., entirely extraneous to the Acciaioli.

The letters were therefore abstracted, before the Certosa documents were transferred to the State Archives, and it is very likely that they ended in the celebrated collection of Sig. Libri, and then in the not less celebrated Ashburnham collection, of which the greater part of the Italian element returned to Italy on their purchase by the government, and was deposited in the Laurentian Library. Here there really exist fifteen large envelopes containing papers and letters of the Acciaioli; on one of the envelopes is written on the front and back with pencil the indication ' Sir John Hawkwood" and on the other envelopes is marked ' Letters and papers concerning Giovanni Acuto — relating to G. Acuto " extracted in the date 1873-74 etc. Had there been perhaps a special pile formed of all that related to our Condottiere? We cannot assert this, none of the fifteen envelopes contain the letters, seen by Manni himself; but we have found, instead, some documents relative to him, and a note from the Englishman John Beltoft, which recommends his comrade John Liverpool to Donato Acciaioli. Therefore without absolutely excluding the hypothesis that the Ashburnham collection has been sifted on behalf of English libraries or archives, and Hawkwood's letters kept in England, we may with more probability hold that Manni was mistaken about the above mentioned papers ' relative to Acuto."

1892. that I may have 1000 florins which are owing of my pension, either in money or in note of hand, that Madonna Donnina may dress my wife for the wedding on the 24th of this month. Madonna Donnina writes that nothing is wanting except the money to dress her. I have ordered them to make great *fêtes,* but they have put off so long the purchase of gowns for the maiden, who from what Madonna Donnina writes is more to you than your own child, and she tells me that for her there is no one like you, for she owes you more than her own father. I am always prepared to obey your every command.

" Bologna, January 9th.

" CONRAD DE PROSPERGH
knight and captain."

This document in good truth makes us doubt whether Hawkwood, now an aged man, had not given way to the sordid passion of avarice, which when it becomes habitual is often apt to increase in the old age of men who have gained and accumulated much in life. On the other hand we know that if Hawkwood had gained much, he had saved little, for his patrimonial condition is noted and documented. Facts are not wanting to prove that he knew how to be liberal with his money; Cavalcanti recounts that in one of the frequent occasions in which Hawkwood had to treat with Spinello Alberti, when the compact was concluded he made a present of 6000 florins to Spinello, who religiously passed it into the treasury of the Commune; but even if we choose to imagine the anecdote inexact, and that the 6000 florins had been saved by the ability of Alberti* in making negotiations, there is nothing

---

* It is certain that the honesty of the treasurer Alberti was exemplary: in the *Chronicle* of Giovanni Morelli we read: ' He was loyal and faithful to our Commune, and after his death his portrait was placed in the Chamber of the Commune to do him honour. He died so poor that his family could not give him the honorable funeral that he well deserved.' — (*Translator.*)

in the life of Hawkwood which authorises us to see in
him the avarice of a Harpagon. Prospergh's letter might
rather contribute to prove that which we have already
seen, and shall find Hawkwood himself asserting, that his
financial position was not at all a brilliant one.

XXXIX.

MONUMENT TO THE LIVING HAWKWOOD.

[*Consulte e pratiche e Provvisioni* of the Commune, in the State Archives of Florence —
D. M. Manni, Biography of Hawkwood in v. II of the *Appendix* to the *R. I. S.* of
Muratori — Giovanni Cavalcanti, Anecdotes in the Appendix to his *Storie Fioren-
tine* published amongst the *Documents for Italian history* — Richa, *Historical notices
of the Florentine churches* — Gregorovius, *History of Rome in the Middle-ages* —
Franco Sacchetti, *Novelle* — *Chronicle of Treviso* — *Letter* of Pier Paolo Vergerio.]

The old Condottiere was now drawing near the end of   1393.
his life, and the Florentines, though they could not expect
any more signal services from him, were yet generous in
shewing him honor and conferring favours.

"Let a proper provision be made to reward Hawkwood's services, in a manner which will display the gratitude we owe him; we will give him 25 lances, and   March.
observe all the compacts stipulated with him; and let the
Signoria make this provision as soon as possible."

In fact he was immediately hired with twenty five lances including archers.   April 2.

There was a general feeling, that not only ought all
the agreements made with him to be observed, but that
it would be right to procure him some prerogative besides.   April 6.

Meanwhile he gave his attention to regulating the
affairs of his patrimony in the best manner, as one who
feels death approaching is anxious to leave his family
without embarrassments. He had a settling of accounts   June 2.
with his former secretary Ser Francesco da Milano, and

1393. on the same day, at San Donato in Polverosa, his wife Donnina Visconti with her husband's order and consent signed an act of notary nominating Donna Agatina, daughter of Messer Cuccolo da Giussano, as the agent for her affairs at Milan; a choice which Hawkwood ratified in his own name.

These interests at Milan, — whether referring to her marriage portion, or hereditary or other possessions, — must have been very unsafe under Gian Galeazzo Visconti.

December 2. Hawkwood also gave a power of attorney to Antonio di Porcaria to receive certain sums not yet paid him by the Commune of Bologna. Nor were property taxes and financial difficulties lacking to Hawkwood in Florence.

July 11. He represents to the Priors that on the 10th of September 1392 the extraordinary accountants of the Commune had declared him to be debtor to the Commune for the sum of 1834 florins, on the original sum of 3000, of which he had paid the rest with the money received during his stay in the Kingdom of Naples, and they had intimated to him that " the 1834 florins must be paid within three months and fifteen days under penalty of a quarter of the sum in addition."

He added that he had not been able to pay, because the Commune had not disbursed to him the annuity of 2000 gold florins. He therefore asked that the debt against him should be annulled, that the cancelling thereof should be free of charge. He also explained that he had in pledge at Venice and Bologna some worked silver and jewels of no slight value, for which he paid very heavy usury, but from want of money was unable to redeem them; that considering the innumerable daily expenses his income was not sufficient for the support of his family. He was therefore obliged to sell his property, and having no bail for the sales he prayed that Guido Lippi, Davanzato Davanzati, Andrea Vettori, Niccolò da Uzzano and

Ser Benedetto di Lando might be made syndics for the purpose.

We remember that in 1387 Hawkwood had made an analogous request to the Commune, but he could not in the meantime have effectuated any sale in Tuscany, as the description of the property alleged in this petition of 1393 is identical with that of 1387,* the only difference in the more recent catalogue being that some of these possessions are placed in the name of John, son of Hawkwood, or in that of Donnina his wife. It is not strange that the alienation should be difficult, if we reflect that the continuous and costly wars had impoverished the citizens, either on account of the imposts or the suspension of commercial transactions.

From these documents it would appear that at the end of a career, apparently lucrative, Hawkwood had only a limited and compromised patrimony: that Tuscany and Italy had given him means to live in good style with his numerous family and to marry his daughters well, but his military habits had not allowed him to save much capital. Or he might also have sent some of his savings to invest in his own country.

---

* Neither is there in this second appeal any sign that Hawkwood possessed any house or habitation within the walls of Florence, and this is confirmed by what Giovanni Cavalcanti says: ' This esteemed man stayed in Santo Antonio inside the Porta di Faenza.' That is to say that when he visited the city from his suburban residence of San Donato, he lodged at Sant'Antonio, which was a vast convent, belonging to the regular ' canons hospitaller ' of Sant'Antonio of Vienne in France. The prior of Sant'Antonio had the title of *commendatore*; the fraternity possessed a large block of houses with gardens and fields and every convenience just within the Faenza gate. Both church and house were magnificent and noble buildings: among others Buffalmacco and Lippi painted frescoes in them. A bull of Calixtus III (1455) distinguished the monastery, the hospital, the mansion and the annexes. We understand then that it served as a free hospital for the poor, and as an hostelry for those who were able to give alms as an equivalent. The Commune of Florence had taken Sant' Antonio under its protection; Cardinal Giovanni de' Medici, afterwards Leo X, was its *commendatore*. But it was completely destroyed in 1534 by Duke Alessandro to build there that fortress *da basso* which still remains as a monument of Medicean tyranny.

1393.

However this may be, the Florentines, before he died, displayed an affection, gratitude and honor, so solemn and extraordinary, that the most sordid of mercenaries must have been touched; — how much more then must it have been appreciated by him, who, on the scales of conscience, had always given good weight of fidelity and honor compatible with his calling.

August 22.

In the Council of the Podestà and Commune the following deliberation was carried by a majority of 177 votes, against a minority of 8 — almost unanimously in fact:

" The magnificent and potent Lords, the Signori Priors of the Arts, and Gonfaloniere of justice of the people and Commune of Florence, being desirous that the magnificent and faithful achievements of the here-written Sir John, his fidelity to the honor and grandeur of the Florentine Republic, should not only be rewarded by remuneration during his life, as was done in his pension, but perpetually shown to his glory after death ; and above all that brave men may know that the Commune of Florence recompenses true service with her recognition and beneficent gratitude.... deliberate that the members of the *Opera* (Board of works) of Santa Reparata, i. e. the greatest of the Florentine churches — or even two parts of them if the other should be absent, or not forthcoming, or dissentient, or unwilling, — shall as soon as possible, beginning at the coming year, cause to be constructed and made in the said church, and in a conspicuous place, high and honorable, as shall appear best to them, a worthy and handsome tomb for the ashes of the great and brave knight Sir John Hawkwood, English captain-general of war to the said Commune, and who has more than once in the wars of the said Commune been captain-general. And the said sepulchre, in which the body of the said Sir John and no other body may be placed, shall be adorned with such stone and marble figures and armorial ensigns as shall seem convenient, either to the magnificence of the Commune of Florence, or to the honor and lasting fame of the said Sir John. And they may and ought to spend.... as much, how and whensoever they will."

Here Gregorovius exclaims with indignation, that " Florence who denied Dante a resting place, should erect an honorable monument in her Duomo to that robber of a Hawkwood ! "

But though this action may at first sight seem monstrous, there is nothing in it which should excite our wonder. The exiled Alighieri was not to his fellow-citizens and contemporaries that Dante who in years to come was to subdue the universe by admiration of his " divine Comedy; " he was a man of great genius, much culture, bold character and above all a man who, implicated in the political contests of his Commune, was left among the vanquished and exiled ones, who in exile continued to agitate for the restoration of the ghibellines in his city where the great majority were guelphs.

As to Hawkwood, we may judge his trade of a mercenary to be dishonest, but in those times it was a necessity created by circumstances: the Italian states were not accustomed to provide for their political needs by any other means. Hawkwood had several times efficaciously defended the Florentine Republic against external enemies, and more than once had he secured internal order; he had done his duty almost conscientiously, and certainly to the satisfaction of the Florentines who hired him. It would be an exaggeration to say that the Florentines considered him as a patriotic hero, but it would be unjust to pretend that they ought to consider him as a brigand.

It is also certain that sensible people knew how much better it would be for the Italian princes and communes not to be subjected to the forced services of condottieri. Franco Sacchetti thus concludes his 181" Novella, which

we have already referred to, and which speaks of Hawkwood
by name : — " Woe to those men and people who trust
too much in men of this kind. In them there is neither
love nor faith. They often do more harm to those who
pay them, than to their adversaries' soldiers ; and this
because, although they make a show of wishing to fight
and combat one against the other, they love each other,
better than they like the people who hire them, and they
seem to say : You rob on that side, I will rob well on this."

But this same Sacchetti, in his 36ᵗʰ Novella, must needs
ridicule the stupidity of the Priors of Florence in the war
of 1363, when Hawkwood fought for the Pisans, recognising
that " those who are used to commerce can never know
what war is, and therefore the Communes who do not live
in peace are undone." Now, municipalities did not know
how to keep the peace, and being composed of merchants
knew not how to make war; they were therefore constrained
to submit to the mercenary and untrustworthy arms of
adventurers.

Hawkwood's general reputation as captain of war in
Italy is easily gathered from the exaggerations of chroniclers and contemporaneous rhetoricians. The " Chronicles
of Treviso " say that Hawkwood " had fought in Italy
twenty three times in regular battles as a leader of men-
at-arms, and had always been victor except once when he
was vanquished."

Vergerio proclaims him " a man of generous spirit and
long experience," and does not hesitate to compare him " for
valour and glory almost equal to the ancient Imperators."

fortifications either at Migliari or at Pino, and we only have these slight mentions of the places; that Migliari in Val d' Ambra was a village dependent on the neighbouring Abbey of Agnano till 1384, in which year the Abbey (under the date of May 9th) placed itself under the Florentine Republic which soon after become master of Arezzo.

1394.

The Abbey of Pino was a more important possession. In the 10th century it was a dependency of the Abbot of Santa Fiora, was raised to a *Commenda* * in the 15th century; after that it passed to the nuns of St. Bridget in the Pian di Ripoli and finally to the Florentine hospital of Bonifazio.

1734.

We have already seen that Hawkwood, on returning from the Kingdom of Naples into central Italy, and fighting against Siena, had taken "certain places," regarding which he had made some proposals to the Florentines which they at the time excused themselves from answering.

1384.

It is very likely he had proposed to sell them, and that the places treated of were Migliari, del Pino, and Montecchio. The latter is in our own days a most remarkable and well preserved monument of ancient fortification, and as Hawkwood liked to stay there, as we see in Franco Sacchetti's 181st Novella, it merits a short description.

The castle of Montecchio-Vesponi rises above a hill on the northern boundary of the Val di Chiana, between the town of Castiglion Fiorentino and the city of Cortona.** It was already existing in the beginning of the 11th century, and during the 13th was enlarged, so that the " an-

---

* A *Commenda* was land belonging to the Church, the income of which was given to a priest or a knight. — (*Translator*.)

** The traveller who goes by rail from Florence towards Perugia and Rome cannot fail to see, on his left hand, between the stations of Castiglion Fiorentino and Cortona, the beautiful view of Montecchio with its picturesque battlemented towers. — (*Translator*.)

cient " and " modern " parts were distinguishable one
from the other, and it enclosed within its walls as many
as fifty six habitations which were rented by tenants, the
little church of San Biagio and a communal palace with
the relative courts ; it had, in its dependencies, moats and
*carbonaie,** suburbs and outskirts, fields and woods, land
and vines, and belonged to the Commune of Arezzo.
Towards the middle of the 14th century it was, like Castiglione, held by the Perugians, and it is probable that
having been damaged in the preceding wars, it was at
1351.   that time transformed and fortified so as to take the
distinct character of a fortress which it still preserves, for
it sustained a long siege by the Tarlati of Arezzo, the
Casali of Cortona, and the troops of archbishop Visconti,
after which it returned into the power of Arezzo.

Pignotti evidently errs when he states that the Florentines became masters of it in 1360 and confided the
government to Hawkwood, — who had not then crossed the
Alps. We are on the contrary confirmed in the opinion
1384.   that Hawkwood assumed the lordship on his own account,
and with the consent of the Florentines, for the Signoria
1387.   commanded the Podestà of Castiglione to allow three mule
loads of armour and implements which Hawkwood intended
to send to Montecchio to pass without toll. And when
1394.   Florence, after Hawkwood's renunciation, obtained posses-
May.
sion of Montecchio, she absolved this Commune from the
customs, taxes and fees which it should have paid to Arezzo,
as well as from all denunciations, condemnations and reprisals before the month of December 1384.

From the *Capitoli* relating to it we also find that
Hawkwood, as lord of Montecchio, received the introits of
customs, imposts, contracts, duties, loans, taxes, and a no-
minal toll, which was however rather important, on cattle

---

* *Carbonaia*, i. e. *dry-ditch*, in Latin *Pomœrium.* — (*Translator*).

and sheep, for the receipts of three years were destined to make a moat and other enclosures in the neighbourhood of Arezzo; that the keep of Montecchio was kept well supplied with ammunition and provisions : that a syndic presided over the Commune and that the inhabitants made regular provision of salt and wine, and possessed large and small cattle of their own, and a *soccida* * with the people of Cortona.

Whether Hawkwood in the ten years of his dominion worked at the restoration and modification of the walls, towers and keep of Montecchio is not proved; in any case the fortress preserved a certain military importance almost to the end of the 17th century. At that time, owing to the changed conditions of strategy, it became too antiquated and useless to form a good weapon of war; so the keep with its lofty tower, which some years before had been esteemed at 500 lire, was sold for 100 lire to a sergeant named Orazio Nocci.

1623

In 1641 Montecchio was raised to a marquisate by the Grand Duke Ferdinand II in favor of Tommaso Capponi; but his son the Marquis Lorenzo dying without offspring, Montecchio reverted to the State, and in the succession of governments in Tuscany it remained the property of the Crown until in our days it was purchased by the noted financier Giacomo Servadio together with vast demesnial estates in the neighbouring hills, and in the plain below, and it now belongs to his heirs.

A description written in 1575 mentions that the tower had several stories with vaulted ceilings and a good roof; it contained a dove-cot, and a bell; that it was a square tower, the sides of which were eight *braccia* ** wide, and

---

* A *soccida* is a contract for hiring out cattle on a similar principle to that adopted by our dairymen on English farms. — (*Translator.*)

** The *braccio* is about 23 inches. — (*Translator.*)

the height fifty braccia ; it was well preserved, and in good
condition. The keep, which was joined to the tower on
one side, measured on the other sides, respectively twelve,
twenty, and twenty five braccia ; the rooms which first
existed there had been already demolished. The moats
outside the walls surrounded the castle on all sides except
the west, where the gate was situated. They were
fifty braccia wide and occupied a superficies of twenty
thousand square braccia.

Another description dates from 1640 and gives a circum-
ference of four hundred and fifty braccia to the external walls
and a diameter across of a hundred and forty seven braccia.
The fortress contained nineteen *fuochi* (hearths or family
dwellings) and fifty three souls, the greater part under the
cure of a vicar, — all being peasants except the sergeant
Nocci who lived on a private income at the tower. The
people went to work in the fields lying below, and exercised
no industry, excepting that the women spun wool and flax ;
three of the inhabitants were inscribed in the infantry
militia, but were more adapted to peace than to arms.

Inside the circuit were two churches, the *pieve* (vi-
carage) of San Biagio, and the " company " of the Holy
Sacrament. For the rest there was much poverty, good
air, abundant hunting and fishing in the plain. " As to
the habitations inside the fortress they are almost all huts,
low, dark, and very ill kept, and in many places they are
in ruins. There is a small house for the officials, which
serves also as a council chamber, and is very bad. "

On this picture if we allow for the wear and tear of
the elements, and the permanent neglect of men, for another two centuries, we may have an idea of what Montecchio has become in our day. Its last proprietor restored
the great tower which had been split by a thunderbolt,
and replaced the Ghibelline battlements of the boundary
walls and seven towers which rise from them ; thus from

without, the fortress even now presents an imposing aspect, both military and picturesque, high on that hill covered with olives and pines, and thick underwood, in which the wild pomegranate predominates. But the moat is filled up, and within the enclosure the aspect of poverty disputes the space with the ruins. No more over the arched gateway are seen the figures of the protecting saints of Montecchio, St. Biagio, Martin and Egidio; they have completely disappeared. The parish church, which served also as a cemetery, has been dismantled; nothing remains of the keep but its walls, and we can hardly find a trace of the projecting gallery with its *piombatoi* * which anciently defended the gates. By a broken stairway we may with difficulty ascend to the only part of this gallery which remains on the boundary wall, towards the west, in which loop-holes had been pierced at the epoch when fire arms were first used. A very good wooden staircase entirely modern conducts us to the platform of the tower, from which the view is magnificent. It overlooks the Val di Chiana as far as Monte Amiata, across a branch of Lake Thrasymene, and the picturesque country town of Castiglione Fiorentino, but the bell no longer disturbs the rest of the pigeons, falcons and swallows whose abode it is.

The few poor houses surrounding it are as miserable as possible; only two human families reside there, with some fowls and a donkey, who may chose his meals among the chestnut burrs, acorns, poppies and nettles in the shadow of the wild *ailanthus*. Some vines, figs, and olive trees seem to vegetate there only to emphasize, by reminding one of fruitful culture, the almost sepulchral loneliness of that place, where, between one campaign and another, the

---

* *Piombatoi* were a species of loop-holes made in the floor of a projecting gallery in the battlements of an ancient fortress for the purpose of throwing down stones or heavy missiles on the assailants. — (*Translator*.)

old English Condottiere repaired for brief repose and to refurbish his arms, and where charity was denied to the monks who dared to ask it in the name of peace.

XLI.

DEATH AND FUNERAL OBSEQUIES.

[*Provvisioni e Regesto dei Capitoli* of the Commune in the State Archives of Florence — PIERO MINERBETTI, *Chronicle* — D. MARIA MANNI, Biography of Hawkwood in the II v. of the *Appendix* to MURATORI [*H. I. S.*] — *Song on the death of Messere Giovanni Aguto* published by ANTONIO MEDIN in the *Archivio storico italiano* of 1886 — *Chronicle* of BENEDETTO DEI.]

1394. The Commune of Florence had favorably received the proposal of Hawkwood as to the alienation of Montecchio, and of his other fortresses in the province of Arezzo, but the negotiations were complicated, as he wanted at the same time to liquidate his annuity for a fixed sum.

After many discussions the affair was concluded by the *provvisione*, approved by the Council of the Commune with 181 votes against 24 ; — here is the substance of it:

" Considering that Hawkwood, weary by reason of his great age, and, as he asserts, weighed down by infirmity, wishes to return to his old country, and to dispose of his pension, as well as the under mentioned among others of his possessions, and hence to make an exchange or composition (*staglum*); taking into account the negotiations which for some months we have been making, both on the part of the Commune and on that of Sir John; and wishing to dispose of them as seems most advantageous to the Commune, the council of the Gonfalonieri together with that of the twelve Buonomini after serious deliberation ordain,

" That the recipient Commune shall by public act be liberated and absolved from the here written pensions and sums due to Sir John, in such a manner that they shall not last longer than the present month of March, and from thenceforward shall no longer be due, but from that moment the Commune shall be free of them;

" The chamberlains of the Commune shall pay to Sir John or his procurator six thousand golden florins without any deduction, and without other formalities except the present provision, the payment of which sum shall be made as will be declared below;

" With the addition, however, that the herein mentioned fortresses, strongholds and possessions shall be held by the Commune, and to this end that all the rights appertaining to them shall be conceded by Sir John or his procurator, placing the Commune in their possession and custody.

" *Pensions and sums owing, above mentioned.*

" 1" of 1200 gold florins annually for the duration of his life, granted in 1375;

" 2ⁿᵈ of 2000 gold florins yearly for his life, conceded on April 1" 1391;

" 3ʳᵈ of 1000 gold florins granted to the Lady Donnina wife of Sir John, as long as she lives with her children in the city, country or district of Florence (April ditto);

" 4ᵗʰ sum of 2000 gold florins assigned as ' dote ' to the third daughter of Sir John (April ditto).

" *Fortresses and Places.*

" Castle of Montecchio;
" Stronghold or Castle of the Abbey of the Pino;
" Stronghold of *Migliaris;*
with the rights, jurisdictions, appurtenances, tribunals, men and persons etc.

" Of the said sum of six thousand gold florins two thousand to be paid immediately, the other four thousand

1394.

in three rates, the first within four months, the second within eight months, the third and last within a year.

" Moreover, as it is said that Sir John wishes to leave us, and with his family to go to England whence he had his origin — that the Signoria shall appropriate a thousand gold florins to purchase the objects with which they think well to honor Sir John and his son, according to the credit and magnificence of the Commune.

" That the sums to be paid as above cannot in any manner or for any claim be sequestered under penalty of a thousand small florins.

" All questions which might arise, concerning the execution of that which is above mentioned, shall be settled by the Signoria and their decision shall have absolute force.

" That the Signoria shall dispose as to the custody, government and administration of the three castles which are ceded.

" Finally, that the contracts or acts which are stipulated in order as above shall be free from all and every tax."

Man proposes and God disposes: five days after this *provvisione*, Hawkwood, who had for some time been reduced to pass his time between the bed and the couch, instead of setting out for his fatherland, departed for that journey which has no return.

How Messer Giovanni 'Acuto captain of war of the Commune of Florence died, and how the Commune paid him the greatest honors and he was interred in Santa Maria del Fiore; thus runs the title of a chapter in the chronicle of Piero Minerbetti, which assigns the date of March 16th as the day of his death, while the 17th results from documents. It may have been during the night between the 16th and 17th. It says that Hawkwood was ill at his place outside the city (without doubt it was San Donato), but that he died from a stroke of apoplexy.

The Priors elected a commission of citizens to order

and provide splendid obsequies, without regard to expense, and they proved really grand.

All the priests of the city attended, meeting in Santa Maria del Fiore; the catafalque was gorgeous; the choir, and other convenient places of the church were full of lighted torches.

The Signoria provided handsome black dresses for his son, wife and daughters, and all the numerous household.

The bier, adorned with very rich drapery of crimson velvet and gold, was first placed on the Piazza della Signoria, where the funeral procession formed, and to which all the magistrates contributed; i. e. the Signoria sent a hundred large wax torches, a banner with the arms of the Commune, another with the arms of the people, a standard with the arms of the Commune, and the shields pertaining thereto, a helmet with a golden lion with a lily in his claw as a crest. This was a Florentine ensign, and would seem to symbolize the valour of the Condottiere who was so faithful to the Commune.

The captains of the Guelph faction sent twenty wax torches, a pennon with the Guelph arms, and a helmet with the same design as a crest.

The " Six of the Mercanzia " sent twenty wax torches, and moreover they personally attended, together with the consuls of the Arts.

The soldiers of Hawkwood's lances with fourteen caparisoned horses carried several flags and pennons with his arms, his helmet with its crest, and the pennon with the Harpy (an ensign almost too eloquent), his sword and his shield.

The bier was raised by the cavaliers of Florence, none of whom were missing, as it was to do honor to such an illustrious comrade, and was carried to fetch the corpse where it lay (probably from San Donato it had been placed in some church in the city). It was laid on the open

1394.

bier robed in cloth of gold, and the cavaliers carried it to San Giovanni (the Baptistery) and placed it on the holy baptismal font covered with cloth of gold. Here Hawkwood was wept for by the women * in the presence of a great crowd, for all the shops of Florence were closed.

He was then carried into the Duomo, and placed under the catafalque, where the clergy recited the office, and a funeral oration was pronounced.

Finally he was interred in the place temporarily ordained, and the Signoria ** and people returned to their houses.

The place chosen was in the choir, and here Manni observes: " This was not the present choir but the first and more ancient wooden one, " and supposes every vestige of the sepulchre was lost, either when the new choir was made, or when the pavement was re-covered with marble (1519-1524).

But it is also likely that the temporary place of sepulture in the choir had no especial mark, the definite tomb having been decreed seven months before. It was not built however, as the remains were sent to King Richard II in England.

Minerbetti's description in prose is precisely analogous to that of a contemporaneous *Cantare* in *rima ottava*.

---

* Manni observed how Dante desired similar solemn funeral rites in the Baptistery, when he said in *Paradiso* XXV:

. . . . ed in sul fonte
Del mio battesmo prenderò il cappello.

He noted the error of those who arbitrarily amplified the women weeping (*donne piangenti*) over Hawkwood's bier into noble matrons (*nobili matrone*); these were nothing more than a derivation from the Roman *preficæ*, and the custom is still kept up in many places on the Mediterranean.

** The diarist Simone della Tosa observed that the Signoria were accustomed never to go out of the Palace unless on occasions of the greatest solemnity.

If the *Obsequies and honors made for Messer Giovanni*   **1394.**
Aguto our captain of war furnished the argument for
popular poesy, and inspired a poem of ingenuous but decidedly elegiac character, it shows that the man was sin-
cerely loved and esteemed in Florence. There was nothing
now to hope or to fear from the dead man : the sumptuous official observances decreed by the magistrates might
have been the fruit of political prudence, to shew to future condottieri, that the Commune knew how to value
and recompense their fidelity; but the verses correspond
to a heartfelt sentiment, to the sincere opinion of the
citizens.

This is the more valuable in that the verses retained
their popularity for many years afterwards. Benedetto Dei,
who wrote his chronicle late in the 15th century, remarked
that he knew them by heart. The poet is not known,
but this matters little : he was the interpreter of all the
people.

To the details described by Minerbetti the *Cantare*
adds his own, from which we learn that the ensigns, flags,
and helmets with crests were carried on large war chargers, draped with housings and breast plates; it is specified that the flags offered by the wife and family of
Hawkwood were six in number; that the general closing
of shops was ordered under penalty, and many men dressed
in black by the Commune followed the bier with their
heads covered with hoods, as a sign of great grief; and that
a multitude of priests walked behind bearing torches and
candles and singing psalms. There were the minor friars,
the Servite monks, those of San Marco, Ognissanti, Monte
Uliveto, the Dominicans, the monks of the Angioli, the
Carmine, San Miniato and "all the rest" (*tutti quanti*),
and all the bells rang out a death peal.

At the holy font of the Baptistery, the corpse was
exposed on the bier, which was surrounded by thirty wax

1394. torches; a drawn sword was laid on the breast, and the *bâton* of command in the hand.

The obsequies in the Duomo being finished, the priests carried the body into the sacristy.

The *Cantare* ends by invoking from the Lord and the Madonna eternal life and supernal glory for him who had lived under the wings of victory.

XLII.

THE MONUMENT IN SANTA MARIA DEL FIORE.

[*Provvisioni* of the Commune in the State Archives of Florence — CAVALLUCCI, *Documental history of Santa Maria del Fiore* — D. MARIA MANNI, Biography of Hawkwood in v. II of the *Appendix* to MURATORI [*R. I. S.*] — VASARI, *Lives* etc. — FOSSOMBRONI, *Memoria sul moto degli animali* — CICOGNARA, *History of painting* — BECKER, *Adventurous Lives — Familiar letters* of SER LAPO MAZZEI published by CESARE GUASTI — RICOTTI, *History of the mercenary companies.*]

April 14. The state ceremonials of Hawkwood's funeral were costly in proportion to their grandeur: the account was made up, with a result of 410 gold florins, 1 lira, 11 soldi. There still remained to provide the monumental tomb, in conformity to the deliberations taken during Hawkwood's life, and as in those days no public work of any importance was admitted in the city unless it fulfilled the exigencies of art, the following " provision " was taken, 1395. which is mentioned by C. I. Cavallucci:

" Being desirous of renewing in a more decent manner the tomb of Piero Farnese* and satisfying the provision of

---

* Piero Farnese, a worthy captain, died, in the service of Florence against the Pisans, in 1362 the year before the English came into Tuscany. He also was honored by the Florentines with a sepulchral monument in Santa Maria del Fiore: there is still seen his marble sarcophagous over the first lateral door to the right, adorned with the lily and the cross of Florence, the arms of the Guelph party and the Farnese lilies: formerly the sarcophagous supported a canopy over the statue of Piero Farnese mounted on a mule, to

the Commune respecting the monument *incliti militis Domini Joh. Augut olim honorati capitanei guerre Comunis Florentie et honoris et status ipsius communis iamdiu continui et solliciti defensoris* — the operai * wishing to place the said tombs in the façade which is between the two doors towards Via dei Cassettai ** will cause to be made *honorabiliter quantum decet, deliberaverunt: Primo in ipsa facie ipsas sepolturas designare per pictores bonos, ut omnibus civibus ad ipsam ecclesiam venientibus ostendatur et super eas maturius et honorabilius et cum deliberatione omnium volentium consulere, postea ad ipsarum perfectionem procedatur:* and they commission Agnolo di Taddeo Gaddi and Giuliano d'Arrigo, painters, to design and paint them for the price of thirty florins."

But then a request came to the Commune of Florence, which truly honored the memory of John Hawkwood: the King of England demanded that the body of the warrior should be restored to his native country; and the Commune did not refuse it, perhaps remembering that a little time before his death Hawkwood was arranging everything for his return home. The consent of the Signoria was given in the following letter dated June 3ʳᵈ 1395 : ***

" Most serene and invincible prince, most reverend lord and our especial benefactor.

" Our devotion can deny nothing to the eminence of your highness. We will leave nothing undone that it is possible to do, that we may fulfil your good pleasure. And therefore,

---

record that in the day of his victory over the Pisans his horse had been killed and he had continued to fight mounted on a mule; but both statue and canopy, which were of wood painted and gilt, tumbled to pieces in 1842 when they were removed to clean the inner walls of the Cathedral.

* Members of the ' Opera ' of the Duomo, a large society of influential citizens, artists and architects, who superintended the works of the Duomo. — (*Translator.*)

** On the north side of the Cathedral.

*** The text has been published by Manni.

although we hold that it reflected glory on us and on our people to keep the ashes and the bones of the late brave soldier, and most remarkable leader Sir John Hawkwood (*Haukkodue*) who, as commandant of our army, fought most gloriously for us, and whom at the public expense we interred honorably in the principal church of our city, nevertheless, according to the tenor of your request, we freely concede permission that his remains shall return to his native land, so that it shall not be said that your sublimity has uselessly and in vain demanded anything from the reverence of our humility...."

The ashes of Hawkwood having been transported to England, it no longer appeared urgent to erect his tomb and that his memory would be sufficiently honored by the fresco which had been painted to serve as a model on the wall of the Duomo. Time went on to 1436, when they were setting the Duomo in order for the solemn consecration which was to be given by Pope Eugene IV who was in Florence for the famous council. Either because the picture had suffered or they wanted it to be a little more decorous, the "operai" deliberated "to repaint the figure of Sir John Hawkwood in the same manner and form as it was before painted." A few days afterwards the idea prevailed of erecting the monument: "Let us make the tomb of *Signor Giovanni Hauto* according to the decisions of the councils of the People and the Commune of Florence, and hasten them in the work for the honor of the Commune and the Opera."

But this proposal only lasted a few hours; for reasons it is allowable to suppose of economy, they returned to the idea of the fresco: and Paolo Uccello was commissioned to paint the figure of Hawkwood in *terra verde* (a colour that imitated bronze) where it was at first, and with the salary which shall be determined.

1436.
May 18.

May 26.

May 30.

Neither ability nor reputation were wanting in Paolo   1436.
Uccello ; he was however unfortunate, as we read of him
in Vasari : he executed the commission rapidly it is true,
but with little success. In fact it was deliberated in
council : " That the head master of the works of the   June 28.
Duomo should cause the horse and figure of Sir John
Hawkwood done by Paolo Uccello to be destroyed, because
it is not painted as it should be." We must admit that
some kind of merit was acknowledged even in that first
work, for the commission was renewed to the same artist.   July 6.
" Paolo Uccello shall again paint and portray in *terra
verde* the figure of *Signor Giovanni Hauto* and of the
horse of the said Sir John, for the salary and price which
shall be established." This time Uccello employed an extra
fortnight and no objection was raised : the " operai " com-   August 31.
missioned two of their number, Francesco di Benedetto di
Caroccio Strozzi and Simone di Noferi Bonaccorsi, " to
put a price on the picture of the horse and person of
Sir John Hawkwood, painted in the principal Florentine
church."

" This work," says Vasari, " was then thought, and is
still considered, one of great beauty of its kind ; and if
Paolo had not made the horse move his legs on one side
only, which horses do not naturally do, since they would
fall if they did (which happened, perhaps, because the
artist was not accustomed to ride, or to see so much of
horses as of other animals), the work would have been
perfect. The proportions of the horse, which, as has been
observed, is of immense size, are extremely beautiful. On
the basement are inscribed the following letters : *Pauli
Uccelli opus.*" *

For the rest the criticism of Vasari on the horse does
not hold, as Fossombroni and several other competent

---

* Bohn's edition of Vasari, vol. I, page 356. — (*Translator.*)

observers cited by Cicognara have shown: Hawkwood's horse has the pace of the *ambio* (amble).

The fresco was transferred to canvas about 1845 and moved from the northern to the western wall of the Duomo over the lesser door on the left, while above the right door is, also in fresco, the equestrian figure of another condottiere much esteemed in Florence — Niccolò Tolentino.

Paolo Uccello's grand picture of Hawkwood, with a stone cornice in the style of the decorations of the Duomo, occupies almost all the wall; the cornice rests on two half capitals with rich foliage of acanthus leaves. The equestrian statue stands out from the reddishpurple back-ground, framed in a wide and elegant frieze of " grotesques," and other renaissance mouldings painted in grey " chiaroscuro " on gold colour. Hawkwood has a cap on his head, and a short doublet over the armour; he holds in his right hand the *bâton* of captain of war. A sarcophagous, resting on a fine architectural base of two grades, serves as a pedestal for the statue. The whole is in a monotone bronze green, except the arms, the housings and harness of the horse which are of a scarlet colour with large silver bosses. So this picture gives no authority for the assertion that Hawkwood was of a ruddy complexion, with brown hair and eyes: we can only see that he was of more than medium height, with broad shoulders, powerful chest, and the very build of a warrior. His face seems to have been entirely shaved (a custom taken probably from the Bretons in Lombardy, where the word *britonare* long remained, meaning " to shave," but the usage was general in Tuscany a long while before the English came there).

We may admire the regular and sculpturesque features, in which the English may recognize not only the type of their own race, but see that in character they especially resemble the hereditary physiognomy of the Stanley family.

The epigraph, composed by Bartolommeo di Ser Filippo Fortini, says:

JOANNES ACUTUS EQUES BRITANNICUS
DUX ÆTATIS SUÆ CAUTISSIMUS ET REI
MILITARIS PERITISSIMUS HABITUS EST.

It is a modest and reserved epigraph, whose truth-fulness we cannot doubt, and to which we, who have studied the life of the Condottiere, may even find something to add. It is decidedly preferable in every way to the bombastic epigram with which Giulio Feroldo pretended to celebrate the imaginary portrait of Hawkwood, published among the " Illustrious warriors " by Paolo Giovio.

The short biography compiled by the famous bishop of Como is merely fantastic, but it proves that the fame of the English adventurer survived for several generations in Italy.

Nor was the memory of his achievements soon extinguished in the popular tradition: for several years after his death his name * was not only still extolled, but the details of his feats of arms were generally known.

" I like a man who is subtile and long sighted. Perhaps that is what my friend does when he quotes to me the ruse of Sir John Hawkwood when he wanted to flee (*lo spianare di Messer Giovanni Auto quando volea fuggire....*)

" .... You who give out that I like to live in disorder, do you not remember that story of Sir John Hawkwood! (*quella novella di Messer Giovanni Auto*).

" .... Is it not true.... that John Hawkwood was not

---

* We have already noticed and the reader of this story will have verified the multitude of variations with which the documents and the contemporaneous chroniclers wrote the name of Hawkwood. — Some chroniclers even mistook his nationality : the *Chronicle of Rimini* called him ' a great German commander.' — And even learned men of modern times had a difficulty in finding the orthography of the esotic surname : Michele Luigi Malpeli, publishing in 1806 the *Dissertations on the ancient history of Bagnacavallo*, speaking of *Acuto*, observes in a note : ' This English surname was *Karcoud*.' — (*Translator*.)

worth 500 lances (*che Messer Giovanni Auto non valesse per cinquecento lance....*) "

These allusions are found here and there in the interesting " Familiar letters of Ser Lapo Mazzei " written at the beginning of the 15th century.

In fact the best Italian condottieri who bore arms in Italy after Hawkwood, i. e. Alberico da Barbiano, Attendolo Sforza, Braccio da Montone, not less than Carlo Malatesta, Paolo Orsini, and Mostarda, may be considered as his disciples in the art of war, for if not wholly pupils they fought with or against him. As Ricotti justly observes : " I do not know if *Giovanni Acuto* were the last of the foreign condottieri or the first of the Italian ones, that is the first who designed and perfected those military factions with a certain science. Next in rank came Braccio and Sforza with their two schools," the *Braccesque* and the *Sforzesque*.

XLIII.

HEREDITARY LIQUIDATION.

[*Consulte e pratiche* and *Provvisioni* of the Commune, in the State Archives of Florence — Article on the death of John Hawkwood by ANTONIO MEDIN in the *Archivio storico italiano*, 1886 — LAROUSSE, *Dictionary of the 19th century*, article Hawkwood — Registers of the *Chamber* of the Commune of Florence — *Capitoli* of ditto.]

The illustrious Condottiere being honorably interred, the Florentine Commune gave its attention to the execution of the compacts made with him almost *in articulo mortis*. The mercantile spirit of the citizens suggested the expedience of procuring some advantage, some *prerogative,* while giving effect to those stipulations, seeing that *chi muore giace* (he who dies lies still), they thought it urgent beyond everything to go directly and take possession of the Castle of Montecchio.

1394.
April 6.

They easily induced the widow Donnina to write to the castellan that he should consign the fortress to them, and accompanied the letter with the following message which we translate : *

1394.

" To Richard Kell, castellan of Montecchio.

" Our well beloved ! According to the agreement which we made not long ago with the magnificent Sir John 'Haucud' when he was in this life, his noble consort the lady Donnina writes that you may concede to us the fortress of Montecchio, with its guard and garrison. We require therefore that you consign the same, with all the munitions of war which it contains, to Antonio Materio, our well-beloved familiar, whom we send for this purpose, and who will receive it in the name of our Commune by public act of notary. Then, as soon as may be without inconvenience to yourself, we beg you to come into the presence of our Signoria, to the effect that we may know what is due to you for stipend and *provvigione,* which we shall pay integrally, and send you without delay."

April 25.

We see that if Florence demanded her dues, she did not refuse to give the same to others. The last contract was to the effect that the engagement of the twenty five lances, and the stipend of 1200 florins, and the pension of 2000 florins would not cease till the end of March.

It was therefore requested of the Signoria on behalf of his children that the payment might be effected for the whole month, although Hawkwood died on the 17th, subtracting only the payment of the fifteen lances, who were serving the Commune at Mantua, and were there directly paid by it ; and that the required payments should be made to any procurator of the late Sir John, who should have permanent power of attorney since his death. The petition

---

* See the text of Document LXVIII.

was made " so that the said children may pay the expenses of the funeral and the domestics who had served Hawkwood during his life." On the whole it was a claim founded on justice, and was accepted with 188 votes against 28.*

Had Hawkwood made a will? It was asserted that he had, and it was even added (for example in the " Dictionary of the 19th century ") that he left a legacy to found in Rome a hospital for English pilgrims, as though in expiation for the rapacity of his career, and for not having taken the cross against the infidels as he had promised. It is certain that this problematic foundation had not a canonical institution. If he ever made a last testament, he did not make it in Florence; the archives of Florentine notaries exist in a complete and well-arranged condition, classified by quarters; the indices of the testator's name drawn up in Florence after 1350, were taken from the " Opera of the Duomo," which exacted a small tax for each will. We have found a mention of the will of John Berwick (*Giovanni Berichie*) *anglicus stipendiarius comunis Florentiæ* in 1385, but no sign of that of John Hawkwood.

Nor does his name figure in the registers of the hospital of St. Maria Nuova, to which it was the custom in those days to leave some alms in every will.

But although he intended to return to England, he feared his end was drawing nigh; a deed executed on January 10th 1395, of which we shall soon see the substance, commenced by recalling the transaction of March 1394, with these particulars, " that Hawkwood, weighed down by old age and a certain singular infirmity (?) which almost continually keeps him in bed or in the house, not being able to fulfil his military or other duties, *but rather fearing a speedy death,* is prudently induced " etc.

---

* *Provvisione* published by Antonio Medin.

Nor did Hawkwood die without leaving a general power *1394.*
of attorney in the interest of his children, to Giovanni
di Iacopo Orlandini : and his faith was fully justified,
for Orlandini executed the trust with much zeal.

The final compact with Hawkwood reserved to the
Signoria the resolution of eventual questions, and these
were not long in rising up.

By force of that contract the Commune was to pay
1000 florins to honor the departure of Hawkwood, who
intended to go to England: death prevented the journey,
— ought those 1000 florins to be paid notwithstanding?

And how could they pay the 2000 florins of wedding
portion to Anna third daughter of the deceased? as she
was under age, and had no guardian or possibility of
having one, and being a minor she was not empowered to
give a receipt? In every way the Signoria and the Councils, acknowledging the propriety of faithfully observing
the agreement, deliberated to consider Orlandini as procu- Decemb. 15.
rator of Anna the minor, and to pay to him her portion
and the donation of 1000 florins.

Through Orlandini's zeal and the good will of the
Signoria, the liquidation of accounts between Hawkwood's
heirs and the Commune proceeded expeditiously. The
Commune decided " that the noble man John *fils,* and the Decemb. 22.
daughters of the deceased John Hawkwood, and therefore
his inheritance and estates, and the estates of the said
John his son, shall not at any time nor by any claim be
summoned, taxed or molested either in the city, country
or district of Florence, by any one who is not of Florentine birth or of Florentine parentage on the male side,
for any obligation contracted in his life by the aforesaid
quondam John Hawkwood."

· This was according to international private right, as
it then existed, but it might happen that some Florentine

would buy the credits and in that case the benefit would all go to the usurers.

The widow Donnina, to obtain power of administration, declared that she required a tutor (*mundualdus*) who could authorise her legal acts instead of her deceased consort, and begged that the notary would allow Orlandini to be this legal guardian. This being done and drawn up, she, " with the consent, authority, and permission of the guardian, being certified by the notary of her rights, and of that which she was about to do, accepted the transaction of March 12th, inasmuch as regarded her annual pension of 1000 florins, and gave a receipt in full with a promise *in perpetuo* never to demand it again, under penalty of 2000 florins.

It is noteworthy that the deed was executed " in the house of habitation of the before mentioned lady — in the parish of Santa Maria di Quarto, *pieve* di Santo Stefano in Pane. She lived then in the suburbs, but not at San Donato, which confirms that Hawkwood must have effected the sale of his possessions in preparation for his intended return home, only reserving the temporary use of San Donato. Correlative to the above, Giacomo Orlandini as agent to the deceased Hawkwood gave on the following day a full receipt and promise never again to demand the annual pensions of 1200 and 2000 florins, nor the 2000 florins for Anna's wedding portion and the 1000 florins of yearly pension to the widow Donnina. He moreover ceded and transferred to the Commune the proprietorship and possession of the fortresses in the Arezzo territory. The said Orlandini besides, of his own spontaneous will, moved thereto by affection for the son of Sir John for whom he had long conducted negotiations, and so that the 1000 gold florins might be paid by the Commune besides the 6000 (according to the contract of March 12th and the declaration of December 15th 1394), en-

gaged that Anna's wedding portion of 2000 florins should
never be required of the Commune, he being himself the
guarantee to hold the Commune indemnified for any preten-
sion to the whole or a part of this claim.

A last difficulty arose, derived from a new law of December 1394, respecting the payment of stipends, which
was resolved by abrogating this law for the occasion; consequently, recognising that to the late (*olim*) John Hawkwood 7000 gold florins, in all, are due, of which his agent
has as yet received 5000, the chamberlains are authorised
to place on the side of expenditure the payment of the
entire sum.

In fact the registers of the Chamber show that the
payments, begun October 1ˢᵗ 1394, were completed and regu-
lated under the two dates of March 4ᵗʰ and 10ᵗʰ 1395, i. e.:

March 4ᵗʰ	florins	2000				
	➤	1333	soldi	6	danari	8
	➤	1333	➤	6	➤	8
March 10ᵗʰ	➤	1000				
	➤	1333	➤	13	➤	4
	➤	6999	➤	25	➤	20

The 1000 florins, as we know, were those destined
to compliment the departure of Hawkwood for England:
but in the register of the chamberlains they are entered
to *honor the son of Sir John.*

And in truth Hawkwood's son was flattered and favoured
by the Commune in regard for the merits of his father.
Whilst the suits relating to the liquidation of the paternal estate were pending, *Giovanni Augud junior* was
engaged with two lances, comprising his own person and
lance, from January 4ᵗʰ to the end of March 1395, with a
stipend of 16 gold florins a month each lance. There is
nothing to show that he was already a man of war, and
this appears to be merely a mark of honorary courtesy.

1395.   Having terminated the arrangements of the patrimonial affairs in Italy, the widow Donnina decided to go to England with her children (i. e. John and the young girl Anna), for her husband had also left possessions in his native land, which required the eye of a master in those times which were so hard for orphans and widows.

The Signoria of Florence did not fail to introduce the widow and her children to the King of England by the following letter of recommendation, which we here translate : *

     " *To the King of England.*

     " Most serene and most glorious prince, and our lord and singular benefactor.

     " We cannot in any way neglect the posterity of your subject, the noble and brave knight Sir John Hawkwood, who for a long time has faithfully and with true honesty fought in our service, nor may we omit to render honor and service to him in every possible manner, the more so that the progeny of that man, whose glorious celebrity reflected honor on all the English nation,** are left far away from their fatherland, and since the death of that worthy sire find themselves as strangers and pilgrims in Italy, although for the merits of the father, our city is disposed to embrace them, and welcome them as our own children. Therefore it is that their mother — a consort truly worthy of such a husband — having decided, as soon as the age of her children will allow of it, to transfer herself with them to England; we with all possible devo-

---

     * See the text of Document LXIX.
     ** How much Hawkwood's achievements raised the reputation of the English in the Florentine minds, is seen in the negotiations (see Documents LXX and LXXI) about the hiring of Nicholas Clifton, recommended by the King of England, and who had before been in the Florentine service (see Chapter XXI).

tion recommend the children and family of the aforesaid
Sir John to your Highness, with every reverence, and with
all the affection in our power, supplicating the clemency
of your Sublimity, that from the height of your exalted
state you will deign to receive these wards with benevolence, and aid their undertakings with your royal favor.
And verily the estates under wardship are those of the
widow and orphans, whom divine laws ordain shall be
taken care of by the princes of the world, and judges of
the earth. Therefore we add that it becomes your royal
majesty to remember with grateful memory, even after
death, the virtue of those subjects who shed honor on your
country, so that the minds of others may be inspired to
show themselves equally great, and the reward of their good
works may be transferred to their heirs; so that they
may hope to live in fame even after death, seeing that
by the merits of their fathers the children of the brave
receive especial favors and grace. As to us and our devotion, most benevolent prince, we cannot express how
acceptable and pleasing any thing which may be done
for the family of the aforesaid Sir John will prove to us.
" Given from Florence, March 29th. III indiction (1395)."

XLIV.

HAWKWOOD'S DESCENDANTS. — THE TWO ROSES.

[D. MARIA MANNI, Biography of Hawkwood in v. II of *Appendix* to MURATORI [*R. I. S.*] —
Transactions of the Essex Archæological Society, v. III — *Ancient wills* by H. W. KING,
The will of Sir Thomas Tyrell of Heron Knight ob. 1476 — CORIO, *Milanese history* —
WRIGHT's *History of Essex* — MUILMAN's *History of Essex* — GOUGH, *Additions to Bri-
tannia* — JOHN WEEVER, *History of Essex* — MORANT, *Ancient funeral monuments* —
FULLER, *Worthies of England* — Parliament Rolls — *Feet of Fines County dieerses* — *Close
Rolls*, 10th year of Henry IV — *Letters of St. Catherine of Siena*, commentated by NIC-
COLÒ TOMMASEO — SHAKESPEARE, *First part of Henry VI*, act II, scene IV; *Measure
for measure*, act I, scene II, edition 1623.]

Notwithstanding the warm recommendation of the Florentines, it is not known precisely whether Donnina Vis-

conti put into effect that removal into England which she had planned. The letter in which the Commune of Florence granted * to King Richard the remains of John Hawkwood for which he had asked, concludes with the

following expressions, without mentioning the widow: " The son and the posterity of the said Sir John, who rendered famous the name and glory of Eglishmen ** in Italy, and also our merchants and citizens, we recommend to the benevolence of your highness with all due reverence and with all possible supplication."

Perhaps the widow remained in Italy, where her kinship and the high esteem inherited from her husband *** enabled her to marry her third daughter as well as the others. The latter in fact (as we know from a book of *Riforma-gioni* of 1418 cited by Manni) married Ambrogiuolo di Piero della Torre, of the great Milanese family, a relative of Buonamico della Torre, who was captain of the people at Florence in 1420, and *podestà* in 1431 ; the marriage was not ill-assorted, as the Torriani had already fallen not only from the Signoria of Milan, but also from the successive patriarchal splendor of Friuli.

Manni supposes that from this same Anna was born another Donnina, who afterwards married the Milanese captain Giovanni Casati, and was the mother of the humanist Scipio Casati : but Manni was sometimes at fault in his suppositions, as for instance when he thought that Hawkwood was the son of a certain Anizzo because he had sometimes found the name *Anisi* united with that of

---

* See Chapter XLII.

** Just as the name *Francesco* in Italy increased after Italian intercourse with the French, so the military predominance of the English in the second half of the 14th century gave rise to the names *Inghilesco* and *Inghilese ;* a daughter of Bernabò Visconti was also called *Inglesia.*

*** From Document LIX it seems that Hawkwood asked Niccolò one of the illustrious and rich Sienese family of the Salimbeni to be godfather to one his children, and his friendship with Acciaioli is also well-known.

John Hawkwood in matters of war; but we know that this was no other than the German *Anisi di Rieten.*

And were there not some romancing genealogists who wanted to trace the descent of the Lords of *Montauto* and Anghiari from Hawkwood?

It is not known whether Hawkwood's race was perpetuated in Italy through Catherine wife of the valiant German Conrad Prospergh. As to Janet who had married Brezaglia di Porcia, some documents in Friuli (which from her place of residence call her *Zannetta di Castell' alto*), state that in 1425 she was left a widow without children.

In the "Transactions of the archæological society of Essex" we find named as the wife of Sir William de Coggeshall "*Antiocha,* daughter and heiress of the famous warrior Sir John Hawkwood, and of *Aufricia* his wife, the natural daughter of Bernabò Duke of Milan." Let us pass over the fact that Bernabò was not a duke, let us pass over the name of Aufricia given to the wife of Hawkwood, and merely note that the silence of the Florentine documents entirely excludes the existence of a fourth daughter from that marriage.

For the same reason we cannot admit a fifth, *Fiorentina* who, according to Corio, was married to Lancelot of the noble Milanese family del Mayno. Perhaps *Fiorentina* was the daughter of Hawkwood's first wife, whose name is entirely unknown, and who is not *documentally* proved to be his legitimate wife. That she was a legal wife rather than mistress is however confirmed by the memorial on the monument erected to Hawkwood in his native place.

At Sible Hedingham, near *Hawkwood's Manor,* in the parish church of St. Peter, may be still seen a part of a canopy under an arch, where there once rose a noble cenotaph; the arch bore the allusive heraldic decoration of a hawk flying amidst trees (Hawk-wood), and several figures of hawks are sculpured in other parts of the church. This suffices to make it clear that the monument belonged to a Hawkwood, and that the church, whose architecture answers to the epoch of Edward III, but whose foundations are much more ancient, was rebuilt or restored, at the expense, or by liberal contributions from one of the Hawkwood family, in the last half of the 14th century. There seems no doubt that the monument was precisely the tomb of our John Hawkwood.

It had been for some time destroyed for the substitution of benches in 1631, when John Weever wrote, but both he and Morant agree that with the abundant (?) money yielded by the heritage of Hawkwood, and sent to England, his friends erected the cenotaph: and Morant (who must have seen some old design) adds: " From the effigies on this monument it would seem that he had two wives."

Weever even gives the names of these zealous friends, who were Robert Rokeden sen.', Robert Rokeden jun.' and John Cook, — perhaps the man whom Italian chroniclers called *Cocco* and who was amongst the leaders in Hawkwood's Company. And not content with perpetuating the memory and providing a tomb for the captain, they also took thought for his soul, by founding a chapelry in the same church, and another in the Priory of Hedingham castle " to pray for the souls of Sir John Hawkwood, and of Thomas Oliver * and John Newenton Esquires, two of his comrades who died in Italy.

The priest of the chapelry of Sible Hedingham lived in a house close by, called the Hostage (anciently Hostelage) because it formerly served as a hospice for pilgrims.

Thus the man who in his life time had always renounced peace, had solemn repose after death with many prayers and requiems.

---

* There are still Olivers in Essex.

As to his son, the father's reputation and the recommendations of the Florentines, united to his patrimonial heritage, rendered him good service in his fatherland. He was created knight and naturalized in the eighth year of King Henry IV, as appears from the Record *Johannis filius Johannis Hawkewood, miles, natus in partibus Italiæ, factus indigena anno 8 Henrici IV: mater ejus nata in par-* 1407. *tibus transmarinis,* and from the textual privilege which we publish among the documents.*

These favors, like the homage rendered by King Richard II to the memory of Hawkwood, in asking the Florentines for his remains, shew that if there had been circumstances in the fortunate life of the Condottiere which caused him to fall into disgrace with his natural sovereign, the position achieved by him in Italy had entirely rehabilitated him.

We speak thus because in the English Parliament Rolls, in the 51ˢᵗ year of Edward III, is registered a "petition of Sir John Hawkwood to the King demanding a 1376-77. patent of pardon as the King has promised to Sir Robert Knolles,** *for God and charity.*" We must however confess that there is no proof of the result of the petition, nor even whether it received an answer, and that we are not in a position to throw any light on the cause, or significance of the facts to which it refers, for at that time Hawkwood had been fighting fifteen years in Italy, where the King of England had no rights, nor interests, or disputes. We can only risk a supposition: we already know that when 1368. the Duke of Clarence, son of Edward III, died in Lombardy a short time after having married Violante Visconti, and her father Galeazzo lost no time in retaking possession of the places in Piedmont which had been given her

---

* See Document LXXII.
** Respecting Knolles, Hawkwood's comrade. see page 15.

as her portion, Hawkwood, without mixing himself in the
contest, continued to serve the Visconti elsewhere. It
might be that his conduct in this circumstance being considered by Edward III as incompatible with the loyalty
of a subject, may have been declared to be criminal and
punished as such, for example by banishing Hawkwood
from the Kingdom.

It is not probable that the petition was from John
Hawkwood the elder brother of our Condottiere, because he
would have been distinguished as *senior :* there is in fact
1370-71. a document of the 45ᵗʰ year of Edward III, referring to
a judicial sentence, respecting divers possessions, between
Thomas de Vere Earl of Oxford and his wife Matilda on
one part, and several persons qualified as usurpers on the
other, *John de Hawkwood senior* being named among the
usurpers.

To return to Hawkwood's son, who unlike his father had
no history after his elevation to knighthood, we only
1409. learn from English papers that in the 10ᵗʰ year of Henry IV
he had possessions to let at Padbury in Buckinghamshire,
and that he married a certain Margaret with whom he
lived to extreme old age. In 1464 the couple were still
alive at Sible Hedingham, where they enjoyed the life-
hold possession of eighty acres of land, probably under
the high dominion of the Earls of Oxford.

At that epoch there were neither adventurers, condottieri, knights nor lances of English birth in Italy. The
military forces were in the hands of Italian companies.
France on her side had ended by repelling the invasions
(perhaps legitimate but not national) of England, who was
now wearying herself in the civil wars of the " two Roses."

Apropos of this, it was asserted that the emblems of
the white and red Roses were brought back to England
by the adventurers returning from Italy.

Catherine of Siena, writing to Queen Johanna of Naples, deploring the schism and war between the partisans of Pope Urban VI and the antipope Clement, added: "Alas! how can you help your heart breaking when you think that they are divided on your account, and that one holds a white rose and the other a red?"

And Niccolò Tommaseo, the saint's commentator, notes: "They do not seem to be translated ensigns but real ones, there are no other mentions of them; and we only know that the arms of one of Urban's nephews were six red roses; perhaps Clement's French partisans had taken the white rose for opposition or in memory of the lily. Burlamacchi suspects that the English adventurers, dispersed from Count Alberico, carried those ill-omened ensigns to England after Hawkwood's death."

All these are mere fantasies: the lily of France was a golden one, not white: Count Alberico da Barbiano dispersed the Bretons and not the English: the Prignani, nephews of Urban VI, had not six roses for their arms. We do not know the origin of the symbols to which Catherine of Siena refers; and only find that white and red roses were taken as factional emblems in several of the southern Italian cities, for example at Benevento and Amalfi.

As to the origin of the two English roses, the history has been well told, and put on the stage with exquisite elegance by Shakespeare.

As we are quoting this universal poet, we may find in him a passage exactly applicable to John Hawkwood.

"Lucio. Thou concludest like the sanctimonious pirate, that put forth to sea with the ten commandements but scraped one of them out of the table.

"2 Gent. Thou shalt not steal?

"Lucio. Aye! that he raz'd.

"1 Gent. Why! 'twas a commandement, to command

the Captaine and all the rest from their functions : they put forth to steal. There's not a souldier of us all, that in the thanksgiving before meate, do rallish the petition well, that praies for peace."

But Italy, who had received from England the curse of rapacious companies, and did not render " Measure for Measure," found her compensation some centuries later, when in the great enterprise of re-establishing her national unity, the English gave her a moral and political support which was truly valuable. And now the two people are the most sincere supporters, in Europe, of that peace whose very name John Hawkwood refused to hear invoked by mendicant friars.

DOCUMENTS.

Among the numerous unedited documents, that have served for this history of John Hawkwood, and which could have been cited, those only have been selected of which the text could add something to the narration and better colour the particulars.

I.

[1363.]

Octavo ydus septembris prime indictionis.

Providerunt domini Anthiani pisani populi, partitu facto inter eos ad denarios albos et giallos secundum formam brevis pisani populi, utentes in hiis generali bailia eis a comuni et populo pisano concessa ut supra constat quod....

Bindus Agliata civis pisanus, partitor prestantie florenorum trigintamilium auri impositorum in civitate pisana hoc anno de mense iunii proxime preteriti pro stipendiando magnam societatem anglicorum pro comuni pisano, possit teneatur et debeat ipsam prestantiam restituere omnibus et singulis illis pisanis civibus qui illam prestantiam solverunt et comuni pisano mutuaverunt, in illa pecunia tantum de qua mutuum ipsum factum fuit ; videlicet illis qui mutuaverunt florenos teneatur et debeat restituere florenos et illis qui mutuaverunt monetam in ea spetie pecunie sive monete quam mutuaverunt comuni pisano, non obstante in hiis quod florenus auri sit maioris valentie quam tempore dicti mutui comuni pisano facti. Et ad hoc, ut nulla deceptio sive fraus commicti possit in valentia florenorum, ex dicta bailia et auctoritate quam a comuni pisano habent, plenarie commiserunt Pellario Grifo camerario camere pisani comunis et dicto Bindo ut singula edomade cuiusque mensis in principio ipsius edomade provideant et deliberent de valentia floreni, et similiter et concorditer determinent et declarent quanto pretio florenus auri ipsa edomada debeat computari, habito respectu ad indempnitatem pisani comunis et illorum qui de prestantia suprascripta solverunt, vigore presentis provisionis contrarietate aliqua non obstante.

(Pisa, State Archives, *Archivio del Comune, Provvisioni degli Anziani, Reg.* 58 *c.* 103 *t.*)

II.

Sicut locutus fui una vobiscum a Pysa, notifico vobis quod veniam ad vos cum quinquaginta lanceis, si vos vultis michi acomodare mille florenos aurei et dare michi supra istos quingentos florenos aurei pro me ipso. Et omnes mei sotii, et ego, quos ducam mecum sint et esse debeant securi et liberi ab omnibus, tam Anglicis quam Theotonicis quam etiam Ytalianis, quascumque rixas vel inimicitias haberemus cum ipsis vel aliquo ipsorum. Ita quod omnis inimicitia sit totaliter remota et placata. Et ea que intenditis facere super ista rescribatur michi per presentium latorem quam citius potestis. Et si ista intenditis facere que ibi superius continent, faciatis ut habeam securitatem veniendi ad vos cum octo sotiis et conferamus ea que intendo et posso adimplere.

Voster JOHANNES DE EBERHART SWILER.

Data in Peruscio die xiij* mensis novembris.

(A tergo.)

Magnifico et Potenti militi Domino Johanni Achuto.

(Siena, State Archives, *Carte di particolari*, Agut.)

(This and the numerous successive documents of the Sienese Archives were communicated to us by favor of the director signor Alessandro Lisini.)

III.

[1367.]

die xxviii mensis aprilis.

Convocato et congregato consilio infrascriptorum prudentium virorum in consistorio palatii residentie dominorum duodecim de mandato prudentis viri Francisci Johannis prioris dictorum dominorum duodecim, facta deinde proposita de infrascriptis per dictum Franciscum priorem de consensu sotiorum suorum, consulente domino Andrea Francisci de Piccolominibus de Senis, fuerunt in plena concordia stantiandi et reformandi et stantiaverunt et reformaverunt quod domini duodecim et capitaneus populi quam citius possunt procurent cum effectu mictere Nannem ser Vannis de Senis in ambaxiatorem et pro ambaxiatore comunis Senarum domino Johanne Agud et aliis caporalibus sotietatis Anglicorum cum illa ambaxiata quam domini duodecim et capitaneus populi eidem commictent ad procurandum iuxta posse quod dicta sotietas vel pars ipsius non intrect in teritorio comunis Senarum; et si ei fuerit possibile hoc facere bene quidem, sin autem possit dictus Nannis de pecunia communis Senarum dare et solvere dicto domino Johanni Agud et aliis caporalibus ut sibi videbitur usque ad quantitatem V florenos auri, non abergando vel stando dicta sotietas vel pars ipsius in comitatu Senarum nisi una nocte et duobus diebus et non aliter vel alio modo. Et predicta stantiaverunt et reformaverunt omni via iure et modo quibus melius potuerunt.

(Ibidem, *Deliberazioni di Concistoro.*)

IV.

[1367.]

Die tertia mensis maij.

Convocato et congregato Consilio....

Laurentius Mini Jacopelli unus ex dominis memoratis mandato dicti prioris proposuit: cum ad presens verisimiliter formidetur de perverse sotietatis Anglicorum incursu et vestri territorij inimicabiliter invasione, et stipendiarij Comunis Sen. non sint ad equitandum habiles propter pecunie eorum stipendii inopiam, et ad presens in comuni Sen. nulla sit pecunia, quod dicto Consilio et consiliariis videatur et placeat providere ordinare et reformare super predictis; in Dei nomine consulatur.

Super quibus et cet.

Petrus domini Jacobi de Tholomeis unus ex consiliariis dicti consilij, in ipso surgens consilio ad arengheriam, arengando dixit et consuluit supra dicta proposita: quod per dominos Duodecim et Capitaneum populi inveniatur et indagetur modus ut eis placuerit et videbitur convenire quod supra kabella vini comunis que venit et restat exempta a prestam restituendo in fine presentis mensis maij vel circa, acquirendi mutuo supra eadem pro illo costo quo melius potuerint usque in quantitate iij flor. aurei etc.

In reformatione et secunda etc. consilii, facto et misso partito et scruptinio per dictum priorem ad lupinos albos et nigros ut est moris, obtemptum reformatum fuit ad dictum et secundum dictum et consilium supradicti Petri consultoris per xxxj ex consiliariis dicti consilii, etc.

(Ibidem.)

V.

[1367.]

Die iiij mensis maij.

Magnifici viri domini Duodecim etc.

. . . .

Similiter ad scruptinium, proposita precedente, eligerunt et nomina-
verunt infrascriptos prudentes cum uno equo pro quolibet ad equitandum per comitatum supra festino exgombero occasione incursus et
invasionis sotietatis Anglicorum nostri territorij. Quorum hec sunt nomina etc.

(Ibidem.)

VI.

[1367.]

Die v mensis maij.

Consilio magnificum et honorabilium virorum dominorum duodecim....
convocato et congregato. In quo prudens vir Petrus Cinuczij unus ex
dictis dominis de mandato supradicti prioris proposuit et dixit: Cum
audiveritis ambaxiatam prudenter per Nannem ser Vannis a sotietate
Anglicorum retractam circa compositionem perverse sotietatis predicte
cum comuni Sen. disponentem, quod dicto consilio videatur et placeat
providere, ordinare et reformare super eandem; iu Dei nomine consulatur.

Super quibus etc.

Ser Franciscus ser Mini Ture unus ex consiliariis dicti consilii, in
ipso surgens consilio ad dicitorium, arengando dixit et consuluit supra
proposita, quod plene remaneat et sit in dominis D. et capitaneo populi quod circa presentem materiam et compositionem tractandam cum
sotietate Anglicorum seu domino Johanne eorum capitaneo per medium
Nannis ser Vannis seu cuiuscumque alterius prout sicut et quomodo
eis videbitur et placebit et pro illa quantitate florenorum que eis videbitur et placebit. Et circa predicta habeant plenam baliam et po-
testatem etc. Qui debeant, omni tarditate posposita, operam dare
quod dicta compositio fiat extra nostrum territorium si potest, sin aut
non, quod tunc et eo casu curetur quod quam citius potest nostrum
territorium egrediatur.

In reformatione et secunda etc. consilii, facto et celebrato partito
per priorem predictum supra consilio predicto ad lupinos albos et
nigros ut est moris, obtentum et reformatum fuit ad dictum et secun-

dum dictum et consilium supradicti Ser Francisci consultoris per **xxxj** ex consiliariis dicti consilii....

Quibus omnibus pro parte domini prioris et capitanei populi preceptum fuit secretum, scilicet per sacramentum et sub maiori pena, et sic iuraverunt in manibus Prioris.

(Ibidem.)

VII.

[1368.]

Exultet Sancta Mater Ecclesia et pro tanta victoria devoti ejus gaudeant universi, sed pre ceteris affluat in letitia et applausu felicissimus populus aretinus in cujus gremio datum est celitus de hostibus triunphari. Sane siquidem hodie xv hujus mensis magne sollicitudinis nostre cura celeriter accersiti magnifici et egregii viri fortes dominus Simon de Spoleto capitaneus gentis Ecclesie, dominus Flaxen de Risach et dominus Johannes de Rieten cum gente strenua bellatorum una cum nostris universis gentibus equestribus et pedestribus, in planu Arretii super strata porte Buje per unum miliare proxime civitati contra compagniam perniciosam et temerariam Anglicorum castramentatam ex adverso in campis, et aciebus hinc inde instructis manibusque consertis ad prelium, bellum terribile inierunt; denique decertato, ipsam debellarunt et miserunt forti brachio victoriosis ictibus in conflictum in quo multi numero et qualitate mortui ceciderunt, ceterisque quasi omnibus captivatis inter quos est capitaneus dominus Johannes Haud capitaneus dicte compagnie et plurimi caporales, ac ictitatus est infelix Dinolus Bindi Monaldi orator comunis Perusii qui dictam compagniam de partibus Ligurie ad tantum eccidium huc conduxit ut tanta temeritas perusina, sic confusa discat, mansuetudine licet tarda, Christi Vicario obedire. In dictoque prelio dictus dominus Johannes de Rieten decoratus est cingulo militari sicut decebat ejus excellentissimam probitatem. Que jucundis animis et mentibus Beatitudini Vestre nuntiare curavimus ad suppositum gaudium omnium gaudiorum.

Arretii xv juni.

(MS. formerly Redi in the Marucellian Library, Florence.)

(This document was indicated to us by professor Gamurrini, and the copy communicated by signor Pasqui, communal librarian of Arezzo.)

VIII.

[1369.]

Magnifici et Generosi Domini. Noveritis per presentes quod Magnificus et Excelsus Dominus Noster dominus Bernabos afficitur toto corde ad Comunem Senarum eius territorium et districtum tamquam ad pupillam oculi sui; et ideo vos rogo precibus quibus valeo quod amore et contemplatione Domini antedicti abstinere velitis a quibuscumque dampnis et noxiis novitatibus inferendis hominibus territorio et districtui Civitatis et Comunis Senarum, scientes a certo quod a Domino nostro prefato ultra comendationem gratam et benevolam eritis laudabilibus muneribus recomissi.

Vester ALBERTUS DE PESAURO   } Senis die XXIJ decembris.
Magnifici domini d. B. Vicarius generalis }

(A tergo)

Magnificis et Potentibus Viris
et Militibus dominis Johanni Agud
et Anexe de Ritene etc.

(Siena, State Archives, *Carte di particolari*, Agut.)

IX.

[1373.]

Dilecto filio nobili viro Johanni Aguti militi, Capitaneo gentis armigere Anglicorum pro Romana ecclesia in partibus Italie existentis, salutem etc.

Dilectum filium nobilem virum Johannem Britz militem, ambaxiatorem tuum tuorumque sociorum, tam mittentium quam missi consideratione gratanter recepimus sepeque audivimus graciose et ad ea que nobis pro parte tua et ipsorum sociorum exposuit benigne respondimus prout ipse miles tibi referet oraculo vive vocis. Quare nobilitatem tuam, de qua plene confidimus et speramus, rogamus attentius et hortamur, quatenus in negotiis Romane ecclesie tamquam vir fidelis et strenuus studeas continue laborare, hostes ipsius ecclesie, presertim sceleratum Bernabovem, qui adhuc in tanta guerra terras non perdidit, fortiter impugnando, ita quod ipsorum hostium cito sequatur depressio et optata victoria; tuque provide preter premium retributoris eterni, pro cuius laboras ecclesia, apostolice sedis amorem et favorem, ac perpetuam gloriam valeas reportare, eandemque ecclesiam de stipendiis tibi et genti tue ac eorumdem sociorum debitis, cum velimus, prout rationis est, et tota solicitudine procuremus quod ea cito habeatis, velis filiali patientia supportare, quia dilectus filius noster Guillelmus Sancti Angeli diaconus cardinalis, quem nuper loco dilecti filii nostri cardinalis Bituricensis redituri ad Romanam Curiam nostrum Vicarium ordinavimus generalem, super hiis providebit in partibus illis ad quas venire celeriter se disponit. Et ad supportationem huiusmodi dictos socios et gentem velis inducere providis modis tuis.—Datum Avinione, xv Kal. ian. anno tertio.

(Vatican Archives, *Regestum* 269 (Gregorii XI) fol. 100ᵃ.)

(This and the successive documents extracted from the Vatican Archives were communicated to us by favor of the Archivist, the very Reverend Don Gregorio Palmieri.)

X.

[1373.]

Dilecto filio nobili viro Johanni Aguti militi, capitaneo gentis armigere Anglicorum pro Romana ecclesia in partibus Italie existentis, salutem etc.—Cum dilectus filius Berengarius Abbas monasterii Lesatensis, Rutenensis diocesis, apostolice sedis nuncius in partibus placentin., sicut audivimus, habiturus sit aliquos tractatus in partibus illis, pro quorum perfectione erunt necessarie gentes tue, nobilitatem tuam rogamus attentius et hortamur, quatenus cum idem nuncius super hiis te requisierit velis secrete ac subito equitare cum tota tua gente, aut eius partem mittere sine dilacione ac difficultate quacumque; oportet enim, sicut nosti, talia secretissime teneri et fieri festinanter. — Datum Avinione, xv Kal. Januarii, anno tertio.

(Ibidem, fol. 100ᵇ.)

XI.

[1373.]

Dilecto filio nobili viro Johanni Acuti militi, Capitaneo gentis armigere Anglicorum in partibus Italie nostris et Romane ecclesie obsequiis insistentium salutem, etc. :

Quantum honoris et laudis tibi et aliis gentibus armigeris Anglicorum in partibus Italie nostris et Romane ecclesie obsequiis insistentium, quantumque utilitatis et exaltationis eidem Romane ecclesie ac

rei publice provenit de tua et ipsarum gentium armigerarum solicitu-
dinibus et laboribus indefessis, quos contra iniquitatis filios Bernabovem
et Galeatium de Vicecomitibus de Mediolano ac alios viros et eiusdem
Romane ecclesie inimicos, tamquam ipsius ecclesie pugiles et virtuosi,
in preliis exhibuistis hactenus, et exhibentur incessanter tua et ipsarum gentium armigerarum strenua et magnifica opera manifesta. In
hiis igitur nobilitatem tuam cum gratiarum actionibus multipliciter
commendantes, ipsam rogandam duximus et hortandam, quatenus bene
cepta prout plene confidimus pugili cura continuans, ubicumque poteris predictos inimicos impugnes, et ad dilectum filium nobilem virum
Amedeum Comitem Sabaudie, una cum dictis gentibus armigeris, cum
hoc summe cordi nobis sit, accedere non postponas. Dilectum autem
filium nobilem virum Petrum de Murlis, domicellum, familiarem nostrum ad partes illas destinamus, cui in hiis que ex parte nostra
tibi dicet plenam fidem adhibere sinceritas tua velit.

Datum apud Pontemsorgie, Avinionensis diocesis, vii Idus Junii,
anno tertio.

(Ibidem, fol. 175ᵃ.)

XII.

[1373.]

Dilecto filio, nobili viro Johanni Agud, militi Anglicano, capitaneo
gentium Anglicanarum servientium Romane ecclesie in partibus Lom-
bardie salutem, etc.

Cum letitia ingenti audivimus dilectum filium nobilem virum Petrum
de Murlis, domicellum, Magalonensis diocesis, nuncium tuum, narratam
nobis victoriam de crudelibus tirannis hostibus et persecutoribus Romane ecclesie tibi et gentibus dicte ecclesie ab exercituum Domino con-
donatam, que tanto gratior nostris venit affectibus, quanto mirabilius
et ex maiori Dei gratia noscitur processisse dum pauciores de pluribus, invasi de invadentibus, et transeuntes de incolis in suo districtu
reportavere triumphum. Letare igitur, fili, quod in obsequiis Dei sueque
ecclesie fideliter strenueque militans, famosam gloriam es adeptus, quam
indesinenter persequendo prefatos hostes donec deficiant, cum in ruina
sint positi, efficies longiorem ut in tuo glorioso nomine egregia tua
posteritas delectetur. Cum autem audivimus te et dictas gentes versus
Bononiam remeasse, et magis censeatur expediens quod iter continuares
inceptum, et dilecto filio nobili viro Amedeo Comiti Sabaudie, guerre
superiorum partium que fit contra dictos hostes capitaneo generali, in

Mediolanensi territorio coniungaris celeriter, ne hostes ipsi vires resu-
mant et a pressura imminenti respirent, nobilitatem tuam rogitamus
attentius et hortamur, mandantes quatenus ubicumque sis non differas
ad prelibatum Comitem proficisci, et ad hoc efficiendum celeriter gentes
ipsas inducas, ut sicut proinde ordinatum est, hostes ipsi absque mora,
que ad se trahit grande dispendium et forsan periculum, intermissio-
nis procedimento quatiantur. Ipsasque gentes velis exhortari efficaciter
ex parte nostra quod de stipendiis eis debitis et in futurum debendis,
si vero non solvantur eis celeriter ut ea debent habere, velint nos et
dictam ecclesiam ac dilectum filium nostrum Petrum tituli Sancte Ma-
rie in Trastiberim presbiterum cardinalem in nonnullis terris prefate
ecclesie vicarium generalem, patienter et filialiter supportare, tenentes
pro certo quod omnia ipsa stipendia, quam cito fieri poterit, solventur
eisdem. Et pro parte nostra dictique cardinalis super hoc omnimode la-
boratur. — Datum Avinione, xi Kal. Junii, anno tertio.

(Ibidem, fol. 51ᵇ.)

XIII.

[1373.]

Dilecto filio nobili viro Johanni Acuti, militi, capitaneo gentis armigere Anglicorum, in partibus Italie nostris et Romane ecclesie stipendiis
militancium salutem etc. — Clare devotionis titulis insignitus, more de-
votissimi filii Romanam ecclesiam revereris ut matrem, sicut operum
effectibus manifestas, dum iniquitatis filios Barnabovem et Galeacium
de Vicecomitibus de Mediolano ac alios nostros et eiusdem Romane
ecclesie inimicos, tamquam ipsius ecclesie pugil ac virtuosus, in preliis
potenter expugnas, et ea que ad nostrum et ipsius ecclesie honorem
pertinent procuras fideliter et utiliter operaris, propter quod apostolice sedis et nostram gratiam sic meruisse dinosceris ut personam
tuam in visceribus caritatis gerere debitum reputemus. Leteris igitur
in Domino quod talia de tua bonitate sentimus, quod nomen tuum laude
dignum ostenditur, et quod in te secure quiescimus ubi prees, confidentes ymmo pro certo tenentes quod ad ea que nobis sunt placita libenter
intendas, et salubrem statum eiusdem Romane ecclesie, tamquam ipsius
exaltationis zelator sincerus, desideras multipliciter et affectas. Verum
miramur quamplurimum quod ipse Belial filius Barnabos supradictus
nullam civitatem fortalitium sive terram adhuc perdiderit, et cum de
strenuitate tua ac tuorum specialiter confidamus, nobilitatem tuam,
quam in adimplendis votis nostris promptam semper invenimus et pa-

ratam, rogamus et hortamur in Domino, eam attentius deprecantes quatenus, pro nostra et apostolice sedis reverentia et sicut nobis placere desideras, modis omnibus quibus tibi magis expedire videbitur, contra predictos perditionis filios viriliter insurgere, ac sinceritatis et strenuitatis tue et tuorum aliquod notabile faciendo vires ostendere. Ac dilecto filio nobili viro Hugoni de Rupe, militi, magistro hospicii nostri, quem ad partes illas presentialiter destinamus, in hiis que ex parte nostra tibi dicet fidem plenariam adhibere sinceritas tua velit; gerimus enim in animo personam tuam nobis peramabilem inter nostra precordia recumbentem vultu sereno prospicere dignisque semper favoribus prevenire, ut apud Deum et ipsam ecclesiam pura devocione preclarus sis et esse possis aliis in exemplum. — Datum Avinione, IIII Nonas Julii, anno tertio.

(Ibidem, fol. 184.)

XIV.

[1374.]

Dilecto filio nobili viro Johanni Acuti, militi, capitaneo gentis armigere Anglicorum in partibus Italie pro Romana ecclesia militantis, salutem etc. — Sicut dilectus filius nobilis vir Johannes Briche miles. socius tuus, nuper tibi debuit parte nostra referre, super oportuna tuarum et aliorum nostris et ecclesie Romane sub te militantium obsequiis solutione pagarum provisionem solertem facimus adhiberi, adeo quod infra breve, Deo previo, poteritis inde merito contentari, nobilitatem tuam precordiose rogantes quatenus, tua fidelia continuando servicia, super territoriis emulorum in partibus placentinis et parmensibus remanere velis donec aliud habueris in mandatis, plenam fidem adhibens eis que dilectus filius cardinalis Bituricensis tibi dixerit vel nuntiaverit nostri parte, sicque ipsius cardinalis monitis et rogatibus de mente nostra prodeuntibus acquiescens, quod inde tibi felicia laudis et honoris proveniant incrementa, nostramque et apostolice sedis benevolentiam pariter et gratiam adhuc uberius tua sinceritas mereatur. — Datum Avinione, nonis Januarii, anno quarto.

(Ibidem, fol. 221.)

XV.

[1374.]

Dilecto filio et nobili viro Johanni Agut, militi, capitaneo gentis Anglicorum existentium in Lombardia ad servicia nostra et Romane ecclesie, salutem etc. — Litteram tuam propriam in villa Romagneri die xxviiii decembris datam nuper benigne recepimus, in qua repetebas ea que per dilectum filium nobilem virum Johannem Briz, militem, ambaxiatorem tuum nobis duxeras intimanda; ad quam quidem literam respondemus quod ad illa omnia per dictum militem, qui a nobis ante festum nativitatis Domini proxime preteritum recessit et eum nunc tecum esse credimus, respondimus seriose et taliter quod, ut speramus, debebis esse contentus. Tuam igitur nobilitatem de cuius fidelitate prudentia et strenuitate specialiter confidimus et speramus, hortamur et rogamus attentius quatenus, tua laudabilia et magnifica opera pro reverentia Dei cuius servis ecclesie ac honore tuo perpetuo conservando, ut semper habeas eiusdem ecclesie amorem et favorem, indesinenter continues hostes ipsius ecclesie viriliter impugnando, et succurrendo in tractatibus et aliis cum et prout ab officialibus dicte ecclesie fueris requisitus, et ad hec Caporales gentis tue ipsamque gentem exhorteris iugiter et inducas. — Datum Avinione, Idus Januarii, anno quarto.

(Ibidem, *Regest.* 270 (Gregorii XI), fol. 3ᵇ.)

XVI.

[1374.]

Dilecto filio nobili viro Johanni Acuti, militi, nonnullarum armigerarum gentium nostris et ecclesie Romane militantium obsequiis capitaneo, salutem etc. — Visis capitulis que nobis dilectus filius secretarius tuus presentium exhibitor nuper pro parte tua porrexit, licet votis obtemperare tuis, prout nobis possibile fuerit, intendamus; que tamen ad petitum per te lancearum augmentum, propter incumbentium expensarum sarcinam qua pro nunc Camera nostra premitur supra modum, ad presens tibi nullo modo possumus complacere, prout idem secretarius tuus latius declarabit. Cui etiam super aliis capitulis plene aperuimus mentem nostram, tibi per eum verbotenus referendam, tenens a certo quod sicut beneplacitorum nostrorum cooperator studiosus existis, teque speramus in huiusmodi fidelitatis vigore continuatione laudabili permansurum, sic personam tuam et tuos intendimus favoribus prosequi gratiosis, adeo quod, favente Deo, tandem letaberis nostris et ecclesie Romane serviciis insudasse. — Datum Salon. iii idus Maii, anno quarto.

(Ibidem, fol. 214.)

XVII.

[1374.]

Dilecto filio nobili viro Johanni Acuti, militi, capitaneo nonnullarum gentium armigerarum in partibus Italie pro nobis et Romana ecclesia, salutem.

Cum dilectum filium nobilem virum Johannem de Canis, domicellum, ad partes Italie pro certis arduis negociis per nos ei commissis presentialiter destinemus, nobilitatem tuam rogamus et hortamur attente, quatenus eidem Johanni in hiis que pro parte nostra tibi dicet vel scribet plenam fidem adhibere et ea adimplere, et pro honore nostro et Romane ecclesie, prout plene confidimus, in hoc salubriter providere sinceritas tua velit.

Datum Sallon. Arelatensis diocesis, vi Kal. iunii, anno quarto.

(Ibidem, fol. 109.)

XVIII.

[1374.]

Dilecto filio nobili viro Johanni Acuti, militi, capitaneo nonnullarum gentium armigerarum in partibus Italie pro nobis et Romana ecclesia, salutem etc.

Anxiatur nos, fili dilectissime, magnus exercitus quem illi Belial filii et iniquitatis allumpni Barnabos et Galeacius de Vicecomitibus de Mediolano in obsidione contra nostram civitatem Vercellensem, in nostrum et Romane ecclesie ac nostrorum fidelium vituperium ac scandalum plurimorum, prout ad tuam credimus devenisse notitiam, tenent de presenti ; sed inter anxietates huiusmodi non modicum doloris addit concursus gentium armigerarum tam de Parma quam de aliis terris quas iidem Barnabos et Galeatius detinent ad dictum exercitum cotidie venientium, penuriaque victualium quam habent gentes nostre in eadem civitate existentes que, prout fertur, cito, quod absit, deficerent, nisi celeriter succurreretur eisdem ; ideo, confidentes in illo qui elata conteret cornua superborum, nobilitatem tuam que, aborrens delicias et otia fugiens, ardua querere et appetere strenua consuevit, rogamus et hortamur in Domino, eam attentius deprecantes ac pro speciali munere postulantes quatenus, que promisimus infra catholici tui pectoris claustra revolvens, ac etiam considerans quod iidem Barnabos et Galeacius in terris nostris propinquis paucas gentes armorum, sicut nobis relatum est, pro nunc tenent, que eisdem terris nostris nocere possunt de presenti, pro nostra et apostolice sedis reverentia ac etiam tui honoris et publice utilitatis intuitu et sicut nobis placere desideras, ad tollenda opprobria eiusdem Romane ecclesie ac nostra et iniurias propulsandas, zelum illum quem ad nos et ipsam Romanam ecclesiam gerere dignosceris per effectum ostendens, ad levandum predictum exercitum et succurrendum celeriter predicte Civitati in tanta necessitate constitute, tanquam bellator fortis et vir strenuus quem hactenus omnipotens Dominus gloriosis decoravit victoriis, cum tuis gentibus armigeris et aliis que iuxta dispositionem dilecti filii nostri Guillelmi Sancti Angeli diaconi cardinalis in eisdem partibus pro nobis et eadem ecclesia in temporalibus vicarii generalis, haberi poterunt, dimissis aliquibus pro custodia civitatis nostre Bononiensis et circumvicinarum partium, iuxta consilium dicti cardinalis, cui in dicendis ex parte nostra adhibere velis plenam fidem, sub spe divini auxilii et favoris personaliter accedere non postponas; confidimus enim in potentia Domini et de beati Petri apostolorum principis, cuius causam gerimus, meritis et intercessione speramus quod sub tua virtute et potencia huiusmodi adversariorum nostrorum elidetur superbia, et quod idem princeps apostolici ordinis tui erit comes itineris ac pro illius directione felici et salute tua efficax apud Dominum et perpetuus intercessor. Ceterum in animo gerimus hoc gratum servicium, si nobis illud, prout plene confidimus, feceris, nunquam oblivioni tradere, sed personam tuam nobis peramabilem intra nostra recumbere precordia, atque tuos vultu sereno prospicere, dignisque semper favoribus et gratiis, quantum cum Deo poterimus, prevenire. — Datum Novis, Avinionensis diocesis, xvii Kal. Augusti, anno quarto.

(Ibidem, fol. 212.)

XIX.

[1374.]

Magnifici et potentes domini amici carissimi. Ne magnificentia vestra admirationem asumat de adventu istius societatis notificamus vobis nos audivisse magnam gentium armorum quantitatem ad fronterias vestri territorij fore congregatam ut nobiscum preliarent, hacque de causa huc accessimus visuri si facta dictis consonabunt. Ex quo si dominationi vestre placet huic societati curialitatem aliquam impendere prout mos est gentibus armigeris fieri debere, abstinebimus a dampnis et territorium vestrum quanto plus poterimus indempne conservabimus:

sin autem dimitemus Sachomanos istius sotietatis facere prout voluerint. Super quibus incenium vestrum nobis indillate placeat inclinare

JOHANNES HAUCCD et
CONRADUS COMES HECHILBERG } capitanei etc.

Datum Montispolis viij augusti xij Indictione.

(A tergo)

Magnificis et potentibus dominis dominis Prioribus Civitatis Senarum amicis carissimis.

(Siena. State Archives. *Carte di particolari*, Agud.)

XX.

[1375.]

Die tertio Julii.

Viri Magnifici domini Defensores et Capitaneus populi Civitatis Senarum nec non quidam viri sapientes et honorabiles cives Senenses electi per dictos dominos Defensores vigore dicti consilii supra retenti et consilii generalis exinde secuti, de quo patet manu Ser Johannis Ture de Prato, in consueto consistorio palatii comunis Sen. convocati pro factis et negotiis dicti comunis peragendis et in eos commissis expediendis, concorditer facta prius de infrascriptis proposita et supra ea diligenti partito ad lupinos albos et nigros secundum formam statutorum et ordinum comunis Sen., fuerunt in plena concordia deliberandi et providendi, et providerunt deliberaverunt et decreverunt: Quod cum compagnia domini Johannis concordia et compositio fiat pro meliori seu minima quantitate florenorum qua fieri poterit, et quod maxime iucludatur terra de Montepolitiano et de Cortonio si possibile est, etsi ultra quantitatem declaratam per Ser Jacobum ser Gani ambaxiatorem opporteat dare dicte compagnie, et cum aliis pactis et tantum utilioribus et honorabilibus pro comuni quantum poterit fieri. Et quod Ser Jacobus predictus redeat ad dictam sotietatem ad concordiam predictam firmandam.

Eodem modo et forma domini defensores et capitaneus populi ac sapientes predicti concorditer deliberaverunt et decreverunt pro habenda pecunia pro solvendo et dando dictis de compagnia hoc modo, videlicet, vigore consilii generalis supradicti,

In primis quod cum bona personarum ecclesiasticarum defendantur et redimantur ab ista feroci compagnia quomodo civium Senensium et suppositorum Comunis Sen. predicti, et sic sit conveniens quod ipsi clerici et persone ecclesiastice conferant cum comuni in hac gravedine, quod, scito modo et habita forma quo et quam Florentini tenent in imponendo clericis, quod solvant pro dicta eadem causa. Quod tunc per illum modum seu per eamdem formam imponatur clericis nostris et personis ecclesiasticis Civitatis Comitatus et iurisdictionis Senarum videlicet quantitas xx florenorum auri pro redimendo se a dicta sotietate domini Johannis Agud. Et quod domini defensores et capitaneus populi eligant quos voluerint ad predicta excipienda.

Item quod ponatur et posita sit presta civibus Sen. et conferentibus cum civitate ad rationem trium florenorum pro M que solvi debeat in terminis et cum modis et modificationibus ac conditionibus quibus solvi debet presta predicta posita per dominos et defensores et capitaneum populi in offitio proximos precessores.

Item quod ponatur et posita sit comitatinis et comunitatibus comitatus Senarum solventibus taxationibus quedam presta xij flor. auri, quam solvere teneantur in paghis et terminis et cum modificationibus declarandis per dominos defensores et capitaneum populi vel per alios quibus ipsi domini commissionem facerent de predictis.

Item quod ponatur et posita sit quedam presta censualibus et recomendatis pro redimendo a dicta sotietate, illius quantitatis quam videbitur et placebit dominis Defensoribus et capitaneo populi seu illis quibus committent, solvenda in termino et cum conditionibus declarandis per dictos dominos seu commissarios supradictos.

Die viiij Julij commiserunt banditoribus quod banniant prestam.

(Ibidem, *Deliberazioni di Concistoro.*)

XXI.

[1375.]

Die dicta [July 30].

Viri Magnifici et potentes domini domini Defensores et capitaneus populi civitatis Senarum convocati et congregati insimul in consueto consistorio palatii Comunis Sen. pro eorum offitio honorabiliter exercendo. Facta prius proposita de infrascriptis per virum prudentem priorem dictorum dominorum Defensorum cum consotiorum eius assensu, et super ea facto et celebrato solempni et secreto scruptinio inter eos ad lupinos albos et nigros et obtenta deinde per duas partes et satis ultra secundum formam statutorum Senensium, facientes hec omnia infrascripta vigore et auctoritate balie eis concesse a generali consilio

campane comunis Sen. manu ser Johannis Ture notarii, pro habenda
aquirenda et procuranda pecunia occasione concordie compagnie Anglicorum domini Johannis Agud et omni via iure modo quibus magis et
melius potuerint, fuerunt in plena concordia providendi et deliberandi.
Et decreverunt et providerunt quod sotietas Johannis ser Dini videlicet Filippus Sardini Franciscus Vannis Bertini et alij sotii solvant iij flor.
auri et deponant penes camerarios Bicherne Comunis Sen., quos ipsi
de dicta sotietate habuerunt in depositum de pecunia domini Jacobi
episcopi olim senensis : cum hoc sit quod procedat de voluntate domini Senensis episcopi. Et quod predicti solventes debeant conservari
yndempnes a Comune Sen. de dicto deposito, facta dicta solutione per
eos camerario Bicherne.

(Ibidem.)

XXII.

[1375.]

Die xij Julij.

Viri Magnifici domini Defensores populi civitatis Sen. in consueto
Consistorio convocati concorditer ut moris est eligerunt infrascriptos
supra victualia procuranda et mictenda ad dominum Johannem Agud
et eius compagniam. Quorum hec sunt nomina etc.

(Ibidem.)

XXIII.

[1375.]

Nos .... Defensores et capitaneus populi civitatis Senarum habentes
ad infrascripta plenam et largam baliam a generali consilio Campane
Comunis Sen. significamus vobis Camerario et Quatuor Provisoribus
Bicherne Comunis Sen. quod detis et solvatis Symoni Mei custodi Bicherne Comunis Sen. de pecunia comunis Sen. sine aliqua detractione
kabelle infrascriptas pecuniarum summas et quantitates quas solvit
infrascriptis personis pro pretio infrascriptarum mercantiarum et rerum
mandato nostro. Et que quidem res date et tradite fuerunt pro parte
Comunis Sen. domino Johanni Agud et aliis caporalibus de compagnia
Anglicorum et dicte compagnie secundum compositionem et concordiam per nostros Ambaxiatores et syndicos factam cum dicta compagnia et pro dicta concordia perficenda et consumanda. Et sic per nos,
vigore dicte balie nobis concesse a dicto consilio generali campane Co-

munis Sen. circa predicta et ab eisdem dependentia, constat manu Ser Johannis Ture Notarii Reformationum dicti comunis, fuit et extit solempniter stantiatum. Datum in nostro Consistorio die **xxx** Augusti Indictione **xiij**.

In primis, pro duobus modiis et duobus stariis vini rubei empti ad rationem sedecim flor. pro modio a Ventura Lenzi vinaiuolo et a Ser Arrigo Nerini, trigintatres flor. auri et vigintisex sol.......... **xxxiij** flor. **xxvj** sol.

Item, pro tribus modiis panis cotti in **xxxvij** taschis emptis in campo fori et a pluribus fornariis, in totum.......... **xlv** lib.

Item, pro **lx** lib. confectorum inter morsellectos et Rageiam trasmissorum in sotietate predicta, in totum........... **lxviiij** lib.

Item, pro **xviiij** barilibus datis cum dicto vino dicte sotietati et pro duodecim taschis datis cum dicto pane et pro funibus datis cum dictis rebus quas solvit, scilicet pretiorum dictarum rerum, in totum........ **xxxiiij** lib. **xvij** sol.

Item, quas solvit pro **iiij** ^{or} schatolis magnis et duabus corbellis et pro chanovaccio et pro cordis pro ligando dictos confectos missos et datos dictis de compagnia, tres lib. et quatordecim sol............. **jii** lib. **xiiij** sol.

Item, quos solvit pro portatura barilorum ad celleria in quibus erat vinum missum compagnie et illis qui iverunt ad carichandum et pro palea pro turacciis et pro expensis factis illis qui caricaverunt panem et dictas salmas, in totum quadraginta quatuor sol. et quatuor den.... **ij** lib. **iiij** sol.

Item pro vectura **xxvj** bestiarum et sedecim hominum qui eas duxerunt cum dictis rebus ad dictam compagniam pro duobus diebus, sedecim sol. pro homine quolibet et pro bestia qualibet **vj** sol., in totum viginti lib. **xij** sol.... **xx** lib. **xij** sol.

(Ibidem, *Apodisse.*)

XXIV.

[1375.]

In nomine Domini Amen. Strenuus magnificus et potens miles dominus Johannes Haukeddod anglicus Anglicorumque Societatis in partibus Ytalie nuper militantium Capitaneus generalis per se ipso et vice et nomine dicte societatis Anglicorum, cum consensu presentia et voluntate nobilium militum dominorum Johannis Torneberi, domini Johannis Briz ipsius Sotietatis mereschalcorum, Guilly Gold conistabilis eiusdem comi-

tive et infrascriptorum Caporalium et Consiliariorum, videlicet dominorum Johannis Biston, Johannis For, Philippi Puer, Johannis Cliffordt,
Petri Stoneer militum, nobiliumque virorum Ricciardi Romisey, Roberti
Selver, Guillelmi Tilli, David Rozze, Johannis Dent, Niccolai Tansild,
Johannis Maberve consiliariorum. Et ipsi Capitaneus Mariscalchi Conistabilis et Consiliarii et quilibet eorum in solidum habentes cum eodem
domino Capitaneo plenam auctoritatem et bayliam a dicta Sotietate
hec et alia fatiendi. Pro qua sotietate promiserunt ipsi et quilibet eorum
in solidum et convenerunt de rato in singulis capitulis infrascriptis. Sub
pena obligata infrascriptis hoc publico Instrumento fuerunt consessi et
publice guarentaverunt Nobili viro Rugerio filio nobilis viri Adoazzi
Canis de Casali de Luagij pedemontium presenti et stipulanti vice et
nomine Comunis lucani et michi Jocobi notario tamquam persone publice offitio publico fungenti stipulanti et recipienti vice et nomine
comunis lucani et singulorum ipsius comunis et eorum successorum et
omnium quorum interest seu interesse posset, habuisse et recepisse
sexmilia florenorum auri boni et recti ponderis tempore debito et pro-
misso : quos honorabiles cives Franciscus Busolini et Iuffredus Cen-
nami sindici et Ambassiatores lucani Comunis, de quorum mandato
publice dixerunt contineri manu Ser Petri Saraceni de Luca notarii
et tunc cancellarii dicti comunis, vice et nomine dicti lucani comunis
promiserunt et convenerunt dicto domino Capitaneo stipulanti vice et
nomine dicte sotietatis et per se et dicta sotietate, pro eo quia dictus
dominus Capitaneus marescalchi conistabilis et consiliarii pro se ipsis
et dicta sotietate promiserunt suprascriptis Francisco et Iuffredo quod
predicti Capitaneus Mariscalchi conistabilis et consiliarii Sotietatis Caporales et alii de dicta sotietate presentes et futuri inde ad quinque
Annos proxime futuros habebunt tenebunt et tractabunt lucanum Comunem et eis subditos pro amicis et amicabile et ipsum lucanum Comunem aut terras vel teritorium seu subditos eius non invadent vel
occupabunt seu offendent per modum Sotietatis, prout de predictis continetur et apparet publico instrumento manibus Ser Andree quondam
Contis de Lugiano facto et rogato anno nactivitatis millesimo trecen-
tesimo septuagesimoquinto die tertia Julii sive sub alio tempore vel
data et facto reperiretur. Renumptiantes prefati Capitaneus Mareschalchi
et Consiliarii per se vice et nomine sotietatis predicte et quilibet eorum
in solidum exceptioni dictorum sexmilium florenorum non habuitorum
non receptorum non ponderatorum et non numeratorum et penes eos
non remansorum et omnibus aliis exceptionibus juris vel facti et defen-
sionibus quibus se possent a predictis quoquomodo tueri vel juvari. Qua-
propter dictus dominus Capitaneus mereschalchi et Constabilis et Consiliarii predicti per se ipsis et vice et nomine sotietatis prefate liberaverunt

et absolverunt lucanum Comunem et eius subditos et omnia eorum et
cuiuscumque ipsorum bona presentia et futura et suprascriptum Ruge-
rum stipulantem vice et nomine lucani comunis et me Jacobum notarium
infrascriptum stipulantem et recipientem ut supra de dicta quantitate
sexmilium florenorum auri : tantum per aquilianam stipulationem prece-
dentem et acceptillationem legiptimis verbis juris propositam et legiptime
subsecutam ; fatiens supradictus dominus Capitaneus et alii prelibati
et quilibet eorum in solidum dicto Rogerio presenti stipulanti et recipienti vice et nomine lucani Comunis et michi notario infrascripto ut
supra stipulanti et recipienti finem remissionem refutationem quieta-
tionem absolutionem et pactum de ulterius in perpetuum non petendo
seu amplius imbringando, ymo semper erunt taciti et contenti de predictis et quantum pro quantitate antedicta, reservato omni jure quod
haberent ad maiorem quantitatem vigore pactorum predictorum. Que
quidem omnia suprascripta et infrascripta promiserunt et convenerunt
supradicti dominus Capitaneus mariscalchi conistabilis et consiliarii
nominibus quibus supra suprascripto Rugerio presenti et recipienti et
michi Jacobo notario infrascripto ut supra stipulantibus pro lucano
Comuni perpetuo firma rata et grata et incorrupta habere et tenere et
contra non facere vel venire in judicio vel extra de jure vel de facto
sub infrascriptis penis et obligationibus. Pro quibus omnibus et singulis sic firmiter observandis firmis et ratis habendis et tenendis et pro
dampnis et expensis contingentibus suprascriptus dominus Capitaneus
mareschalchi conistabilis et consiliarii et quilibet eorum in solidum per
se et vice et nomine suprascripte Sotietatis obligaverunt dicto Rugerio
et michi Jacobo notario infrascripto pro lucano comuni stipulanti ut
supra sese ipsos dictam sotietatem et eorum et cuilibet eorum succes-
sores et bona omnia presentia et futura ad penam duppli suprascripte
quantitatem florenorum sollempni stipulatione premissa. Constituentes
et speciali pacto promictentes predicta omnia et singula actendere et
observare et solvere Luce Pisis Janue et alibi ubicumque locorum et
fori ubi predicta fuerint postulata, nulla originis vel domicilii aut in-
competentis exceptione per eos vel alterum ipsorum modo quolibet op-
ponendo. Renumptiantes fori privilegio benefitio solidi de duobus seu
pluribus rei debendi, epistole divi Hadriani autenticorum novo iuri et
desdemissoribus et mandatoriis et omni legum et statutorum auxilio
quo se a predictis vel aliquo predictorum tueri vel juvari possent: et
rogaverunt me Jacobum notarium infrascriptum ut de presentibus publicum presens facerem Instrumentum quod eorum consuetis capitanei
mareschalcorum et conistabilis sigillis iusserunt ad maiorem fidem fir-
missime roborari. Et quod supra in undecima linea presenti computato
interlineatum et hoc verbum mea propria manu scripsi.

Actum in Abatia Ysule comitatus Senarum in campo antedicte sotietatis, millesimotrecentesimo septuagesimoquinto quartadecima indictione
secundum modum et cursum civitatis lucane die septimo mensis Octu-
bris, presentibus nobilibus viris Spinello quondam Luce Alberti civi flo-
rentino et Dionisio quondam Francoli de la Strata, Zannino quondam
domini Petri de Octobellis de Alexandria cancellario prefati Rugerii,
Emont Ubit et Johanne Gubiono Anglicis de Anglia et pluribus aliis
ad hæc vocatis et rogatis.

Ego Jacobus Taddei Simonis de Terrincha vicinatus Petrasante,
publicus imperiali auctoritate notarius et judex ordinarius et nunc notarius et cancellarius prefati domini Capitanei Sotietatis et in hac parte
ipsius Comunis lucani, predictis omnibus et singulis interfui et roga-
tus sic bene scripsi signum quoque meum apposui consuetum et ad
fidem premissorum me in testem subscripsi. Et quod est in quadragesi-
masesta linea interlineatum et hoc verbum notarile mea propria manu
scripsi

D. capitan. D¹ JOHANNIS TORNEBERI D. JOHANNIS BRIS GUILLI GOLD conistabilis

(L. S.) (L. S.) (L. S.) (L. S.)

(Lucca, State Archives.)

XXV.

[1376.]

Domino Johanni Haucud.

Octo.

Magnifice miles, frater et amice karissime.

Intelleximus que nobis pro parte vestre nobilitatis exposuerunt nobilis vir Roggerius Canis nec non Cancellarius vester et Spinellus. Et
circa ea providimus prout idem Roggerius vobis plenius referet viva
voce, cui tamquam nobis placeat in omnibus credere et fidem plenis-
simam tribuere. Sperantes per nos ordinata talia fore, quod poteritis
merito contentare; et certissime tenendo quod ea omnia sine defectu
faciemus firmiter observari.

Dat. Florentie die VIII mensis Junii XIIII Indictionis MCCCLXXVI.

(Florence, State Archives, *Signori, Carteggio, Missive, Cancelleria*, n° 15, c. 66.)

XXVI.

[1376.]

Domino Bernabovi.
Octo.

Magnifice et excelse Domine frater karissime.

Licteras spectabilitatis vestre ad nostra brevia responsivas tanto letius accepimus, quanto quotidie vestrum perfectum animum clarius intuemur. Et quoniam opus est facto non verbis, nobis videtur quod si conducere possumus Dominum Johannem Haucud, simus extra cunta pericula, et quod adventus Bretonum sit futurus ad eorum confusionem : et ideo placeat vobis Roggerio Cani rescribere quod conducat et firmet dictam gentem in minori quantitate quam poterit usque in lanceas mille quingentas et arcerios octingentos, et pro minori tempore ac minori stipendio quam poterit, dummodo congruis pactionibus conducantur. Et quamvis vos offeratis etiam ultra quam tangat hanc expensam facere, de quo vobis regratiamus, tamen nos sumus parati subire una vobiscum expensarum onus pro rata, secundum lige taxationem . . . .

Sed quia visis capitulis Anglicorum satis vobiscum dubitamus ipsos nobiscum ad concordiam non venturos quia res omnino denegabiles postulant et nos in intolerabiles sumptus inducunt, attamen utile credimus quod commodis et habilibus conventionibus conducantur ; ad quod faciendum Spinellum nostrum secretarium transmittimus, et ideo vos super hoc quod expediens visum fuerit Roggerio placeat intimare : et quo simus in tuto, firmare nobis necessarium videtur Ducem Austrie cum sua Brigata, ut celeriter furori Britonum opponatur.

Dat. Floren. xvi Junii xiiii Indic. mccclxxvi.

(Ibidem.)

XXVII.

[1376.]

Magnifico et Egregio militi Domino Johanni Hauchwd, Capitaneo Societatis Anglicorum ad presens Italie militantium, Priores Artium et Vexillifer iustitie Populi et Communis Florentie, salutem et prosperos ad vota successus cum honorum felicibus incrementis. Quoniam vestra nobilitas exigit declarari quod, omissis oblivionique traditis iniuriis damnis et offensionibus quibuscunque quas hactenus Commune nostrum a vobis vel vestris gentibus recepisset, sincerum erga vos animum osten-

damus, Ecce quod tenore presentium omnes offensiones contra nos et
nostrum Commune aut nostros subditos quomodocunque et ubicunque
terrarum et loci, per vos aut gentes vestras, dicto vel facto, personaliter vel in bonis factas quomodolibet vel illatas usque in presentem
diem, sub modo et titulo societatis seu ad aliena stipendia militando,
vobis plene remittimus, et ab eisdem vos integraliter absolvimus et li-
beramus. Recipientes vos, omnibus depositis rancoribus, in nostram
gratiam et in animorum nostrorum sincerissima caritate. Nobilitatem
vestram affectuosissime deprecando, quatenus similem nobis remissionem facere placeat versa vice. In quorum testimonium has litteras nostras patentes per Coluccium scribam nostre Cancellarie notari fecimus
et nostrorum sigillorum impressione munitas in nostris actis pubblicis
registrari. Dat. Florentie die xx mensis Junii, xiv Ind. mccclxxvi.

(Ibidem, c. 69.)

XXVIII.

[1376.]

Domino Joanni Haucud.

Nobili ac egregio militi Domino Johanni Haucud Capitaneo Societatis Anglicorum in Italia militantis.

Priores Artium et Vexillifer iustitie Populi et Communis Florentie
salutem cum honorum felicibus incrementis. Maiestati nostri Populi
congruit viros strenuos probitatis atque virtutum luce conspicuos honorare, ut quantum in nobis est egregias mentes ad studia virtutum ar-
dentius animemus. Quo circa, amice carissime, cum anno preterito, de
mense Julii, vobis quamdiu essetis in partibus Italie provisum fuerit
per nostra oportuna consilia quod annuos mille ducentos florenos auri
a nostra Camera percipere deberetis, nos provisionem predictam tenore
presentium, sicut vestra virtus exigit, ampliantes, vos toto tempore
vite vestre, ubicumque terrarum, citra montes vel ultra montes vos
contigerit militare, in provisionatum nostri Communis, libera et mera
nostra voluntate, et ex certa scientia solemniter acceptamus harum
virtute litterarum vobis mille ducentos auri in Civitate Venetiarum
singulis annis de mense Julii numerandos, nostri Communis nomine
deputantis, sublataque omni alia provisione quibuscunque verbis vobis
per Commune nostrum aut nostros antecessores hactenus constituta,
et omnibus ad presentem reductis; pro predictis observandis, vobis
erarium nostrum publicum ac Commune Florentie efficaciter obliga-
mus. In cuius rei testimonium has nostras patentes litteras per Coluccium Pieri scribam nostre Cancellarie registrari fecimus atque scribi,

nostrorumque sigillorum apprensione iussimus roborari. Dat. Florentie die decima mensis Julii, xiiii Indictione Anno Domini MCCCLXXVI.

(Ibidem, n° 17, c. 45.)

XXIX.

[1378.]

Magnifici et potentes Domini tamquam fratres carissimi.

Significamus vobis quod Dominus Summus Pontifex nobis rescrissit quod pro ambassiatoribus ipsius procuremus habere unum salvum conductum a vobis et a Dominis florentinis per omnibus gentibus Lige, quod ipsi possint adcedere per quascumque terras Lige cum ducentis equitibus armis valisiis et rebus aliis quibuscumque indeque Romam redire, valiturum duobus mensibus ; quare Magnificentiam vestram deprecamur quod dictum salvum conductum nobis mittere non tardetis, in tali forma et ordine quod aliquid in eo opponi non possit. Data in Sancto Quiricho die iii Februarii.

JOHANNES HAUKOWOD
Capitaneus etc.

(A tergo)

Magnificis et potentibus Dominis, Dominis Defensoribus populi Civitatis Senarum fratribus carissimis.

(London, British Museum, Harleyan MSS., 6989, f. I.)

XXX.

[1378.]

Magnifici et potentes Domini, honorandi amici carissimi. Habemus a certo per literas egregii militis domini Johannis Torneberi, Thome de Edwarston et Almerici de Interminellis quod hoc sero ambaxiatores Domini Summi Pontifficis Radicoffanum applicuerunt, et cras in prandio venient Sanctum Quiricum bona hora, quibus obviam ibimus usque ad Hospitale Valdurze bona hora, que vobis significare curavimus per presentes.

Apud Sanctum Quiricum, xxvii Februarii, hora 3ᵃ noctis.

JOHANNES HAUCWOD
Capitaneus etc.

(A tergo)

Magnificis et potentibus Dominis, Dominis Defensoribus Civitatis Senarum honorandis amicis carissimis.

(Ibidem.)

XXXI.

[1379.]

Magnifici et potentes domini; ut noscatis nos in omnibus vigilare, sentimus et a certo habemus quod vos una cum aliis comunitatibus Tuscie nostram procuratis omnino recipere comitivam et nonnullos ex nostris ad vestra stipendia recipere, de quo amiratione multa movemur, ob quod rogamus ut nullos ex nostris accipere vellitis donec vobis aliqua utilia vobis et nobis rescribemus. Nam si tantum omnes gentes istas ad vestra stipendia reciperetis nou propterea deficerent nobis alie gentes in numero grandiori quas undecumque habere possumus: de quibus vos reddere volumus provixos et munitos ut eligere possitis quod vobis videbitur pro meliori. Data in campo nostro Luliani **xxj martij**

LUCIUS COMES DE LANDO et }
JOHANNES HAUKUTD   } Capitanei etc. etc.

(A tergo)

Magnificis et potentibus dominis dominis defensoribus Civitatis Senarum amicis nostris Carissimis.

(Siena. State Archives, *Carte di particolari*, Agud.)

XXXII.

[1380.]

Magnifici et potentes domini et fratres carissimi. Mictimus ad vos nobilem virum Antonium de Porcaria sotium nostrum presentium ostensorem, de nostra intentione super quibus vestre dominationi horetenus explicandis plenissime informatum, relatibus cuius tanquam nobis placeat indubiam dare fidem. Parati ad omnia grata vobis. Data Florentie die VIII octobris.

JOHANNES HAUKCWOD
capitaneus etc.

(A tergo)

Magnificis et potentibus dominis dominis defensoribus civitatis Senarum fratribus carissimis.

Amerycus.

(Ibidem.)

XXXIII.

[1381.]

Magnifici et potentes domini et fratres carissimi. Quia dominus Johannes Banus venturus est Florentie per mare vos rogamus ut ordinare vellitis quod pecunia vestra que est provisa veniat Florentiam ut quando ipse venerit possimus negotium expedire, rogantes etiam vos ut supra materia comitis Conradi de Lando ut vobis scripserunt ambasciatores vestri vellitis assumere bonum partitum, quoniam cognoscimus quod ipse cum brigata sua erit bonus pro vobis; et de ipsis placeat nobis respondere. Offerentes nos ad grata vestra. Florentie XXVIII decembris.

JOHANNES HAUKUTD
capitaneus etc.

(A tergo)

Magnificis et potentibus dominis dominis defensoribus civitatis Senarum ut fratribus precarissimis.

(Ibidem.)

XXXIV.

[1382.]

Magnifici et potentes domini et amici carissimi.

Recepimus licteras vestras ut vobis significaremus nova de progressibus ytalicorum, quibus respondemus quod, ut credimus vos audivisse, Arizzium redierunt; nos autem speramus omnes gentes nostre [haberi?] in partibus vallis Arni de supra ut advenienti simili casu in una possimus die esse insimul. Ex quo rogamus ut vestras gentes armigeras mittere vellitis versus Lucignanum et Ambram ut in casu necessitatis possimus insimul subito conveniri. Et alia non scribimus quia vestri scribunt ambassiatores, ad plenum parati perpetua ad beneplacita vestra.

Dat. Florentie die xj Januarij

JOANNES HAUKUTD
Capitaneus generalis.

(A tergo)

Magnificis et potentibus dominis dominis Defensoribus Civitatis Senarum dominis et amicis Carissimis.

(Ibidem.)

XXXV.

[1382.]

Magnifici et potentes domini et amici carissimi. Juxta informationem vestrorum ambassiatorum firmavimus **xx** lanceas bonas que sunt parate quandocumque habuerint pecunias ; et immo placeat providere quod pecunias solvatur ipsis hic (*sic*) prestantia et venient sine mora ; sed si placeret habere plus usque in **xxv** vel **xxx** lanzeas nobis rescribatis et mictemus usque ad numerum prelibatum ; ultra vero hic iam diu virum strenuum Henricum Actimbergh retinuimus, et si placeret ipsum ad vestra servitia habere cum centum vel **lxxx** lanzeis nobis rescribatis et ipsum facemus cum bona brigata venire. Et de omnibus placeat per Godardum latorem presentium respondere. Parati ad grata vestra.

Florentie **xxij** Januarij

JOHANNES HAUKUTD
Capitaneus generalis.

(A tergo)

Magnificis et potentibus dominis dominis Defensoribus Civitatis Senarum amicis carissimis.

(Ibidem, *Lettere al Concistoro.*)

XXXVI.

[1382.]

Magnifici et potentes domini et amici carissimi. Jam per plures nostras literas magnificentie vestre rescripsimus supra liberatione egregii militis domini Petri de Gaetanis de Pisis et nunc percepimus ipsum fore antedicto (*sic*) captivatum quem credebamus vos iam relapsasse. Et ob id, cum noster sit intimus amicus et carus, magnificentiam prelibatam grate rogamus quod licet in aliquo fefellerit, quod nullo modo credere possumus, eundem ex gratia et dono singulari petimus et personam suam postulamus quantum affectius possumus, nam gratiam ipsam quam credimus apud amicitiam vestram liberaliter obtinere nunquam nostris tradebimus temporibus oblivioni. Et pro huiusmodi liberatione vobis et comunitati illi ad queque gratuita et honoranda obtulimus ecce nos paratos. Datum Florentie **xxiv** Januarii.

JOHANNES HAUKUTD
capitaneus generalis.

(A tergo)

Magnificis et potentibus dominis dominis defensoribus civitatis Senarum amicis nostris carissimis etc.

(Ibidem, *Carte di particolari*, Agud.)

XXXVII.

[1382.]

Magnifici et potentes domini. Quia nuper inteleximus gentes societatis Italicorum Sancti Georgii Aretium exivisse et equitasse versus territoria vestra, Magnificentiam Vestram rogamus actente ut nobis scribere placeat iter eorum, ut si equitassent versus partes maretime statim exire contra eos possimus in vestri auxilium. Et si citra Senas equitassent ordinetis quod gentes vestre se reducant versus Podio Bonizum et alias partes ad finem quod ipsos ibidem invenire valeamus. Insuper, ut alio Magnificentie Vestre scripsimus, dignemini nobis ex gratia largiri dominum Petrum de Gaytanis vestris carceribus mancipatum. Parati ad singula gratuita votis vestris. Dat. Florentie xxiiij Januarij hora ij noctis. Et taliter providere quod vestre gentes parati sint quod veniendo nobiscum ad fronterias ad facendum honorem nostrum et vestrum (sic).

JOHANNES HAUCUD
Capitaneus generalis etc.

(A tergo)

Magnificis et potentis dominis. D. Defensoribus Civitatis Senarum etc.

(The seal bears the impress of a hawk.)

(Ibidem.)

XXXVIII.

[1382.]

Magnifici et potentes domini et amici carissimi. Recepimus literas vestras quibus respondemus quod infra duos dies cum omnibus gentibus venire erimus certe parati, iuxta tamen mandata dominorum nostrorum, ex gratia et dono preterea petentes personam domini Petri de Gaytanis. Datum Florentie xxv Januarii.

JOHANNES HAUKUTD
capitaneus generalis.

(A tergo)

Magnificis et potentibus dominis dominis defensoribus civitatis Senarum amicis carissimis.

(Ibidem.)

XXXIX.

[1382.]

Magnifici et potentes domini. Recomendatione premissa. Quia nobilis vir Henricus Cher est cum Ciono Sandri quem cognoscimus probum
virum, ipsum si gentes faceretis totis affectibus commendamus. Nam
ab ibso fructuosa servitia reportabitis. Et honore parati ad singula
M. V. grata. Dat. Florentie xxv. Januarij

JOHANNES HAUCUD
Capitaneus Generalis etc.

(A tergo)

Magnificis et potentibus dominis dominis Defensoribus Civitatis Senarum dominis precarissimis.

(Ibidem.)

XL.

[1382.]

Magnifici et potentes domini. Ut novistis pridie, pro firma illarum
xx lancearum miximus ad vos Conradum de Laudebach latorem presentium quem, ut reportavit, benigniter firmavistis ad vestra servitia;
et pro incurso casu istorum inimicorum ipsas xx lanceas in campo nobis-
scum retinuimus, nunc vero ad vestram presentiam destinamus partem;
et alia pars ibit Florentiam pro rebus et bonis eorum, ventura illico
Senas; et ob id ipsos magnificentie vestre affectuose recomendamus ut
ipsis pro damnis receptis in campo fieri facere vellitis prestantias duorum mensium et facere subito ipsos scribere et collocare prope confines istos, ut in casu quo inimici equitarent possimus contra ipsos viriliter equitare. Et similiter placeat semper gentes vestras equestres et
pedites ac balistrarios in punto equitandi retinere, quoniam si venerint
versus partes vestras aut Florentiam, intendimus, favente altissimo, contra ipsos nostras vires demonstrare; rogantes ut propter dilationem
eorum non ammictant stipendium; parati semper ad beneplacita vestra. Dat. apud Castrum Novum die primo februarii.

JOHANNES HAUKUTD
capitaneus generalis.

(A tergo)

Magnificis et potentibus dominis dominis defensoribus civitatis Senarum dominis et amicis carissimis.

(Ibidem.)

XLI.

[1382.]

Magnifici et potentes domini. Recomendatione premissa. Sentientes vestram Magnificentiam gentes velle facere de presenti, Ecce ad presentiam vestram se transferet vir nobilis atque probus Rubinus de Borset Britonus qui cum lanzeis ẍx fideliter dominationi vestre servire curabit. Ipsum eidem dominationi totis affectibus commendantes.

Dat. Florentie xxiiij februarii.

JOHANNES HAUCUD

Capitaneus generalis etc.

(A tergo)

Magnificis et potentibus dominis dominis Defensoribus Civitatis Senarum dominis precarissimis.

(Ibidem.)

XLII.

[1382.]

Magnifici et potentes domini. Recomendatione premissa. Audientes Magnificam dominationem vestram gentes velle firmare ad sua servitia de presenti, Ecce Miles Egregius et in armorum ministerio comprobatus dominus Goz theutonicus lator presentium ad vestram se dirrigit presentiam, qui cum certa quantitate brigate vestre dominationi servire fideliter procurabit. Quem contemplatione nostri dignemini suscipere comendatum. Dat. Florentie xxiiij februarij.

JOHANNES HAUCUD

Capitaneus generalis etc.

(A tergo)

Magnificis et potentibus dominis dominis defensoribus Civitatis Senarum dominis precarissimis.

(Ibidem.)

XLIII.

[1382.]

Magnifici et potentes domini. Sentientes vestram magnificentiam gentes armorum velle facere de presenti, Ecce ad presentiam vestram accedit vir nobilis atque probus Aymericus ungarus qui cum certa brigata vestre magnificentie fideliter servire curabit; ipsum dominationi vestre totis affectibus comendantes. Datum Florentie die xxiv februarii.

JOHANNES HAUCUD
capitaneus generalis etc.

(A tergo)

Magnificis et potentibus dominis dominis deffensoribus civitatis Senarum dominis precarissimis.

(Ibidem.)

_____

XLIV.

[1382.]

Magnifici et potentes domini fratres carissimi. Conquesti sunt nobis Anglici qui de anno preterito et presenti ad servitia vestra fuere, quod in eorum rationibus tempore firme finite fuerunt fortiter defalcati et dapnificati contra formam pactorum indebite et iniuste. Quod contra vestri conscentiam processisse putamus si verum est M. V. care precantes ut Dionixio de la Strata Cancellario nostro mittere placeat unam literam fidantie per quam venire valeat Senas et inde redire cum sex equitibus, contradictione aliqua non obstante et aliqua molestia sibi quomodolibet inferenda octo dierum spatio duraturam, quamquam frustratoriam nobis videatur; dispositi semper ad singula M. V. grata. Dat. Florentie xxvij Aprilis.

JOHANNES HAUCUD
Capitaneus generalis etc.

(A tergo)

Magnificis et potentibus dominis dominis Defensoribus Civitatis Senarum fratribus precarissimis.

(Ibidem.)

_____

XLV.

[1382.]

Magnifici et potentes domini fratres carissimi.

Pridie scripsimus Magnificentie vestre eandem M. rogitando ut pro Dionixio de la Strata cancellario nostro mittere debeatis unum salvum conductum cum quo venire tute valeret Senis pro conferendo cum fraternitate vestra super quibusdam. Iterato rogamus ut ipsum salvum conductum concedere placeat et Carolo Speziario consignare.

Parati et dispositi ad quelibet consona votis vestris. Datum Florentie xj May.

JOHANNES HAUCUD

Capitaneus etc.

(A tergo)

. Magnificis et potentibus dominis dominis Defensoribus Civitatis Senarum fratribus precarissimis.

(Ibidem.)

XLVI.

[1382.]

Magnifici et potentes Domini et amici carissimi. Providendo logiamenta istarum partium huc appullimus, dispositis in vestris partibus omnes gentes armigeras. Et ut advenienti casu possimus subito esse insimul vos rogamus ut omnes vestras gentes equites pedites et balistrarios in maiori quo potestis numero mittere velitis sub ductu vestri Capitanei ad partes Lucignani et aliorum vestrorum locorum quum facta Arizzii procedunt per modum quod poteritis contentari. Et in hoc vestram festinam sollicitudinem imploramus vice ista parati ubilibet ad grata vestra. Datum Civitelle primo Maji.

JOHANNES HAUKUTD

Capitaneus generalis ec.

(A tergo)

Magnificis et potentibus Dominis Dominis Defensoribus Civitatis Senarum amicis carissimis.

(London, British Museum Cottonian Charters, IV. 16.)

XLVII.

[1383.]

Die vjj mensis decembris

Magnifici et potentes domini, domini defensores Capitaneus Populi, Prior Reformationum et septem ex octo offitialibus Comunis Sen.....

Pro evidenti utilitate, honore, comodo Comunis et populi Civitatis Sen. predicte et pro reparatione quam plurium scandalorum et periculorum que pro futuro de facili possent contingere, etc. Fuerunt in plena concordia deliberandi et deliberaverunt quod sit remissum ex nunc in Ser Ghanum Biondi notarium, Mannoccium Guidi de Ranconibus de Senis et Bencivennem Gani, ambaxiatores dicti comunis, ituros ad dominum Johannem Augut capitaneum Sotietatis (*interruption in the MS.*), qui ambaxiatores possint libere componere et pacisci et compositionem et concordiam facere cum dicto domino Johanne Augut et cum Johanne Azzi et cum omnibus aliis caporalibus dicte societatis, cum illis capitulis pactis articulis et limitationibus quibus et prout et sicut dictis ambaxiatoribus videbitur et placebit, de non offendendo Civitatem vel Comitatum Sen. durante pro illo tempore et modis quibus eisdem ambaxiatoribus placuerit etc. Et pro dicta compositione fienda et concordia habenda, possint vice et nomine Comunis Sen. dictis Domino Johanni capitaneo et aliis caporalibus dicte sotietatis pro se et pro dictis de Sotietate etc. promictere dare et solvere tria millia vel quinque millia florenorum auri et etiam promictere usque ad quantitatem et summam otto millia florenorum auri inclusive prout et sicut eisdem ambaxiatoribus videbitur et placebit ; et quidquid per eos in predictis factum fuerit et compositum sive gestum valeat et teneat ac si factum esset per dictos de balia predicta etc.

(Siena, State Archives. *Deliberazioni di Concistoro.*)

XLVIII.

[1383.]

Die xjj de mense decembris

Magnifici et potentes domini, domini defensores, Capitaneus populi, prior Reformationum Civitatis Sen. et septem ex otto offitialibus Comunis Sen. super Balia deputati, in solito consistorio congregati, solepnitatibus debitis osservatis etc. vigore eorum balie etc. fuerunt in plena concordia deliberandi et deliberaverunt quod Dominus Johannes Agut, Capitaneus Sotietatis (*interruption in the MS.*) habeat provisionem a Comuni Sen. pro tempore unius anni proximi secuturi, incipiente dicto anno in calendis decembris proximis preteritis et ut sequitur finiendo, ad rationem pro quolibet mensi dicti anni centum florenorum auri neptorum sine aliqua detractione kabelle : et hec pro remuneratione quamplurium servitiorum factorum per eum Comuni Sen. etc. et ut ejus animus in posterum ferventius sit ad serviendo dicto Comuni, maxime nunc in pace et concordie et compositione fienda inter ipsum Comune ex una parte et eumdem Dominum Johannem et ejus caporales et sotietatem ex altera parte. que nunc tractatur etc.

(Ibidem.)

XLIX.

[1384.]

Magnifici et potentes domini fratres carissimi. Recomandatione pre-missa. Exigunt virtuosa opera sapientis viri domini Petri de Boncom-pagnis de Pinu legum doctoris dignis honoribus 'sublimari; considerantes igitur prefati domini Petri nobis intimissimi sufficientiam, audemus pro ipso tanquam benemerito apud magnificentiam vestram interponere partes nostras; magnificentiam vestram, quam erga nos semper invenimus liberalem, non cessamus cordialiter deprecari ut eidem domino Petro, nostri amoris intuitu, de officio sindicatus vestre nobilissime civitatis pro semestri et tempore ellectionis primere begnigniter subvenire. Tenentes a certo quod quicquid eidem nostra gratia et amore impensum fuerit personis propriis ascribemus. Ideoque erga ipsum taliter se habere dignetur magnificentia antedicta quod idem dominus Petrus mediante vestro suffragio gaudeat nostras literas destinasse vestreque dominationi teneamur grata vicissitudine respondere. Super quibus placeat per latorem presentem destinare vestrum gratiosum responsum. Parati semper ad quelibet conformia votis vestris. Dat. Florentie III septembris.

JOANNES HAUCUD
capitaneus generalis etc.

(A tergo)

Magnificis et potentibus dominis dominis defensoribus civitatis Se-narum fratribus precarissimis.

(Ibidem, *Carte di particolari*, Agud.)

L.

[1384.]

Magnifici et potentes domini. Mittimus ad vos ser Guicciardinum de Bononia cancellarium nostrum cum pleno mandato pro illa pecunia quam nobis dare debetis ex causa vobis nota, quem placeat ad nos re-mittere expeditum et cum dicta pecunia, quia ipsa ut plurimum pre-

sentialiter indigemus. Dat. in campo nostro in comitatu Cortone
XXIII septembris VII indictione.

JOHANNES HAUCHUTD miles
JOHANNES DE UBALDINIS } capitanei societatis rose.
RICIARDUS ROMUSEN

(A tergo)

Magnificis et potentibus dominis defensoribus populi civitatis Senarum dominis carissimis.

(Ibidem.)

Ll.

[1384.]

Priores artium et vexillifer Iustitie populi et Communis Florentie.
Vogliamo e comandiamo che voi messer Donato rimagnate a fare
quello che aveste in commessione e perchè il ragionamento di messer
Giovanni Aguto per lo quale foste mandati voi, Bartolomeo e Jacopo,
non vengono a dire nulla, fate che vedute le presenti tornate alla nostra presentia. Dat. Florentie die 27 octobris VII Indict.

(Florence, Laurentian Library, Ahsburnham MSS. n° 1751 of the catalogue.)

LII.

[1384.]

Magnifici et potentes domini et amici carissimi.
Ad vestre presentie Magnificentiam accedit vir nobilis Vituccius de
Pisis mercator lator presentium cui sum in certa pecunie quantitate
veridice obligatus; et ob id ad ipsam vestram dominationem necessario
cogor confidenter recurrere, rogans ut ipsi Vituccio dare facere vellitis
illos quingentos florenos quos pro resto illius mee provixionis mihi
dare debetis. Nam erit mihi tantum gratum quod licteris explicare non
possem. Et exinde ero vobis in omnibus obligatus; queso intuitu meo
deficere non vellitis. Paratus ad singula grata vestra. Dat. Florentie
primo Novembris vij Ind.

Vester JOHANNES HAUKUTD miles etc.

(A tergo)

Magnificis et potentibus dominis dominis Defensoribus Civitatis Senarum dominis et Amicis precarissimis.

(Siena, State Archives, Carte di particolari, Agud.)

LIII.

[1385.]

Copia lictere trasmisse per dominum Carolum Vicecomitem etc.
domino Johanni de Agud.

Magnifice et extrenue amice nostri carissime. Notificamus vobis quod hodie summo mane dominus comes Virtutum in Mediolano cepit et detenuit magnificum et excelsum dominum dominum genitorem nostrum et magnificum fratrem nostrum carissimum dominum Lodovicum Vicecomitem etc. Nos liberi sumus in Crema cittadella nostra et castrum Porte Romane tenetur nostro nomine. Quare fraternam probitatem vestram affettuose rogamus ut statim cum illis gentibus armigeris quas a vobis et ab amicis recuperare poteritis veniatis personaliter nobis in subsidium per Parmam; et denarios opportunos in quantitate habemus paratos pro numerari faciendos prout ordinabitis; tempus est enim ut ostendatis virilitatem vestram et quod scitis facere et estis consueti Rescribentes statim etc.

Datum Creme die vi maii.

CAROLUS VICECOMES etc.

(Ibidem.)

LIV.

[1385.]

Magnifici et potentes domini carissimi. Recomendatione premissa. Ad Magnificientiam Vestram providum et discretum virum Ser Jacobum de Petrasanta carissimum meum de meis intentione plenarie informatum trasmicto, cui tamquam proprie persone mee placeat fidem credulam hadibere. Paratus et dispositus ad omnia vobis grata. Datum Florentie xvij Augusti millesimo ccclxxxv

JOHANNES HAUCUD
miles, Anglicorum etc.

(A tergo)

Magnificis et potentibus dominis dominis Prioribus et Vexilliferis Iustitie civitatis Senarum dominis precarissimis.

(Ibidem, *Lettere al Concistoro.*)

LV.

[1386.]

Die quinta settembris.

Convocato certo consilio richieste centum octo civium civitatis Sen. in dicto numero predictis dominis prioribus computatis, ad richiestam factam per famulos eorumdem dominorum fuit in dicto consilio de licentia propositi per Andream Francisci Purghiani de numero dictorum dominorum priorum dictum et propositum in hac forma, videlicet: Cum audiveritis licteram et ambaxiatam domini Jóhannis Agud super quibus et contentis quarum alias in simili consilio fuit propositum. Et quod cum Antonio de Porcari post dictum retentum consilium fuerit habita certa pratica et colloquio, quibus comprehendi potest quod dominus Johannes Agud hiis temporibus venturus est ad partes nostri comitatu. Iterum et de novo supra predicta materia petiit sibi pro comuni Senarum sanum utileque consilium exiberi.

Ventura Andree unus ex consiliariis dicti consili, surgens in dicto consilio et ad consuetum existens dicitorium, supra dicta proposita et contentis in ea dixit et consuluit: quod Monaldus Mini Monaldi ambaxiator jam electus pro predictis vadat et mictatur per dominos priores ad dictum dominem Johannem Agud, qui eidem clarificet et dicat impossibilitatem nostram et nostri comunis Sen., qua mediante excuset Comune Sen. quod sibi de petitis per eum non potest sibi complacere solummodo per nostram impossibilitatem. Qua exposita ambaxiata, dictus ambaxiator actente audiat quod respondebitur per dictum dominum Johannem et omnem eius quantum possit presentem intentionem, et omnia que habuerit et presumserit referat et notificet dominis prioribus ; et quod dictus Monaldus vadat quo citius poterit cum dicta ambaxiata vel alia qua domini priores per se vel per illos in quos comictere volunt super predictis.

In cujus summa consilii et reformatione, dato, facto et misso solepni scrutinio ad lupinos albos et nigros secundum formam statutorum Sen., fuit in dicto consilio obtentum et solepniter reformatum per centum tres consiliarios qui reddiderunt eorum lupinum album pro sic, non obstantibus quinque eorum qui reddiderunt nigros lupinos pro non, quod predicta omnia faciantur et exequantur prout superius continetur.

(Ibidem. *Deliberazioni di Concistoro.*)

LVI.

[1386.]

Die primo mensis novembris.

Viri magnifici et honorabiles domini domini priores Comunis et Populi Civitatis Sen. et offitiales balie in sufficienti numero convocati et congregati in consueto consistorio palatii comunis Senarum, residentia dictorum dominorum priorum, pro eorum offitio laudabiliter exercendo, de mandato viri prudentis Jacobi Fei honorabilis propositi dictorum dominorum, facta prius super infrascriptis solenni et diligenti proposita per dictum Dominum propositum de assensu suorum collegarum, et super ea dato facto et misso secreto partito et scruptineo inter eos ad lupinos albos et nigros secundum formam statutorum Senarum, uniformes conformes et unanimes statuerunt et decreverunt: quod Georgius Coltini de Senis, electus in ambassiatorem iturus ad dominum Johannem de Agut ex parte Comunis Senarum, omni postposita mora equitet et se transferat ad dictum Dominum Johannem eidemque referat quod quantitas florenorum de auro, quos tenetur et debet habere a Niccolao domini Spinelli de Piccolominibus, est protinus preparata. Nec non roget eundem dominum Johannem ex parte et intuito Comunis Senarum quod eidem placeat quod iter suum non fiat per territorium Senarum per se vel suos complices. Et in quantum idem Dominus Johannes velit aliud iter carpere quantum per Comitatum Senarum, quod tunc et eo casu dictus Georgius orator possit et sibi liceat largiri eidem Domino Johanni de Agut, in quantum aliud iter ipse et sui complices caporales et sequaces tenere velint quantum per comitatum Senarum, usque in quantitatem quingentorum florenorum de auro de florenis et pecunia comunis Sen. sine aliquo suo preiudicio. Et quod ipse Georgius habeat ed ducat pro honore Comunis Senarum et sue persone tres equos. Et hec fecerunt et decreverunt vigore eorum bailie et omni via jure modo et forma quibus melius poterint. In cujus reformatione consilj dato facto et misso partito, fuit victum optentum et reformatum quod plene sit fiat et exequatur prout et sicut superius continetur, per sedecim lupinos albos del si, non obstantibus duobus lupinis nigris del no in contrarium.

(Ibidem.)

LVII.

[1386.]

Die quarto mensis Novembris.

Viri magnifici et honorabiles domini domini priores et offitiales de
bailia civitatis Senarum, in consueto consistorio palatii comunis Senarum convocati pro eorum offitio laudabiliter exercendo, vigore eorum
bailie, concorditer decreverunt, respectu habito ad inoppinatum adventum domini Johannis de Agut cum suis complicibus armigeris: quod,
omni postposita mora, per proprium gerulum scribatur ambassiatoribus
comunis Senarum qui in civitate Cortonij moram trahunt quatenus,
ipsis inspectis licteris, se cum omnibus stipendiaris comunis Senarum
celeriter Senas transferant primo cum domino Cortonense licentia bene-
vola ac curiali capta. Et hec decreverunt etc.

(Ibidem.)

LVIII.

[1386.]

Die vij mensis novembris.

Viri magnifici et honorabiles domini, domini priores Civitatis Sen.
et offitiales de bailia ejusdem Civitatis in consueto consistorio, palatii
comunis Sen. convocati pro eorum offitio laudabiliter exercendo, vigore
eorum bailie etc. decreverunt quod ex parte comunis Sen. gratis re-
quirantur comunia Florentie, Perusii, Pisarum et Luce de ipsorum et
cujuslibet ipsorum potentia armigera equestri, eisdem comunibus noti-
ficando adventu domini Johannis de Agut cum sua armigerum comitiva in territorium Jurisdictionis Sen., consulente Checo petri Guccii
uno ex dominis prioribus et optentus per sedecim del si, nemine in
contrarium disponente.

(Ibidem.)

LIX.

[1386.]

Dicta die (november 7).

Viri magnifici et honorabiles domini, domini priores et officiales bailie
civitatis Sen. in consueto consistorio palatii comunis Sen. convocati pro
eorum offitio honorabiliter exercendo, vigore eorum balie concorditer

decreverunt, quod cum Georgius Coltini de Senis, comunis Sen. orator translatum ad Dominum Johannem de Agut, redierit et eisdem dominis retulerit dictum Johannem prefatum protinus velle quod suis caporalibus armigeris et complicibus suis aliis fiat a comuni Sen. curialitas de mille flor. auri, sibique etiam illa curialitas que comuni Sen. placet et videtur, et ab hijs comune Sen. non valeat resilire sine maximo danno sui comitatus, quod dominus Niccolus de Salimbenibus scribat eidem domino Iohanni, quia conpater suus est, ista forma: videlicet quod, eodem ipso domino Niccolo ad pedes dominorum priorum Civitatis Senarum, inter numerum quorumdam quandam bailiam habentium pro quibusdam debito fine in comuni Sen. terminandis, interfuit cuidam relationi Ambassiate ipsius domini Johannis relate eisdem dominis prioribus per Georgium Coltini de Senis, referentem ipsum dominum Johannem petere Comuni Sen. nomine curialitatis mille flor. auri pro suis complicibus et pro sua persona id quod Comunis Sen. placeret et videretur. Igitur cum comune Sen. occasione iniqui retrohacti regiminis reformationis ad presens impotens sistat den., sibi Dño Johanni, gratia et comtenplatione sui, placeat remanere contento de quingentis flor. auri quos idem Dominus Niccolus vere de suis propris den et flor. mutuat comuni Sen. Et nihilominus Georgius Coltini orator predictus, in quantum dominus Johannes non staret contentus probationi domini Niccoli, plenam habeat auctoritatem et bailiam se pro comuni Sen. componendi cum dicto domino Johanne usque in quantitatem mille flor. de auro, si et in quantum ipse dominus Johannes et sui complices non ingrediantur in comitatum Senarum. Et hoc fecerunt etc. ut patet latius etc.

(Ibidem.)

LX.

[1386.]

Die xij mensis novembris.

Viri Magnifici et honorabiles Domini, Domini priores et offitiales Bailie Civitatis Sen. consueto consistorio pallatij Comunis Sen. convocati pro eorum offitio honorabiliter exercendo, vigore eorum bailie concorditer decreverunt, cum Georgius Coltini civis ambassiator et commissarius comunis Sen. redierit a domino Johanne de Agut et cum eo composuerit sibi domino Johanni et suis complicibus et armigerum comitive nomine curialitatis largiri de pecunia et florenis comunis Senarum octingentos florenos de auro. Et eumdem dominum Johannem et suos caporales et complices eidem Georgio promisisse pro comuni

Sen. recipienti non ingredi comitatum Senarum neque invadere neque in ipsum territorium intrare usque ad unum annum proximum venturum, et Senas idem Dominus Johannes miserit Bartholomeum de Gonzaga et Johachinum Bartalato caporales suos pro dictis octingenti florenis auri. Quod camerarius et quatuor provisores biccherne comunis Sen. dent et solvant eisdem caporalibus de pecunia et florenis comunis Sen. sine aliqua detentione kabelle et sine aliquo eorum danno periculo vel preiudicio, dictos octingentos florenorum auri. Et hec fecerunt etc.: ut patet latius etc.

(Ibidem.)

LXI.

[1386.]

Dicta die (november 12).

Viri magnifici et horabiles domini, domini priores et offitiales de balia Civitatis Sen. in consueto consistorio palatii Comunis Sen. convocati pro eorum offitio honorabiliter exercendo etc., decreverunt quod domino Johanni de Agut fiat salvum cunductum pro sua persona et xl vel l sotiis equestribus quod libere possint accedere ad civitatem Sen. et inde discedendi pro eorum libito voluntatis tute et sicure etc. Hec fecerunt etc. ut patet latius etc.

(Ibidem.)

LXII.

[1386.]

Die xv mensis decembris

Viri magnifici et honorabiles domini, domini priores gubernatores reipublice civitatis Sen. et officiales de balia civitatis ejusdem in consueto consistorio pallatij comunis Sen. convocati pro eorum officio laudabiliter exercendo. vigore eorum balie concorditer decreverunt quod ex parte dominorum priorum scribatur Jacobo Johannis Arighecti ambassiatori pro comuni Sen. Florentie moram trahenti, quod postulet comunis Sen. parte prioribus florentinis quod aut separari faciant gentes armigeras de partibus vallis Ambre domini Johannis de Augud, aut nobis prestent in nostrum subsidium de eorum gentibus armigeris equestribus. Et hec fecerunt etc. ut patet latius etc.

(Ibidem.)

LXIII.

[1388.]

Die tertia mensis settembris.

Convocato et congregato certo consilio richieste quorumdam civium Civitatis Sen.......

Cum audiverit legere quamdam licteram et narrare quamdam ambaxiatam pro parte domini Johannis Agud transmissas, quibus in effectu ipse dominus Johannes Agud requirit comune Senarum de quatuor millibus florenorum mutuo, et posse stare cum eius brigata per usque decem dies supra territorio Senarum etc.

Super quibus omnibus Dominicus Guiducci Ruffaldi unus ex consiliariis dicti consilii in dicto surgens consilio ad dicitorium consuetum, dixit et consuluit quod ad dictum dominum Johannem Agud destinetur unus ambaxiator comunis Senarum, qui eidem domino Johanni excuset comune Sen. pro presenti est impotens et eius cives sunt multum gravati et quod etiam comitatini nostri comitatus sunt multum oppressi multis gravedinibus maxime sotietatum et gentium armorum, quod eidem non potest nostrum comune subveniri de hiis que petit; et quam plus potuerit verbis placabilibus excuset de predictis dictum nostrum comune Sen. adeo quod remaneat contentus. Hoc addito consilio dicti domini per Meium Johannis Juntini unum ex dictis consiliariis, videlicet quod si dictus ambaxiator, habito responso a dicto domino Johanne, comprehenderet ipsum non fore contentum, possit dictus ambaxiator componere cum dicto domino Johanne componere et concordare non intrando in comitatu Sen. usque quantitatem mille vel duorum milium florenorum, possit in hoc spendere et eidem promictere et dare quantitatem predictam.......

In cujus summa Consilii et Reformatione dato facto et misso solepni partito ad lupinos albos et nigros secundum formam statutorum Senarum, victum et obtentum fuit solepniter et reformatum.......

(Ibidem.)

Die dicta.

Magnifici domini, domini priores supradicti, more solito coadunati in eorum solito consistorio, volentes exequi supradicti consilii stabilita, precedentibus solepnitatibus opportunis cum precedenti solenni scruptineo, de ipsorum plena concordia eligerunt in eorum et comunis Senarum ambaxiadorem qui vadat ad dominum Johannem Agud, infrascriptum civem Sen. cuius nomen hoc est: Monaldus Mini Monaldi.

(Ibidem.)

LXIV.

[1388.]

Die dicta (september 5).

Magnifici Domini.... coadunati etc....

Simili modo domini priores et sapientes consistorii predicti deliberaverunt.......

Scribatur ambaxiatoribus comunis Sen. Florentie existentes ea que
dominus Johannes Agud petit comuni Sen. in mutuo quatuormilia flor.
et stare in comitatu Sen. cum ejus comitiva per aliquos dies. Et quod
de predictis dicti Ambaxiatores conferant in comuni Florentie, qui rogent priores Florentie quod velint assitere eis in talibus petitionibus,
asserendo dictis dominis prioribus quod se certos reddunt quod si in
hoc se voluerit intromictere comune Florentie, ipse Dominus Johannes
desistet ab hujusmodi petitionibus, et cessabit talis petitio dicti domini
Johannis, etc.

(Ibidem.)

LXV.

[1389.]

Nota e informatione a voi Andrea Vettori e Giovanni di Giovanni
     Iacobi di quello che avete a fare con messer Giovanni Aguto, fatta
     per li Dieci della Balia del Comune di Firenze nel MCCCLXXXVIIII
     adì VIII di giugno.

Andrete a ritrovare messer Giovanni Aguto, il quale colla sua Brigata dovrà essere verso il Borgo a San Sepolcro o Città di Castello.
E dopo le saluti gli direte come noi ci maravigliamo dello essere egli
tanto soprastato a venire avendo avute da noi tante richieste e per
tanti nostri Ambasciadori, dicendogli che questa non è la speranza la
quale noi abbiavamo in lui, che pensavamo come essendoci egli obligato
che dovesse venire a nostra richiesta, non che avendo i patti sì chiari
con lui.

E dipoi direte come voi andate per scrivere lui e sua Brigata e
vedere la mostra, e in modo di Compagna. E così farete.

E il modo dello scrivere sia questo come è d'usanza, cioè che messer Giovanni può fare scrivere infino in Lance mille, s'egli l'a seco,
computati gli arcieri, e infino in v^c tra fanti e balestrieri. E così stanno
i patti. E intendesi la Lancia di tre huomini e tre cavalli per Lancia,

e non femine. E allo scrivere e alla mostra farete d'avere continua-
mente con voi presenti messer Giovanni Aguto, Gianichino Bottigliere
e parecchi altri Caporali huomini da bene e tra gli altri Liverpol, pre-
gandogli che proveggano che noi non siamo ingannati, perciocchè aven-
dogli a adoperare, tornerebbe pur a loro danno e vergogna non avendo
la gente che dessono a divedere.

Poi procederete nello scrivere; e comincerete a messer Giovanni e
subsequentemente a gli altri Caporali, mettendo i nomi e soprannomi
de' Caporali e la quantità delle Lance e Arcieri che diranno avere ve-
ramente : e farete jurare ciascuno di servire bene e lealmente e observare i patti, e che nella mostra eglino avranno loro cavalli e non al-
trui, e che non presteranno i loro a persona, nè faranno la mostra
più che una volta. E così farete de' fanti e balestrieri.

E fatto questo scrivere e dati i giuramenti, ordinerete uno luogo
dove s'abbia a fare la mostra, che sia tale che vi si passi strecto e
ch'e' cavalli passati non possino ritornare a mostrarvisi più che una
volta. E questo sia o ponte sopra fiume o qualche foce di valli stretta.
E se vi bisognasse fare qualche sbarra, fatela fare. E di questi tali
luoghi pigliate informatione da' paesani.

E cominciate questa mostra una mattina per tempo, sì che in uno
dì sanza fallo si spacci, tegnendo ogni modo che saprete perchè siamo
ingannati il meno che si può. E annovererete tutti i cavalli e ronzini,
scrivendo il numero a piedi di ciascuno Caporale. E simile si scrivono
i muli e ronzini.

E porrete mente che cavalli eglino anno e come sono armati, e tra
l'altre cose farete notare per scriptura quanti bacinetti e armature di
capo saranno nella detta Brigata.

E questo fatto. tornerete alla nostra presentia, dicendo a messer
Giovanni che lasci la Brigata in buon'ordine, e venga a noi prestamente
con parecchi Caporali con mandato pieno e sufficiente, perchè con lui
vogliamo fare alcuno ragionamento.

E se messer Giovanni dicesse volere scrivere le mille Lance e desse
indugio, direte che scriva quelle ch'egli a al presente, che secondo i
patti non si dovrebbero scrivere se non quelle ch'egli avesse quando
fu richiesto. E quando egli sarà quà, noi ragioneremo con lui di questa
materia e d'altre cose.

Pregheretegli strettamente che non offendano Castello nè Cortona
nè Montepulciano, e ancora in singularità Perugini nostri fratelli.

(Florence. State Archives. *Classe* x, *dist.* 3. n° 1. — *Dieci di Balìa, Legazioni,
vol.* 1, c. 197.)

LXVI.

[1389.]

Pietro di Barna da Siena. Pietro di Biagio da Montepulciano de-
vono avere a dì primo di settembre fior. venticinque den. netti di ca-
bella. e quali den. sono per remuneratione premio e provisione de la
presura che fecero d'Antonio d'Abisso corriere e messo del Comune
di Firenze e Giannino di Larginino e di Goro di Broglio del contado
di Fiorenza. e' quagli di mandato del detto Comune di Fiorenza por-
tavano brevi a la compagnia di misser Giovanni Aguto e del conte Cu-
rado ostegianti in sul contado di Siena e quali erano in pericolo e
danno del Comune, e quali presi condussero nella forza del Comune.
Avemone poliza da' Priori et officiali di Balía.

(Siena. State Archives. *Biccherna, Memoriali delle spese.*)

LXVII.

[1389.]

Nota e informatione a te Matteo di Iacopo Arrighi di quello ai a fare
con messer Giovanni Aguto e col Conte Currado, fatta per li Dieci
della Balia del Comune di Firenze nel MCCCLXXXVIIII adì primo
d' ottobre.

Andrai a detti messer Giovanni e Conte Currado, e dopo le saluti,
dirai loro come tu vai per scrivere e vedere la mostra delle loro brigate in forma di Compagna come furono richiesti ......
Il Conte Currado deve scrivere in fino in Lance cccc.
E messer Giovanni Aguto insino in Lance vc, avendole ora, inten-
dendo tre huomini e tre cavalli per lancia, e non femine. E allo scrivere e alla mostra farete d'aver presenti i Capitani e parecchi Caporali
de' migliori, pregandoli che provveggano che noi non siamo ingannati,
per loro honore e per fortificatione della Brigata ......
E dirai a' Capitani che, fatta la decta scriptura, mandino quà loro
procuratori e della Brigata, e noi daremo loro le loro paghe. E se di-
cessono volerle prima, dirai che nè si può nè si dee fare, però che, non

sappiendo il numero de' Cavalli che sono, non sapremmo quanti danari avessimo a dare.

Sollicitagli quanto puoi ch' eglino escano del nostro terreno. E se per questo bisognassono danari, mandino i loro procuratori per essi.

Avrai teco a far la mostra Cocchi Albergotti.

(Florence, State Archives, *Classe* x, *dist.* 3, n° 1. — *Dieci di Balìa, Legazioni, vol.* 1, *c.* 218.)

LXVIII.

[1394.]

Riccardo Chel Castellano Monticulj

Carissime noster. Secundum concordiam quam hactenus fecimus cum magnifico domino Johanne Haucud cum degeret in humanis, nobilis quondam uxor sua Domina Donnina tibi scribit quod arcem custodiam atque presidium Monticulj nobis tradas. Ea propter volumus quod ipsarum cum omnibus munitionibus que sunt ibidem, nomine nostri comunis Antonino Materio, familiari nostri dilecto, quam ob hanc causam mittimus, debeas consignare, faciens fieri de cunctis pubblicum instrumentum. Deinde quanto citius commode facere poteris ad presentiam nostre dominationis accedas. Quicquid enim pro tuis stipendis et provvisione recipere debes tibi faciemus integre solvi et, ne tenearis in tempore, celeriter expediri.

25 aprilis.

(Ibidem. *Carteggio della Signoria, lettere interne.*)

LXIX.

[1395.]

Regi Anglie.

Serenissime atque gloriosissime princeps et singularissime benefactor et domine noster. Non possumus posteritatem nobilis et strenui militis domini Johannis Haucud fidelis vestri, qui longis temporibus fideliter multaque cum probitate in nostris servitiis militavit, aliquo modo diserere et ipse utilitatem et honorem non modis omnibus procurare, et eo maxime quia tanti viri progenies, qui tam celebri gloria totam linguam anglicam honoravit, extra patriam est, et post illius optimi parentis obitum in Italia degunt tamquam hospites et peregrini, quamvis propter patris merita disposita sit nostra civitas ipsos amplecti et tamquam ex nobis genitos confovere. Quamobrem cum decreverat ipsorum mater, uxor veraciter tanto digna marito, quum primum etas filiorum patietur, cum ipsis in Angliam transfretare, filios prefati domini Johannis eiusque familiam celsitudini vestre quanta cum devotione possumus commendamus, omni cum reverentia quantaque cum affectione valimus sublimitatis vestre clementie supplicantes quod dignetur vestri culminis altitudo pupillos istos cum benignitate recipere, et ipsorum negocia regiis favoribus communire. Res equidem pupillaris est orfanorum et vidue, quibus iubent divinarum legum oracula mundi principes et terre iudices providere. Accedit ad hec quod decet regiam majestatem virtutis suorum fidelium qui patriam honoraverunt etiam post mortem grata cum memoria reminisci, ut accendant animos aliorum ut se tales exhibeant quod in heredes ipsorum favor honorum operum transfudatur, et sperent etiam post mortem se per famam vivere cum viderent virtuosorum filios, ob parentum merita, singulares favores et gratiam impetrare. Nobis autem et devotioni nostre, benignissime princeps, dici non posset quantum erit acceptum et gratum quicquid familie prefati domini Johannis fuerit impensum.

Datum Florentie die 29 martii III indict.

(Ibidem. Miss. 23.)

———————— — —

LXX.

[1395.]

Regi Anglie.

Serenissime atque invictissime princeps et onorandissime domine benefactor noster benignissime. Quum serenitas vestra concesserit nobili et strenuo militi domino Nicolao Clyfton, fedeli sacratissimi vestri dyadematis, facultatem atque licentiam ad nostra servitia venendi, videmus a benivolentia regali quam semper erga nostram renpublicam habuistis hoc processisse. Et ob id devotis affectibus dignissimas gratias culmini vestre celsitudinis agimus et habemus. Nunc atqui, quum per dei gratiam in pace sumus, non est necessarium nobis gentes aliunde conducere nec majoris potentie brachium implorare. Nulla quidem in orbe terrarum gens est quam per armorum gloria et fidelitate servitii libentius quam Anglicos sumeremus, quorum prestantissima in bello virtus domesticis et externis experientie non ignoramus exemplis. Quamobrem si necessitas imminebit, prefatum dominum Nicholaum, vestre sublimitatis respectu suarumque consideratione virtutum et amore gentis, super omnes alios requiremus.

Data Florentie die 4 augusti III indict.

(Ibidem.)

LXXI.

[1395.]

Dno nicholao Clyfton

Nobilis et strenue miles. Quanta sit erga nos vestra dilectio facillime patuit per ea que Simon Salesburi nobis explicavit. Et ob id certa sit vestra nobilitas quod quoties in rebus arduis ad qualia nos requiri convenerit maiorem potentiam gentibus egerimus, linguam rogabimus anglicam super omnes et amicitiam vestram curabimus honorare. Quam per tam gratis oblationibus digni gratiarum persequimur actione. Dat ut supra (august 4).

(Ibidem.)

LXXII.

8th year of Henry IV [1407]

Per Johannem filium Johannis Hawkwood militis.

Rex omnibus ad quos, etc., salutem.

Sciatis quod de gratia nostra speciali concessimus dilecto nobis Johanni filio Johannis Hawkwode militis defuncti, qui quidem Johannes filius in partibus Italie natus et procreatus extitit, quod ipse de cetero homo ligeus noster et indigena existat et pro tali in omnibus tractetur et teneatur, et quod ipse maneria terras seu redditus servicia feuda advocaciones franchesias libertates et alias possessiones quascunque infra regnum nostrum Anglie de quibuscumque personis et de tanto valore prout sibi placuerit in feodo simplici seu in feodo talliato ad terminum vite vel aliter adquirere, ac etiam impetitare et impetitari in quibuscumque Curiis nostris et alibi infra regnum nostrum predictum, ac hereditatem et alia emolumenta quecumque taliter et eodem modo sicut aliqui ligeorum nostrorum infra regnum nostrum predictum oriundiorum tenere possit, eo quod predictus Johannes filius et Donnina mater sua infra dictum regnum nostrum nati et procreati non extiterunt aut aliquo alio statuto seu ordinacione in contrarium facta non obstante; in cuius etc. H R apud Westminster tertio die November.

per bre (?) de privato sigillo et per quadraginta solidis solutis in Hanaperio.*

(Patent Rolls.)

---

* *Hanaperio* from the English *Hanaper* or *Hamper* (basket).

In the ancient simplicity of forms, the papers and patents relating to the affairs of private persons susceptible of taxation by the imposition of the royal seal, were placed in a basket: those relating to affairs in which the Crown was directly or indirectly interested were placed in a little sack (*parca bargâ*) *petty bag*.

Hence were derived the two departments, *Hanaper-office* and *Petty bag-office*, which, according to English tenacity in matters of tradition, still have the same names in the *Courts of Common Law*, and *Chancery*.

THE END.

CONTENTS.

————

DOCUMENTS.

Printed in the United States
86286LV00005B/26/A